The BIG BOOK of LOGOS 4

David E. Carter

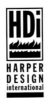

HDi

HARPER
DESIGN
international

An Imprint of HarperCollins*Publishers*

The Big Book of Logos 4

Copyright © 2004 by David E. Carter and Harper Design
International

First published in 2004 by:
Harper Design International,
An imprint of HarperCollins*Publishers*
10 East 53rd Street
New York, NY 10022

Distributed throughout the world by:
HarperCollins International
10 East 53rd Street
New York, NY 10022
Fax: (212) 207-7654

HarperCollins books may be purchased for educational, business,
or sales promotional use. For information, please write: Special
Markets Department, HarperCollins Publishers Inc., 10 East 53rd
Street, New York, NY 10022.

Book design by **Designs on You!**
Suzanna and Anthony Stephens

Library of Congress Contol Number: 2004110152

ISBN 0-06-074806-0

Printed in Hong Kong by Everbest Printing Company through Four
Colour Imports, Louisville, Kentucky.
First Printing, 2004

Number 4.

Three sequels now to the original *Big Book of Logos*.

Logo designers all over the world know the importance of keeping "in the loop," of having a source that shows the fresh new designs that are being produced by outstanding creative people.

The Big Book of Logos series IS that source.

The Big Book of Logos 4 is packed full of new designs that will inspire you, challenge you, and serve as a creative springboard.

For all those who create logos, this book will be your constant source for "solitary brainstorming."

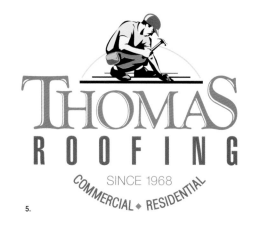

1.

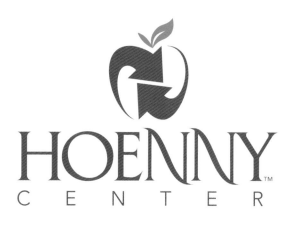

2.

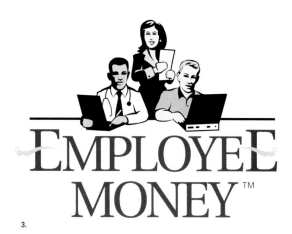

3.

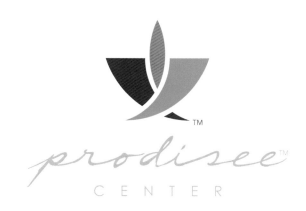

4.

5.

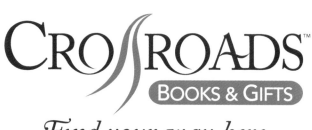

6.

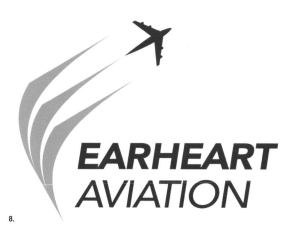

7.

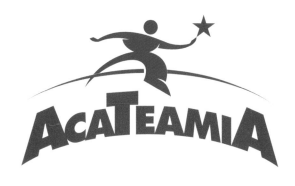

8.

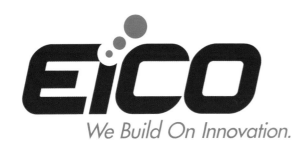

9.

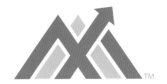

The MAXAlliance™

Trans*Action*™

10.

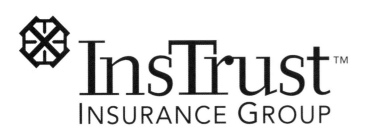

InsTrust™
INSURANCE GROUP

11.

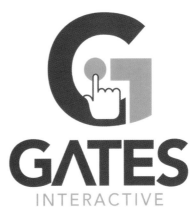

GATES
INTERACTIVE

12.

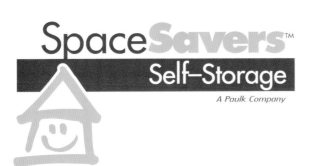

13.

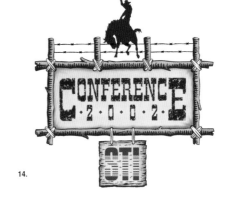

14.

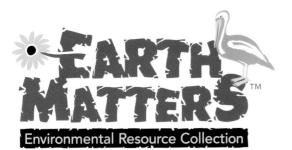

15.

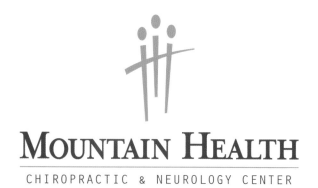

MOUNTAIN HEALTH
CHIROPRACTIC & NEUROLOGY CENTER

1.

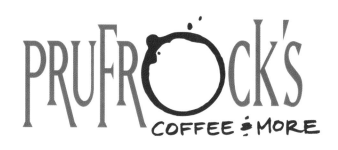

2.

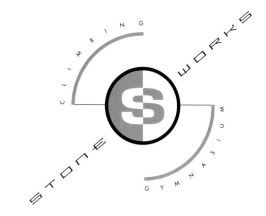

3.

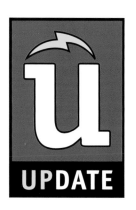

UPDATE

4.

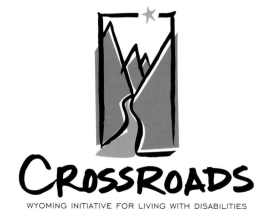

CROSSROADS
WYOMING INITIATIVE FOR LIVING WITH DISABILITIES

5.

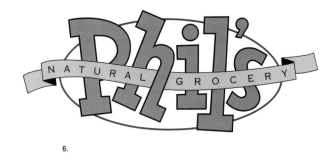

6.

orion pacific
plastics reprocessing

7.

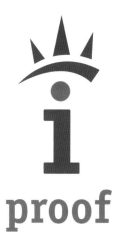

proof

8.

6

FIRST AMERICAN FUNDS™

9.

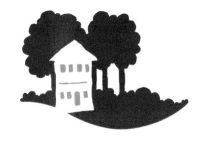

ARCOLA MILLS

10.

LANDMARK
C E N T E R

11.

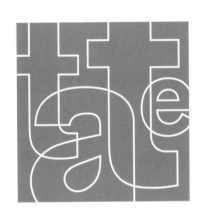

12.

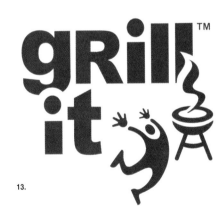

13.

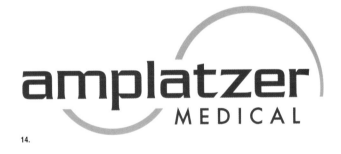

14.

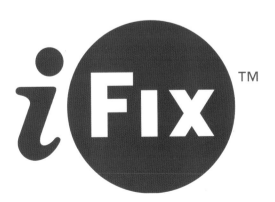

15.

1 - 8
Design Firm **Catalyst Creative**
9 - 15
Design Firm **Larsen Design + Interactive**

1.
Client   *Mountain Health Chiropractic*
Designer Jeanna Pool

2.
Client   *Prufrock's Coffee*
Designer Jeanna Pool

3.
Client   *Stoneworks Climbing Gym*
Designer Jeanna Pool

4.
Client   *Update*
Designers Jeanna Pool, David Coleman

5.
Client   *Wyoming Initiative for
          Living with Disabilities*
Designers Jeanna Pool, David Coleman

6.
Client   *Phil's Natural Food Grocery*
Designer Jeanna Pool

7.
Client   *Orion Pacific*
Designer Jeanna Pool

8.
Client   *I-Proof*
Designers Jeanna Pool, David Coleman

9.
Client   *First American Funds*
Designer Todd Nesser

10.
Client   *Arcola Mills*
Designer Michelle Solie

11.
Client   *Landmark Center*
Designer Bill Pflipsen

12.
Client   *Tate Capital Partners*
Designer Bill Pflipsen

13.
Client   *Target Corporation*
Designer Michelle Solie

14.
Client   *AGA Medical Corporation*
Designer Michelle Solie

15.
Client   *Target Corporation*
Designer Peter de Sibour

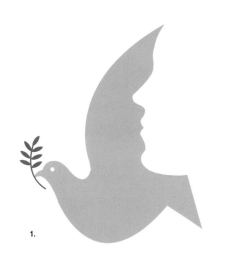

1.

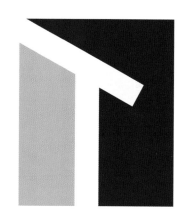

2.

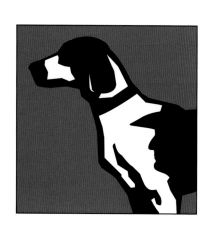

3.

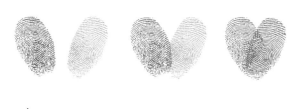

4.

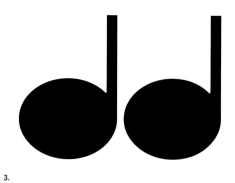

5.

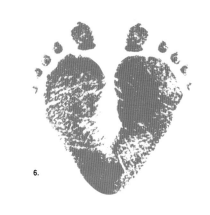

6.

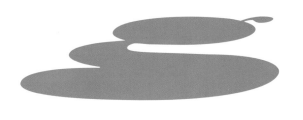

7.

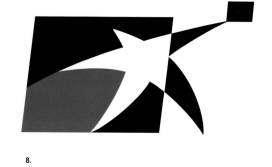

8.

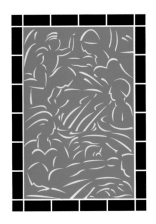

9.

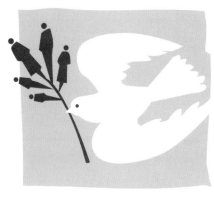

10.

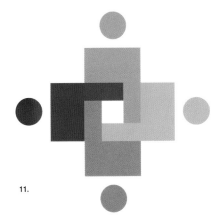

11.

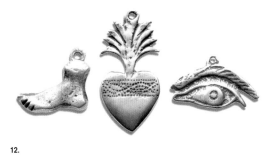

12.

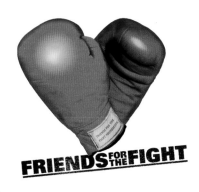

FRIENDS FOR THE FIGHT

14.

13.

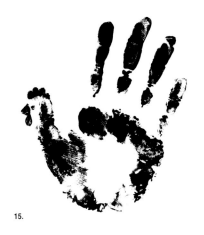

15.

1 - 15
Design Firm **Bradford Lawton Design Group**

1.
   Client   *New Heights Methodist Church*
   Designer   Jody Laney
2.
   Client   *True Slate*
   Designers Bradford Lawton, Jody Laney
3.
   Client   *KPAC Texas Public Radio*
   Designers Jody Laney, Bradford Lawton
4.
   Client   *Marriage and Family Counseling*
   Designer   Bradford Lawton
5.
   Client   *Rick Smith Dog Training*
   Designer   Jody Laney
6.
   Client   *Sav-A-Baby*
   Designers Becky Haas, Bradford Lawton
7.
   Client   *Gary Pools*
   Designers Becky Haas, Bradford Lawton

8.
   Client   *Lone Star Overnight*
   Designer   Bradford Lawton
9.
   Client   *Alamo Heights Pool*
   Designers Jody Laney, Bradford Lawton
10.
   Client   *Family Violence Prevention Service*
   Designer   Jody Laney
11.
   Client   *University Physicians Group*
   Designers Bradford Lawton, Jody Laney
12.
   Client   *Texas Diabetes Institute*
   Designer   Bradford Lawton
13.
   Client   *Air Force Federal Credit Union*
   Designer   Jennifer Zinsmeyer Murillo
14.
   Client   *Friends for the Fight*
   Designer   Leslie Magee
15.
   Client   *Wing Basket*
   Designer   Jennifer Zinsmeyer Murillo

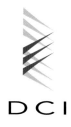

DESIGN COMMUNICATIONS INC

3.

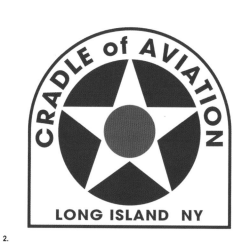

4.

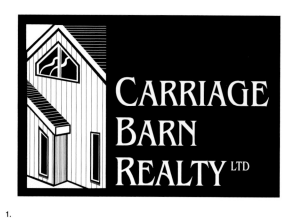

MS BALLIN

5.

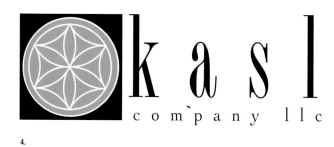

TRIANGLE
PROPERTIES

6.

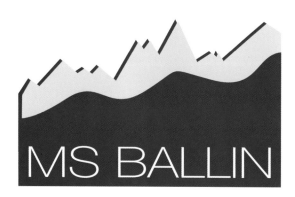

7.

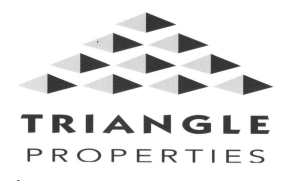

1 - 6
Design Firm **Guarino Graphics &
Design Studio**
7
Design Firm **Monderer Design**

1.
Client   *Carriage Barn Realty*
Designer   Jan Guarino
2.
Client   *Cradle of Aviation*
Designer   Jan Guarino
3.
Client   *DCI Communications*
Designer   Jan Guarino
4.
Client   *KASL Company LLC*
Designer   Jan Guarino
5.
Client   *MS Ballin*
Designer   Jan Guarino

6.
Client   *Triangle Properties*
Designer   Jan Guarino
7.
Client   *Lightbridge*
Designers Jason CK Miller,
            Stewart Monderer
(opposite)
Client   *Flying Star Cafe*
Design Firm **Vaughn Wedeen Creative**
Designer   Pamela Chang

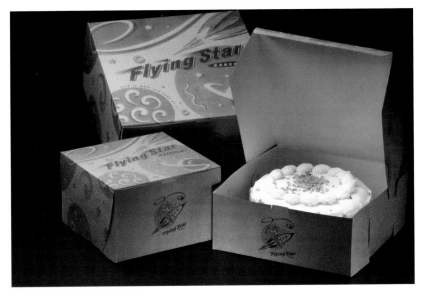

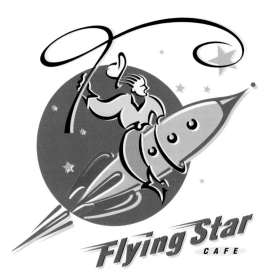

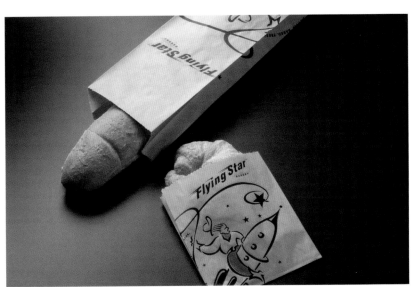

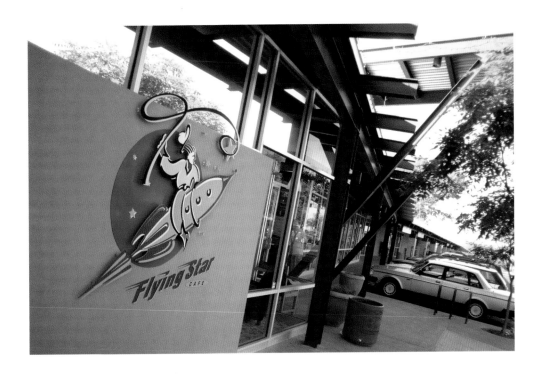

SPACE

1.

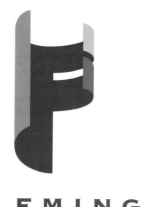

FLEMING

2.

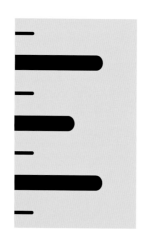

3.

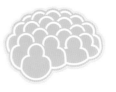

CREATIVE CLUB *of* SAN ANTONIO

4.

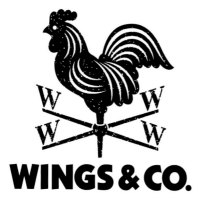

WINGS & CO.

5.

SAN ANTONIO RIVER FOUNDATION

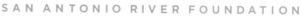

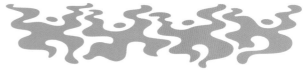

6.

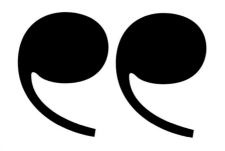

7.

The Birth Place

AT SOUTHWEST GENERAL HOSPITAL

8.

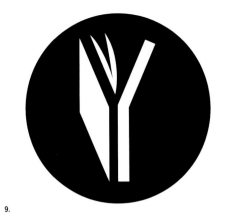

9.

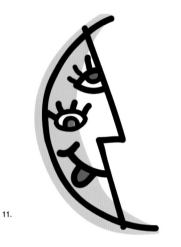

10.

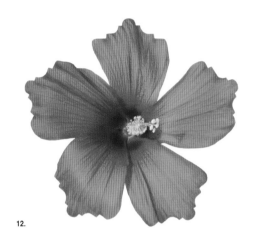

11.

12.

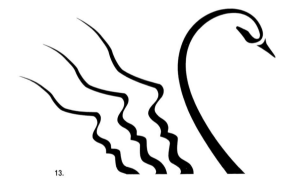

13.

cielos

14.

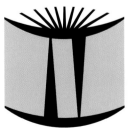

15.

1 - 15
Design Firm **Bradford Lawton Design Group**

1.
Client   *BBtt*
Designer   Bradford Lawton

2.
Client   *Fleming*
Designer   Bradford Lawton

3.
Client   *Easy Inch Loss Program*
Designer   Leslie Magee

4.
Client   *Creative Club of San Antonio*
Designer   Rolando M. Murillo

5.
Client   *Wings Basket*
Designer   Rolando M. Murillo

6.
Client   *San Antonio River Foundation*
Designers   Rolando M. Murillo, Bradford Lawton

7.
Client   *KSTX Texas Public Radio*

8.
Client   *Southwest General Hospital*
Designers   Bradford Lawton, Jody Laney

9.
Client   *San Antonio Youth Literacy*
Designer   Jennifer Zinsmeyer Murillo

10.
Client   *Williams Landscaping*
Designer   Bradford Lawton

11.
Client   *Luna C Restaurant*
Designers   Bradford Lawton, Jody Laney

12.
Client   *San Antonio Botanical Society*
Designer   Bradford Lawton

13.
Client   *Creative Surgeons*
Designers   Bradford Lawton, Jody Laney

14.
Client   *Frontier Ent.*
Designers   Rolando Murillo, Bradford Lawton

15.
Client   *Gemini Ink*
Designers   Leslie Magee

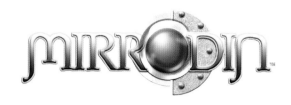

1.

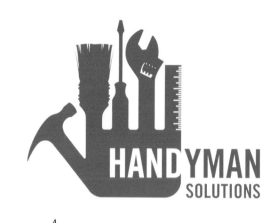

2.

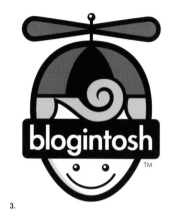

3.

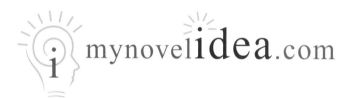

4.

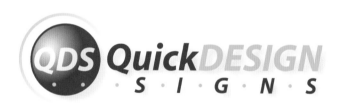

5.

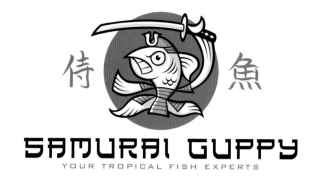

6.

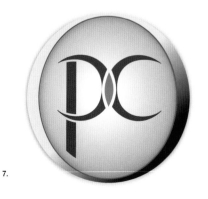

7.

1
        Design Firm **Wizards of the Coast**
2 - 4
        Design Firm **Glitschka Studios**
5 - 7
        Design Firm **End2End Integration, LLC**
1.
        Designers   Jeremy Cranford,
                    Yasuyo Dunnett
2.
        Client   *Samurai Guppy*
        Designer   Von R. Glitschka
3.
        Client   *www.blogintosh.com*
        Designer   Von R. Glitschka
4.
        Client   *Handyman Solutions*
        Designer   Von R. Glitschka

5.
        Client   *My Novel Idea*
        Designer   Scott Wyss
6.
        Client   *Quick Design Signs*
        Designer   Scott Wyss
7.
        Client   *Party Campus*
        Designer   Scott Wyss
(opposite)
        Client   *Satellite Coffee*
        Design Firm **Vaughn Wedeen Creative**
        Designer   Pamela Chang

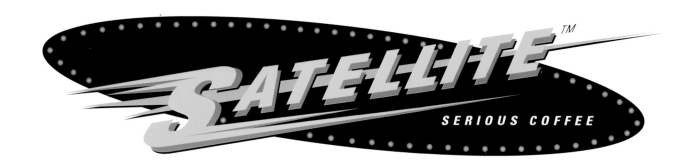

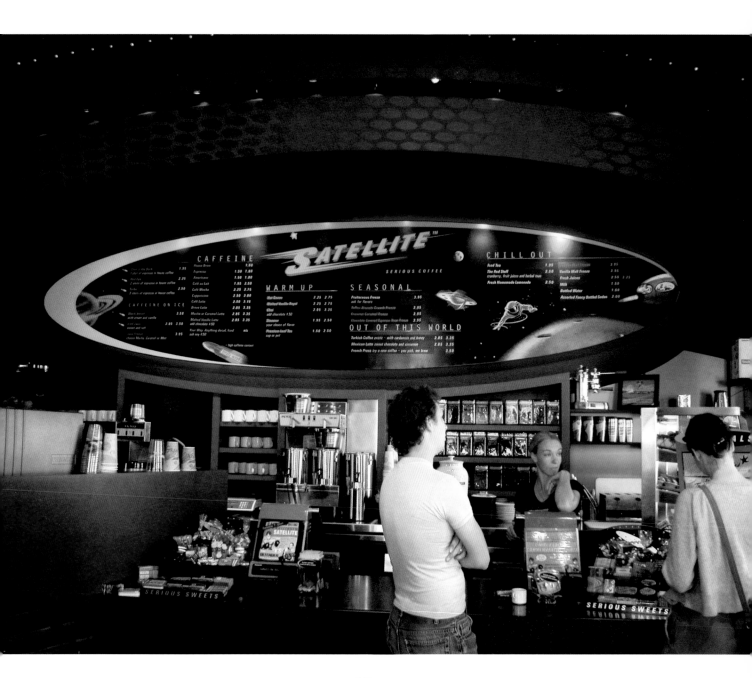

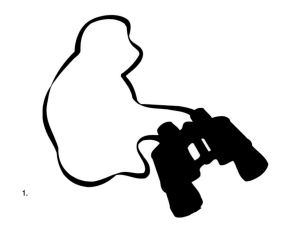

1.

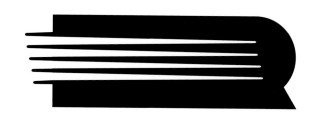

2.

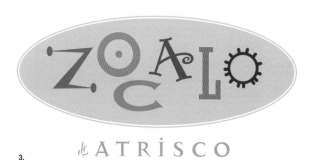

ZOCALO

de ATRISCO

3.

MODRALL SPERLING
ROEHL HARRIS & SISK, P.A.

L A W Y E R S

4.

Amy Biehl

High School

5.

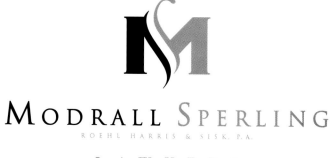

nCube

POWER ON DEMAND

6.

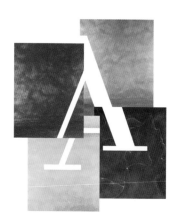

7.

A G U A V I D A

8.

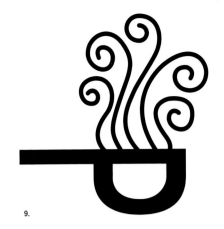

9.

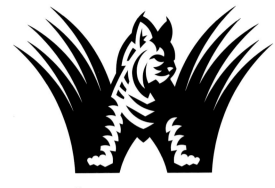

10.

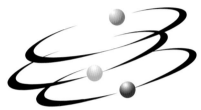

bios group
science for business

11.

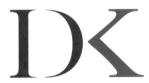

DK

DENISH + KLINE ASSOCIATES

12.

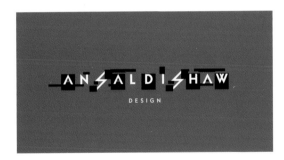

ANSALDISHAW

DESIGN

13.

National Hispanic Cultural Center

14.

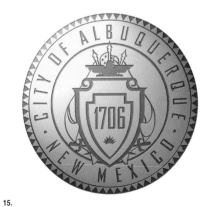

15.

1, 2, 9, 10
Design Firm **Bradford Lawton Design Group**
3 - 8, 11 - 15
Design Firm **Vaughn Wedeen Creative**

1.
Client *Texas Primate Observatory*
Designer Bradford Lawton

2.
Client *Railtex*
Designers Bradford Lawton, Jody Laney

3.
Client *Zocalo LLC*
Designer Rick Vaughn

4.
Client *Modrall Sperling Lawyers*
Designer Pamela Chang

5.
Client *Amy Biehl High School*
Designers Steve Wedeen, Pamela Chang

6.
Client *nCube*
Designer Pamela Chang

7.
Client *Academy Printers*
Designer Pamela Chang

8.
Client *AguaVida*
Designer Pamela Chang

9.
Client *Premier Catering*
Designers Bradford Lawton, Jody Laney

10.
Client *Wildlife Rescue & Rehabilitation*
Designer Rolando Murillo

11.
Client *BiosGroup*
Designer Pamela Chang

12.
Client *Denish + Kline Associates*
Designer Pamela Chang

13.
Client *Ansaldi Shaw Design/Architecture*
Designer Steve Wedeen

14.
Client *National Hispanic Cultural Center*
Designers Steve Wedeen, Pamela Chang

15.
Client *City of Albuquerque, New Mexico*
Designer Rich Vaughn

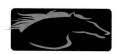

CALIFORNIA HORSE PARK

A STATE OF THE ART EQUINE SHOW FACILITY

1.

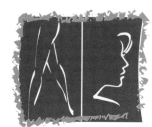

total vein care

vein and aesthetic laser center

2.

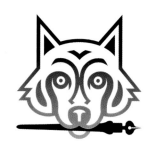

Randi Wolf
D E S I G N

3.

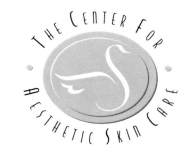

The Center For Aesthetic Skin Care

Marc S. Cohen, MD, FACS • Nancy G. Swartz, MS, MD, FACS
Ophthalmic Plastic and Cosmetic Surgeons

4.

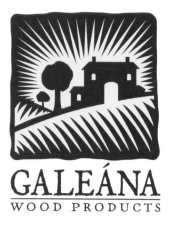

GALEÁNA
WOOD PRODUCTS

5.

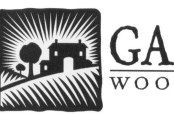

GALEÁNA
WOOD PRODUCTS

6.

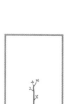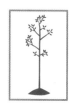

LITTLETON PUBLIC SCHOOLS FOUNDATION

If You Want Oak Trees, You Have To Plant Acorns

7.

1, 2
Design Firm **Market Street Marketing**
3, 4
Design Firm **Randi Wolf Design**
5 - 7
Design Firm **Hat Trick Creative, Inc.**
1.
Client · *California Horse Park*
Designer · Kathleen Downs
2.
Client · *Total Vein Care*
Designer · Kathleen Downs
3.
Client · *Randi Wolf Design*
Designer · Randi Wolf
4.
Client · *Dr. Marc Cohen,*
Dr. Nancy Swartz
Designer · Randi Wolf

5, 6.
Client · *Galeána Wood Products*
Designers · Charlie Pate, Lance Brown
7.
Client · *Littleton Public Schools*
Foundation
Designers · Lance Brown, Charlie Pate
(opposite)
Client · *Albuquerque Isotopes*
Design Firm **Vaughn Wedeen Creative**
Designer · Pamela Chang

18

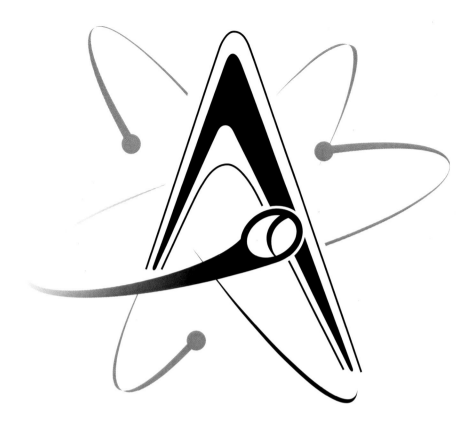

Albuquerque

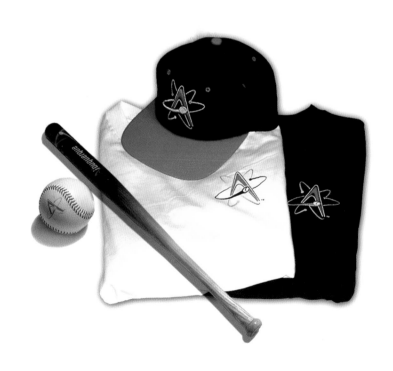

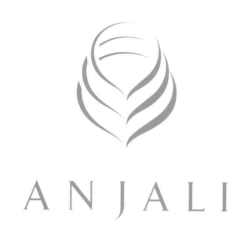

A N J A L I

1.

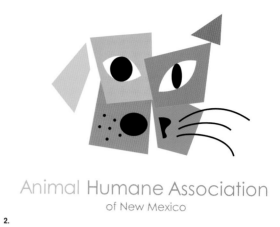

Animal Humane Association
of New Mexico

2.

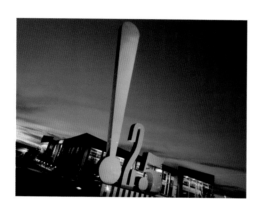

3.

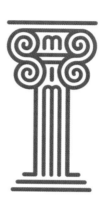

4.

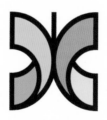

5.

6.

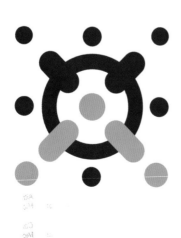

7.

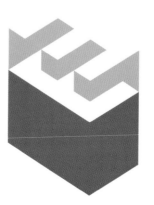

8.

9.

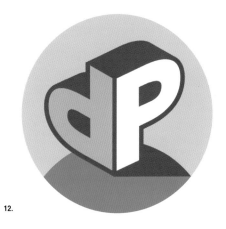

10.

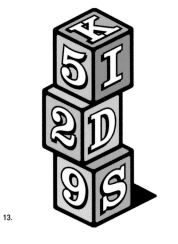

11.

12.

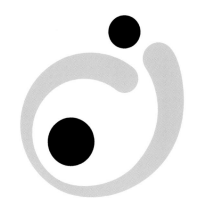

13.

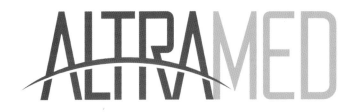

14.

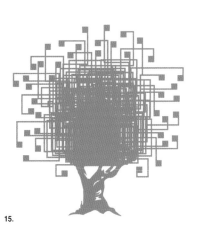

15.

1 - 3		
Design Firm	**Vaughn Wedeen Creative**	
4 - 15		
Design Firm	**Ramp**	

1.
Client — *Anjali Living Community Center*
Designer — Pamela Chang

2.
Client — *Animal Humane Association of New Mexico*
Designer — Pamela Chang

3.
Client — *Provident Realty*
Designer — Rich Vaughn

4.
Client — *Mark Stewart Securities*
Designer — Michael Stinson

5.
Client — *DirectColor*
Designer — Michael Stinson

6.
Client — *b&beyond*
Designers — Michael Stinson, Rachel Elnar

7.
Client — *Canon Development Americas*
Designers — Michael Stinson, Rachel Elnar

8.
Client — *Evans & Evans Construction Services*
Designer — Michael Stinson

9, 10.
Client — *Safety Syringes*
Designer — Michael Stinson

11.
Client — *Canon Development Americas*
Designers — Michael Stinson, Rachel Elnar

12.
Client — *Dave Perry*
Designer — Michael Stinson

13.
Client — *Mark Stewart Securities*
Designer — Michael Stinson

14.
Client — *Altramed*
Designer — Michael Stinson

15.
Client — *CompLife*
Designer — Michael Stinson

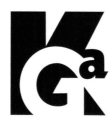

Kensington | GLASS ARTS | Incorporated

1.

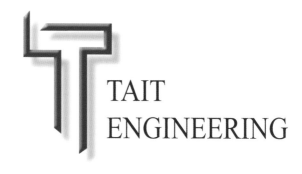

2.

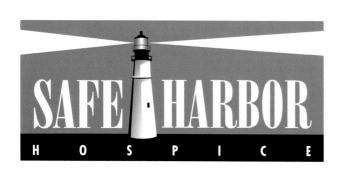

3.

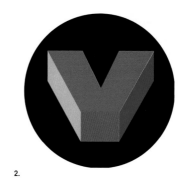

TAIT
ENGINEERING

4.

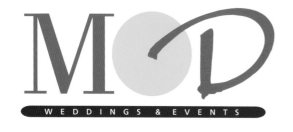

WEDDINGS & EVENTS

5.

CAIRNS + ASSOCIATES

6.

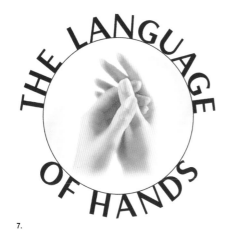

7.

1
Design Firm **Jill Tanenbaum**
Graphic Design & Advertising
2, 3
Design Firm **VanPelt Creative**
4
Design Firm **Erisa Creative**
5, 6
Design Firm **Ethan Ries Designs**
7
Design Firm **Cairns + Associates**
1.
Client   *Kensington Glass Arts*
                Incorporated
Designer   Sue Sprinkle
2.
Client   *VanPelt Creative*
Designer   Chip VanPelt

3.
Client   *Safe Harbor Hospice*
Designer   Chip VanPelt
4.
Client   *Tait Engineering*
Designer   Erin May
5.
Client   *MOD Weddings & Events*
Designer   Ethan Ries
6.
Client   *Cairns + Associates*
Designer   Ethan Ries
7.
Client   *Vaseline Intensive Care Lotion*
Designer   Ethan Ries
(opposite)
Client   *Goldline Controls, Inc.*
Design Firm **DynaPac Design Group**
Designer   Lee A. Aellig

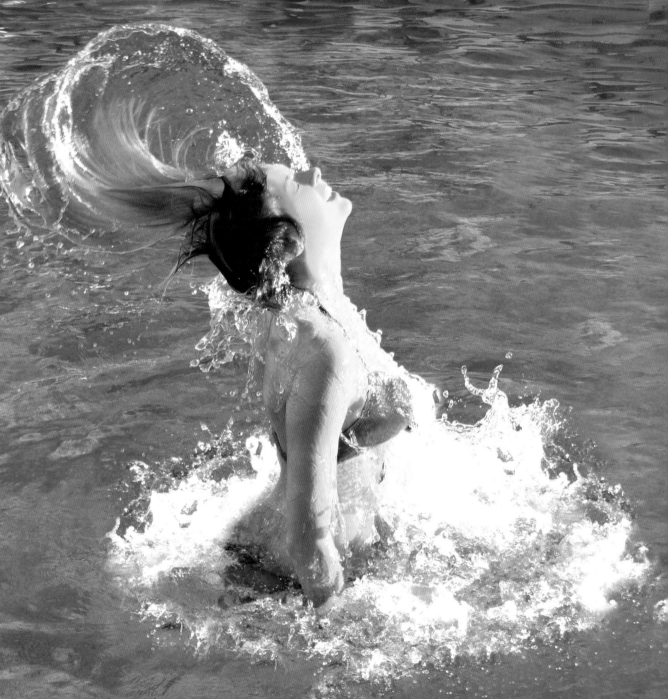

Aqua Logic
Automation and Chlorination

THE LOGICAL SOLUTION
FOR PURE SWIMMING PLEASURE

GOLDLINE
CONTROLS INC.

IMAGINE

changing the world

1.

BURNS
AND COMPANY
CONSULTING

2.

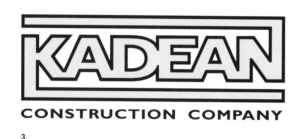

KADEAN

CONSTRUCTION COMPANY

3.

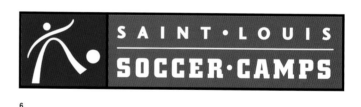

WEINBAUER & *ASSOCIATES, INC.*
Tax & Financial Services

4.

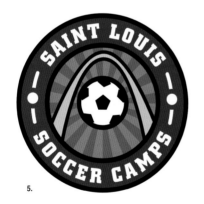

SAINT LOUIS

SOCCER CAMPS

5.

SAINT · LOUIS

SOCCER · CAMPS

6.

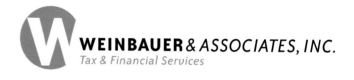

LIVE ANOTHER DAY

7.

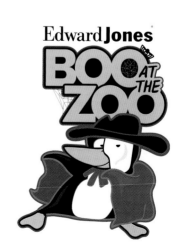

Edward **Jones**

BOO AT THE ZOO

8.

24

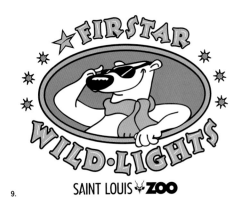

9.

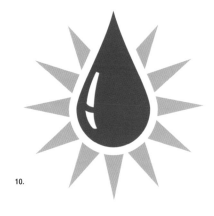

10.

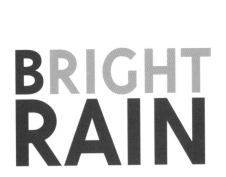

11.

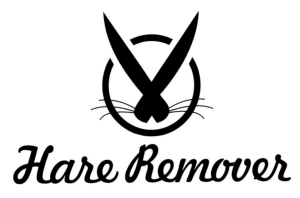

12.

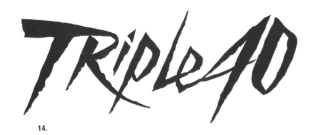

13.

14.

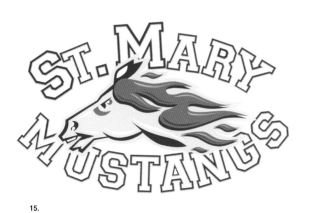

15.

1 - 13
Design Firm **Bright Rain Creative**
14, 15
Design Firm **Pixallure Design**

1.
Client   *St Louis Young Presidents Organization*
Designer   Matt Marino

2.
Client   *Burns and Company Consulting*
Designer   Kevin Hough

3.
Client   *Kadean Construction Company*
Designer   Matt Marino, Bill Rice

4.
Client   *Weinbauer & Associates, Inc.*
Designer   Matt Marino

5, 6.
Client   *St. Louis Soccer Camps*
Designer   Matt Marino

7.
Client   *Saint Louis Zoo*
Designer   Kevin Hough

8, 9.
Client   *Saint Louis Zoo*
Designer   Matt Marino

10, 11.
Client   *Bright Rain Creative*
Designers   Kevin Hough, Matt Marino

12.
Client   *Bob Abrams Idea Company*
Designer   Matt Marino

13.
Client   *Clayco Construction Company*
Designer   Kevin Hough

14.
Client   *Triple 40*
Designer   Steven Lutz

15.
Client   *St. Mary Catholic School*
Designer   Terry Edeker

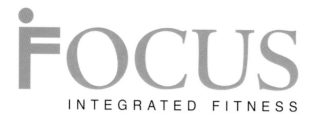

1.

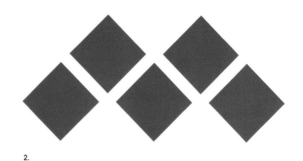

2.

FOSTER/SEARING

consultants in executive search

3.

H2

LAND COMPANY

4.

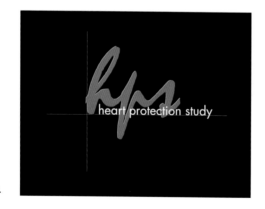

5.

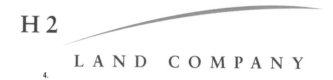

6.

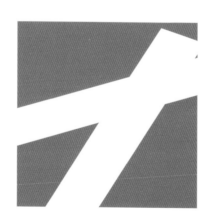

7.

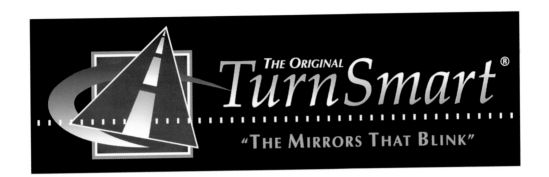

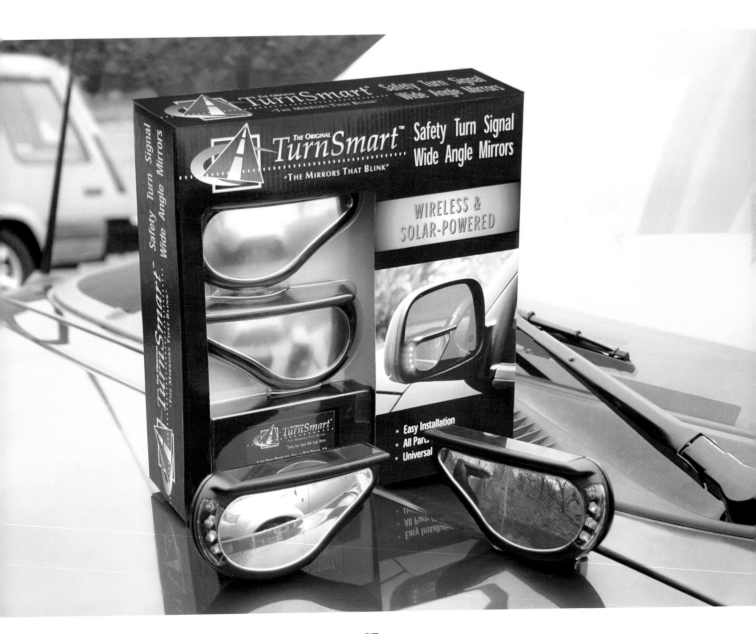

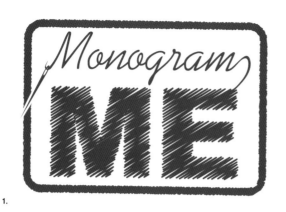

1.

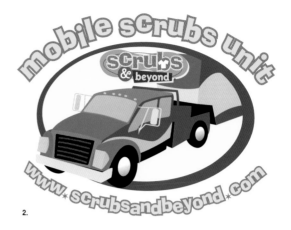

2.

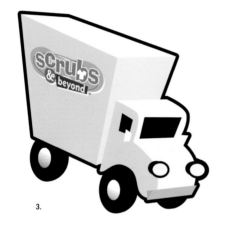

3.

Collections

4.

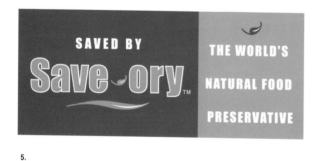

SAVED BY
Save-ory™

THE WORLD'S
NATURAL FOOD
PRESERVATIVE

5.

St. Luke's
FAMILY PRACTICE

6.

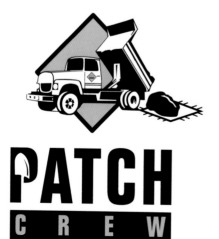

PATCH
CREW

7.

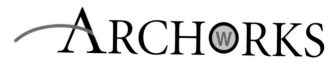

ARCHORKS

Architectural Essentials

8.

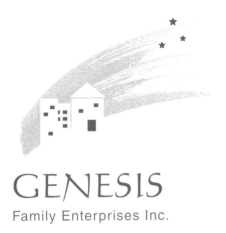

GENESIS

9. Family Enterprises Inc.

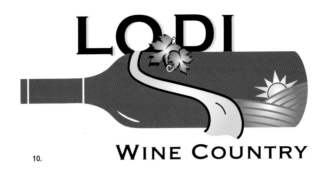

10.

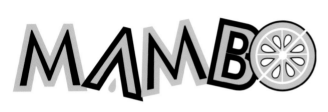

Marketing With A Twist!

11.

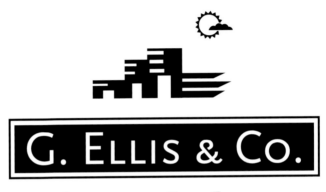

12.

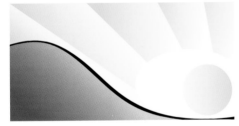

Eggs can't get any fresher.

13.

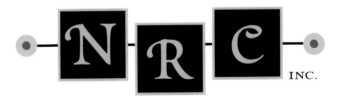

14.

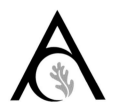

AGILE OAK ORTHOPEDICS

15.

1 - 4
Design Firm **Bright Rain Creative**
5 - 15
Design Firm **Marcia Herrmann Design**
1, 2.
Client   Scrubs & Beyond
Designers   Kevin Hough, Matt Marino
3, 4.
Client   Scrubs & Beyond
Designer   Matt Marino
5.
Client   Meitetso Corporation
Designer   Marcia Herrmann
6.
Client   St. Lukes Family Practice
Designer   Marcia Herrmann
7.
Client   Patch Crew
Designer   Marcia Herrmann
8.
Client   Archworks
Designer   Marcia Herrmann
9.
Client   Genesis Family Enterprises
Designer   Marcia Herrmann

10.
Client   Lodi Wine Country
Designer   Marcia Herrmann
11.
Client   Mambo
Designer   Marcia Herrmann
12.
Client   G. Ellis & Co.
Designer   Marcia Herrmann
13.
Client   NuCal Eggs
Designer   Marcia Herrmann
14.
Client   NRC Insurance Agency Inc.
Designers   Marcia Herrmann,
              Sylvia Magdelena
15.
Client   Agile Oak Orthopedics
Designer   Marcia Herrmann

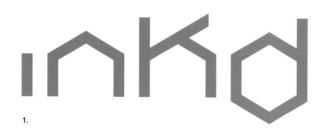

1.

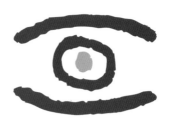

T H E K E E N E Y E

2.

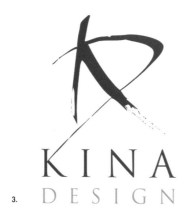

K I N A
D E S I G N

3.

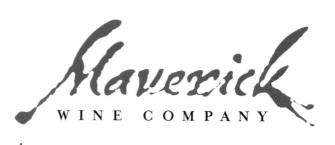

W I N E C O M P A N Y

4.

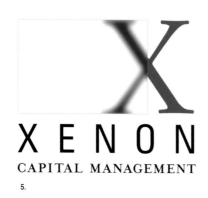

X E N O N
CAPITAL MANAGEMENT

5.

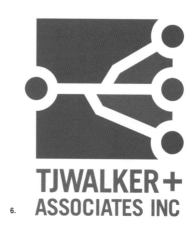

TJWALKER+
ASSOCIATES INC

6.

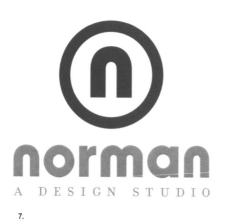

norman
A D E S I G N S T U D I O

7.

1
Design Firm **Lahn Nguyen**
2 - 7
Design Firm **Norman Design**
1.
Client   *INKD Clothing*
Designer   Lahn Nguyen
2.
Client   *The Keen Eye*
Designer   Claudia Renzi
3.
Client   *Kina Design*
Designer   Armin Vit
4.
Client   *Maverick Wine Company*
Designer   Armin Vit
5.
Client   *Xenon Capital Management*
Designer   Armin Vit

6.
Client   *TJ Walker & Associates Inc.*
Designer   Armin Vit
7.
Client   *Norman Design*
Designer   Armin Vit
(opposite)
Client   *Putt Meister, Inc.*
Design Firm **DynaPac Design Group**
Designer   Lee A. Aellig

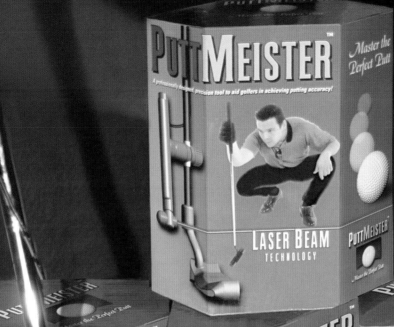

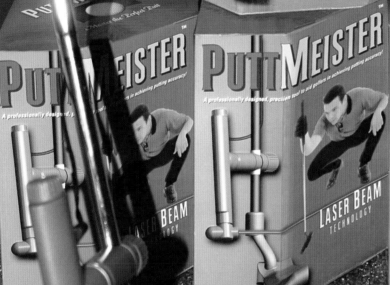

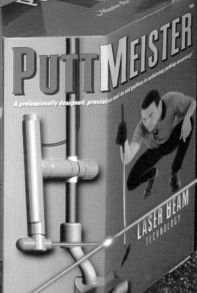

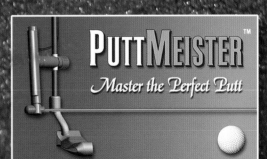

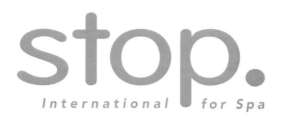

stop.
International for Spa

1.

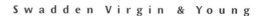

Swadden Virgin & Young

2.

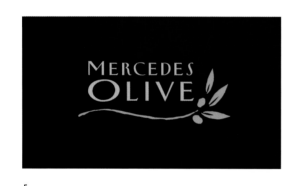

WILDEN LOFTS

3.

**HEALTH
POINT**

▼

The new model
of Primary Care

4.

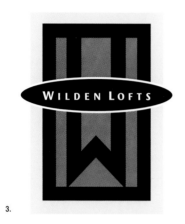

MERCEDES
OLIVE

5.

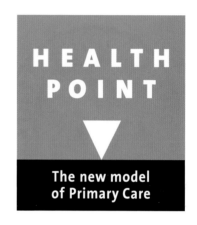

MARIA MANNA LIFE SPA

6.

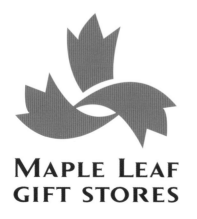

MAPLE LEAF
GIFT STORES

7.

2020

**DOWNTOWN VICTORIA
2020**

8.

32

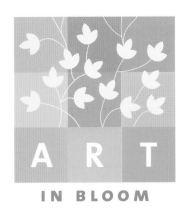

A R T

IN BLOOM

9.

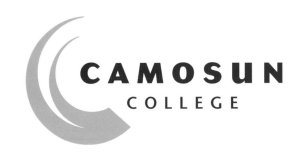

CAMOSUN
COLLEGE

10.

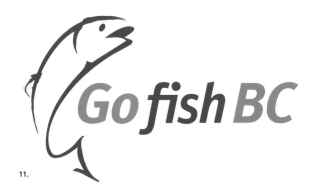

Go fish BC

11.

Glazin Sisco

executive search

12.

together we care

H

GREATER
VICTORIA HOSPITALS
FOUNDATION

13.

Hard·Hats®

Job training • Job filled • Job done

14.

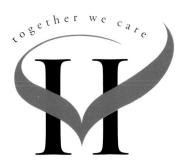

INSPECTECH

Building Inspection Services

15.

1 - 15
Design Firm **Trapeze Communications**

1.
Client   *Stop. Hand & Foot Spa*
Designer   Mark Bawden

2.
Client   *Swadden, Virgin & Young*
Designer   Mark Bawden

3.
Client   *Wilden Lofts*
Designer   Mark Bawden

4.
Client   *Vancouver Island Health Authority*
Designer   Mark Bawden

5.
Client   *Mercedes Olive*
Designers   Mark Bawden, Joe Hedges

6.
Client   *Maria Manna*
Designer   Neil Tran

7.
Client   *Maple Leaf Gifts*
Designer   Joe Hedges

8.
Client   *Downtown Victoria 2020*
Designer   Marianne Unger

9.
Client   *Art Gallery of Greater Victoria*
Designers   Mark Bawden, June Paulovich

10.
Client   *Camosun College*
Designer   Mark Bawden

11.
Client   *Freshwater Fisheries Society of British Columbia*
Designer   Joe Hedges

12.
Client   *Glazin Sisco*
Designers   Mark Bawden, Marianne Unger

13.
Client   *Greater Victoria Hospitals Foundation*
Designers   Mark Bawden, Marianne Unger

14.
Client   *Grant Thornton*
Designer   Neil Tran

15.
Client   *Inspectech*
Designers   Mark Bawden, June Paulovich

33

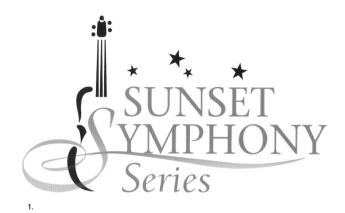

1.

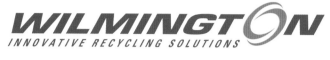

2.

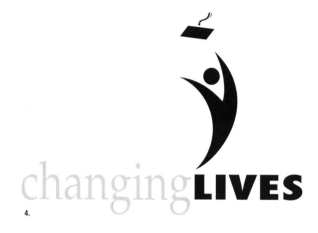

KETTERING

3. TOWER

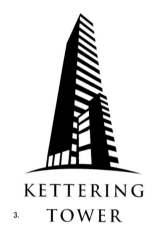

changing **LIVES**

4.

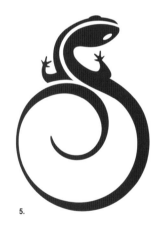

5.

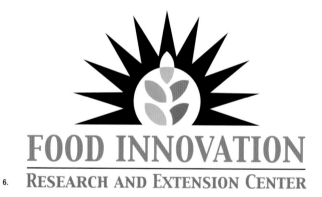

FOOD INNOVATION

6. RESEARCH AND EXTENSION CENTER

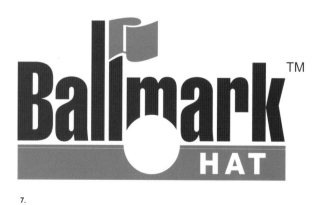

7.

1 - 4
Design Firm **Nova Creative Group**

5
Design Firm **Grafik Marketing Communications**

6
Design Firm **Rutgers University**

7
Design Firm **Fleming & Roskelly, Inc.**

1.
Client — Dayton Philharmonic Orchestra
Designer — Dwayne Swormstedt

2.
Client — Wilmington Iron & Metal
Designer — Jack Denlinger

3.
Client — Miller Valentine
Designer — Jack Denlinger

4.
Client — Sinclair Community College Foundation
Designers — Dwayne Swormstedt, Ben Robinson

5.
Client — Market Salamander
Designers — Michelle Mar, Judy Kirpich, Heath Dwiggins

6.
Client — Food Innovation Research and Extension Center
Designer — John Van Cleaf

7.
Client — Adams Headwear
Designers — Tom Roskelly, Deb Moniz
(opposite)
Client — Mexotic Foods
Design Firm **DynaPac Design Group**
Designer — Lee A. Aellig

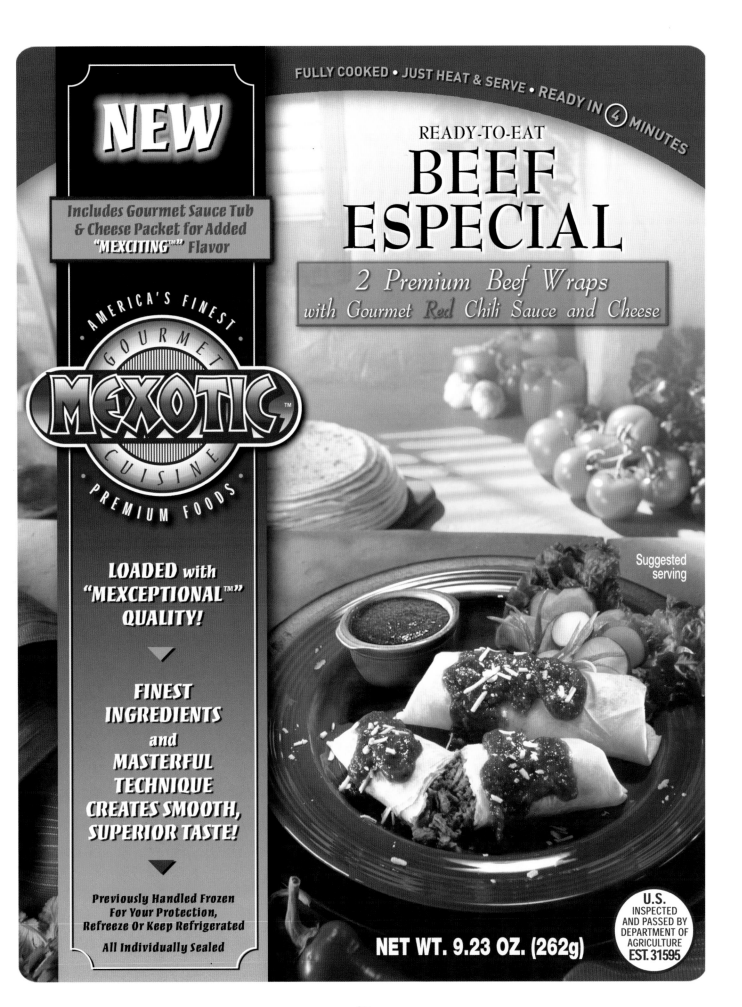

NEW

Includes Gourmet Sauce Tub
& Cheese Packet for Added
"MEXCITING™" Flavor

AMERICA'S FINEST

GOURMET
MEXOTIC™
CUISINE

PREMIUM FOODS

LOADED with
"MEXCEPTIONAL™"
QUALITY!

▼

**FINEST
INGREDIENTS**
and
**MASTERFUL
TECHNIQUE
CREATES SMOOTH,
SUPERIOR TASTE!**

▼

Previously Handled Frozen
For Your Protection,
Refreeze Or Keep Refrigerated

All Individually Sealed

FULLY COOKED • JUST HEAT & SERVE • READY IN ④ MINUTES

READY-TO-EAT
BEEF
ESPECIAL

2 Premium Beef Wraps
with Gourmet Red Chili Sauce and Cheese

Suggested
serving

NET WT. 9.23 OZ. (262g)

U.S.
INSPECTED
AND PASSED BY
DEPARTMENT OF
AGRICULTURE
EST. 31595

Read
Learning
Centre

1.

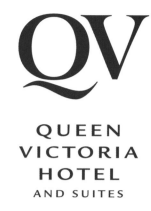

QUEEN
VICTORIA
HOTEL
AND SUITES

2.

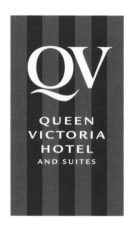

3.

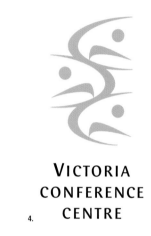

VICTORIA
CONFERENCE
CENTRE

4.

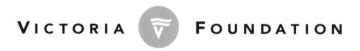

5.

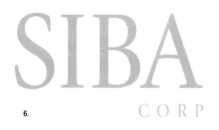

6.

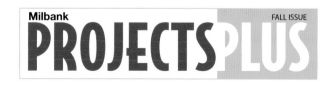

7.

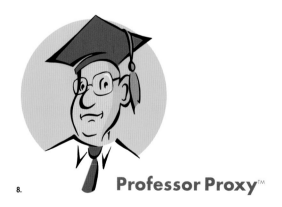

8.

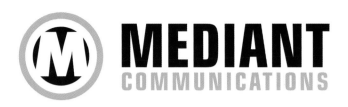

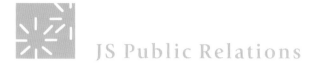

10.

9.

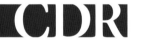

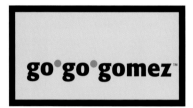

11.

Cantor **SEINUK**

STRUCTURAL ENGINEERS

12.

CDR

Credit Derivatives Research LLC

Gimme Credit™

14.

13.

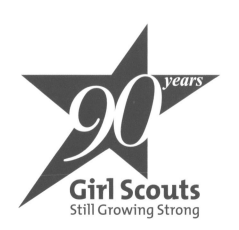

90 *years*

Girl Scouts
Still Growing Strong

15.

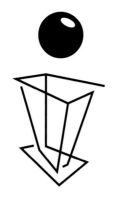

industrial modeling corporation

1.

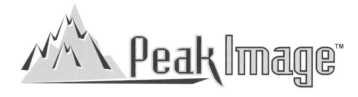

2.

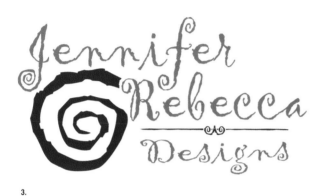

3.

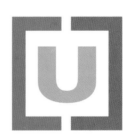

UNIVERSITY SQUARE

4.

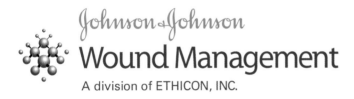

5.

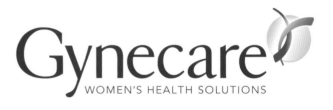

6.

LIFE & HEALTH of AMERICA®

7.

1
Design Firm **DrrtyGrrl Designs**
2, 3
Design Firm **JenGraph**
4 - 7
Design Firm **The Bailey Group**

1.
Client   *Industrial Modeling Corporation*
Designer   Debbi Murray

2.
Client   *Guentherman Consulting, Inc.*
Designer   Jennifer A. Niles

3.
Client   *Jennifer Rebecca Designs*
Designer   Jennifer A. Niles

4.
Client   *University of Pennsylvania*
Designers Jerry Corcoran, Steve Perry,
                Dave Fiedler

5.
Client   *Ethicon*
Designers Steve Perry, Wendy Slavish,
                Lizzy Lee

6.
Client   *Ethicon*
Designer   Ann marie Malone

7.
Client   *Life & Health of America*
Designers Dave Fiedler, Jerry Corcoran

(opposite)
Client   *Nestle Chocolates*
Design Firm **TD2, S.C.**
Designers Rafael Rodrigo Córdova,
                Rafael Treviño M.

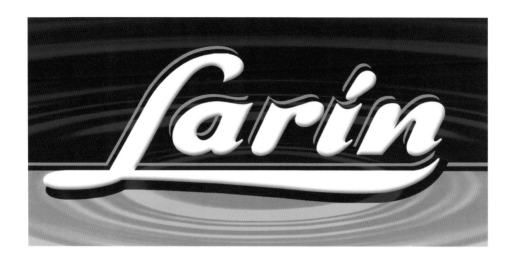

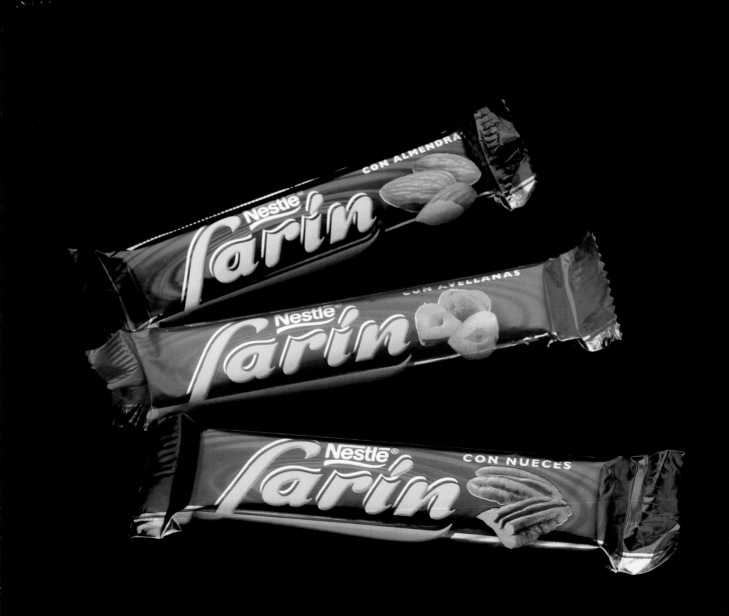

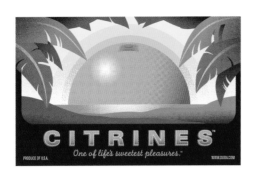

1.

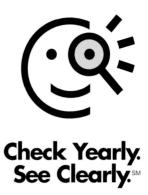

2.

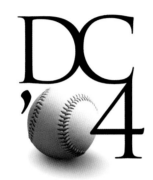

3.

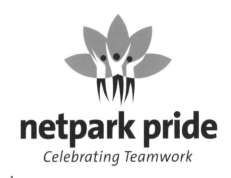

netpark pride
Celebrating Teamwork

4.

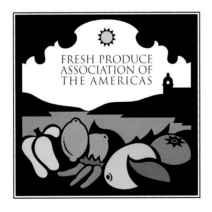

5.

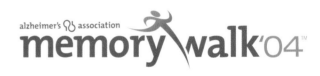

6.

   Paperboard PackagingSM
a natural for innovation

7.

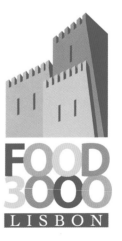

8.

40

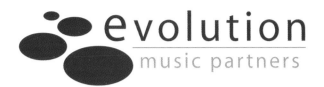

9.

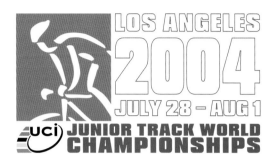

10.

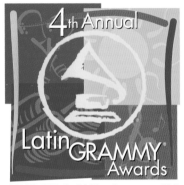

11.

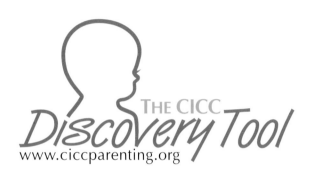

12.

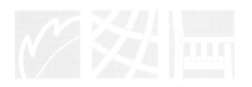

13.

BREWER & TOMINAGA

14.

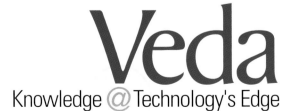

15.

1 - 8
Design Firm **Porter Novelli**
9 - 15
Design Firm **Mark Deitch & Assoc., Inc.**
1.
   Client   *DUDA*
   Designer Todd Metrokin
2.
   Client   *Vision Council of America*
   Designers Penny Rigler, Peter Buttecali
3.
   Client   *Washington DC Baseball*
   Designers Rebecca Mabie, Matt Stevenson
4.
   Client   *Medco*
   Designers Todd Metrokin, Penny Rigler
5.
   Client   *Fresh Produce Association
             of the Americas*
   Designer Todd Metrokin
6.
   Client   *Alzheimer's Association*
   Designers Todd Metrokin, Allyson Hummel
7.
   Client   *American Forest & Paper
             Association*
   Designers Todd Metrokin, Mike Gallagher,
             Penny Rigler

8.
   Client   *Food Forum 3000*
   Designer Penny Rigler
9.
   Client   *Evolution Music Partners*
   Designer Dvorjac Riemersma
10.
   Client   *AEG*
   Designer Lisa Clark
11.
   Client   *Latin Academy of Recording
             Arts & Sciences*
   Designer Lisa Clark
12.
   Client   *Center for Improvement of
             Child Caring*
   Designer Dvorjac Riemersma
13.
   Client   *Mackworks*
   Designer Dvorjac Riemersma
14.
   Client   *Brewer & Tominaga*
   Designer Dvorjac Riemersma
15.
   Client   *VEDA*
   Designer Dvorjac Riemersma

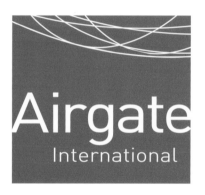

1.

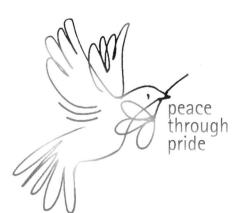

2.

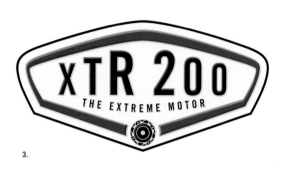

3.

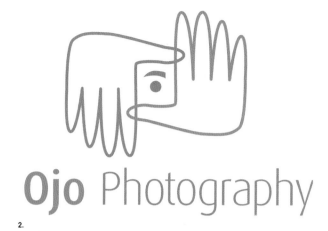

4.

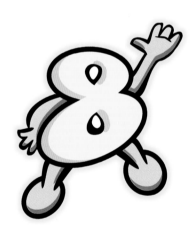

5.

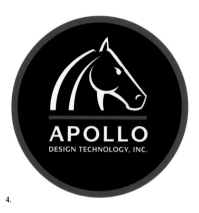

6.

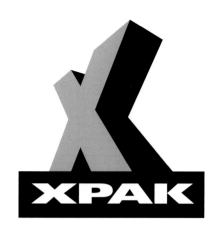

peace
through
pride

7.

1
Design Firm **Proximity Canada**
2
Design Firm **Jenny Kolcun Design**
3
Design Firm **Brad Terres Design**
4
Design Firm **Boyden & Youngblutt**
5
Design Firm **Strategy One, Inc.**
6, 7
Design Firm **Stephen Burdick Design**

1.
Client   *Polyair Envelope Manufacturer*
Designers   Paul Wiersma, Curtis Wolowich
2.
Client   *Ojo Photography*
Designer   Jenny Kolcun

3.
Client   *Casablanca Fan Company*
Designers   Brad Terres, Matt Meehan
4.
Client   *Apollo Design Technology*
Designer   Todd Lemley
5.
Client   *Airgate International*
Designers   Brian Danaher, Jason Thompson
6.
Client   *Technical Assistance Collaborative*
Designer   Stephen Burdick
7.
Client   *Wainwright Bank*
Designer   Stephen Burdick
(opposite)
Client   *Printegra*
Design Firm **TD2, S.C.**
Designer   Rafael Rodrigo Córdova

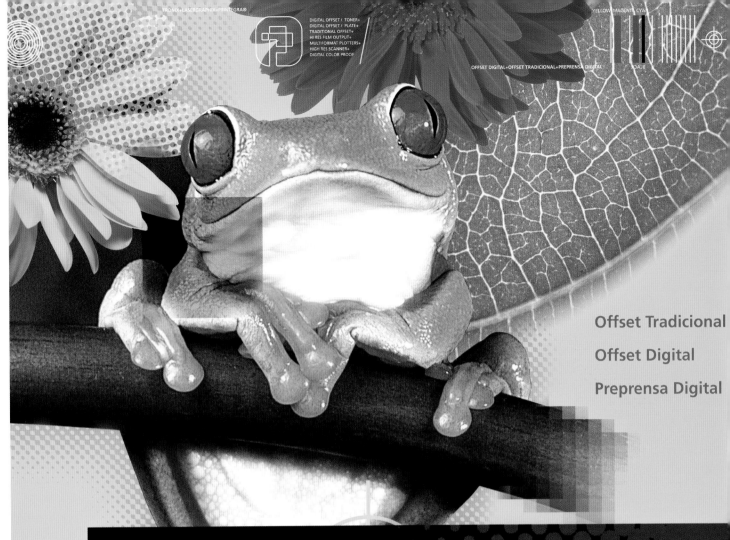

Offset Tradicional

Offset Digital

Preprensa Digital

Trabajando juntos

Ahora somos **Printegra®**.

Trónix y Lasergraphix nos unimos multiplicando nuestras capacidades.

Nos mantenemos a la vanguardia poniendo en tus manos la tecnología de impresión más adecuada para cada tipo de proyecto. Ahora no importará el tamaño, el tiraje, la técnica o el sustrato... En **Printegra®** nuestro trabajo será tu satisfacción.

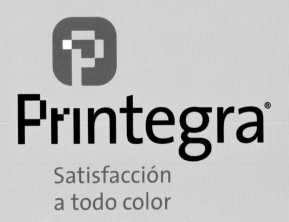

Printegra®

Satisfacción
a todo color

1.

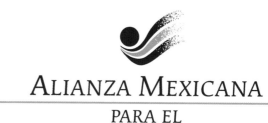

ALIANZA MEXICANA
PARA EL
DESARROLLO SOCIAL, A.C.

2.

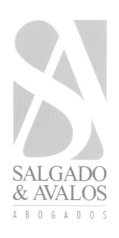

3.

SALGADO
& AVALOS
ABOGADOS

4.

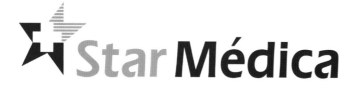

5.

6.

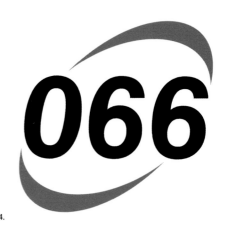

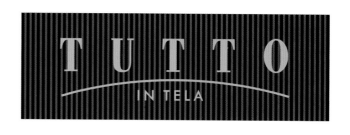

7.

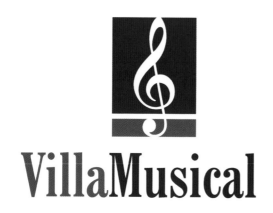

VillaMusical

8.

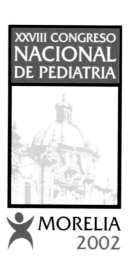

XXVIII CONGRESO
NACIONAL
DE PEDIATRIA

MORELIA
2002

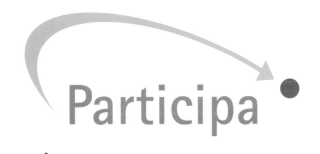

9.

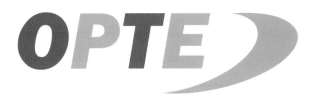

10.

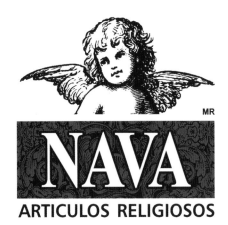

11.

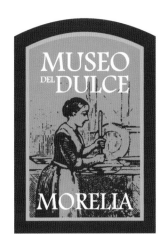

12.

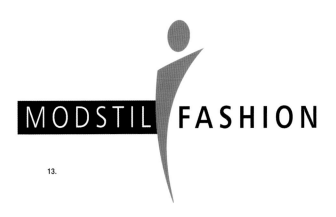

13.

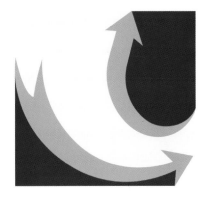

14.

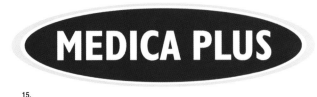

15.

1 - 15
Design Firm **Caracol Consultores SC**

1.
Client   *Aplicación y Comercializadora de Pinturas*
Designer   *Luis Jaime Lara*

2.
Client   *Alianza Mexicana para el Desarrollo Social*
Designers   *Luis Jaime Lara, Mario A. Lara*

3.
Client   *Salgado Avalos Abogados*
Designers   *Luis Jaime Lara, Nora Rodriguez Velasco*

4.
Client   *Gobierno del Estado de Michoacán (Emergencias)*
Designer   *Luis Jaime Lara*

5.
Client   *Hospitales Star Médica*
Designers   *Luis Jaime Lara, Elizabeth Viveros*

6.
Client   *Tutto in Tela*
Designers   *Luis Jaime Lara, Myriam Zavala*

7.
Client   *Villa Musical*
Designers   *Luis Jaime Lara, Myriam Zavala*

8.
Client   *Congreso Nacional de Pediatría 2002*
Designer   *Luis Jaime Lara*

9, 10.
Client   *Gobierno del Estado de Michoacán (Participa)*
Designer   *Luis Jaime Lara*

11.
Client   *Artículos Religiosos Nava*
Designers   *Luis Jaime Lara, Myriam Zavala*

12.
Client   *Museo del Dulce de Morelia*
Designers   *Luis Jaime Lara, Myriam Zavala*

13.
Client   *Modstil Fashion Group*
Designer   *Luis Jaime Lara*

14.
Client   *Coord. Gral para la Atencíon al Migrante Michoacano*
Designers   *Luis Jaime Lara, Laura De la Vega*

15.
Client   *Médica Plus SC*
Designers   *Luis Jaime Lara, Myriam Zavala*

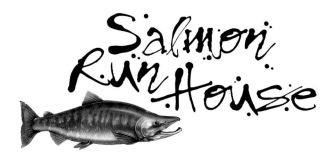

1.

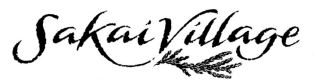

2.

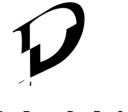

3.

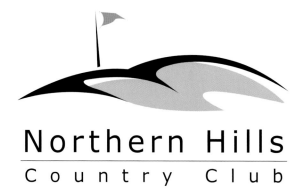

4.

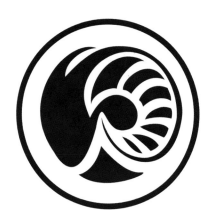

5.

CIBO NATURALS

6.

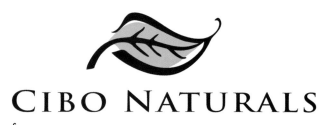

7.

1 - 7
Design Firm **Daigle Design**
1.
Client   *Salmon Run House*
Designers   Candace Daigle, Jessi Carpenter
2.
Client   *Sakai Village*
Designer   Jane Shasky
3.
Client   *Rockford Asset Management*
Designer   Paul Dunning
4.
Client   *Northern Hills Country Club*
Designer   Dan Thompson
5.
Client   *Daigle Design*
Designer   Kim Tebb

6.
Client   *Cibo Naturals*
Designers   Candace Daigle, Jane Shasky,
             Gloria Chen
7.
Client   *Bainbridge Island Performing Arts*
Designers   Candace Daigle, Paul Dunning
(opposite)
Client   *Nestle*
Design Firm **TD2, S.C.**
Designer   Rafael Rodrigo Córdova,
             Liliana Ramírez

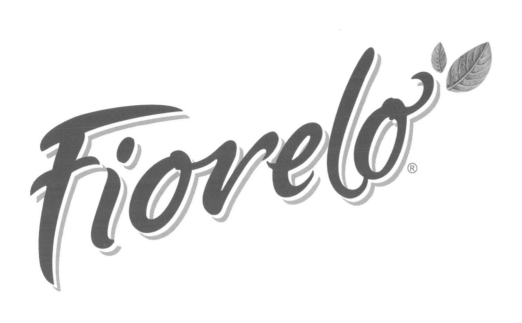

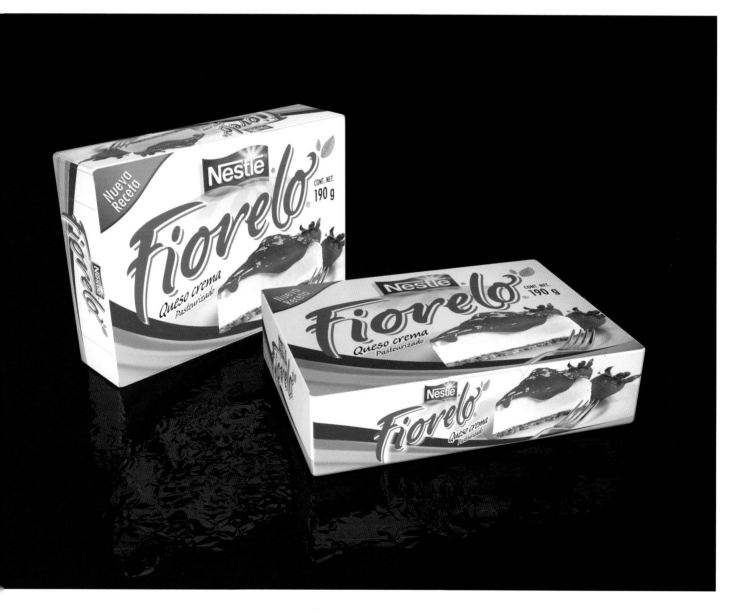

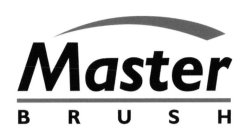

1.

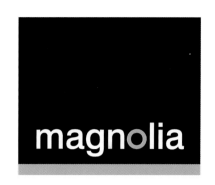

2.

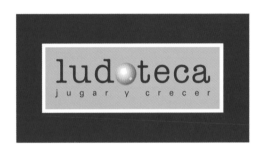

3.

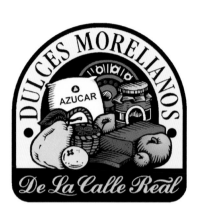

4.

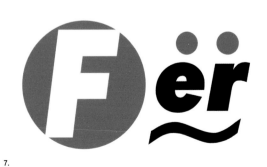

5.

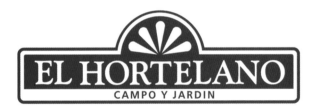

6.

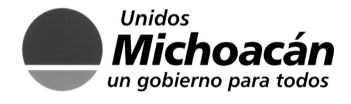

7.

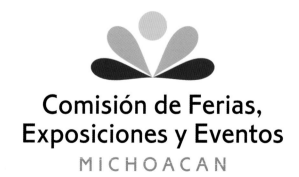

8.

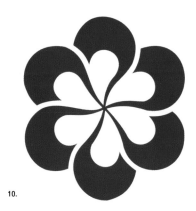

EXIMPORT

9.

10.

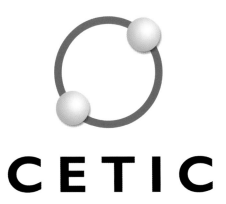

CETIC

11.

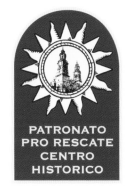

PATRONATO PRO RESCATE CENTRO HISTORICO

Morelia

12.

Iberotel

14.

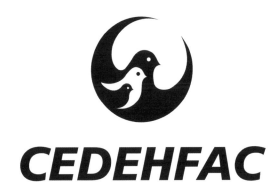

CEDEHFAC

13.

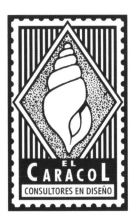

EL CARACOL
CONSULTORES EN DISEÑO

15.

1 - 15
Design Firm **Caracol Consultores SC**

1.
Client · Master Brush
Designer · Luis Jaime Lara

2.
Client · Magnolia Pisos y Recubrimientos
Designers · Luis Jaime Lara, Myriam Zavala

3.
Client · Gobierno del Estado
de Michoacán (Ludotecas)
Designers · Myriam Zavala, Luis Jaime Lara

4.
Client · Dulces Morelianos De La Calle Real
Designer · Luis Jaime Lara

5.
Client · Hortelano Campo y Jardín
Designers · Luis Jaime Lara,
Georgina Luengas M.

6.
Client · Gobierno del Estado
de Michoacán
Designer · Luis Jaime Lara

7.
Client · Fer Material Didáctico Infantil
Designer · Luis Jaime Lara

8.
Client · Comisión de Ferias y
Exposiciones de Michoacán
Designer · Luis Jaime Lara

9.
Client · EXIMPORT
Designer · Luis Jaime Lara

10.
Client · Congreso Nacional de
Escuelas particulares
Designer · Luis Jaime Lara

11.
Client · Gob. del Estado de Michoacán
(Centro de Informática)
Designers · Luis Jaime Lara, Raúl Elizondo,
Carlos Chávez, Victor Rodríguez

12.
Client · Patronato pro—rescate del
Centro Histórico
Designers · Luis Jaime Lara,
Elizabeth Viveros S.

13.
Client · Centro de Desarrollo
Humano y Familiar
Designer · Luis Jaime Lara, Elizabeth Viveros

14.
Client · Ibertol
Designer · Luis Jaime Lara

15.
Client · Caracol Consultores SC
Designers · Luis Jaime Lara, Georgina Luengas

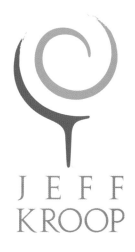

J E F F
KROOP

1.

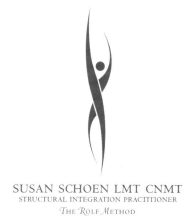

SUSAN SCHOEN LMT CNMT
STRUCTURAL INTEGRATION PRACTITIONER
The Rolf Method

2.

LaTIN access

3.

SnorkelPro®
BY SCUBAPRO®

4.

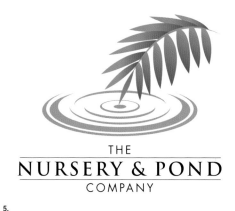

THE
NURSERY & POND
COMPANY

5.

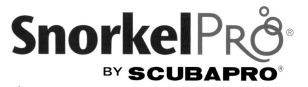

AMERICAN
NATIONAL BANK

6.

primavera
ITALIAN EATERY

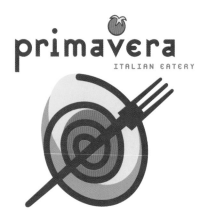

7.

1, 2
Design Firm **Gouthier Design**
3
Design Firm **Smith Design**
4
Design Firm **Laura Coe Design**
5
Design Firm **Rick Cooper, Inc.**
6
Design Firm **Dotzler Creative Arts**
7
Design Firm **Dana Design**
1.
    Client   *Jeff Kroop, Inc.*
    Designers Jonathan Gouthier, Mami Awamura
2.
    Client   *Susan Schoen LMT, CNMT*
    Designers Jonathan Gouthier, Kiley Del Valle

3.
    Client   *Filmation*
    Designer Eileen Berezni
4.
    Client   *Scub Pro*
    Designers Tracy castle, Laura Coe Wright
5.
    Client   *The Nursery & Pond Company*
    Designer Rick Cooper
6.
    Client   *American National Bank*
    Designer Dotzler Creative Arts
7.
    Client   *Primavera, Italian Eatery*
    Designer Dana Ezzell Gay
(opposite)
    Client   *Patricia Gabriela Peláez*
    Design Firm **TD2, S.C.**
    Designer Rafael Rodrigo Córdova

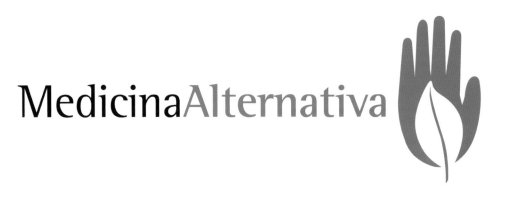

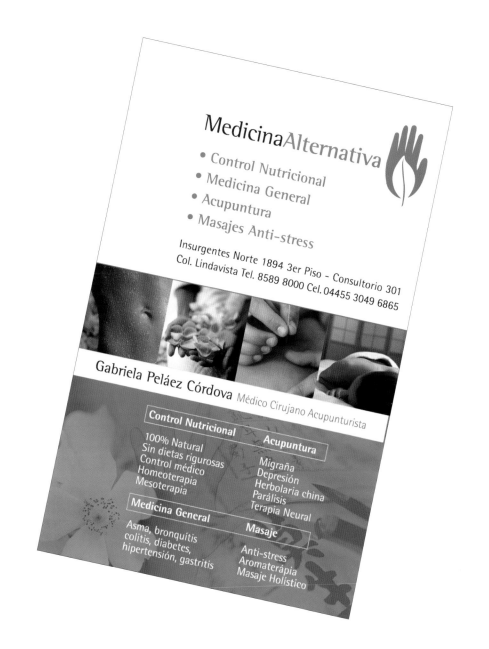

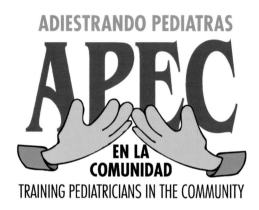

1.

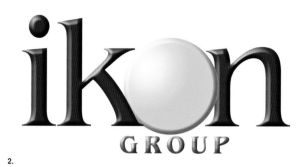

2.

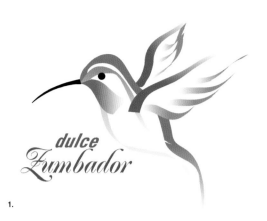

3.

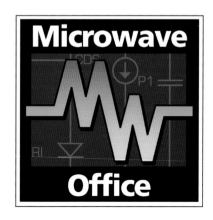

4.

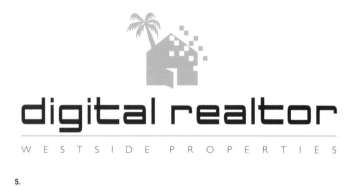

5.

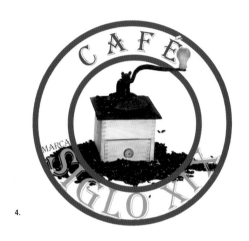

6.

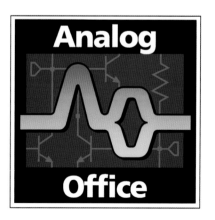

7.

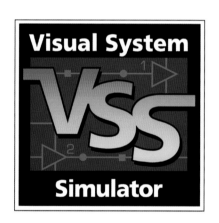

8.

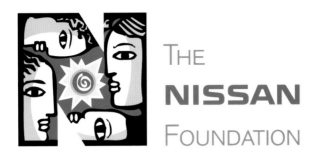

9.

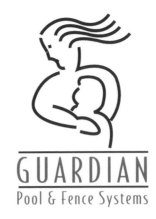

GUARDIAN
Pool & Fence Systems

10.

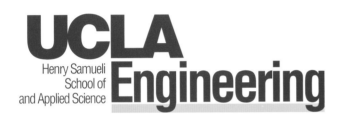

11.

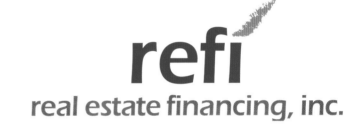
real estate financing, inc.

12.

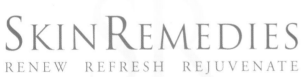

SKIN REMEDIES
RENEW   REFRESH   REJUVENATE

13.

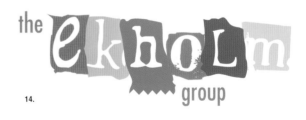
the
group

14.

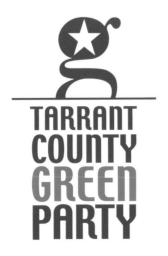

TARRANT
COUNTY
GREEN
PARTY

15.

1 - 4
Design Firm **Maremar Graphic Design**
5 - 13
Design Firm **Poonja Design, Inc.**
14,15
Design Firm **Michael Niblett Design**

1.
| Client | *Lilia Molina* |
| Designer | Marina Rivón |

2.
| Client | *Omar Haedo* |
| Designer | Marina Rivón |

3.
| Client | *UPR Pediatrics Dept.* |
| Designer | Marina Rivón |

4.
| Client | *Ivan Irizarry* |
| Designer | Marina Rivón |

5.
| Client | *Digital Realtor* |
| Designer | Suleman Poonja |

6 - 8.
| Client | *Applied Wave Research, Inc.* |
| Designer | Suleman Poonja |

9.
| Client | *Nissan North America, Inc.* |
| Designer | Suleman Poonja |

10.
| Client | *Guardian Pool and Fence Company* |
| Designer | Suleman Poonja |

11.
| Client | *University of California, Los Angeles* |
| Designer | Suleman Poonja |

12.
| Client | *Real Estate Financing, Inc.* |
| Designer | Suleman Poonja |

13.
| Client | *Skin Remedies* |
| Designer | Suleman Poonja |

14.
| Client | *The Eckholm Group* |
| Designer | Michael Niblett |

15.
| Client | *Green Party of Tarrant County* |
| Designer | Michael Niblett |

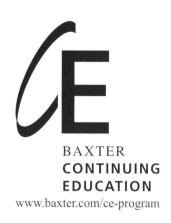

BAXTER
**CONTINUING
EDUCATION**
www.baxter.com/ce-program

1.

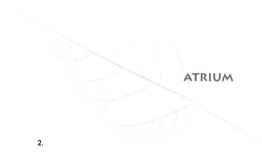

ATRIUM

2.

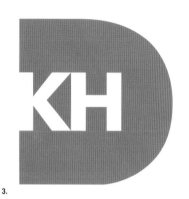

3.

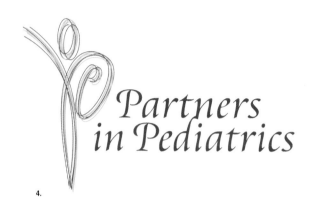

*Partners
in Pediatrics*

4.

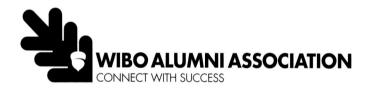

WIBO ALUMNI ASSOCIATION
CONNECT WITH SUCCESS

5.

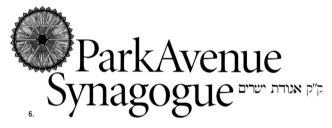

ParkAvenue
Synagogue ק״ק אגודת ישרים

6.

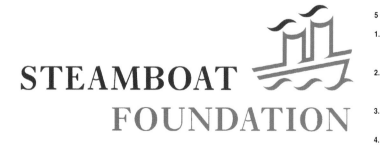

STEAMBOAT
FOUNDATION

7.

1, 2
Design Firm **Design Moves, Ltd.**
3
Design Firm **Kevin Hall Design**
4
Design Firm **Parsons and Maxson, Inc.**
5 - 7
Design Firm **Namaro Graphic Designs, Inc.**
1.
Client   *Baxter Healthcare*
Designers Laurie Medeiros Freed,
          April Weaver
2.
Client   *Atrium Landscape Design*
Designers Laurie Medeiros Freed,
          April Weaver
3.
Client   *Kevin Hall Design*
Designer   Kevin Hall
4.
Client   *Partners In Pediatrics, PC*
Designer   Sean Caldwell

5.
Client   *Workshop in
          Business Opportunities*
Designer   Nadine Robbins
6.
Client   *Park Avenue Synagogue*
Designers Nadine Robbins, Molly Ahearn
7.
Client   *Steamboat Foundation*
Designers Nadine Robbins, Molly Ahearn
(opposite)
Client   *Labatt USA*
Design Firm **HMS Design**
Designer   Josh Laird

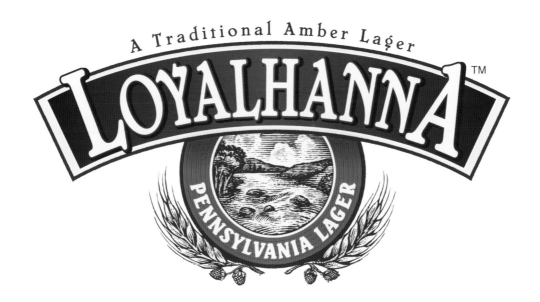

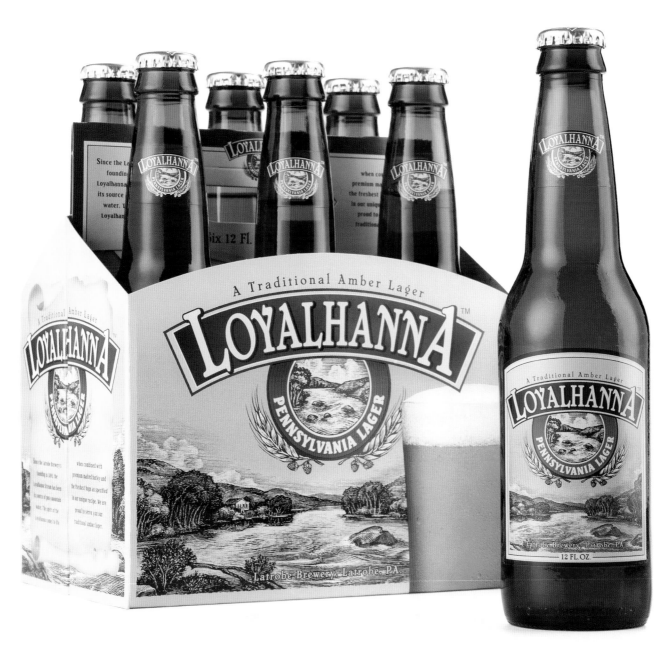

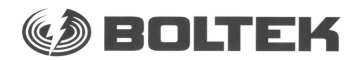

BOLTEK

1.

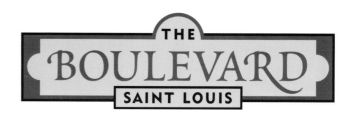

2.

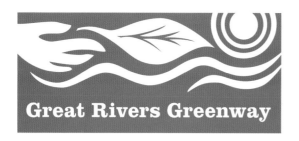

Great Rivers Greenway

Real kitchen ™

3.

4.

St. Louis Mills
SM

PIN-UP BOWL ™

5.

6.

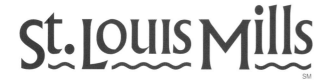

Average Girl
THE MAGAZINE

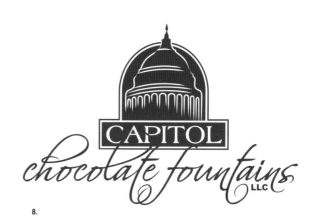

7.

8.

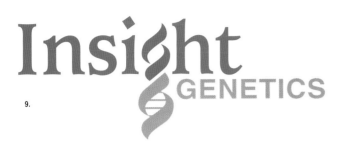

9.

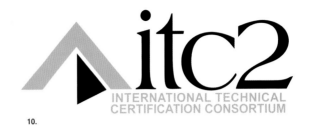

10.

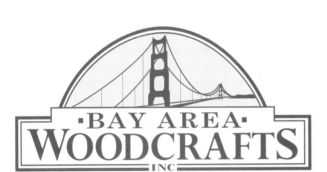

11.

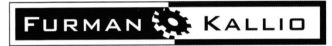

12.

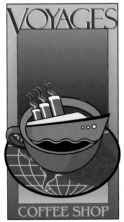

13.

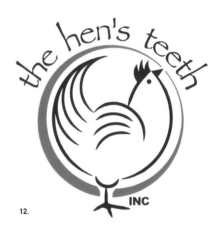

14.

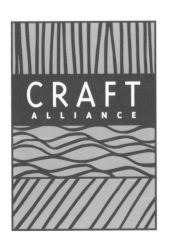

15.

1, 7 - 14
  Design Firm **Nancy Carter Design**
2 - 6, 15
  Design Firm **Kiku Obata & Company**
1.
  Client   *Boltek*
  Designer Nancy Carter
2.
  Client   *Pace Properties*
  Designer Todd Mayberry
3.
  Client   *Great Rivers Greenway*
  Designers Teresa Norton-Young,
            Troy Guzman
4.
  Client   *Real Kitchen*
  Designer Eleanor Safe
5.
  Client   *The Mills Corporation*
  Designer Joe Floresca
6.
  Client   *Pin-up Bowl*
  Designer Rich Nelson
7.
  Client   *Average Girl, The Magazine*
  Designer Nancy Carter

8.
  Client   *Capitol Chocolate Fountains*
  Designer Nancy Carter
9.
  Client   *Insight Genetics*
  Designer Nancy Carter
10.
  Client   *ITC2*
  Designer Nancy Carter
11.
  Client   *Bay Area WoodCrafts*
  Designer Nancy Carter
12.
  Client   *The Hen's Teeth*
  Designer Nancy Carter
13.
  Client   *Voyages Coffee Shop*
  Designer Nancy Carter
14.
  Client   *Furman—Kallio*
  Designer Nancy Carter
15.
  Client   *Craft Alliance*
  Designer Amy Knopf

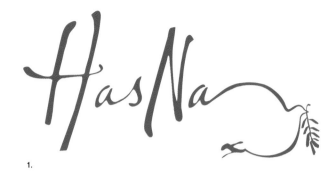

1.

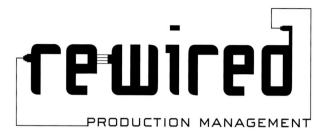

2.

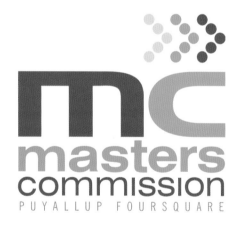

3.

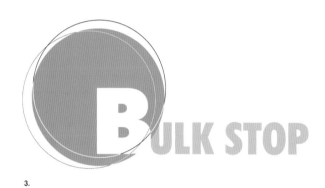

5.

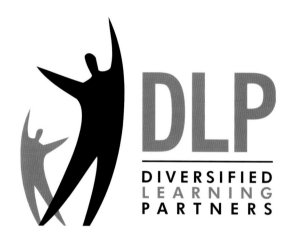

4.

Direct Source

what's in store.

6.

refresh

inspiring results

7.

1, 2
Design Firm **Jill Bredthauer**
3
Design Firm **B² Communications**
4, 5
Design Firm **Drotz Design**
6, 7
Design Firm **Peggy Lauritsen Design Group**
1.
  Client   *Hasna Inc.*
  Designer   Jill Bredthauer
2.
  Client   *Rewired Production Management*
  Designer   Jill Bredthauer
3.
  Client   *Bulk Stop*
  Designer   Brian Berry
4.
  Client   *DLP*
  Designer   Dallas Drotz
5.
  Client   *Puyallup Foursquare*
  Designer   Dallas Drotz

6.
  Client   *Direct Source, Inc.*
  Designer   Michelle Ducayet
7.
  Client   *Lawson Software*
  Designer   John Haines
(opposite)
  Client   *Labatt USA*
  Design Firm **HMS Design**
  Designer   Jeff Meyer

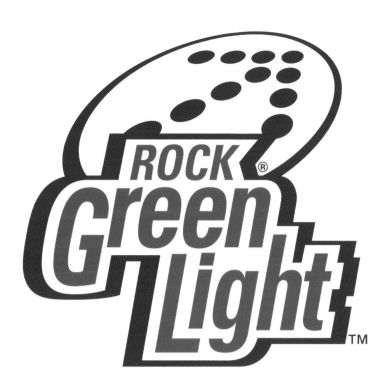

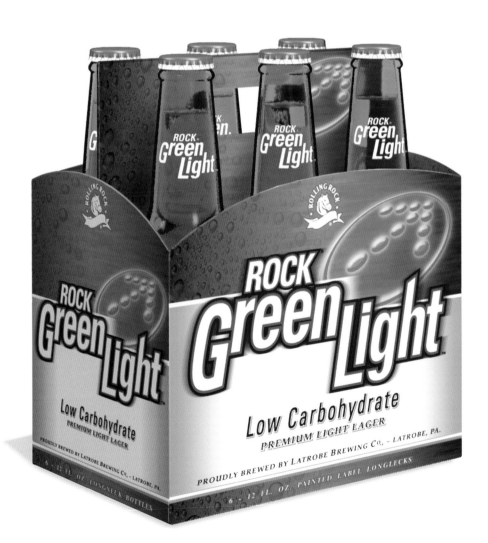

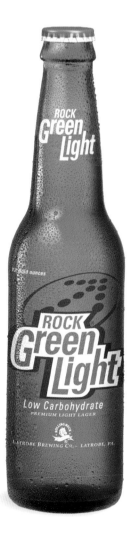

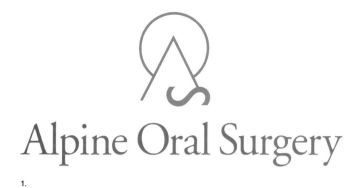

Alpine Oral Surgery

1.

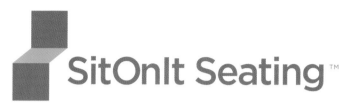

SitOnIt Seating™

2.

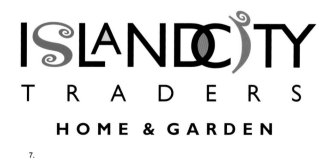

x·rite

3.

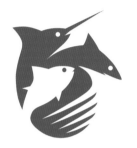

University of Miami
Center for Sustainable Fisheries

4.

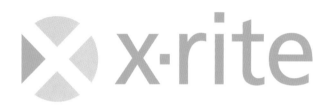

STURGEON
Aqua Farms

5.

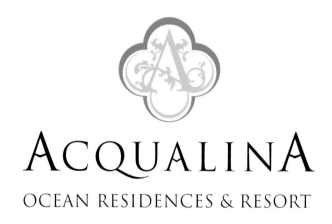

ACQUALINA
OCEAN RESIDENCES & RESORT

6.

ISLANDCITY
TRADERS
HOME & GARDEN

7.

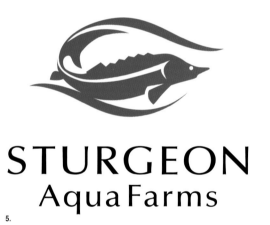

NCORE
National Center for Caribbean
Coral Reef Research

8.

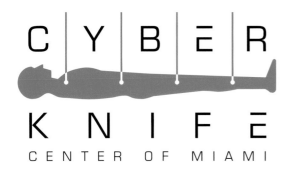

C Y B E R
K N I F E
CENTER OF MIAMI

9.

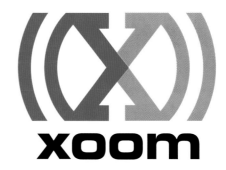

xoom

10.

PEW INSTITUTE FOR
OCEAN SCIENCE

11.

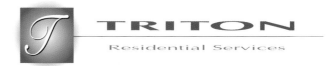

TRITON
Residential Services

12.

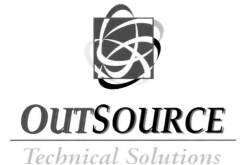

OutSource
Technical Solutions
bringing it all together

13.

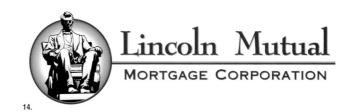

Lincoln Mutual
MORTGAGE CORPORATION

14.

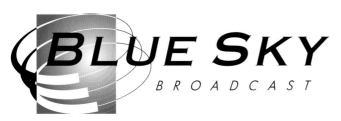

BLUE SKY
BROADCAST

15.

1 - 3
Design Firm **BBK Studio**
4 - 11
Design Firm **Laidlaw Gervais**
12 - 15
Design Firm **Dynapac Design Group**

1.
Client *Alpine Oral Surgery*
Designer Sharon Oleniczak

2.
Client *SitOnit Seating*
Designers Yang Kim, Kevin Budelmann,
Michele Chartier, Alison Popp,
Brian Hauch, Sharon Oleniczak

3.
Client *X-Rite*
Designers Yang Kim, Kevin Budelmann,
Michele Chartier, Alison Popp,
Brian Hauch, Sharon Oleniczak

4.
Client *University of Miami Center for
Sustainable Fisheries*
Designer David Laidlaw

5.
Client *Sturgeon Aquafarms*
Designer David Laidlaw

6.
Client *Acqualina Ocean Residences
& Resort*
Designer David Laidlaw

7.
Client *Island City Traders*
Designer David Laidlaw

8.
Client *NCORE —National Center
for Caribbean Coral Reef Research*
Designer David Laidlaw

9.
Client *Cyberknife Center of Miami*
Designer David Laidlaw

10.
Client *Xoom*
Designer David Laidlaw

11.
Client *Pew Institute for Ocean Science*
Designer David Laidlaw

12.
Client *Triton Residential Services*
Designer Lee A. Aellig

13.
Client *OutSource Technical Solutions*
Designer Lee A. Aellig

14.
Client *Lincoln Mutual
Mortgage Corporation*
Designer Lee A. Aellig

15.
Client *BlueSky Broadcast*
Designer Lee A. Aellig

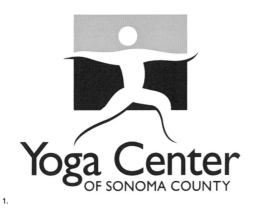

1.

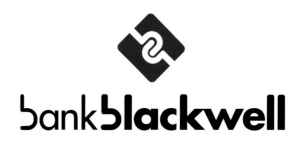

2.

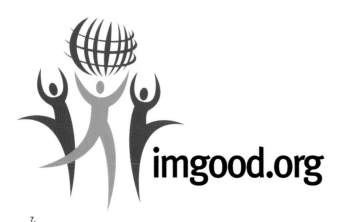

3.

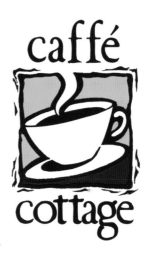

4.

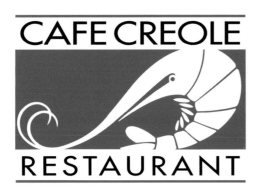

5.

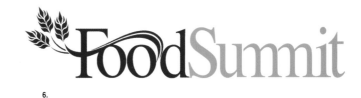

6.

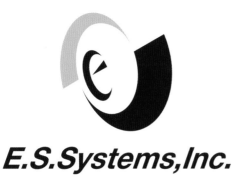

7.

1 - 7
Design Firm **Creative Madhouse**
1.
Client   *Yoga Center of Sonoma County*
Designer   Madelyn Wattigney
2.
Client   *BankBlackwell*
Designer   Madelyn Wattigney
3.
Client   *Cafe Creole Restaurant*
Designer   Madelyn Wattigney
4.
Client   *Caffe Cottage*
Designer   Madelyn Wattigney
5.
Client   *E.S. Systems, Inc.*
Designer   Madelyn Wattigney
6.
Client   *FoodSummit*
Designer   Madelyn Wattigney
7.
Client   *ImGood.org*
Designer   Madelyn Wattigney

(opposite)
Client   *Wm. Bolthouse Farms*
Design Firm **HMS Design**
Designer   Josh Laird

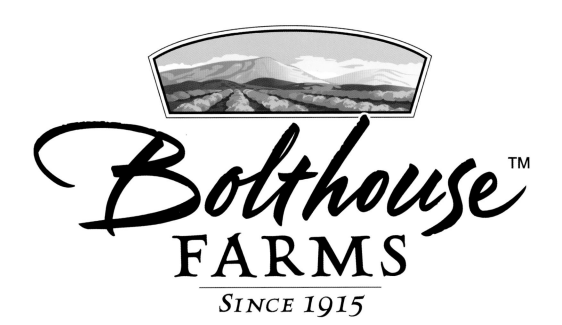

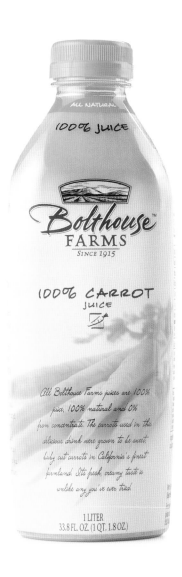

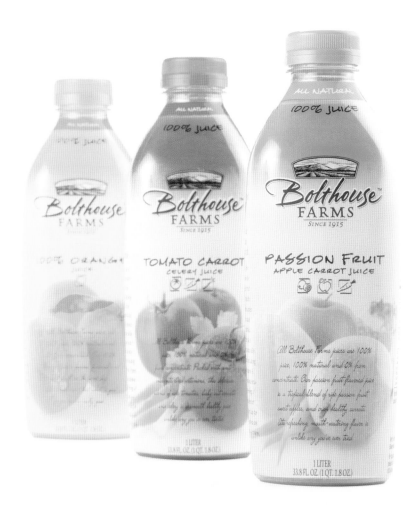

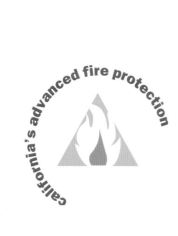

1.

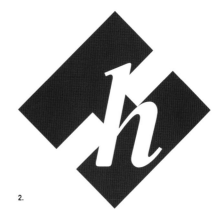

2.

3.

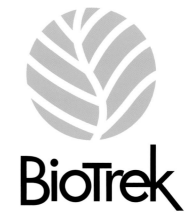

4.

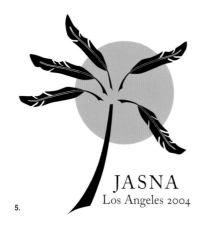

JASNA
Los Angeles 2004

5.

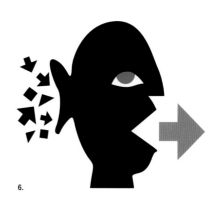

6.

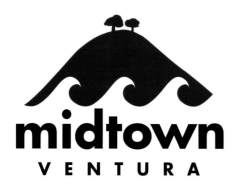

midtown
VENTURA

7.

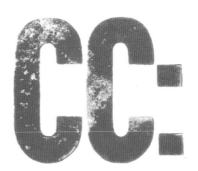

8.

64

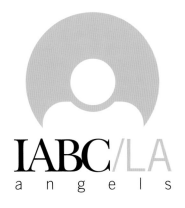

IABC/LA
a n g e l s

9.

Montrachet

PREMIER APARTMENT HOMES

10.

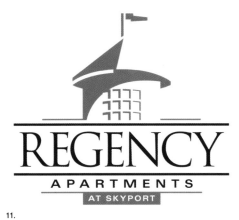

REGENCY
APARTMENTS
AT SKYPORT

11.

BLUESKIES
Marketing & Public Relations Staffing Solutions

12.

Back on Track

13.

CMC

14.

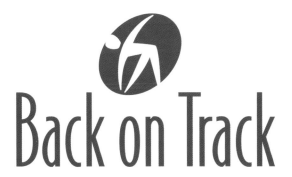

BAYROCK
RESIDENTIAL

15.

1 - 9
Design Firm **Gunnar Swanson Design Office**
10 - 15
Design Firm **Shawver Associates, Inc.**
1.
　Client　　Hanham Consulting
　Designer　Gunnar Swanson
2.
　Client　　Halstead Communication
　Designer　Gunnar Swanson
3.
　Client　　California's Advanced Fire
　　　　　　Protection
　Designer　Gunnar Swanson
4.
　Client　　California State Polytechnic
　　　　　　University Pomona
　Designer　Gunnar Swanson
5.
　Client　　Jane Austen Society of
　　　　　　North America
　Designer　Gunnar Swanson
6.
　Client　　Gunnar Swanson Design Office
　Designer　Gunnar Swanson

7.
　Client　　Midtown Ventura Community
　　　　　　Council
　Designer　Gunnar Swanson
8.
　Client　　County Communicators
　Designer　Gunnar Swanson
9.
　Client　　IABC/LA The Los Angeles Chapter
　　　　　　of the International Association
　　　　　　of Business Communicators
　Designer　Gunnar Swanson
10.
　Client　　Bay Rock
　Designer　Rich Costa
11.
　Client　　SSR Realty
　Designers　Rich Costa, Kyle Ogden
12.
　Client　　Blue Skies
　Designer　Amy Krachenfels
13.
　Client　　Back on Track
　Designer　Amy Krachenfels
14.
　Client　　CMC
　Designers　Rich Costa
15.
　Client　　Bay Rock Residential
　Designers　Rich Costa

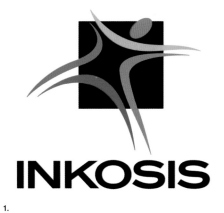

INKOSIS

1.

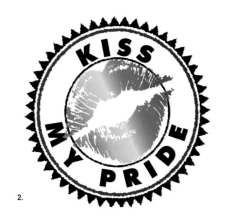

2.

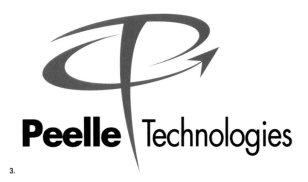

Peelle Technologies

3.

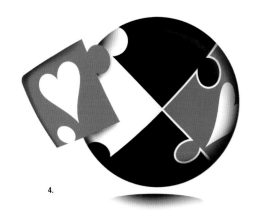

4.

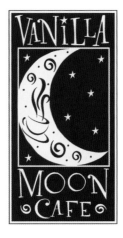

5.

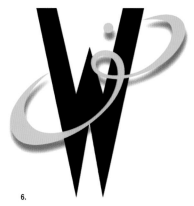

6.

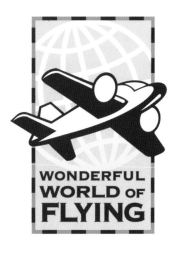

7.

1 - 7
Design Firm **Creative Madhouse**
1.
   Client   *Inkosis*
   Designer Madelyn Wattigney
2.
   Client   *Kiss My Pride*
   Designer Madelyn Wattigney
3.
   Client   *Peelle Technology*
   Designer Madelyn Wattigney
4.
   Client   *Two Topia*
   Designer Madelyn Wattigney
5.
   Client   *Vanilla Moon Cafe*
   Designer Madelyn Wattigney
6.
   Client   *W3 Master*
   Designer Madelyn Wattigney
7.
   Client   *Wonderful World of Flying*
   Designer Madelyn Wattigney

(opposite)
   Client   *Atlantic Maintenance Corp.*
   Design Firm **Fiorentino Associates**
   Designer Andy Eng

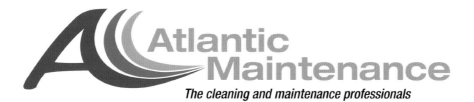

The cleaning and maintenance professionals
that know the outside, inside out.

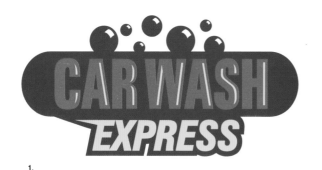

1.

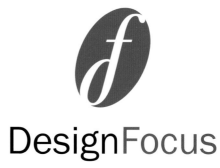

2.

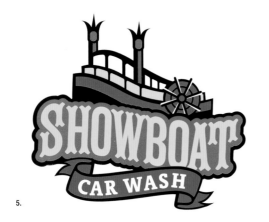

3.

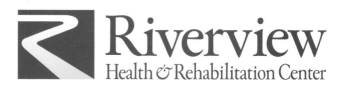

4.

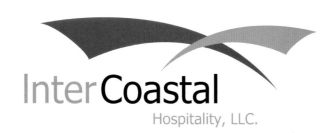

5.

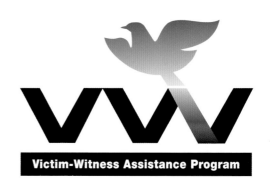

6.

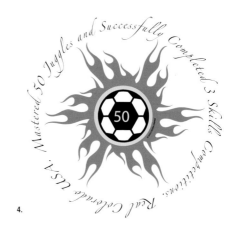

7.

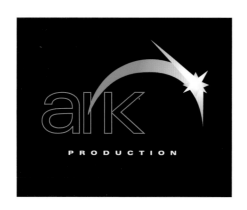

8.

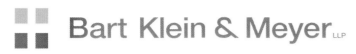

Bart Klein & Meyer LLP

9.

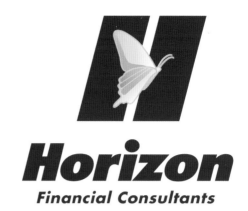

Horizon
Financial Consultants

10.

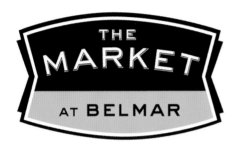

THE
MARKET
AT BELMAR

FARMERS, ARTISANS, FRIENDS

EVERY SUNDAY AT BELMAR

11.

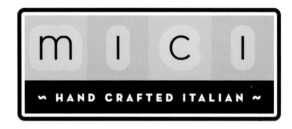

m i c i

~ HAND CRAFTED ITALIAN ~

12.

BRADBURN ROW

URBAN STYLE APARTMENT HOMES

13.

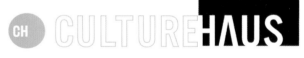

CH CULTURE**HAUS**

14.

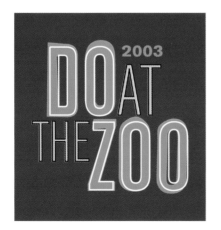

DO AT THE ZOO 2003

15.

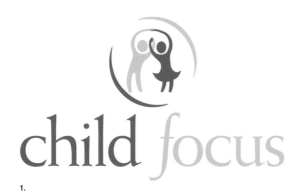

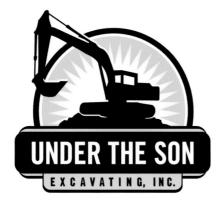

1.

2.

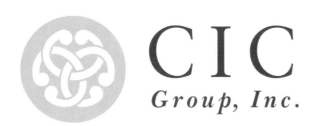

3.

4.

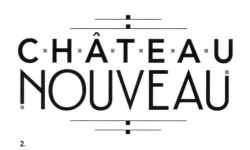

5.

6.

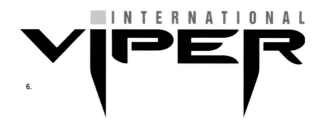

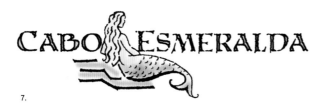

7.

1 - 7
Design Firm **CDI Studios**

1.
Client   *Child Focus of Nevada*
Designer   Henry Martinez III

2.
Client   *Pacific Properties*
Designer   Mackenzie Walsh

3.
Client   *Capital Investment Company*
Designers   Michelle Georgilas,
        Eddie Roberts

4.
Client   *Meridias Capital*
Designers   Michelle Georgilas,
        Eddie Roberts

5.
Client   *Under the Son Excavating*
Designers   Victoria Hart,
        Mackenzie Walsh

6.
Client   *Viper International*
Designer   Casey Corcoran

7.
Client   *Bernard Realty*
Designer   Victoria Hart
(opposite)
Client   *Tasty Baking Company*
Design Firm **Munroe Creative Partners**
Designer   Mike Cavallaro

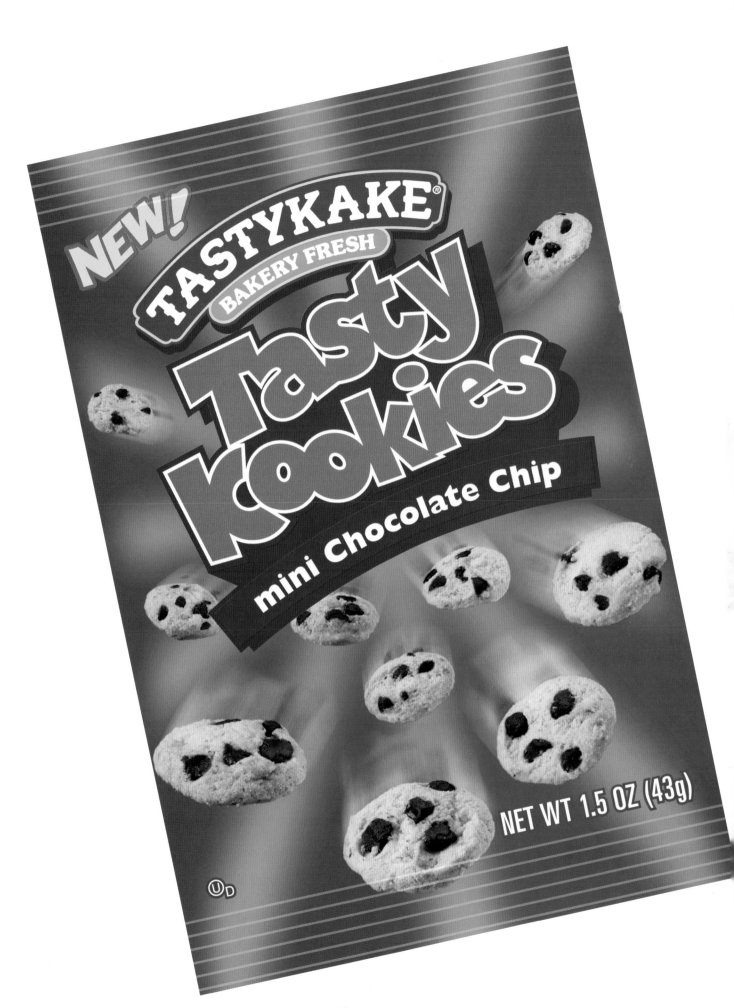

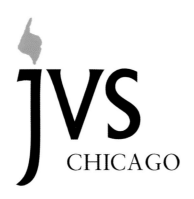

1.

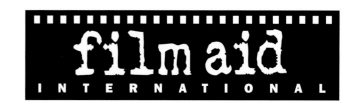

2.

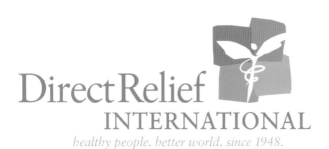

3.

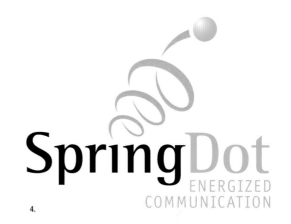

4.

5.

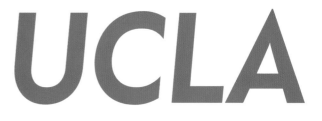

6.

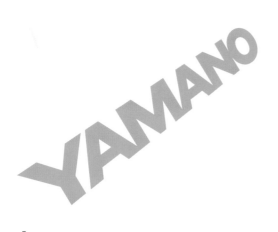

7.

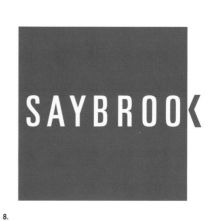

8.

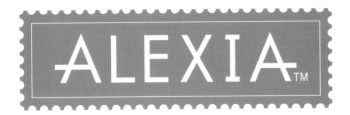

9.

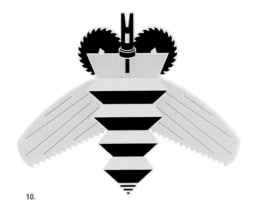

10.

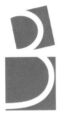

BLOCK CONSULTING

11.

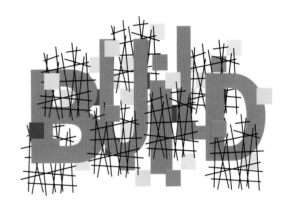

12.

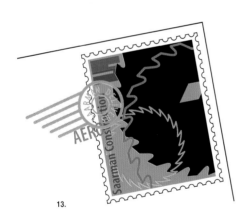

13.

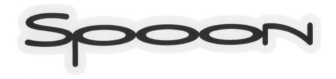

14.

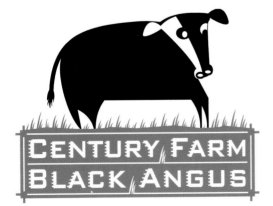

15.

1 - 5		
Design Firm	**Lipson Alport Glass & Assoc.**	
6 - 9		
Design Firm	**Bright Strategic Design**	
10 - 15		
Design Firm	**Bruce Yelaska Design**	
1.		
Client	*Jewish Vocational services*	
Designer	Michelle Palko	
2.		
Client	*Film Aid International*	
Designer	Michelle Palko	
3.		
Client	*Direct Relief International*	
Designer	Michelle Palko	
4.		
Client	*SpringDot*	
Designer	Kevin Wimmer	
5.		
Client	*ARS Rescue Rooter*	
Designer	Lori Cerwin	
6.		
Client	*University of California, Los Angeles*	
Designers	Keith Bright, Denis Parkhurst	

7.	
Client	*Yamano Beauty School*
Designers	Keith Bright, Glenn Sakamoto
8.	
Client	*Saybrooke Capital, LLC*
Designers	Keith Bright, Glenn Sakamoto
9.	
Client	*Alexia Foods*
Designers	Keith Bright, Glenn Sakamoto
10.	
Client	*Saarman Construction*
Designer	Bruce Yelaska
11.	
Client	*Block Consulting*
Designer	Bruce Yelaska
12, 13.	
Client	*Saarman Construction*
Designer	Bruce Yelaska
14.	
Client	*Spoon Restaurant*
Designer	Bruce Yelaska
15.	
Client	*Century Farm Black Angus*
Designer	Bruce Yelaska

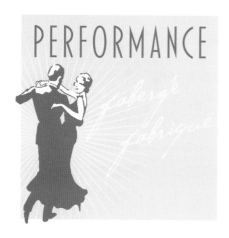

1.

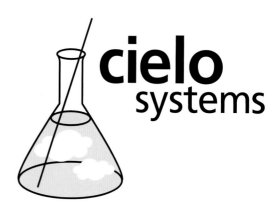

2.

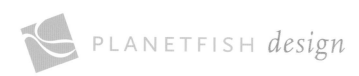

3.

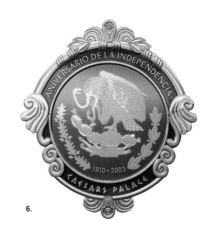

4.

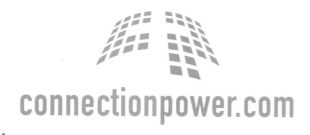

5.

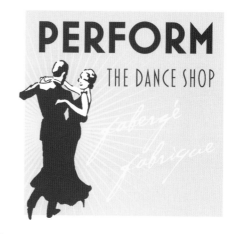

6.

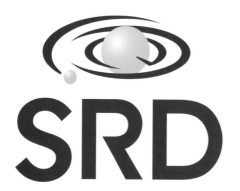

7.

1 - 4
Design Firm **PlanetFish Design**
5 - 7
Design Firm **CDI Studios**
1, 2.
   Client   *Fabergé Fabrique*
   Designer   Felicia Lo
3.
   Client   *PlanetFish Design*
   Designer   Felicia Lo
4.
   Client   *Cielo Systems*
   Designer   Felicia Lo
5.
   Client   *Connection Power*
   Designers Eddie Roberts,
                Victoria Hart

6.
   Client   *Ceasars Palace*
   Designers Victoria Hart,
                Henry Marting III,
                Eddie Roberts
7.
   Client   *Systems Research
                Development*
   Designers Eddie Roberts,
                Victoria Hart
(opposite)
   Client   *Pinnacle Foods*
   Design Firm **Zunda Design Group**
   Designers Todd Nickel, Charles Zunda,
                Tom James

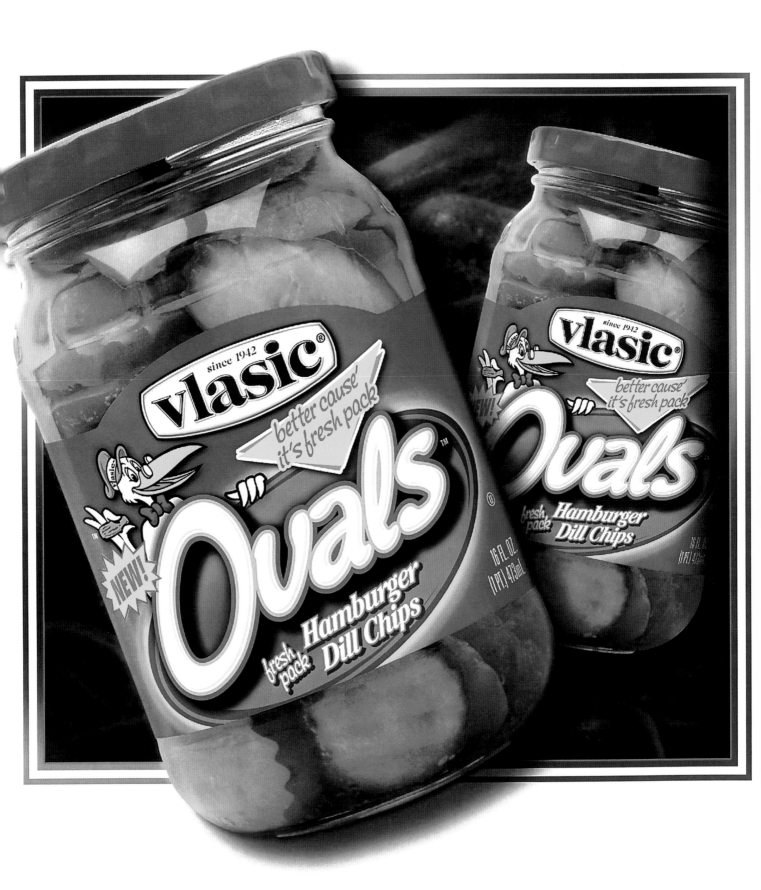

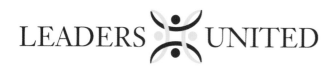

1.

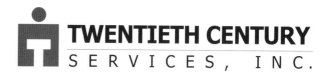

2.

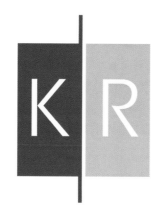

3.

CHICAGO HEALTH
connection

4.

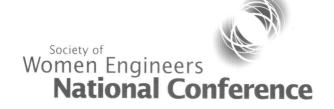

5.

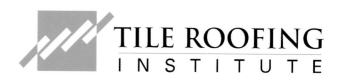

6.

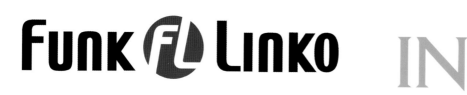

7.

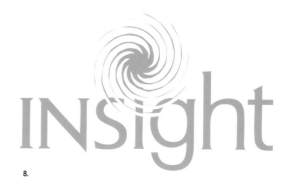

8.

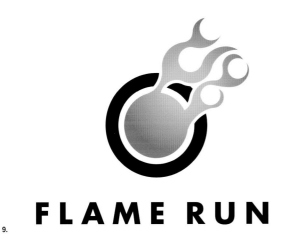

FLAME RUN

9.

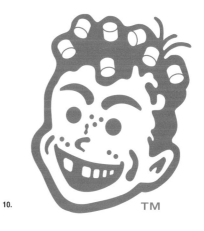

TM

10.

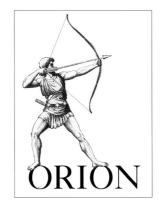

ORION

11.

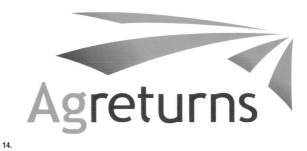

coffeesmiths

12.

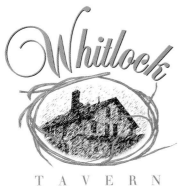

Whitlock

TAVERN

13.

Agreturns

14.

AWAKE

15.

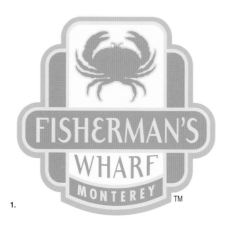

1.

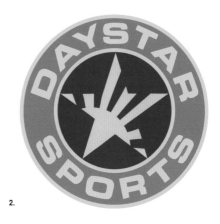

2.

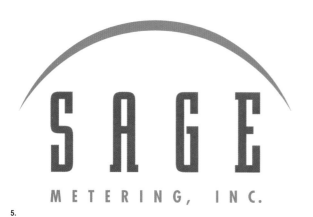

3.

4.

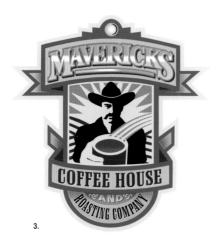

5.

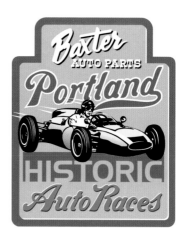

6.

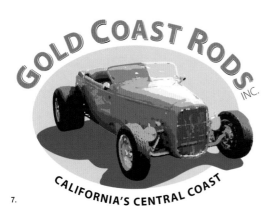

7.

1 - 7
Design Firm **The Wecker Group**
1.
Client   *Fisherman's Wharf Monterey*
Designer   Robert Wecker
2.
Client   *Daystar Sports*
Designer   Robert Wecker
3.
Client   *Mavericks Coffee House &*
            Roasting Company
Designer   Robert Wecker
4.
Client   *Portland Historic*
            Automobile Races
Designer   Robert Wecker
5.
Client   *Sage Metering*
Designer   Robert Wecker
6.
Client   *Greenblock*
Designers   Robert Wecker,
            Matt Gnibus

7.
Client   *Gold Coast Rods, Inc.*
Designer   Robert Wecker
(opposite)
Client   *Drinks Americas, Inc.*
Design Firm **Zunda Design Group**
Designers   Pat Sullivan,
            Charles Zunda

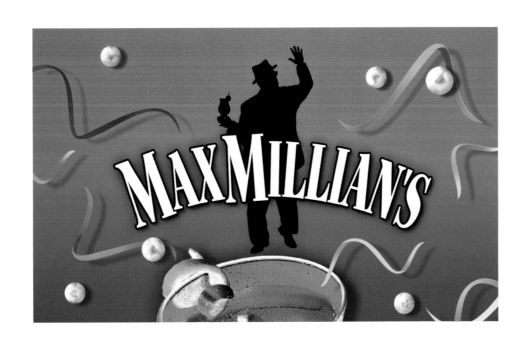

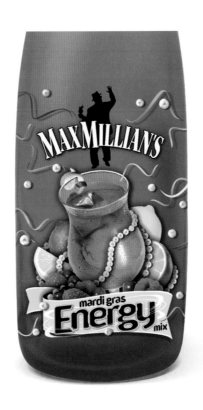

fischers fritzz

1.

Wild World

JAGDCENTER DORSTEN

2.

familyand**friends**
Einfach mehr zurückbekommen.

3.

ascos
ruhrgas positioning services

4.

wortundtat

5.

EDDIE'S MILLION DOLLAR COOK-OFF

6.

CARE
Center for Activity
Research and Education

7.

DAVITA
CHILDREN'S
FOUNDATION

8.

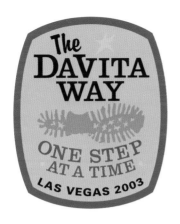

9.

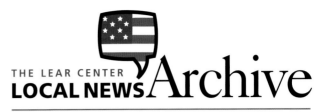

A Project of the USC Annenberg School and the University of Wisconsin

10.

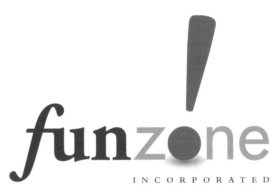

11.

12.

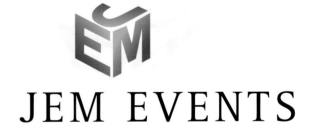

13.

14.

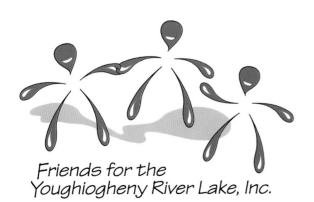

15.

1 - 5
Design Firm **Buttgereit und Heidenreich**
6 - 14
Design Firm **IE Design + Communications**
15
Design Firm **Freelance Visual Artist**

3.
Client   *family and friends*
Designers Michael Buttgereit,
          Wolfram Heidenreich
4.
Client   *Ruhrgas AG, Essen, Germany*
Designer Michael Buttgereit
5.
Client   *Wort und Tat e.v., Essen, Germany*
Designers Michael Buttgereit,
          Wolfram Heidenreich
6.
Client   *Disney*
Designers Marcie Carson, Cya Nelson
7.
Client   *CARE*
Designers Marcie Carson, Amy Klass

8.
Client   *Davita Healthcare*
Designers Marcie Carson, Cya Nelson
9.
Client   *Davita Healthcare*
Designer Marcie Carson
10 - 11
Client   *University of Southern California*
Designers Marcie Carson, Cya Nelson
12.
Client   *Fun Zone*
Designer Marcie Carson
13.
Client   *OnSmile*
Designer Marcie Carson
14.
Client   *JEM Events*
Designer Marcie Carson
15.
Client   *Friends for the Youghiogheny
          River Lake, Inc.*
Designer Chris M. Brioady

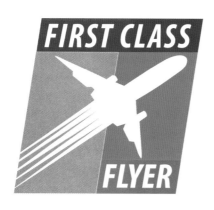

1.

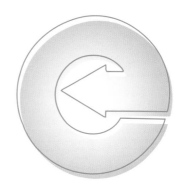

ENTERSPORTS

2.

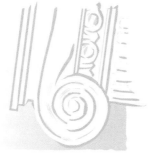

"Here for Good"

Community
Foundation
for Monterey
County

3.

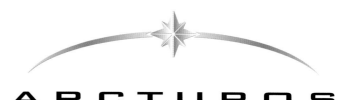

At Home, Around the World

4.

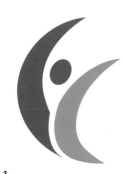

SAMUEL B. BENAVIDES, AIA

5.

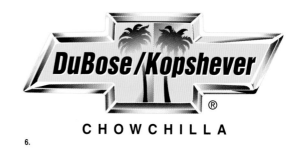

CHOWCHILLA

6.

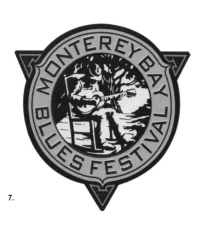

7.

1 - 7
Design Firm **The Wecker Group**
1.
Client — *First Class Flyer*
Designers — Robert Wecker,
Matt Gnibus

2.
Client — *Entersports*
Designer — Robert Wecker

3.
Client — *Community Foundation for Monterey County*
Designer — Robert Wecker

4.
Client — *Arcturos Yachts*
Designers — Robert Wecker,
Matt Gnibus

5.
Client — *Benavides Architects*
Designer — Robert Wecker

6.
Client — *DuBose/Kopshever Chevrolet*
Designers — Robert Wecker,
Matt Gnibus

7.
Client — *Monterey Bay Blues Festival*
Designers — Robert Wecker,
Harry Briggs

(opposite)
Client — *Pinnacle Foods*
Design Firm **Zunda Design Group**
Designers — Todd Nickel,
Charles Zunda,
Tom James

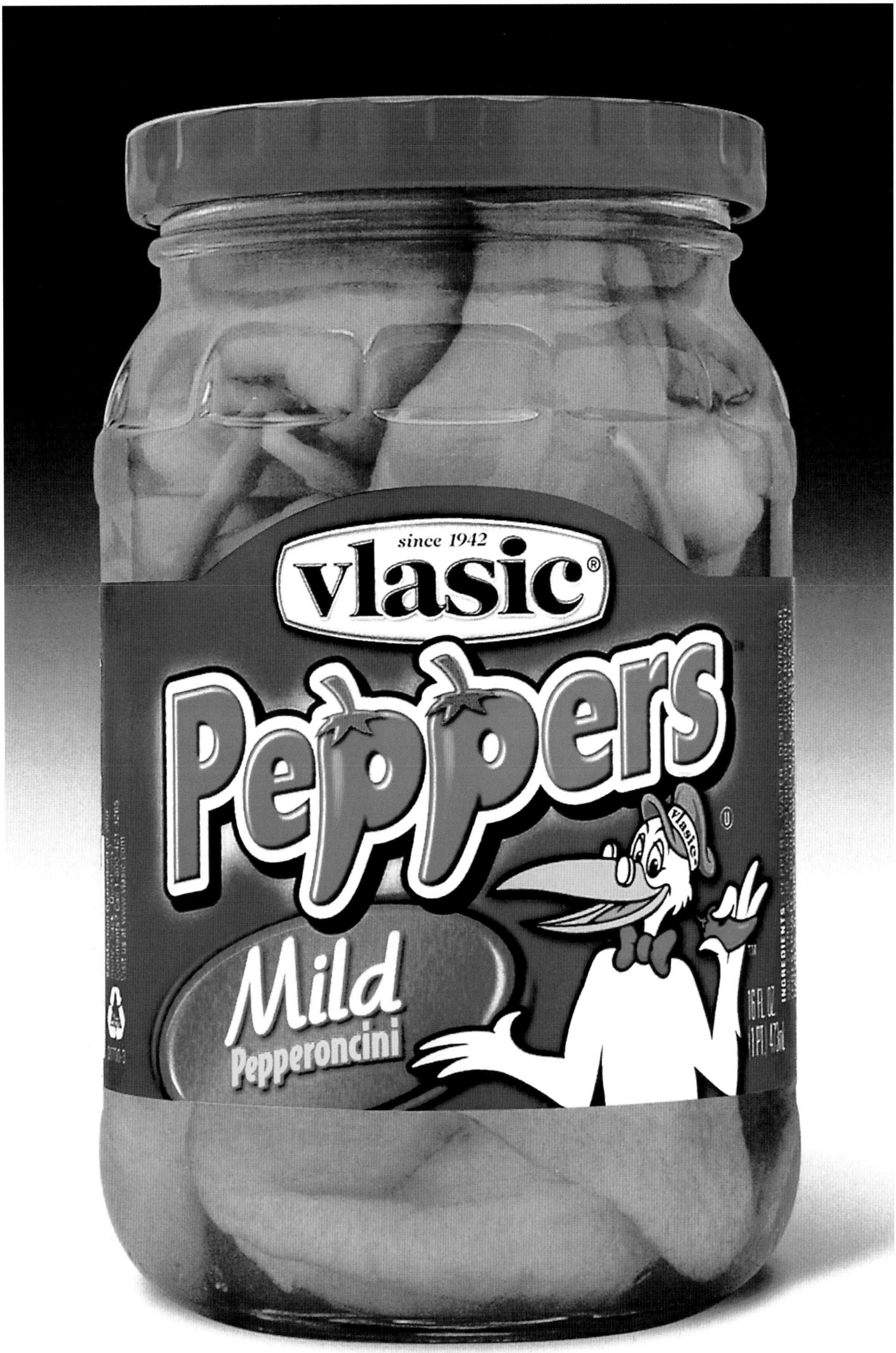
since 1942
vlasic®
Peppers™
Mild
Pepperoncini
16 FL OZ
(1 PT) 473mL

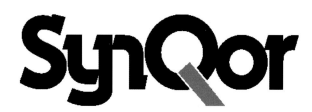

1.

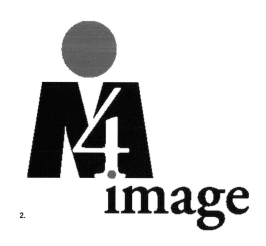

2.

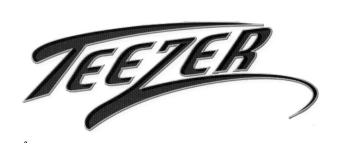

3.

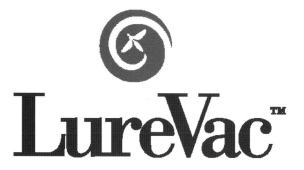

4.

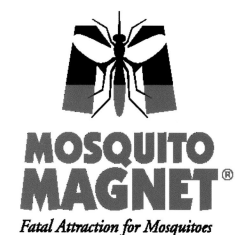

5.

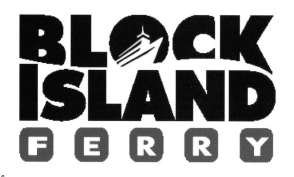

6.

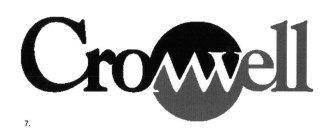

7.

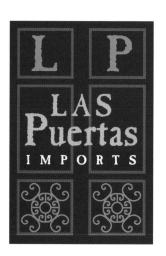

8.

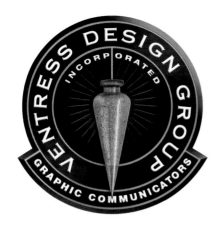

9.

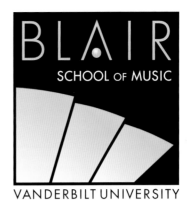

10.

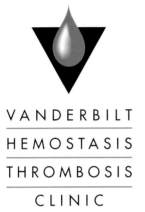

VANDERBILT
HEMOSTASIS
THROMBOSIS
CLINIC

11.

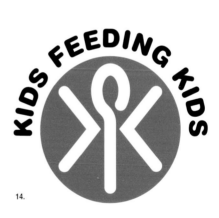

CERTIFIED PUBLIC ACCOUNTANTS

12.

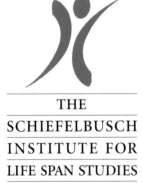

THE
SCHIEFELBUSCH
INSTITUTE FOR
LIFE SPAN STUDIES

13.

14.

15.

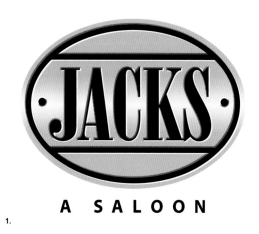

·JACKS·

A SALOON

1.

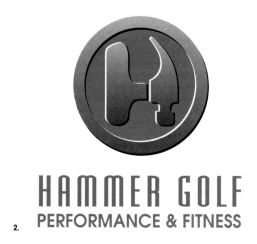

HAMMER GOLF

PERFORMANCE & FITNESS

2.

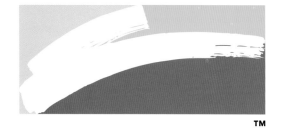

HACKETT
PROPERTIES

3.

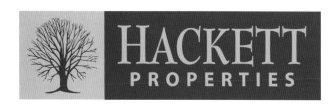

WarnerJoest
BUILDERS

4.

Tools for Decision

™

5.

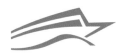

TAYLOR BAY YACHTS, LLC

6.

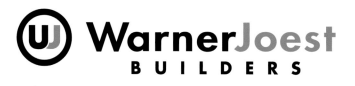

RetReat
Living the Spa Lifestyle

7.

1 - 7
Design Firm **The Wecker Group**
1.
    Client   *Doubletree Hotel/Monterey*
    Designer Robert Wecker
2.
    Client   *Hammer Golf Performance*
    Designers Robert Wecker,
                 Matt Gnibus
3.
    Client   *Hackett Properties*
    Designer Robert Wecker
4.
    Client   *Warner Joest Builders*
    Designers Robert Wecker,
                 Tremayne Cryer
5.
    Client   *Tools for Decision*
    Designers Robert Wecker,
                 Matt Gnibus
6.
    Client   *Taylor Bay Yachts*
    Designers Robert Wecker,
                 Matt Gnibus

7.
    Client   *Retreat*
    Designer Robert Wecker
(opposite)
    Client   *American Heritage Billiards*
    Design Firm **Berni Marketing & Design**
    Designers Carlos Seminario,
                 Stuart Berni

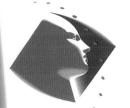

American Heritage

Challenge

To uncover consumer buying habits and reposition the #2 billiards company in the U.S. to stimulate sales growth.

Solution

Repositioned American Heritage through the creation of a new branding strategy and research-based tagline that appeals to consumers looking "For the Finishing Touch" to complete a room's décor. Developed a dynamic corporate identity and website. Designed an innovative kiosk and POP display system that serves as a customizable tool to improve the buying experience.

Result

Right on cue: new positioning and kiosk/sales resonate with target audience yielding exponential sales growth.

Quote

"Our new corporate identity and repositioning have really improved our image. The interactive point of purchase system is a first in the industry and consumers really love it. We look forward to working with Berni for years to come."

Joe Pucci, President

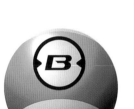

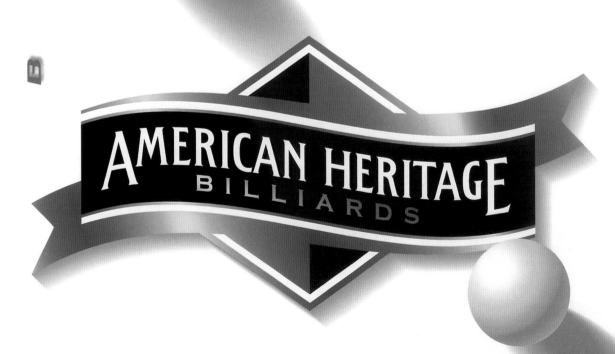

www.bernidesign.com

◆ FOR THE FINISHING TOUCH ◆

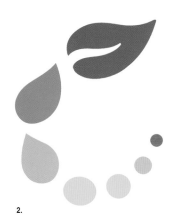

1.

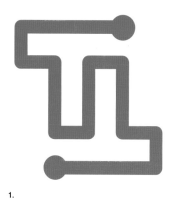

2.

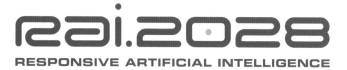

FREEMOTION™

3.

CHURCH CENTERED
MISSION

4.

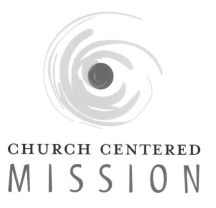

rai.2028
RESPONSIVE ARTIFICIAL INTELLIGENCE

5.

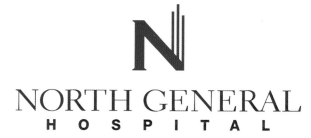

METRIC REPORTS
REPORTING ALIGNED TO YOUR GOALS™

6.

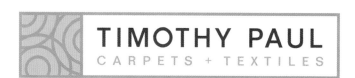

TIMOTHY PAUL
CARPETS + TEXTILES

7.

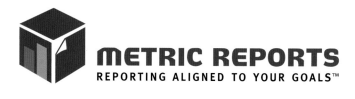

NORTH GENERAL
H O S P I T A L

Growing With Our Community, Caring For Your Health

8.

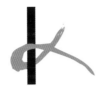

KOOCHES
hand made carpets

9.

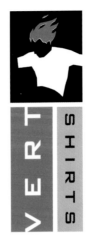

10.

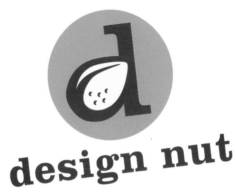

design nut

12.

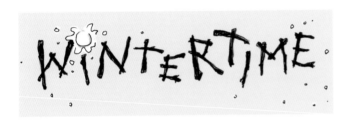

WINTERTIME

11.

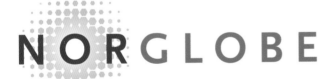

NORGLOBE

13.

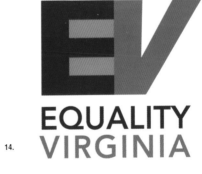

EQUALITY
VIRGINIA

14.

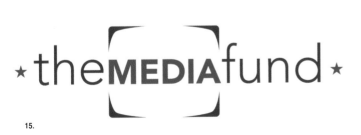

the**MEDIA**fund

15.

1 - 3
Design Firm **Hornall Anderson Design Works**
4 - 6
Design Firm **StudioNorth**
7 - 15
Design Firm **Design Nut**

1.
| Client | TruckTrax |
| Designers | Jack Anderson, Gretchen Cook, Kathy Saito |

2.
| Client | Pace International |
| Designers | Jack Anderson, Sonja Max, Andrew Smith, Kathy Saito |

3.
| Client | FreeMotion |
| Designers | Jack Anderson, Kathy Saito, Sonja Max, Henry Yiu, Alan Copeland |

4.
| Client | Joel Holm Ministries |
| Designers | Allison Misevich, Chris Trinco |

5.
| Client | StudioNorth |
| Designer | Mark Schneider |

6.
| Client | Metric Reports |
| Designer | Allison Misevich |

7.
| Client | Timothy Paul Carpets + Textiles |
| Designer | Brent M. Almond |

8.
| Client | North General Hospital/Sutton Group |
| Designer | Brent M. Almond |

9.
| Client | Kooches Hand Made Carpets |
| Designer | Brent M. Almond |

10.
| Client | David Cohen |
| Designer | Brent M. Almond |

11.
| Client | Round House Theatre/Kircher, Inc. |
| Designer | Brent M. Almond |

12.
| Client | Design Nut, LLC |
| Designer | Brent M. Almond |

13.
| Client | NorGlobe, LLC |
| Designer | Brent M. Almond |

14.
| Client | Equality Virginia |
| Designer | Brent M. Almond |

15.
| Client | The Media Fund/Elevation |
| Designer | Brent M. Almond |

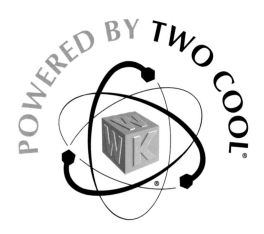

1.

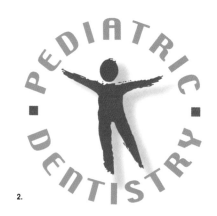

2.

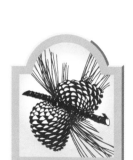

National
Interpreting
Service

3.

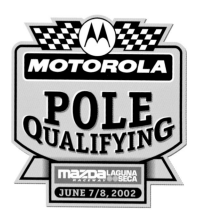

4.

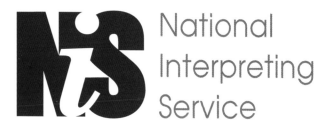

MONTEREY
PENINSULA
COUNTRY CLUB
PEBBLE BEACH, CA

5.

6. The Drink Tank

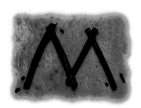

MYTHMAKER
CREATIVE SERVICES

7.

1 - 5
Design Firm **The Wecker Group**
6, 7
Design Firm **Faia Design**

1.
Client — *Wright Williams & Kelly*
Designers — Robert Wecker,
Matt Gnibus

2.
Client — *Monterey Peninsula
Dental Group*
Designer — Robert Wecker

3.
Client — *Language & Line Services*
Designer — Robert Wecker

4.
Client — *Mazda Raceway Laguna Seca*
Designer — Robert Wecker

5.
Client — *Monterey Peninsula Country Club*
Designer — Robert Wecker

6.
Client — *Odwalla, Inc.*
Designer — Don Faia

7.
Client — *Mythmaker Creative Services*
Designers — Don Faia,
Tom Dill

(opposite)
Client — *Owensby Development*
Design Firm — **Berni Marketing & Design**
Designers — Carlos Seminario,
Stuart Berni

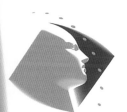

Owensby Development

B E R N I

Challenge

To launch a dynamic
national brand
for a car wash
chain with broad
demographic appeal.

Solution

Creation of shiny, new name and
identity system that is leveraged
into multiple consumer touch-points
to build brand equity.

Result

On time, on target, and on budget.
Positive perception of quality service
achieved with consumers.

Quote

"We needed the look and feel of a national brand
right out of the gate. Berni's expertise and experience
working with startups made all the difference.
We hit the ground running."

Charles Owensby, Principal

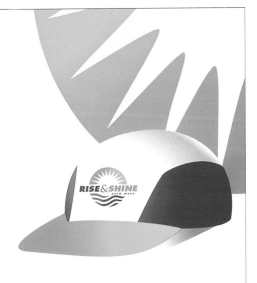

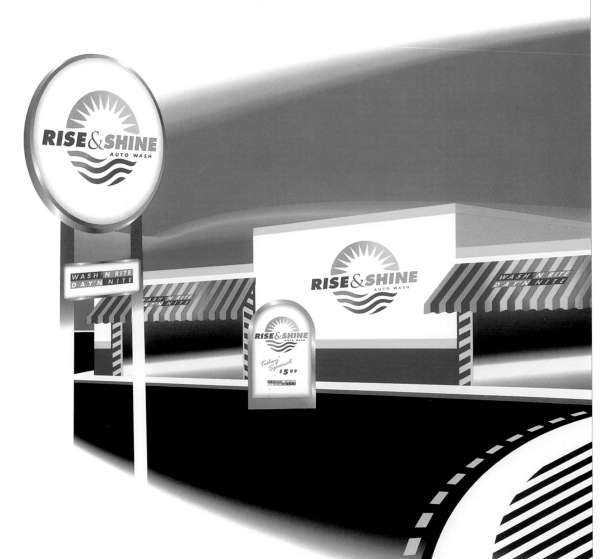

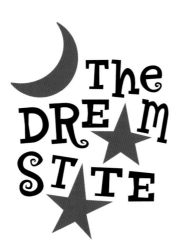

1.

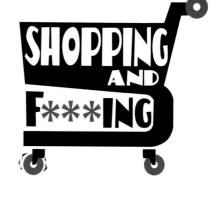

2.

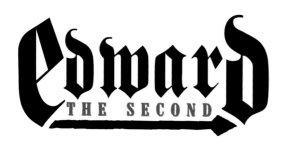

3.

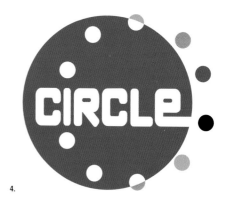

4.

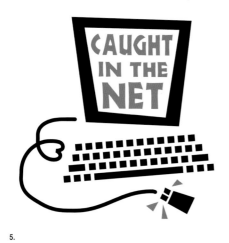

5.

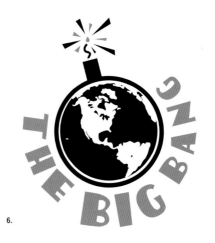

6.

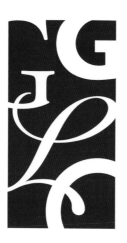

7.

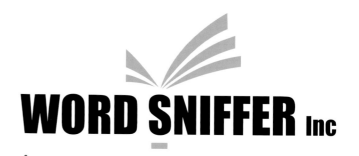

8.

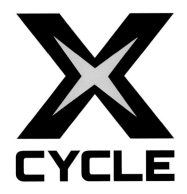

9.

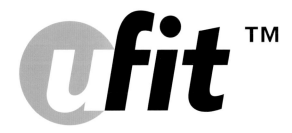

10.

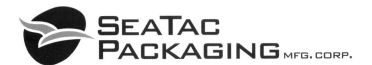

11.

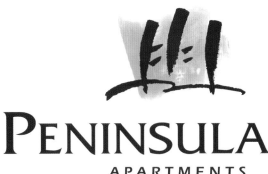

12.

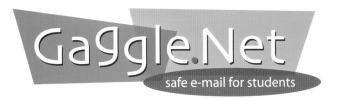

13.

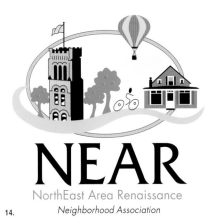

14.

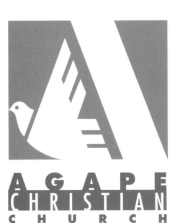

15.

1 - 6
Design Firm **Jeff Fisher LogoMotives**
7
Design Firm **Hornall Anderson Design Works**
8 - 12
Design Firm **Gloria Chen**
13
Design Firm **ZENN Graphic Design**
14
Design Firm **Minx Design**
15
Design Firm **Redpoint Design**

1 - 6.
Client   *triangle productions!*
Designer   Jeff Fisher
7.
Client   *Freerein*
Designers   Jack Anderson, Mark Popich,
            Tobi Brown, John Anicker,
            Bruce Stigler, Steffanie Lorig,
            Ensi Mofasser, Elmer dela Cruz,
            John Anderle, Gretchen Cook

8.
Client   *Word Sniffer, Inc.*
Designer   Gloria Chen
9, 10.
Client   *SportsArt American, Inc.*
Designers   Gloria Chen, David Littrell
11.
Client   *SeaTac Packaging Mfg. Corp.*
Designer   Gloria Chen
12.
Client   *Peninsula Apartments*
Designer   Gloria Chen
13.
Client   *Gaggle.Net*
Designer   Zengo Yoshida
14.
Client   *Northeast Area Renaissance*
Designer   Cecilia Sveda
15.
Client   *Agape Christian Church*
Designer   Clark Most

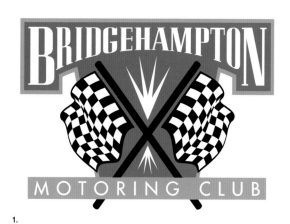

1.

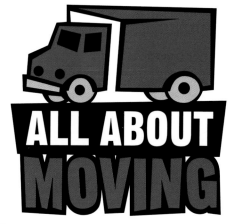

2.

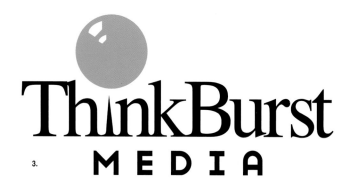

3.

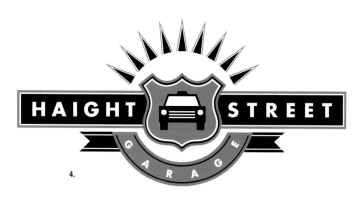

4.

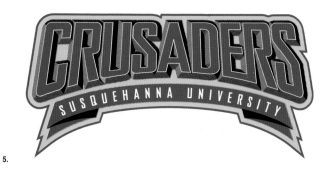

5.

INTERSYMBOL
COMMUNICATIONS

6.

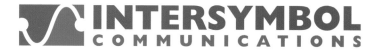

7.

1 - 7
Design Firm **MFDI**

1.
Client   Bridgehampton Motoring Club
Designer   Mark Fertig

2.
Client   All About Moving
Designer   Mark Fertig

3.
Client   Think Burst Media
Designers   Mark Fertig,
            Kevin Pitts

4.
Client   Luxor Cab Company
Designer   Mark Fertig

5.
Client   Susquehanna University
Designer   Mark Fertig

6.
Client   Intersymbol Communications
Designer   Mark Fertig

7.
Client   Labels-R-Us
Designers   Mark Fertig,
            Kevin Pitts

(opposite)
Design Firm **Berni Marketing & Design**
Designers   Carlos Seminario,
            Stuart Berni

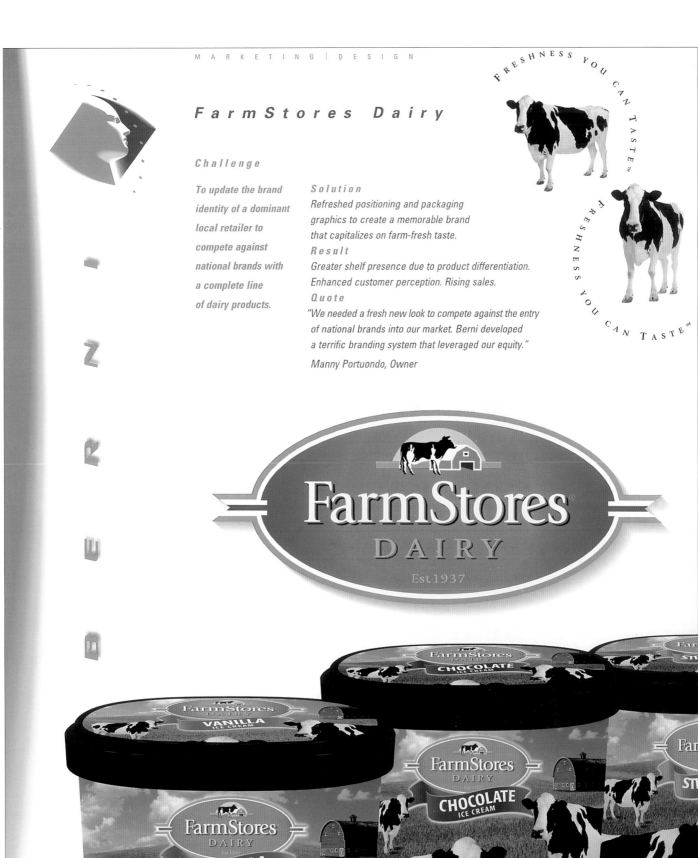

FarmStores Dairy

FRESHNESS YOU CAN TASTE™

FRESHNESS YOU CAN TASTE™

Challenge

To update the brand
identity of a dominant
local retailer to
compete against
national brands with
a complete line
of dairy products.

Solution
Refreshed positioning and packaging
graphics to create a memorable brand
that capitalizes on farm-fresh taste.

Result
Greater shelf presence due to product differentiation.
Enhanced customer perception. Rising sales.

Quote
"We needed a fresh new look to compete against the entry
of national brands into our market. Berni developed
a terrific branding system that leveraged our equity."

Manny Portuondo, Owner

FarmStores®
DAIRY
Est 1937

BERNI

www.bernidesign.com

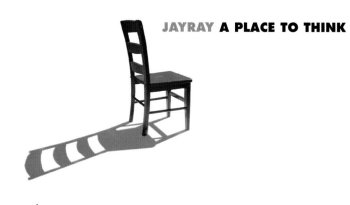

JAYRAY A PLACE TO THINK

1.

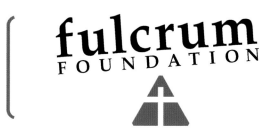

2.

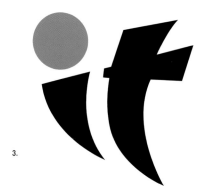

3.

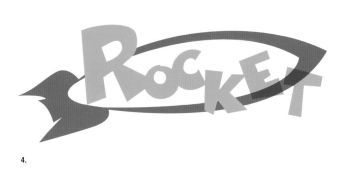

4.

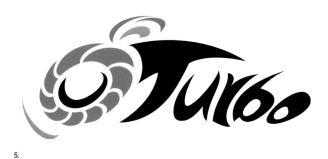

5.

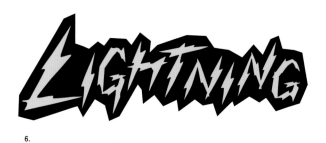

6.

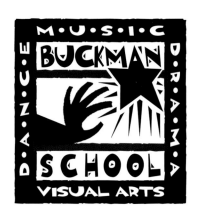

7.

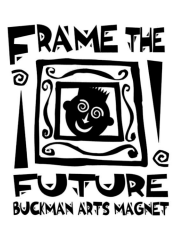

8.

9.

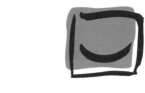

classmates·com®

10.

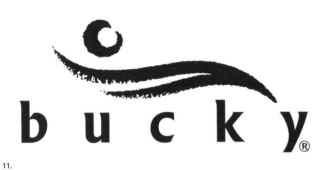

11.

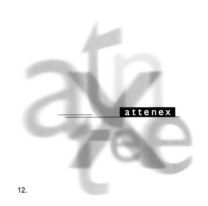

attenex

12.

ORIVO

13.

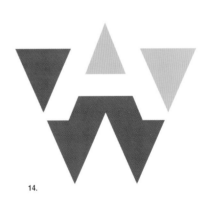

14.

WEST COAST AQUATICS

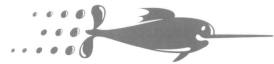

15.

1, 2
Design Firm **JayRay**
3 - 6
Design Firm **Gloria Chen**
7, 8
Design Firm **Jeff Fisher LogoMotives**
9 - 15
Design Firm **Hornall Anderson Design Works**

1.
Client *JayRay*
Designer Tom Cheevers

2.
Client *Fulcrum Foundation*
Designer Craig Wright

3 - 6.
Client *WRFF Corp.*
Designers Gloria Chen, David Littrell

7, 8.
Client *Buckman School*
Designer Jeff Fisher

9.
Client *Erickson McGovern*
Designers John Hornall, Kathy Saito,
Henry Yiu

10.
Client *Classmates.com*
Designers John Hornall, John Anicker,
Debra McCloskey, Gretchen Cook,
John Anderle, Mary Chin Hutchison

11.
Client *Bucky*
Designers Jack Anderson, Mary Hermes,
Gretchen Cook, Henry Yiu,
Elmer dela Cruz

12.
Client *Attenex Corporation*
Designers Katha Dalton, Jana Wilson Esser

13.
Client *Orivo*
Designers Jack Anderson, Andrew Wicklund,
Henry Yiu

14.
Client *Active Wear*
Designers Jack Anderson, Kathy Saito,
Gretchen Cook

15.
Client *West Coast Aquatics*
Designers Jack Anderson, Sonja Max

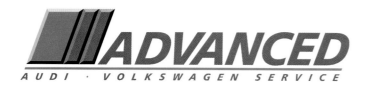

1.

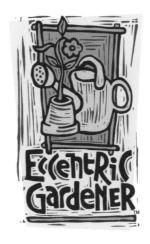

2.

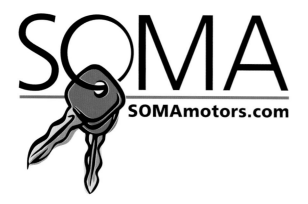

3.

E M B R Y O

4.

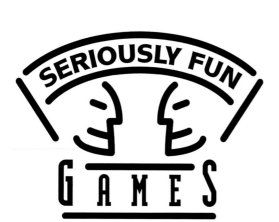

5.

Virtual. reunion

6.

SERIOUSLY FUN
GAMES

7.

1 - 7
Design Firm **MFDI**
1.
Client   *Advanced Audi Volkswagen*
Designer   Mark Fertig
2.
Client   *The Eccentric Gardener*
               Plant Company
Designer   Mark Fertig
3.
Client   *True Hire*
Designer   Mark Fertig
4.
Client   *Embryo Media*
Designer   Mark Fertig
5.
Client   *Soma Motors*
Designer   Mark Fertig

6.
Client   *Chat University*
Designers   Mark Fertig,
               Kevin Pitts
7.
Client   *Seriously Fun Games*
Designer   Mark Fertig
(opposite)
Client   Castleberry Foods
Design Firm **Berni Marketing & Design**
Designers   Carlos Seminario,
               Stuart Berni

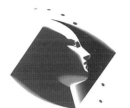

Black Rock Cattle Company

Challenge

To create an entirely new brand that would dominate the premium chili category in today's mass merchandisers.

Solution

Berni develops a compelling new brand name, and then creates the strong and hearty Black Rock brand image which captures the value-conscious consumer looking for a new taste sensation. Results indicated that a western heritage look and feel best supports the overall brand promise.

Result

Right on track: New look, combined with an appetizing multi-pack corralled consumers.

Quote

"The restaurant-quality premium beef Black Rock brand is a gotta have for our stores."

Buyer, Big Box Stores

B E R N I

www.bernidesign.com

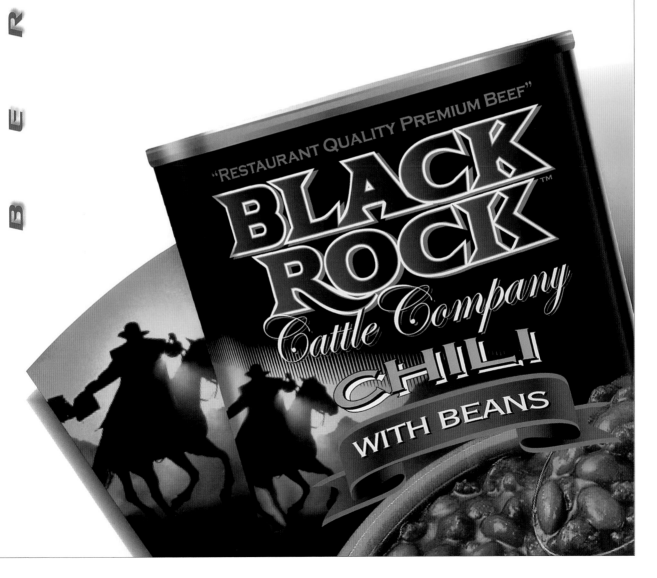

stop.
International **|** for Spa

1.

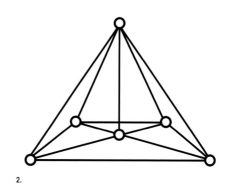

2.

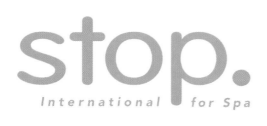

3.

specLogix

4.

b-hive

5.

 aggregate

6.

7.

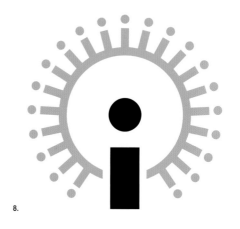

8.

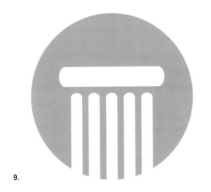

9.

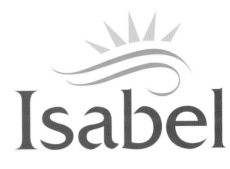

10.

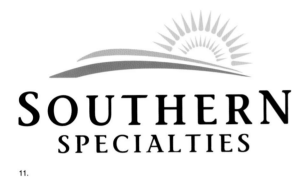

SOUTHERN
SPECIALTIES

11.

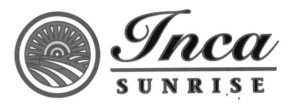

12.

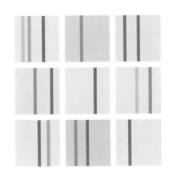

13.

SEÑOR ROOF
TRADITIONAL CRAFTSMANSHIP

14.

15.

1 - 7
Design Firm **And Partners, NY**
8 - 15
Design Firm **Cave**

1.
Client   *National Council of Jewish Women*
Designers   David Schimmel, Susan Brzozowski

2.
Client   *Delta Asset Management*
Designers   David Schimmel, Aimee Sealfon

3.
Client   *NYU Hospital for Joint Diseases
          Center for Children*
Designer   David Schimmel

4.
Client   *SpecLogix, Inc.*
Designers   David Schimmel, Aimee Sealfon,
          Christine Chow, Suzie Brickley,
          Jennifer Gibbs

5.
Client   *Bronstein & Berman Photographers
          B-Hive Productions*
Designers   David Schimmel, Tyler Small

6.
Client   *Aggregate*
Designer   David Schimmel

7.
Client   *BMW of North America, LLC*
Designers   David Schimmel,
          Eugene Timmerman

8.
Client   *Intellibrands*
Designer   Matt Cave

9.
Client   *Policy Funding*
Designer   Matt Cave

10 - 12.
Client   *Southern Specialties*
Designers   David Edmundson, Matt Cave

13.
Client   *Mathew Forbes Romer Foundation*
Designers   David Edmundson, Matt Cave

14.
Client   *Señor Roof*
Designers   David Edmundson, Matt Cave

15.
Client   *Bluefish Concierge*
Designers   David Edmundson, Matt Cave

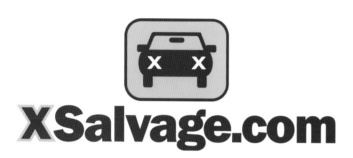

1.

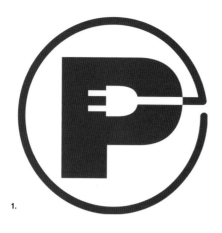

3.

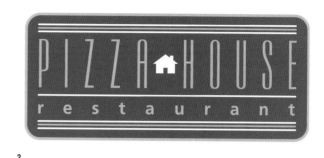

2.

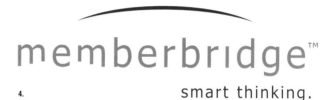

4.

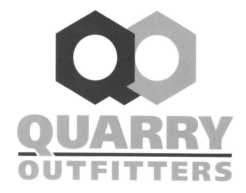

5.

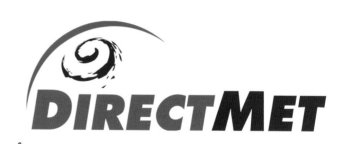

6.

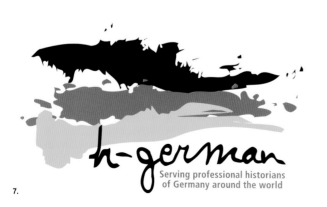

7.

1 - 7
Design Firm **MFDI**

1.
Client   *Computer Environments*
Designer   Mark Fertig

2.
Client   *Pizza House Restaurant*
Designer   Mark Fertig

3.
Client   *XSalvage.com*
Designer   Mark Fertig

4.
Client   *Member Bridge*
Designer   Mark Fertig

5.
Client   *Quarry Outfitters*
Designer   Mark Fertig

6.
Client   *Direct Met*
Designer   Mark Fertig

7.
Client   *H-Net.org*
Designers   Mark Fertig,
    David Imhoof

(opposite)
Client   SDC Designs
Design Firm **Berni Marketing & Design**
Designers   Carlos Seminario,
    Stuart Berni

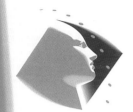

Karishma

Challenge

To launch a new product line with an innovative proprietary brand for a prominent jewelry wholesaler.

Solution

Romancing both jewelry retailers and consumers alike, an elegant and captivating brand name and identity were translated to positioning, POP display, structural packaging and graphics, and supporting sales collateral.

Result

Brilliant success. Dazzled retail target market. Expanded distribution opportunities.

Quote

We needed a partner to launch our first new brand. Berni walked us through the process and we are delighted with the results. Sales are up. The Berni team was great to work with."

Abhay Javeri, Principal

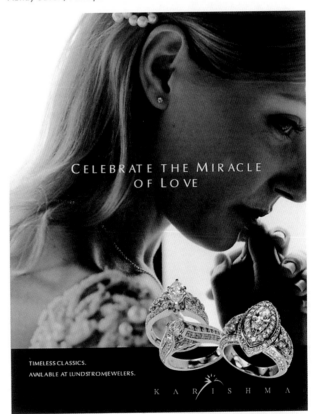

CELEBRATE THE MIRACLE OF LOVE

TIMELESS CLASSICS.
AVAILABLE AT LUNDSTROM JEWELERS.

K A R I S H M A

www.bernidesign.com

K A R I S H M A

TIMELESS CLASSICS

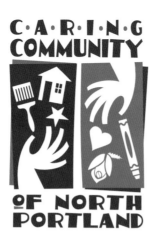

1.

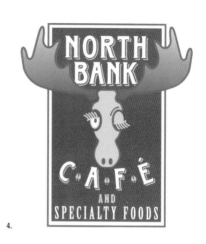

2.

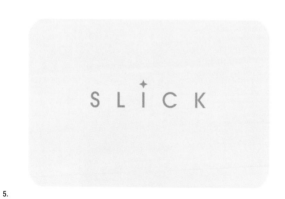

3.

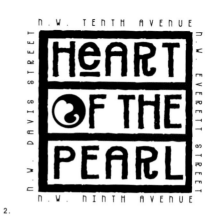

4.

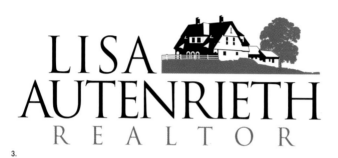

5.

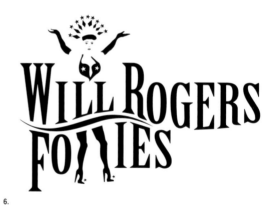

6.

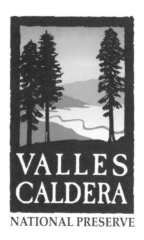

7.

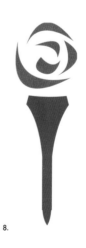

8.

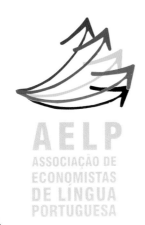

AELP
ASSOCIAÇÃO DE
ECONOMISTAS
DE LÍNGUA
PORTUGUESA

9.

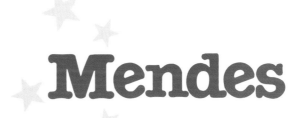
Mendes

10.

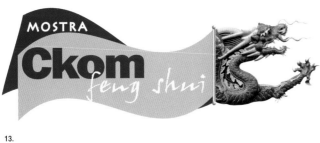

INSTITUTO
CRIANÇAVIDA

11.

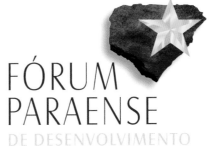

FÓRUM
PARAENSE
DE DESENVOLVIMENTO
50 anos de mineração na Amazônia

12.

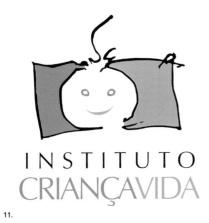

MOSTRA
Ckom feng shui

13.

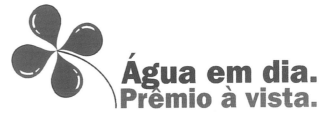

**Água em dia.
Prêmio à vista.**

14.

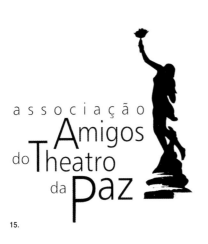

a s s o c i a ç ã o
Amigos
do **Theatro**
da **Paz**

15.

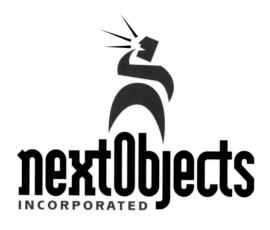

1.

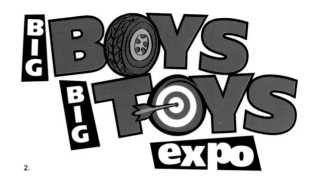

2.

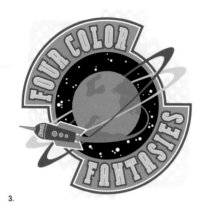

3.

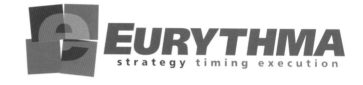

4.

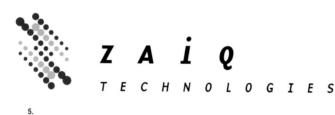

5.

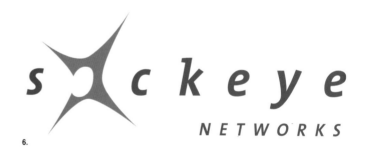

6.

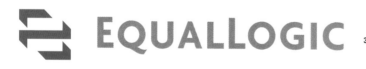

7.

1 - 4
Design Firm **MFDI**
5 - 7
Design Firm **Monderer Design**
1.
Client   *Next Objects Incorporated*
Designer   Mark Fertig
2.
Client   *The Daily Item/Sunbury*
                 Broadcasting
Designers   Mark Fertig, Leslie Imhoof,
                 Scott Spector
3.
Client   *Four Color Fantasies*
                 Collectible Comics
Designer   Mark Fertig

4.
Client   *Eurythma*
Designer   Mark Fertig
5.
Client   *Zaiq Technologies*
Designer   Stewart Monderer
6.
Client   *Sockeye Networks*
Designes   Stewart Monderer,
                 Jeffrey Gobin
7.
Client   *EqualLogic, Inc.*
Designer   Stewart Monderer
(opposite)
Client   *Lennar*
Design Firm **Berni Marketing & Design**
Designers   Carlos Seminario,
                 Stuart Berni

50 Years of Homebuilding

Lennar Corporation

Challenge

How to consolidate over 21 unique brands under one cohesive Brand Architecture System for America's leading home builder.

Solution

Development of a forward looking brand strategy that highlights and promotes Lennar's unique marketing platforms while consolidating twenty-one brands down to two. Update and contemporize corporate identity to build equity with customers and foster teamwork internally.

Old brandmark

Result

Launched in their 50th year anniversary, Lennar is now the "darling of Wall Street" with its stock soaring up 60% since initiating the Brand Strategy Program. Its new image and consumer-oriented positioning of "Quality. Value. Integrity." inspires home buyers, Associates and Wall Street simultaneously.

Quote

"Our new identity and slogan more accurately reflect who we are and what we do. The Berni team did a great job with both our brand strategy and execution. Our entire company is excited about our new image."

Kay Howard
Director of Communications

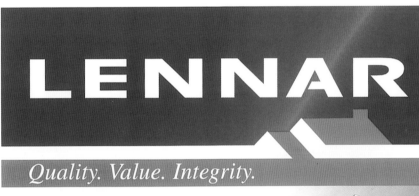

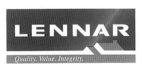

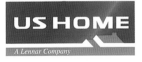

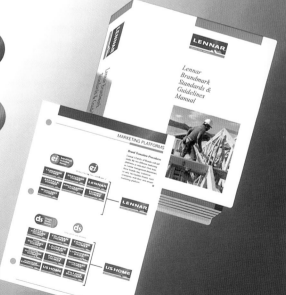

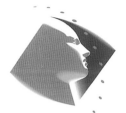

www.bernidesign.com

Stone Crossing

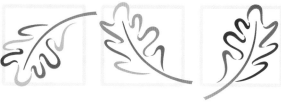

at Middle Creek

1.

MoJo

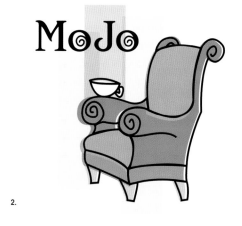

2.

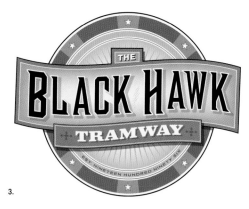

3.

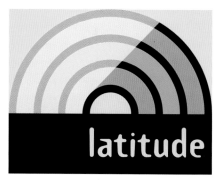

latitude

4.

townhomes for **boundless** living

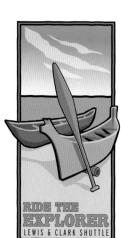

RIDE THE
EXPLORER
LEWIS & CLARK SHUTTLE

5.

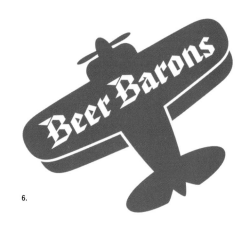

6.

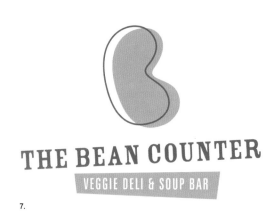

THE BEAN COUNTER

VEGGIE DELI & SOUP BAR

7.

BioZell

8.

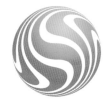

spectrum media

9.

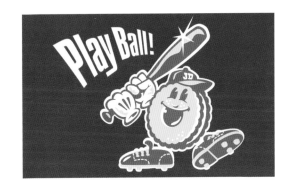

10.

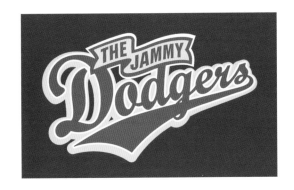

11.

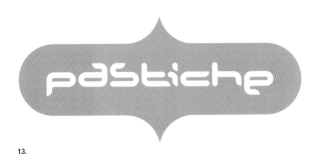

12.

pastiche

13.

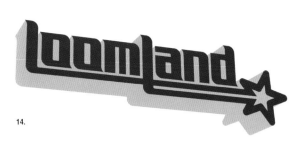

14.

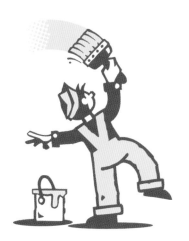

15.

1 - 5
Design Firm **Noble Erickson Inc.**
6 - 15
Design Firm **Imagine**

1.
Client   *Woodmont Development LLC*
Designers   Jackie Noble, Lisa Scheideler
2.
Client   *Mojo Coffee Shop*
Designers   Jackie Noble, Lisa Scheideler
3.
Client   *City of Black Hawk*
Designers   Steven Erickson, Kevin Penland
4.
Client   *Townhomes North LLC*
Designers   Jackie Noble, Robin Ridley
5.
Client   *Destination: The Pacific/N.P.S.*
Designers   Jackie Noble, Steven Erickson,
             Kevin Penland, Jeff Lukes
6.
Client   *Carringtons Wine & Beer Merchants*
Designer   David Caunce

7.
Client   *The Bean Counter*
Designer   David Caunce
8.
Client   *The Visual Connection (TVC)*
Designer   David Caunce
9.
Client   *Spectrum Media,*
             Digital Tele Communications
Designer   David Caunce
10, 11.
Client   *The Jammy Dodgers*
Designer   David Caunce
12, 13.
Client   *Pastiche*
Designer   David Caunce
14.
Client   *Loomland*
Designer   David Caunce
15.
Client   *Adam Day, Decorator*
Designer   David Caunce

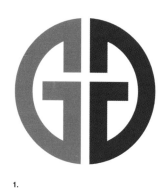

1.

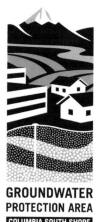

2.

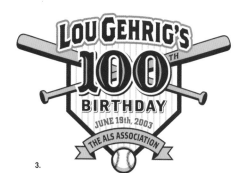

3.

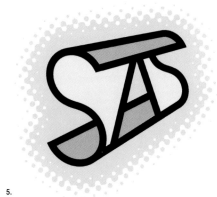

4.

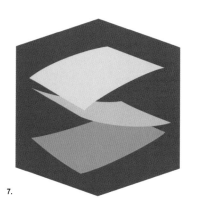

5.

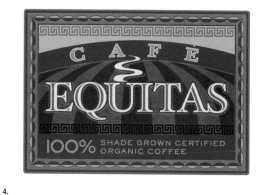

6.

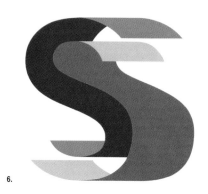

7.

1 - 7
Design Firm **Dotzero Design**
1.
    Client   *Scottsdale Christian Academy*
    Designers Jon Wippich, Karen Wippich
2.
    Client   *Portland Water Bureau*
    Designers Jon Wippich, Karen Wippich
3.
    Client   *ALS Association*
    Designers Jon Wippich, Karen Wippich
4.
    Client   *Davis Agency/Longbottom Coffee*
    Designers Jon Wippich, Karen Wippich
5 - 7.
    Client   *Standard Companies*
    Designers Jon Wippich, Karen Wippich

(opposite)
    Client   *Banco Popular*
                Dominicano, C. por A.
Design Firm **Muts&Joy&Design**
    Designers Katherine Hames,
                Gisele Sangiovanni,
                Tom Delaney

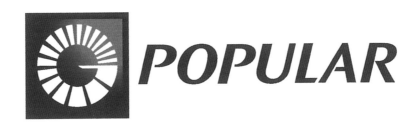

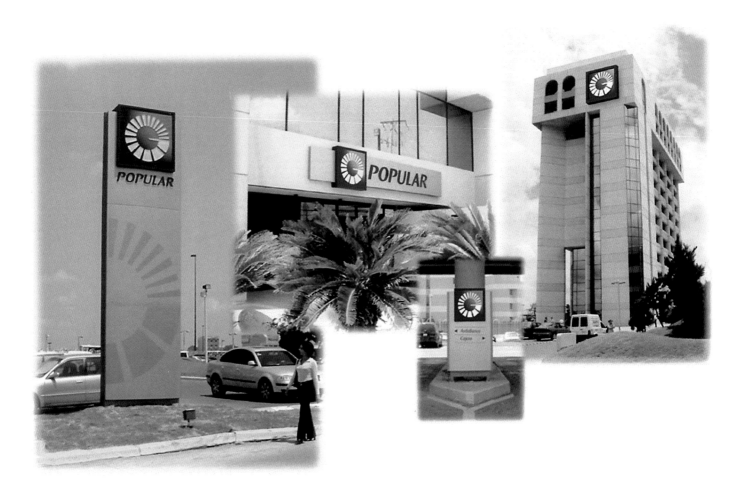

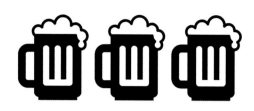

WORLD WIDE BEER FROM THE WORLD WIDE WEB

1.

2.

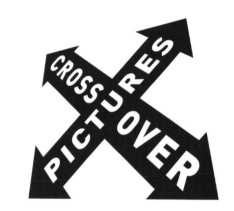

3.

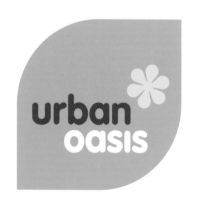

4.

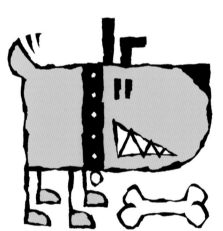

5.

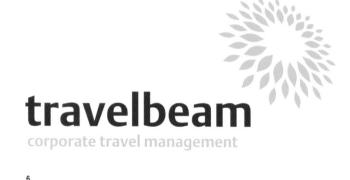

6.

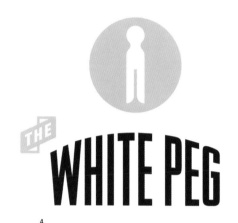

7.

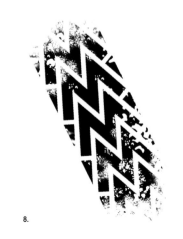

8.

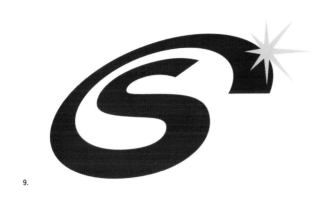

9.

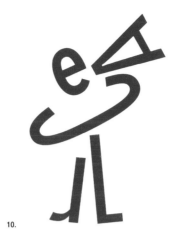

10.

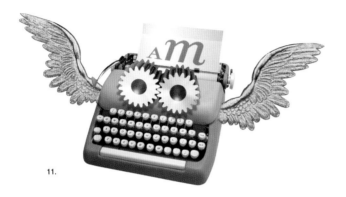

11.

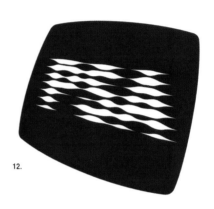

12.

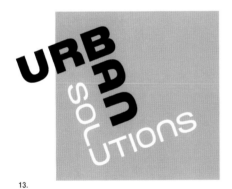

13.

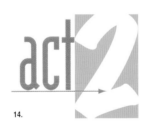

14.

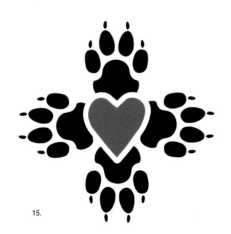

15.

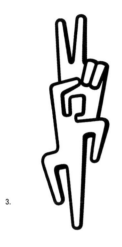

1.

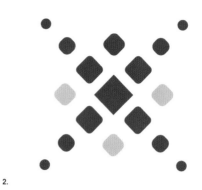

2.

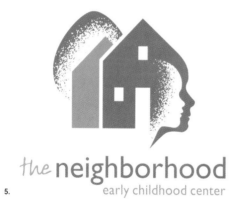

3.

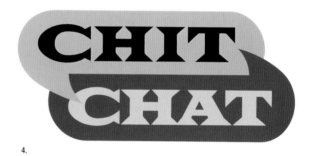

4.

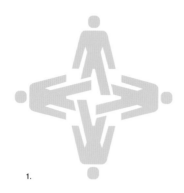

the neighborhood
early childhood center

5.

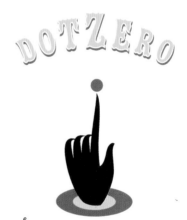

6.

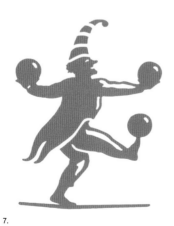

7.

1 - 7
Design Firm **Dotzero Design**
1, 2.
Client   *Unicru*
Designers   Jon Wippich, Karen Wippich
3.
Client   *Do It For Peace*
Designers   Jon Wippich, Karen Wippich
4.
Client   *Chit Chat Coffee Shop*
Designers   Jon Wippich, Karen Wippich
5.
Client   *The Neighborhood*
Designers   Jon Wippich, Karen Wippich
6.
Client   *Dotzero*
Designers   Jon Wippich, Karen Wippich

7.
Client   *CMD/Bridge Port Brewing Co.*
Designers   Jon Wippich, Karen Wippich
(opposite)
Client   *BancoLeón, S.A.*
Design Firm **Muts&Joy&Design**
Designers   Muts Yasumura,
              Katherine Hames,
              Gisele Sangiovanni,
              Tom Delaney

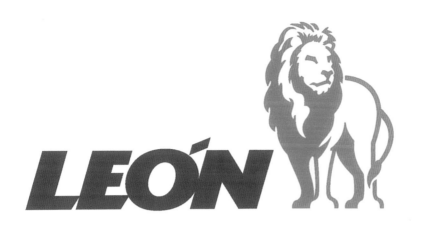

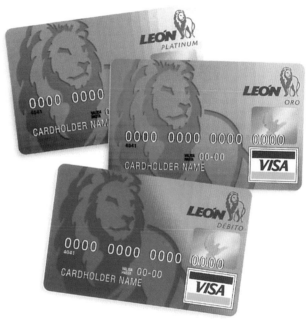

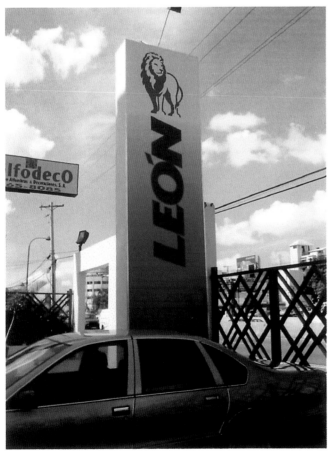

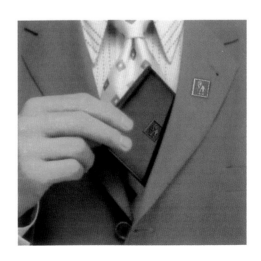

aQuantive

1.

TEAO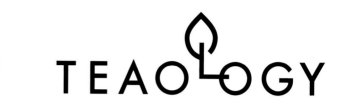OGY

2.

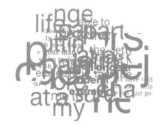

(poetry center san josé)

3.

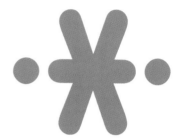

VIAMQ

4.

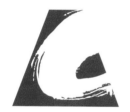

artscouncil

silicon valley

5.

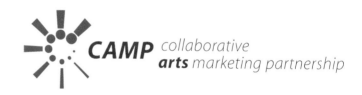

CAMP collaborative
arts marketing partnership

6.

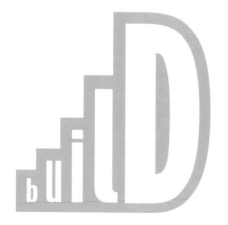

7.

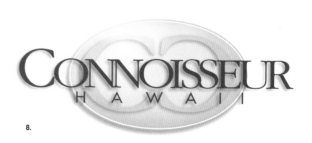

8.

WATERLADIES

9.

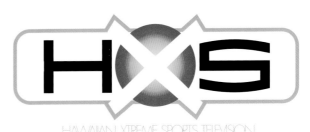

10.

MAUI BAY

11.

HXS
HAWAIIAN XTREME SPORTS TELEVISION

12.

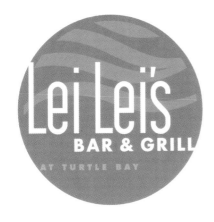

Lei Lei's
BAR & GRILL
AT TURTLE BAY

13.

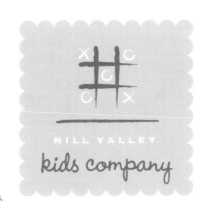

MILL VALLEY
kids company

14.

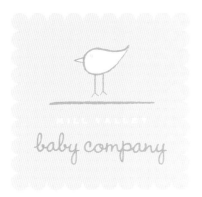

baby company

15.

1, 2.
Design Firm **Hornall Anderson Design Works**
3 - 7
Design Firm **Joe Miller's Company**
8 - 13
Design Firm **John Wingard Design**
14, 15.
Design Firm **Studio Moon**

1.
Client   *aQuantive Corporation*
Designers   Jack Anderson, Kathy Saito,
             Henry Yiu, Sonja Max,
             Gretchen Cook
2.
Client   *Teaology*
Designers   Jana Nishi, Sonja Max,
             Mary Chin Hutchison
3.
Client   *Poetry Center San Jose*
Designer   Joe Miller
4.
Client   *Willow Technology*
Designer   Joe Miller
5, 6.
Client   *Arts Council Silicon Valley*
Designer   Joe Miller

7.
Client   *Build*
Designer   Joe Miller
8.
Client   *Connoisseur Hawaii*
Designer   John Wingard
9.
Client   *The WaterLadies*
Designer   John Wingard
10.
Client   *Alabama Rural Electric Association*
Designer   John Wingard
11.
Client   *Taveuni Development Company*
Designer   John Wingard
12.
Client   *Hawaiian Xtreme Sports Television*
Designer   John Wingard
13.
Client   *Lei Lei's Bar & Grill*
Designer   John Wingard
14.
Client   *Mill Valley Kids Company*
Designer   Tracy Moon
15.
Client   *Mill Valley Baby Company*
Designer   Tracy Moon

1.

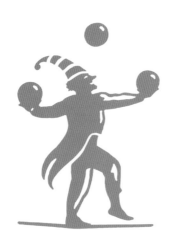

2.

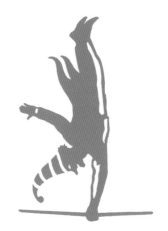

3.

4.

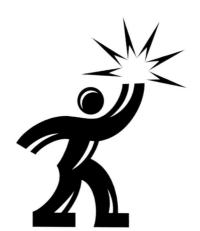

5.

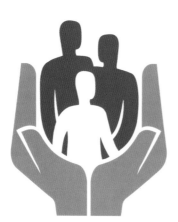

6.

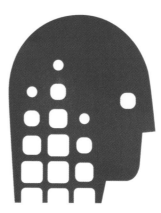

1 - 7
Design Firm **Dotzero Design**
1, 2.
   Client   *CMD/Bridgeport Brewing Co.*
   Designers   Jon Wippich, Karen Wippich
3.
   Client   *Scottsdale Christian Academy*
   Designers   Jon Wippich, Karen Wippich
4.
   Client   *Kalberer*
   Designers   Jon Wippich, Karen Wippich
5.
   Client   *BIA Deaf Translaters*
   Designers   Jon Wippich, Karen Wippich
6.
   Client   *Unicru*
   Designers   Jon Wippich, Karen Wippich

7.
   Client   *Do It For Peace*
   Designers   Jon Wippich, Karen Wippich
(opposite)
   Client   *Varela Hermanos, S.A.*
   Design Firm **Muts&Joy&Design**
   Designers   Tom Delaney,
                 Toni Kurrasch

7.

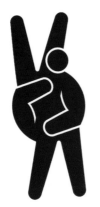

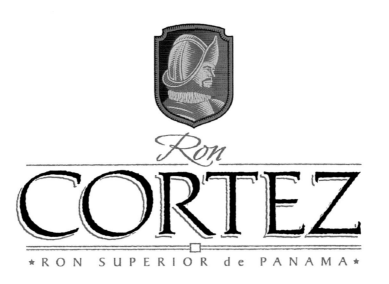

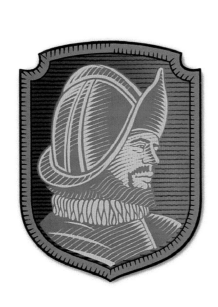

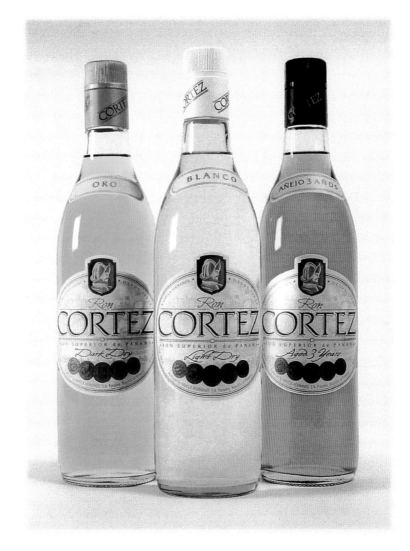

Thermage

Reshaping Your Future

1.

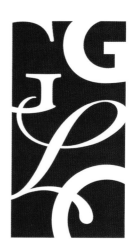

2.

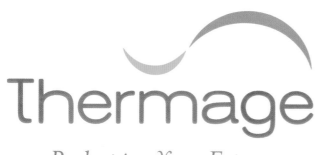

Mindworks

3.

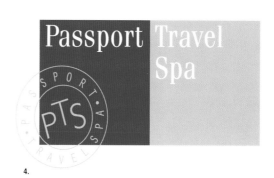

Passport Travel Spa

4.

CHESAPEAKE
· MARKET ·
Regional Food & Wine

5.

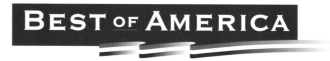

BEST OF AMERICA

6.

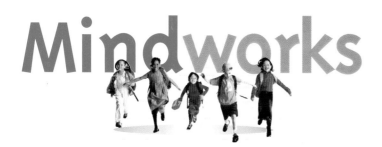

WomenRock

7.

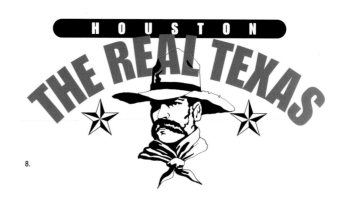

HOUSTON
THE REAL TEXAS

8.

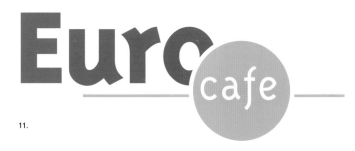

9.

EVERYTHING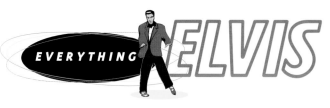

10.

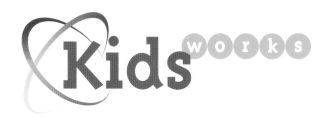

11.

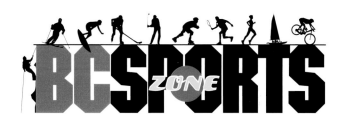

12.

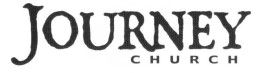

14.

13.

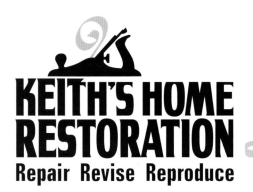

15.

1
  Design Firm **Studio Moon**
2
  Design Firm **Hornall Anderson Design Works**
3 - 13
  Design Firm **Silvester & Tafuro**
14, 15
  Design Firm **Ray Braun Design**
1.
  Client   *Thermage, Inc.*
  Designers   Tracy Moon, Monica Toan
2.
  Client   *GGLO Architects*
  Designers   Debra McCloskey, Tobi Brown,
            Steffanie Lorig, Ensi Mofasser
3.
  Client   *Stellar*
  Designers   Howard York, Monica Kominami
4.
  Client   *Passport Travel Spa*
  Designers   Howard York, Monica Kominami

5, 6.
  Client   *Regional Retail Concepts*
  Designer   Howard York
7.
  Client   *Regional Retail Concepts*
  Designers   Howard York, Monica Kominami,
            Leah York
8 - 12.
  Client   *Hudson Group*
  Designer   Howard York
13.
  Client   *Hudson Group*
  Designers   Howard York, Monica Kominami
14.
  Client   *Journey Church*
  Designer   Ray Braun
15.
  Client   *Keith's Home Restoration*
  Designer   Ray Braun

(j) (w) (d) john wingard design

1.

2.

publicity connections

3.

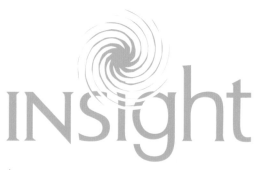

4.

TravelP O R T
A CENDANT COMPANY

5.

TERRA VIDA COFFEE

6.

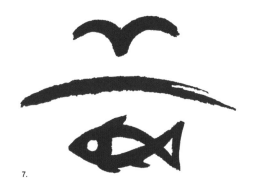

7.

1		
Design Firm	**John Wingard Design**	

2
Design Firm **Cave**

3
Design Firm **Noble Erickson Inc.**

4 - 7
Design Firm **Hornall Anderson Design Works**

1.
Client · *John Wingard Design*
Designer · John Wingard

2.
Client · *Questinghound Technologies*
Designers · David Edmundson, Matt Cave

3.
Client · *Publicity Connections*
Designer · Jackie Nóble

4.
Client · *InSite Works Architects*
Designers · John Anicker, Kathy Saito, Henry Yiu, Sonja Max

5.
Client · *Travelport*
Designers · Lisa Cerveny, Andrew Wicklund, Andrew Smith, Jana Nishi, Hillary Radbill

6.
Client · *TerraVida Coffee*
Designers · Jack Anderson, Sonja Max, James Tee, Tiffany Place, Elmer dela Cruz, Jana Nishi

7.
Client · OneWorld Challenge
Designers · Jack Anderson, John Anicker, Andrew Smith, Andrew Wicklund, Mary Hermes, John Anderle

(opposite)
Client · *Seafarer Baking Co.*
Design Firm · **Sabingrafik, Inc.**
Designers · Tracy Sabin, Bridget Sabin

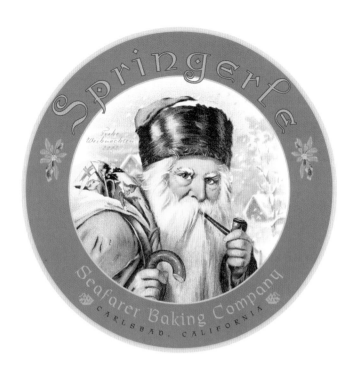

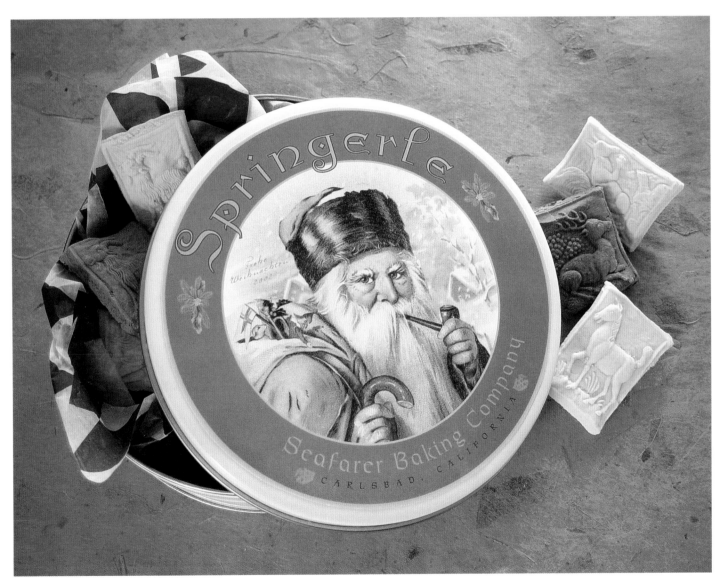

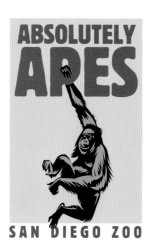

1.

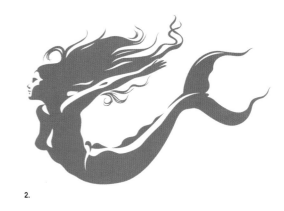

2.

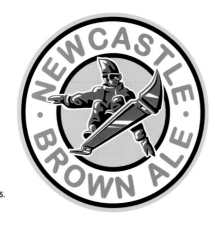

3.

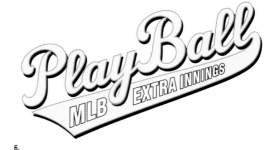

4.

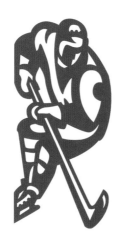

5.

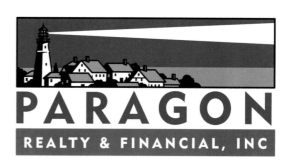

6.

Fitness Equipment Expert

7.

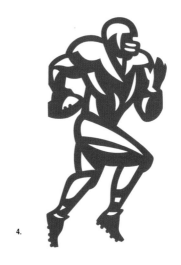

8.

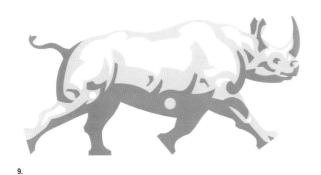

9.

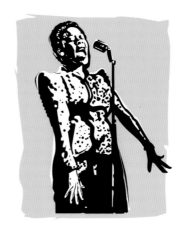

10.

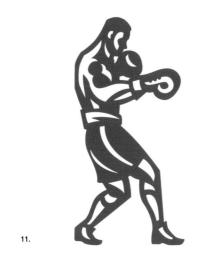

11.

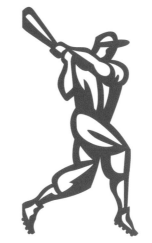

12.

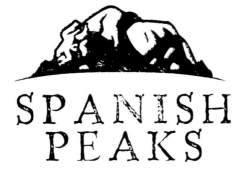

SPANISH
PEAKS

BIG SKY MONTANA

13.

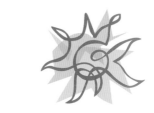

SUNDANCE

14.

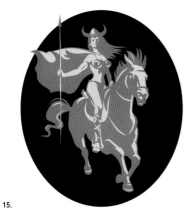

15.

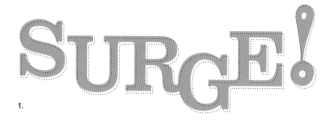

1.

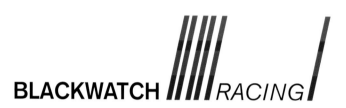

2.

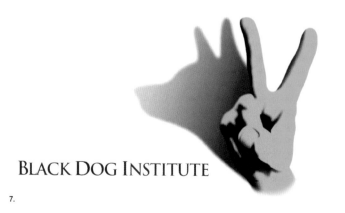

3.

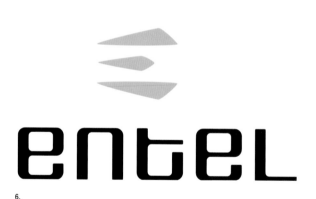

4.

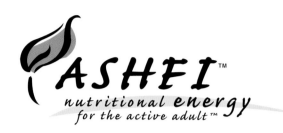

5.

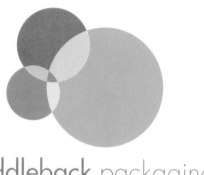

6.

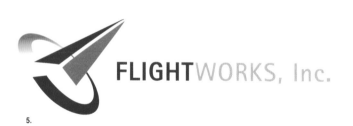

7.

1 - 6
Design Firm **Ciro Design**

7
Design Firm **John Bevins Pty Limited**

1.
Client   *IDSA Western District*
Designer Katrina Luong

2.
Client   *ASHFI*
Designer Alisa Schroeder

3.
Client   *Blackwatch Racing*
Designer Katrina Luong

4.
Client   *Saddleback Packaging*
Designer Juan Valadez

5.
Client   *Flightworks Inc.*
Designer Nora Gard

6.
Client   *Entel*
Designer Jimmy Matsuki

7.
Client   *Black Dog Institute*
Designers John Bevins,
          Cato Purnell Partners

(opposite)
Client   *Adra Soaps*
Design Firm **Sabingrafik, Inc.**
Designer Tracy Sabin

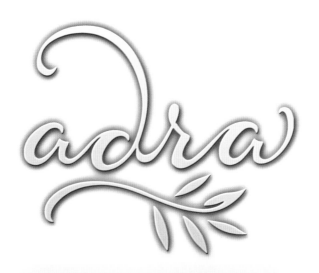

handmade natural soaps

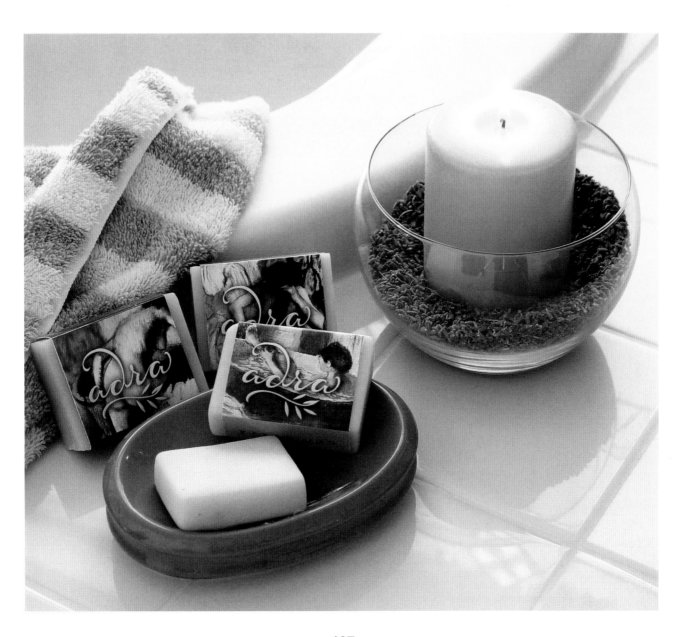

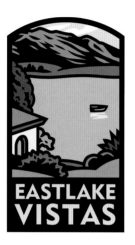

Sabingrafik
INCORPORATED

1.

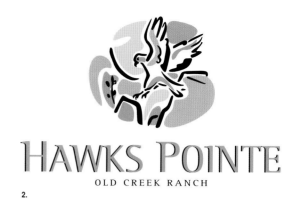

HAWKS POINTE
OLD CREEK RANCH

2.

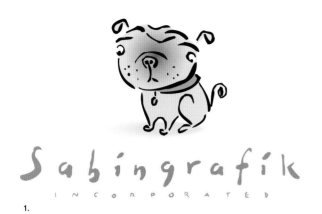

EASTLAKE
VISTAS

3.

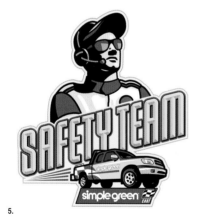

4.

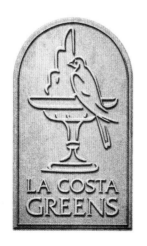

SAFETY TEAM

simple green

5.

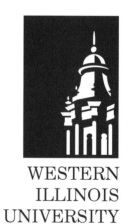

WESTERN
ILLINOIS
UNIVERSITY

6.

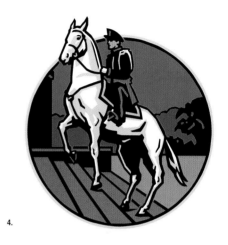

LA COSTA
GREENS

7.

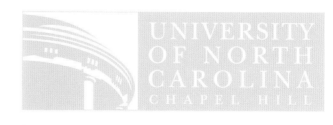

UNIVERSITY
OF NORTH
CAROLINA
CHAPEL HILL

8.

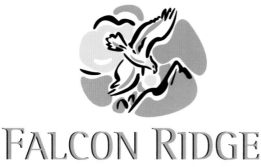

FALCON RIDGE
OLD CREEK RANCH

9.

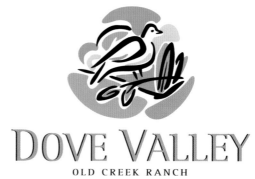

DOVE VALLEY
OLD CREEK RANCH

10.

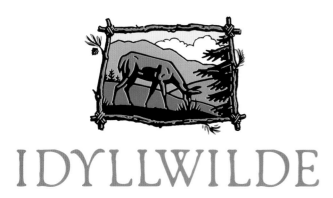

IDYLLWILDE

PARKER COLORADO

11.

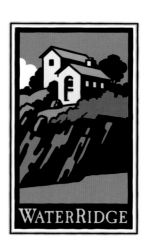

WATERRIDGE

12.

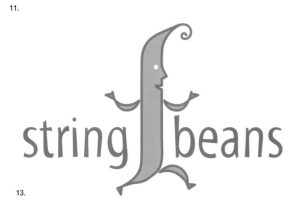

string beans

13.

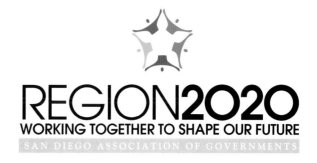

REGION2020
WORKING TOGETHER TO SHAPE OUR FUTURE
SAN DIEGO ASSOCIATION OF GOVERNMENTS

14.

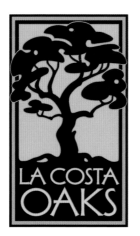

LA COSTA OAKS

15.

1 - 15
Design Firm **Sabingrafik, Inc.**

1.
Client	*Sabingrafik, Inc.*
Designer	Tracy Sabin

2.
Client	*Old Creek Ranch*
Designers	Tracy Sabin, Stephen Sharp

3.
Client	*Eastlake Vistas*
Designers	Tracy Sabin, Dennis Zimmerman

4.
Client	*Sandhurst Foundation*
Designers	Tracy Sabin, James Dewar

5.
Client	*Simple Green*
Designers	Tracy Sabin, Mike Brower

6.
Client	*Western Illinois University*
Designers	Tracy Sabin, Victoria Primicias

7.
Client	*La Costa Greens*
Designers	Tracy Sabin, Stephen Sharp

8.
Client	*University of North Carolina at Chapel Hill*
Designers	Tracy Sabin, Victoria Primicias

9, 10.
Client	*Old Creek Ranch*
Designers	Tracy Sabin, Stephen Sharp

11.
Client	*Idyllwilde*
Designers	Tracy Sabin, Craig Fuller, Sandra Sharp

12.
Client	*WaterRidge*
Designers	Tracy Sabin, Stephen Sharp

13.
Client	*String Beans*
Designers	Tracy Sabin, Mike Nelson

14.
Client	*San Diego Association of Governments*
Designers	Tracy Sabin, Mary McNulty

15.
Client	*La Costa Oaks*
Designers	Tracy Sabin, Stephen Sharp

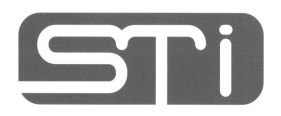

1.

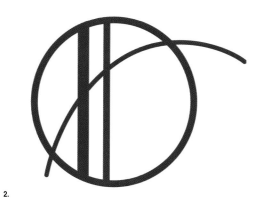

2.

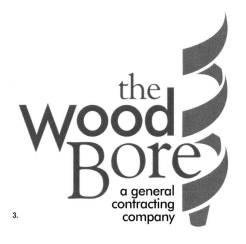

3.

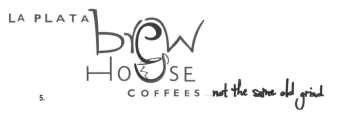

4.

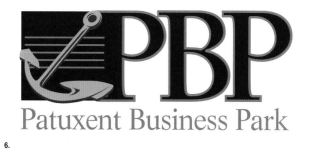

5.

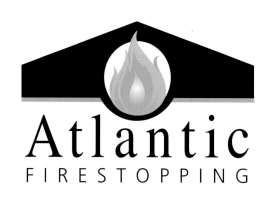

6.

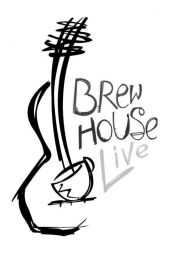

7.

1, 2
Design Firm **The Hayden Group**
3 - 7
Design Firm **Rottman Creative Group**
1.
   Client   *Sti In-Store Merchandising*
   Designer Craig Weber
2.
   Client   *The Hayden Group*
   Designer Ellen Rudy
3.
   Client   *The Wood Bore Co.*
   Designers Gary Rottman,
                Jenna Holcombe
4.
   Client   *Atlantic Firestopping*
   Designer Jenna Holcombe

5.
   Client   *LaPlata BrewHouse Coffee's*
   Designer Jenna Holcombe
6.
   Client   *Calvert County Department of*
                Economical Development
   Designer Gary Rottman
7.
   Client   *LaPlata BrewHouse Coffee's*
   Designer Jenna Holcombe
(opposite)
   Client   *Caffe Ibis*
   Design Firm **One Hundred Church St.**
   Designer R.P. Bissland

CAFFE IBIS

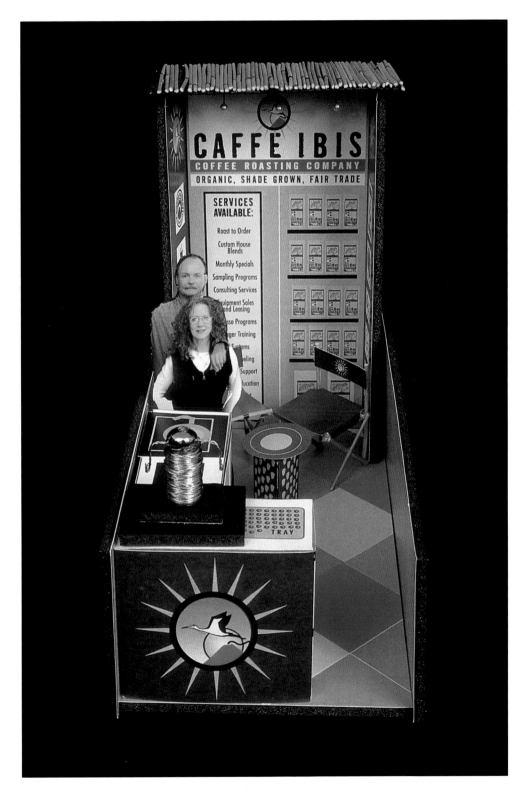

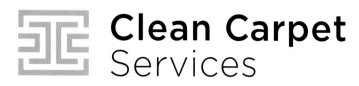 **Clean Carpet**
Services

1.

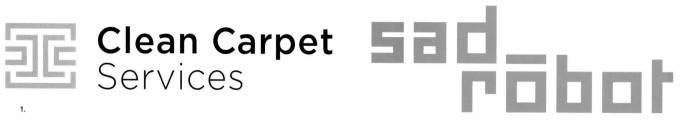

2.

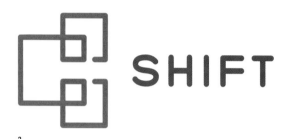 SHIFT

3.

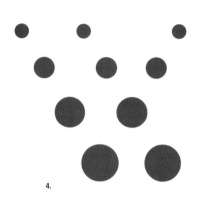

4.

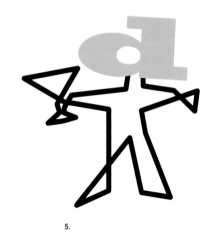

5.

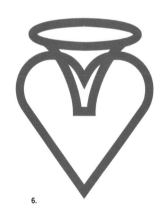

6.

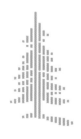 NORTHWEST
BIOTHERAPEUTICS

7.

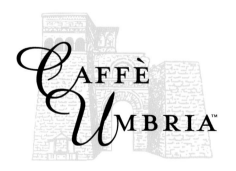

8.

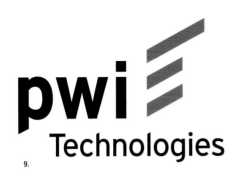

9.

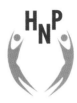

Hemophilia Nurse Partnership

10.

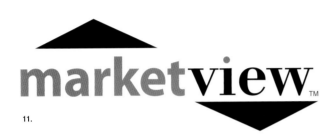

11.

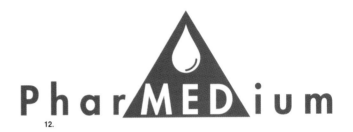

12.

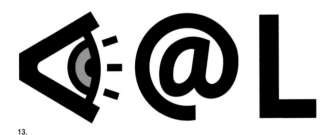

13.

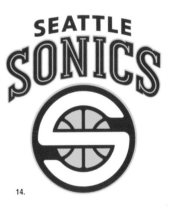

14.

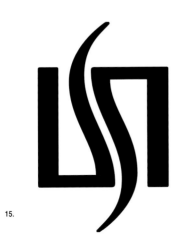

15.

1 - 9
Design Firm **Studio Rayolux**
10 - 12
Design Firm **Design Moves, Ltd.**
13 - 15
Design Firm **Hornall Anderson Design Works**

1.
Client *Clean Carpet Service*
Designer Thad Boss
2.
Client *Sad Robot Records*
Designer Thad Boss
3, 4.
Client *Shift*
Designer Thad Boss
5.
Client *Drunkinseattle.com*
Designer Thad Boss
6.
Client *Vena Cava Records*
Designer Thad Boss
7.
Client *Northwest Biotherapeutics*
Designer Thad Boss
8.
Client *Caffé Umbria Coffee Roasting Company*
Designer Thad Boss

9.
Client *PWI Technologies*
Designer Thad Boss
10.
Client *Baxter Healthcare*
Designers Laurie Medeiros Freed, William R. Sprowl
11.
Client *GlobalView*
Designers Laurie Medeiros Freed, William R. Sprowl
12.
Client *Phar MEDium Healthcare Corporation*
Designers Laurie Medeiros Freed, William R. Sprowl
13.
Client *Seattle Convention & Visitors Bureau*
Designers Lisa Cerveny, Jack Anderson, Bruce Branson-Meyer, Mark Popich
14.
Client *Seattle Sonics*
Designers Jack Anderson, Mark Popich, Andrew Wicklund, Elmer dela Cruz
15.
Client *Lincoln Square*
Designers Jack Anderson, Katha Dalton, Gretchen Cook, Sonja Max

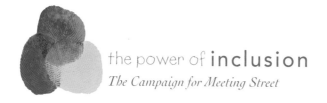

1.

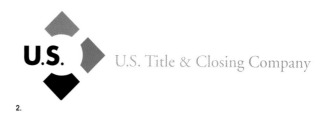

2.

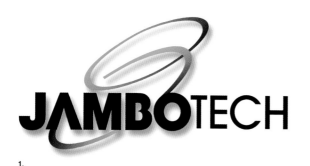

3.

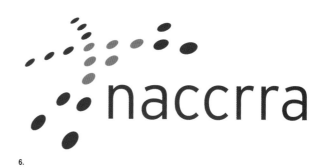

4.

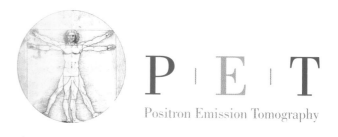

5.

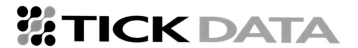

6.

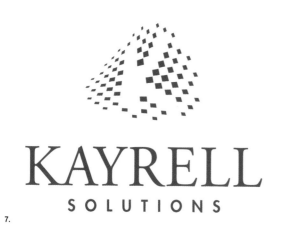

7.

1
Design Firm **Shimokochi—Reeves**
2 - 4
Design Firm **Im-aj Communications & Design, Inc.**
5 - 7
Design Firm **Alliant Studios**

1.
Client   *Jambo Tech*
Designer   Mamoru Shimokochi
2.
Client   *U.S. Title & Closing Company*
Designers   Jami Ouellette, Mark Bevington, Lee Kosa
3.
Client   *Meeting Street*
Designers   Jami Ouellette, Lee Kosa
4.
Client   *Sheilds Health Care*
Designers   Jami Ouellette, Mark Bevington

5.
Client   *Tick Data*
Designers   Mike Domingo, Patrick Dennis
6.
Client   *NACCRRA*
Designer   David McGaw
7.
Client   *Kayrell Solutions*
Designer   Kevin Frank
(opposite)
Client   *Justin Allen Company*
Design Firm **Ciro Design**
Designer   Katrina Luong

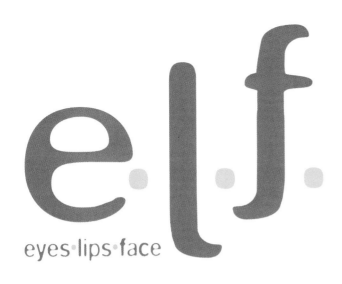

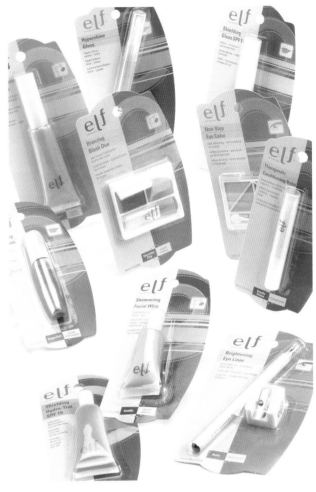

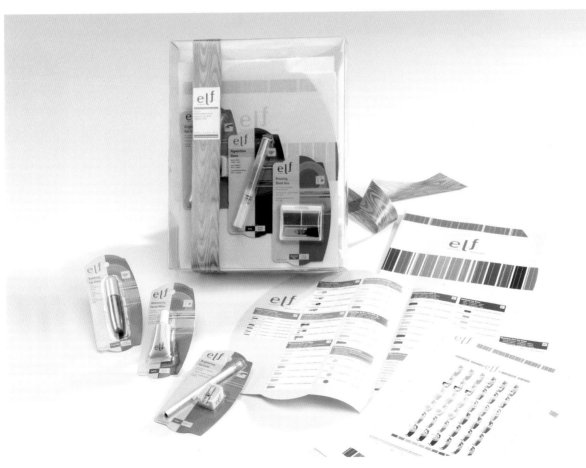

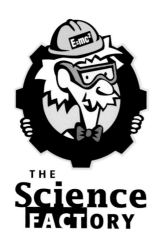

THE
Science
FACTORY

1.

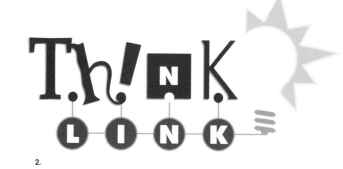

2.

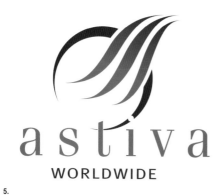

3.

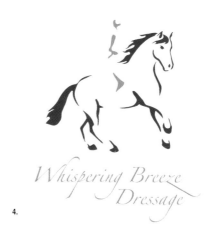

4.

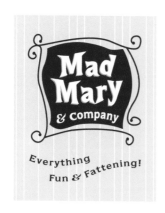

astiva
WORLDWIDE

5.

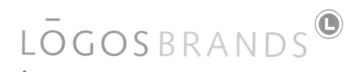

6.

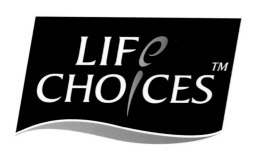

7.

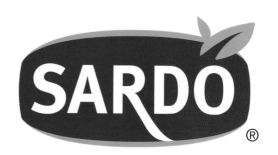

8.

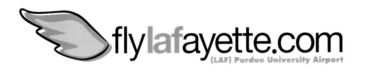

9.

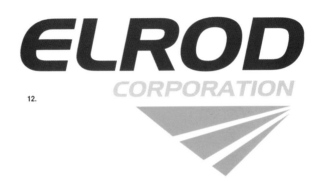

INDIANA PRODUCT DESIGN EXHIBITION

10.

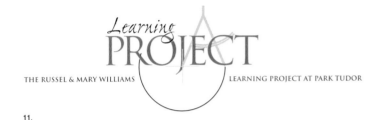

THE RUSSEL & MARY WILLIAMS   LEARNING PROJECT AT PARK TUDOR

11.

12.

ELROD
CORPORATION

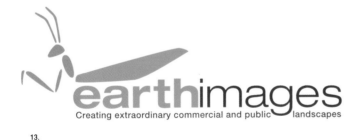

Creating extraordinary commercial and public landscapes

13.

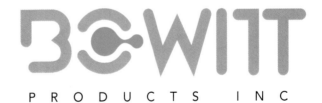

P R O D U C T S   I N C

14.

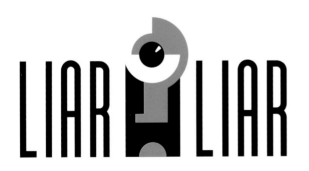

15.

1 - 4		
Design Firm	**j-creative**	
5 - 8		
Design Firm	**LOGOSBRANDS**	
9 - 14		
Design Firm	**Indiana Design Consortium, Inc.**	
15		
Design Firm	**JFDesign**	

1.
Client — *The Science Factory*
Designer — Joan Gilbert Madsen

2.
Client — *Think Link Discovery Museum for Children*
Designer — Joan Gilbert Madsen

3.
Client — *Mad Mary & Company*
Designer — Joan Gilbert Madsen

4.
Client — *Whispering Breeze Dressage*
Designer — Joan Gilbert Madsen

5.
Client — *Astiva Worldwide*
Designers — Gabriella Sousa, Brian Smith

6.
Client — *LOGOSBRANDS*
Designers — Ali Khan, Sunny Chan

7.
Client — *LIFE CHOICES Natural Foods*
Designers — Phil Slous, Franca DiNardo

8.
Client — *SARDO Food Importers*
Designers — Ali Khan, Franca DiNardo

9.
Client — *Lafayette Chamber of Commerce*
Designer — Andrew R. Schwint

10.
Client — *Pro Bono*
Designer — Andrew R. Schwint

11.
Client — *Park Tudor School*
Designer — Kristy Blair

12.
Client — *Elrod Corporation*
Designers — Andrew R. Schwint, Debra Pohl Green

13.
Client — *Earth Images, Inc.*
Designer — Andrew R. Schwint

14.
Client — *Bo-Witt Products, Inc.*
Designer — Andrew R. Schwint

15.
Client — *TDU Toys*
Designer — Josie Fertig

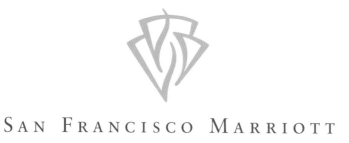

SAN FRANCISCO MARRIOTT

1.

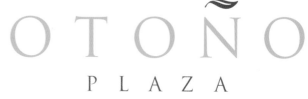

2.

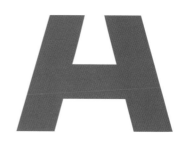

3.

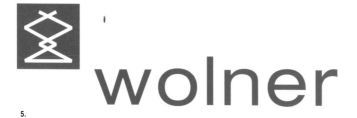

4.

5.

wolner

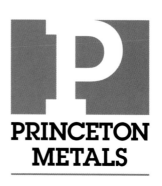

PRINCETON
METALS

6.

Leadership | **Communication**

7.

1 - 4
Design Firm **Hornall Anderson Design Works**
5 - 7
Design Firm **Design Matters, Inc!**
1.
    Client   *San Francisco Marriott*
    Designers Jack Anderson, Kathy Saito,
    Sonja Max, Alan Copeland,
    Gretchen Cook
2.
    Client   *Otoño Plaza*
    Designers John Anicker, Henry Yiu,
    Kathy Saito, Gretchen Cook,
    Sonja Max
3.
    Client   *Mulvanny/G2*
    Designers Jack Anderson, Katha Dalton,
    Jana Nishi, Michael Brugman,
    Hillary Radbill, Henry Yiu, Ed Lee
4.
    Client   *Hornall Anderson Design Works*
    Designers Jack Anderson, John Hornall,
    Henry Yiu, Andrew Wicklund,
    Mark Popich

5.
    Client   *Stephen Z. Wolner, D.D.S.*
    Designers Stephen M. McAllister,
    Gordon Fraser
6.
    Client   *Princeton Metal Company*
    Designer Stephen M. McAllister
7.
    Client   *Leadership Communication*
    Designers Stephen M. McAllister,
    Gordon Fraser
(opposite)
    Client   *Vegewax Candle Worx*
    Design Firm **LOGOSBRANDS**
    Designers Denise Barac, Franca DiNardo

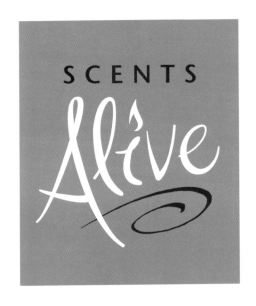

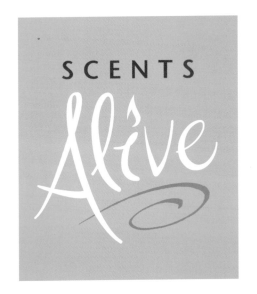

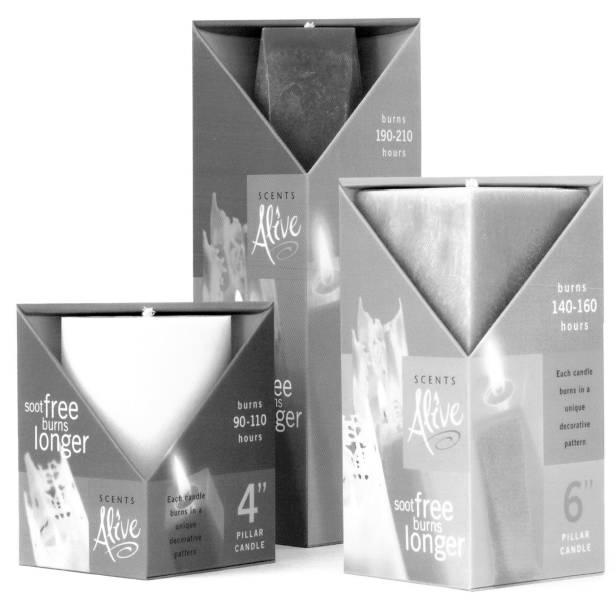

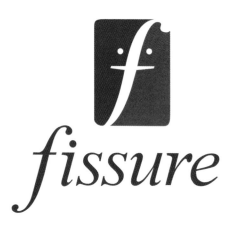

1.

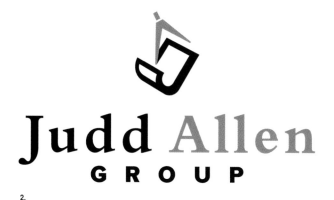

2.

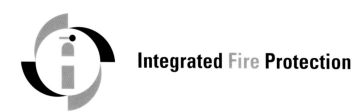

3.

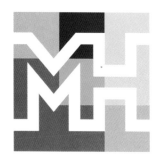

Integrated Fire Protection

5.

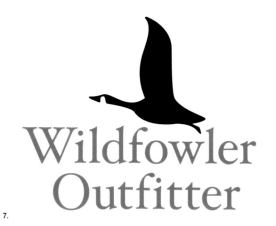

7.

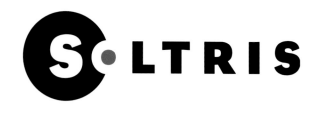

4.

MemberTrust

6.

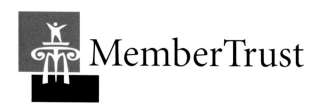

Property Funding Source

8.

140

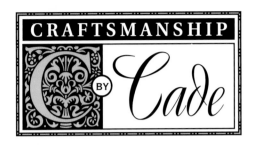

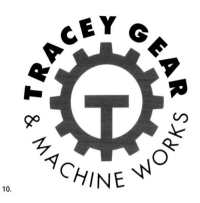

9.

10.

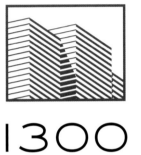

1300
HIGHLAND
CORPORATE DRIVE

11.

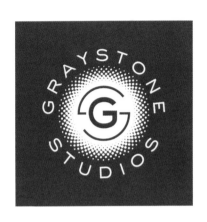

12.

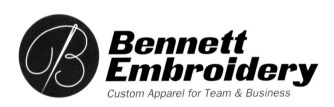

13.

elliot's
ORIGINAL
ALL NATURAL
HOUND SAUCE ®

14.

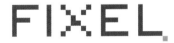

DIGITAL COLOR +
IMAGE MANIPULATION

15.

1 - 9
Design Firm **Design Center, Inc.**
10 - 15
Design Firm **Creative Vision Design Co.**
1.
Client *Fissure*
Designer Chris Cornejo
2.
Client *Judd Allen Group*
Designer Cory Docken
3.
Client *Mohagen Hansen Architectural Group*
Designers Sherwin Schwartzrock, Cory Docken
4.
Client *Soltris*
Designer Cory Docken
5.
Client *Integrated Fire Protection*
Designer Cory Docken
6.
Client *MemberTrust*
Designer Sherwin Schwartzrock
7.
Client *WildFowler Outfitter*
Designer Chris Cornejo
8.
Client *Property Funding Source*
Designer Cory Docken
9.
Client *Cade Moore Carpentry*
Designer Sherwin Schwartzrock
10.
Client *Tracey Gear*
Designer Greg Gonsalves
11.
Client *Peregrine Group*
Designer Greg Gonsalves
12.
Client *Graystone Studios*
Designer Greg Gonsalves
13.
Client *Bennett Embroidery*
Designer Greg Gonsalves
14.
Client *S.J. Corio Company*
Designer Greg Gonsalves
15.
Client *Fixel*
Designer Greg Gonsalves

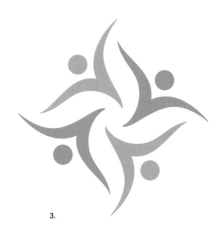

1.

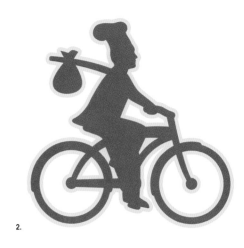

2.

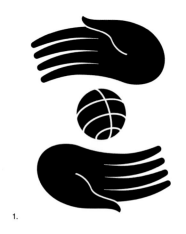

3.

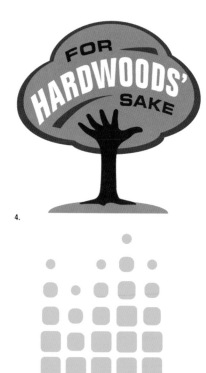

4.

5.

6.

mall
205

7.

1 - 7
Design Firm **Dotzero Design**
1.
  Client   *ALS Association*
  Designers   Jon Wippich, Karen Wippich
2.
  Client   *Peddler Bakery*
  Designers   Jon Wippich, Karen Wippich
3.
  Client   *National Psoriasis Foundation*
  Designers   Jon Wippich, Karen Wippich
4.
  Client   *Healthy Forest*
  Designers   Jon Wippich, Karen Wippich
5, 6.
  Client   *Unicru*
  Designers   Jon Wippich, Karen Wippich

7.
  Client   *Davis Agency/Mall 205*
  Designers   Jon Wippich, Karen Wippich
(opposite)
  Client   Schick Wilkinson Sword
  Design Firm   **Muts&Joy&Design**
  Designer   Gisele Sangiovanni

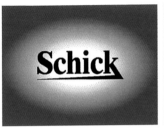 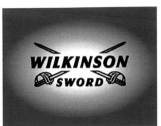

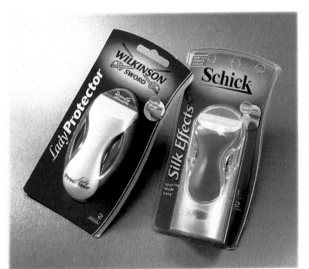 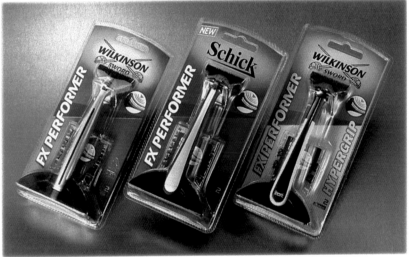

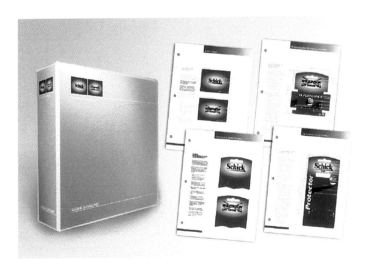

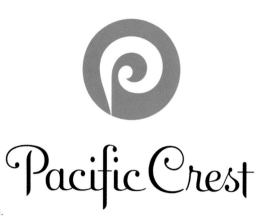

1.

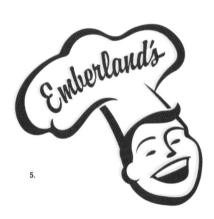

2.

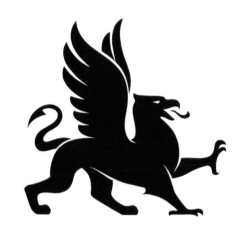

3.

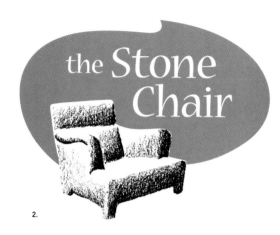

4.

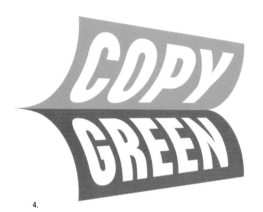

5.

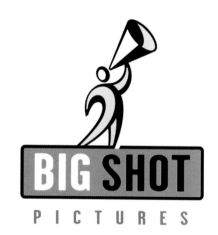

6.

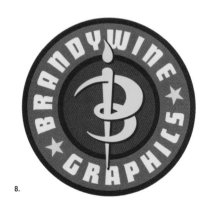

7.

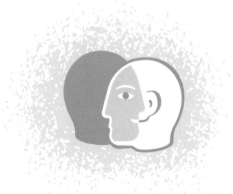

8.

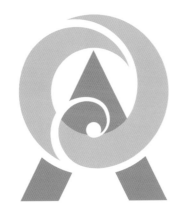

9.

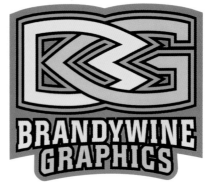

10.

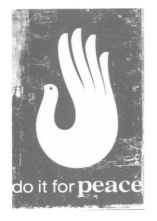

11.

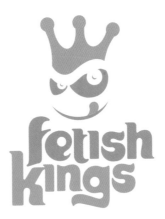

12.

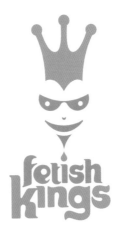

13.

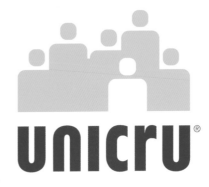

14.

15.

1 - 15
Design Firm **Dotzero Design**

1.
Client   Pacific Crest Hotel
Designers Jon Wippich, Karen Wippich

2.
Client   The Stone Chair
Designers Jon Wippich, Karen Wippich

3.
Client   Davis Agency/Griffin Capital
Designers Jon Wippich, Karen Wippich

4.
Client   Copy Green
Designers Jon Wippich, Karen Wippich

5.
Client   Emberland's
Designers Jon Wippich, Karen Wippich

6.
Client   Big Shot Pictures
Designers Jon Wippich, Karen Wippich

7.
Client   BIA
Designers Jon Wippich, Karen Wippich

8.
Client   Brandywine Graphics
          Silkscreening & Embroidery
Designers Jon Wippich, Karen Wippich

9.
Client   OpenAsia
Designers Jon Wippich, Karen Wippich

10.
Client   Brandywine Graphics
          Silkscreening & Embroidery
Designers Jon Wippich, Karen Wippich

11.
Client   Do It For Peace
Designers Jon Wippich, Karen Wippich

12, 13.
Client   Fetish Kings
Designers Jon Wippich, Karen Wippich

14.
Client   Unicru
Designers Jon Wippich, Karen Wippich

15.
Client   CMD/Bridge Port Brewing Co.
Designers Jon Wippich, Karen Wippich

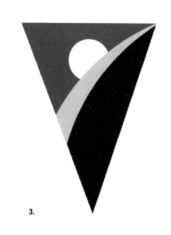

1.

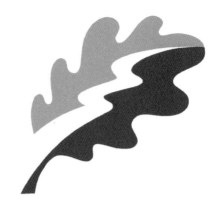

2.

4.

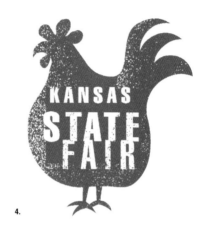

3.

5.

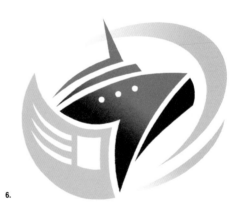

6.

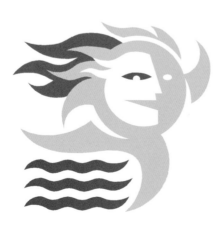

7.

1 - 7
Design Firm **Greteman Group**

1.
Client   *Boise Towne Square*
Designers   Sonia Greteman, James Strange,
Craig Tomson

2.
Client   *Oak Creek Mall*
Designers   Sonia Greteman, James Strange,
Craig Tomson

3.
Client   *Verus Bank*
Designers   Sonia Greteman, James Strange

4.
Client   *Kansas State Fair*
Designers   Sonia Greteman, James Strange,
Craig Tomson

5.
Client   *Butler College*
Designers   Sonia Greteman, James Strange

6.
Client   *Cruise Mailing Services*
Designers   Sonia Greteman, James Strange

7.
Client   *Wichita Festivals*
Designers   James Strange, Sonia Greteman
(opposite)
Client   *Banfi Vintners*
Design Firm **Muts&Joy&Design**
Designers   Katherine Hames,
Muts Yasumura

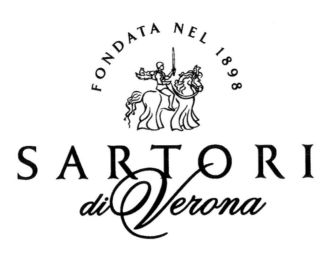

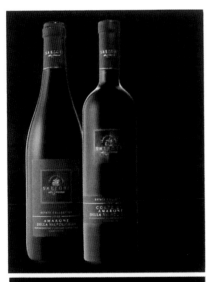

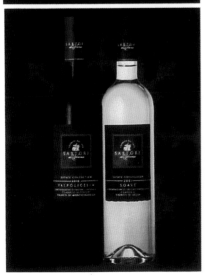

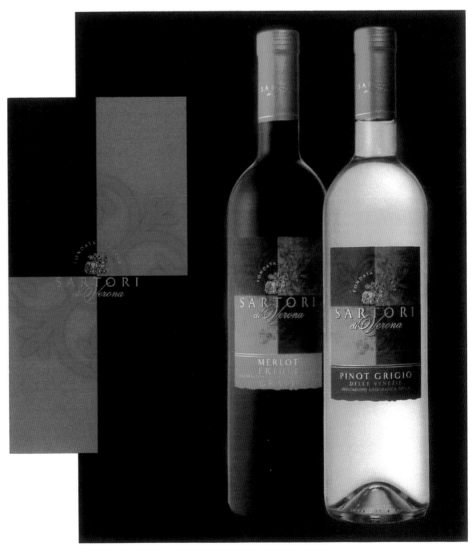

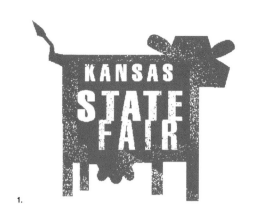

1.

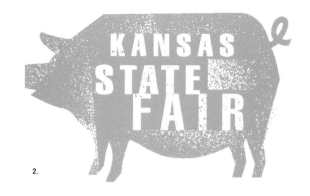

2.

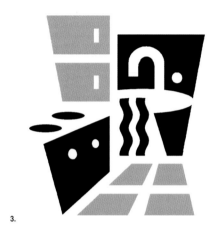

3.

4.

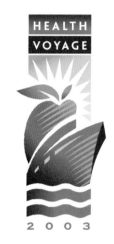

5.

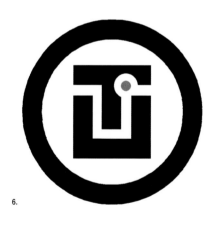

6.

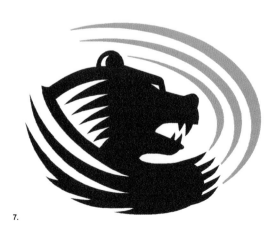

7.

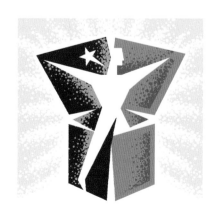

8.

9.

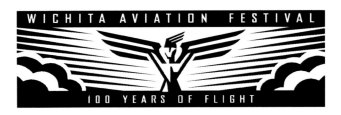

WICHITA AVIATION FESTIVAL
100 YEARS OF FLIGHT

10.

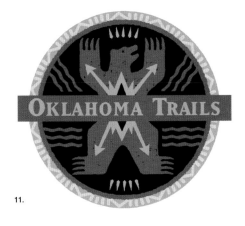

OKLAHOMA TRAILS

11.

12.

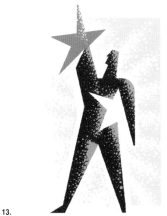

13.

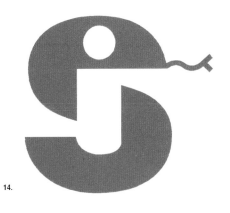

14.

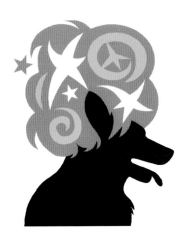

15.

1 - 15		
Design Firm	**Greteman Group**	
1, 2.		
Client	Kansas State Fair	
Designers	Sonia Greteman, James Strange	
3.		
Client	Kitchen & Bath Gallery	
Designers	Sonia Greteman, James Strange	
4.		
Client	Royal Caribbean Cruises Ltd.	
Designers	Sonia Greteman, James Strange	
5.		
Client	Galichia Heart Hospital	
Designers	Sonia Greteman, James Strange	
6.		
Designers	James Strange	
7.		
Client	Butler College Grizzlies	
Designers	Sonia Greteman, James Strange	
8.		
Client	Out of the Box	
Designers	Sonia Greteman, James Strange	

9.	
Client	Kansas Turnpike Authority
Designers	Sonia Greteman, James Strange
10.	
Client	Wichita Aviation Festival
Designers	Sonia Greteman, James Strange
11.	
Client	Oklahoma City Zoo
Designers	Sonia Greteman, James Strange
12.	
Client	Botanica
Designers	Sonia Greteman, James Strange
13.	
Client	Above and Beyond
Designers	Sonia Greteman, James Strange
14.	
Client	Strange Ideas
Designers	James Strange
15.	
Client	Kansas Humane Society
Designers	Sonia Greteman, James Strange

149

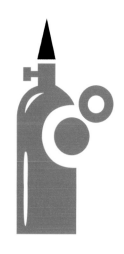

1.

2.

3.

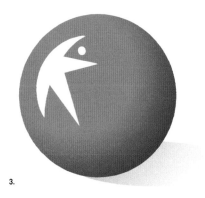

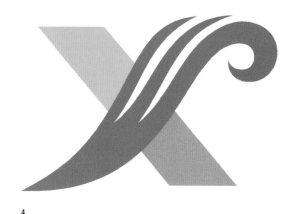

4.

5.

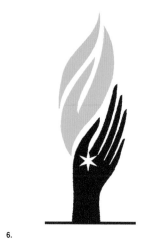

6.

7.

1 - 7
Design Firm **Greteman Group**
1.
   Client   *O2 Design*
   Designers Sonia Greteman, James Strange
2.
   Client   *Shawnee Mission Hospital*
   Designers Sonia Greteman, James Strange
3.
   Client   *Kansas Children's Service League*
   Designers Sonia Greteman, James Strange
4.
   Client   *SeaXpress*
   Designers Sonia Greteman, James Strange
5.
   Client   *Greteman Group*
   Designers Sonia Greteman, James Strange
6.
   Client   *Inspiring Leadership*
   Designers Sonia Greteman, James Strange

7.
   Client   *Wichita Festivals*
   Designers Sonia Greteman, James Strange

(opposite)
   Client   *Symphony Importers LLC*
   Design Firm **Muts&Joy&Design**
   Designers Katherine Hames, Tom Delaney,
                Gisele Sangiovanni

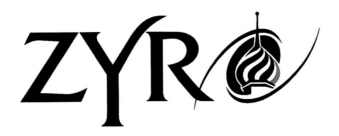

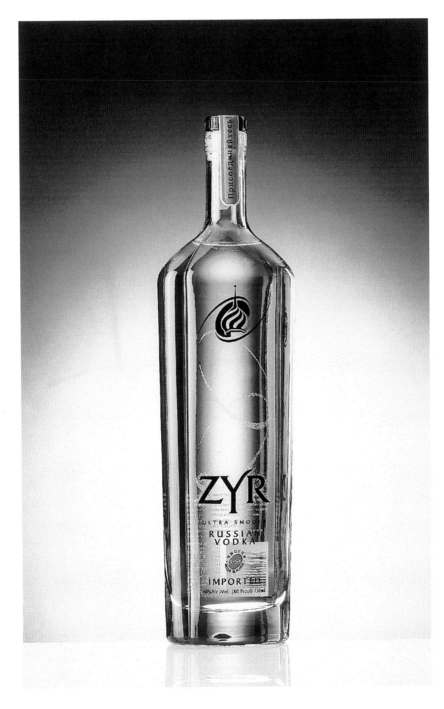

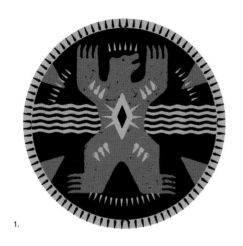

1.

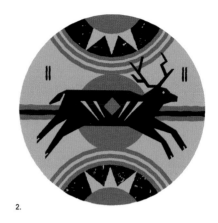

2.

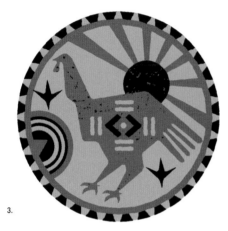

3.

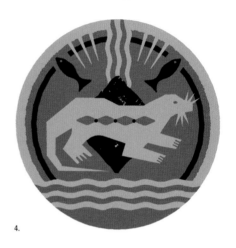

4.

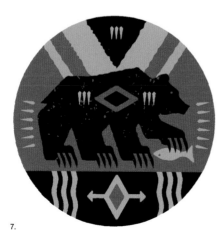

5.

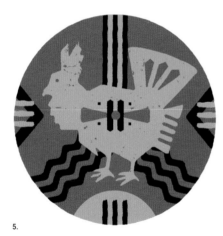

6.

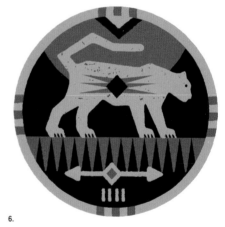

7.

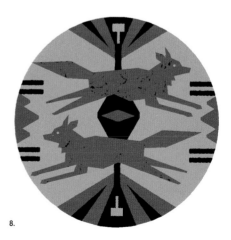

8.

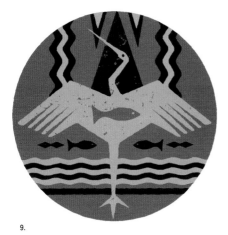

9.

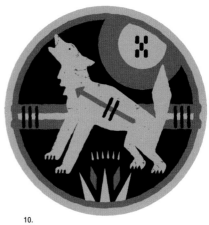

10.

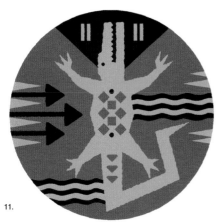

11.

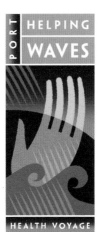

12.

HELPING
PORT
WAVES

HEALTH VOYAGE

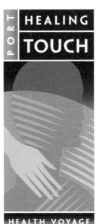

13.

HEALING
PORT
TOUCH

HEALTH VOYAGE

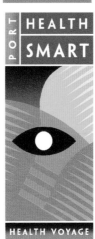

14.

HEALTH
PORT
SMART

HEALTH VOYAGE

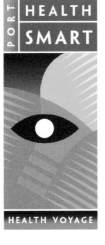

15.

HEALTH
PORT
SMART

HEALTH VOYAGE

1 - 15
Design Firm **Greteman Group**
1 - 11.
  Client   *Oklahoma City Zoo*
  Designers   Sonia Greteman, James Strange
12 - 15.
  Client   *Royal Caribbean Cruises Ltd.*
  Designers   Sonia Greteman, James Strange

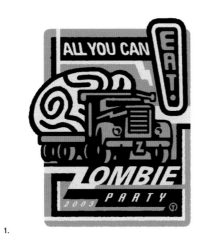

1.

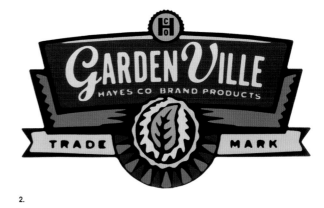

2.

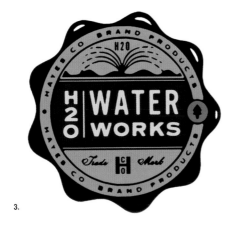

3.

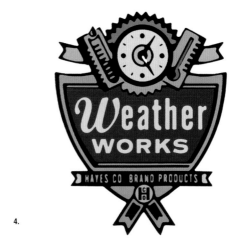

4.

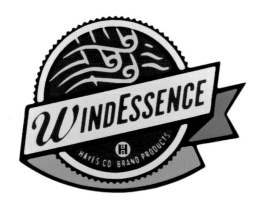

5.

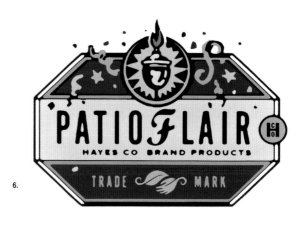

6.

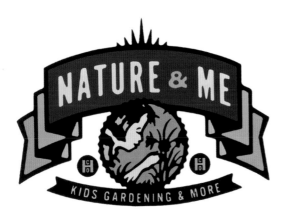

7.

1
  Design Firm **Greteman Group**
2 - 7
  Design Firm **Insight Design Communications**
1.
  Client   *James Strange*
  Designer   James Strange
2 - 7.
  Client   *The Hayes Co., Inc.*
  Designer   Tracy Holdeman

(opposite)
  Client   *Centro Cultural*
              E. León Jimenes
  Design Firm **Muts&Joy&Design**
  Designer   Katherine Hames

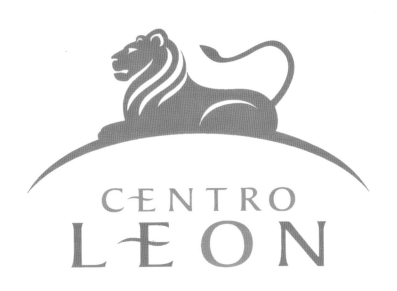

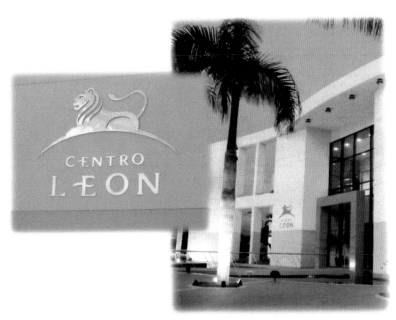

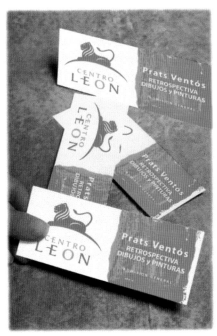

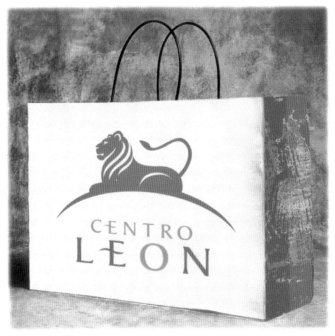

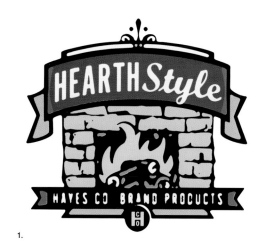

1.

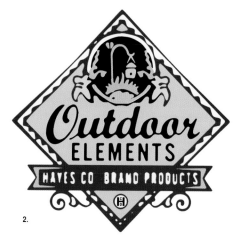

2.

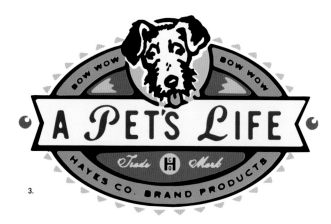

3.

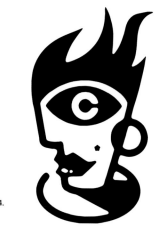

4.

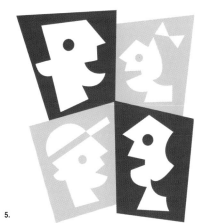

5.

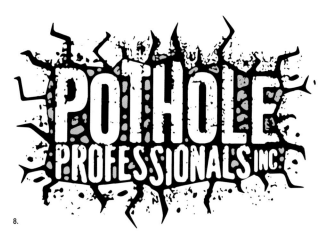

6.

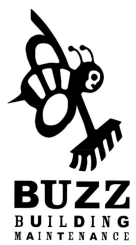

BUZZ
BUILDING
MAINTENANCE

7.

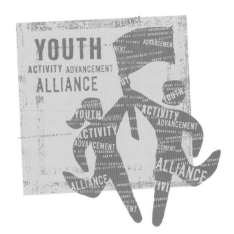

8.

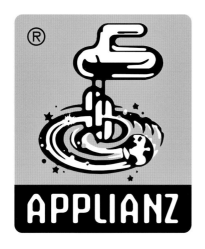

9.

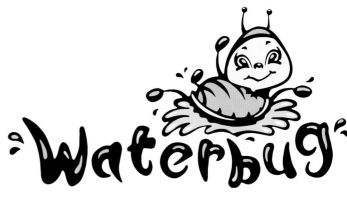

10.

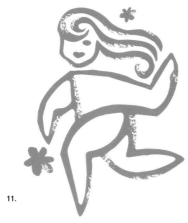

11.

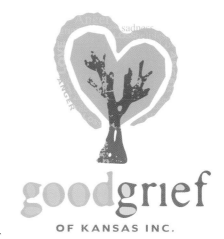

goodgrief
OF KANSAS INC.

12.

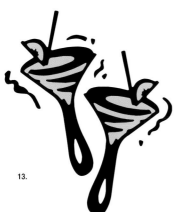

13.

14.

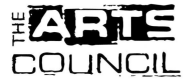

15.

1 - 15		
Design Firm	**Insight Design Communications**	
1 - 3.		
Client	*The Hayes Co., Inc.*	
Designer	Tracy Holdeman	
4.		
Client	*Cosmetic Cafe*	
Designer	Tracy Holdeman	
5.		
Client	*Family Matters*	
Designers	Tracy Holdeman, Lea Carmichael	
6.		
Client	*YMCA*	
Designers	Tracy Holdeman, Lea Carmichael	
7.		
Client	*Buzz Building Maintenance*	
Designers	Tracy Holdeman, Lea Carmichael	
8.		
Client	*Pothole Professionals Inc.*	
Designer	Tracy Holdeman	

9.		
Client	*Applianz*	
Designer	Tracy Holdeman	
10.		
Client	*Floating Swimwear*	
Designer	Tracy Holdeman	
11.		
Client	*YWCA*	
Designers	Tracy Holdeman, Lea Carmichael	
12.		
Client	*Good Grief*	
Designers	Tracy Holdeman, Lea Carmichael	
13.		
Client	*Carlos O' Kelly's*	
Designer	Tracy Holdeman	
14.		
Client	*Marketplace Evangelism*	
Designer	Tracy Holdeman	
15.		
Client	*The Arts Council*	
Designer	Tracy Holdeman	

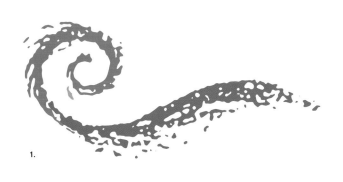

1.

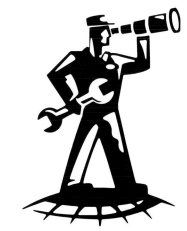

2.

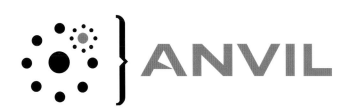

3.

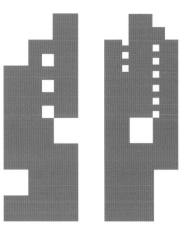

4.

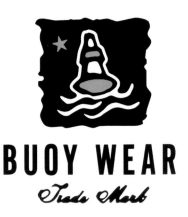

5.

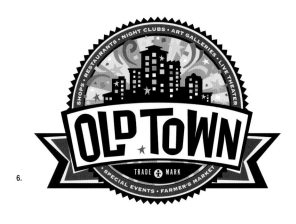

6.

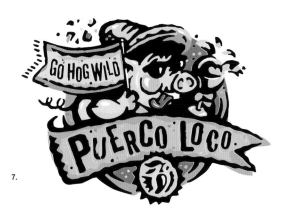

7.

1 - 7
Design Firm **Insight Design Communications**
1.
    Client   *Floating Swimwear*
    Designer Tracy Holdeman
2.
    Client   *B.G. Automotive Products*
    Designer Tracy Holdeman
3.
    Client   *Anvil Corporation*
    Designer Tracy Holdeman
4.
    Client   *Spangenberg Phillips*
    Designer Tracy Holdeman
5.
    Client   *Floating Swimwear*
    Designers Tracy Holdeman, Lea Carmichael
6.
    Client   *Old Town*
    Designer Tracy Holdeman
7.
    Client   *Carlos O'Kelly's*
    Designer Tracy Holdeman

(opposite)
Client   *Banco Del Progreso, S.A.*
Design Firm **Muts&Joy&Design**
Designer   Gisele Sangiovanni

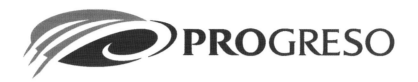

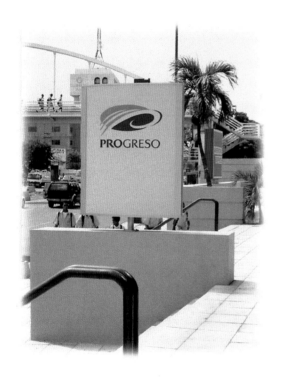

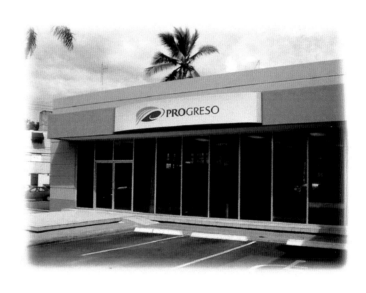

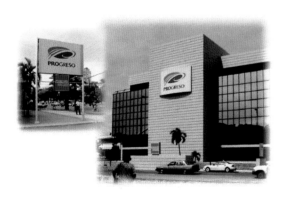

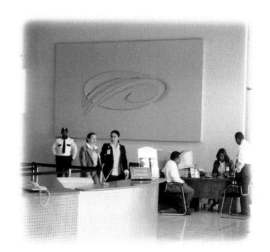

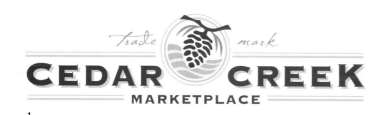

1.

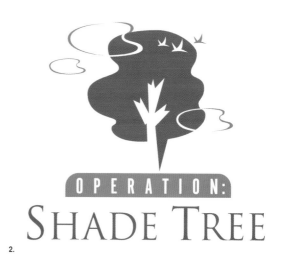

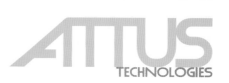

2.

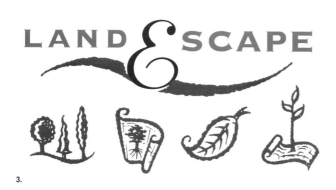

3.

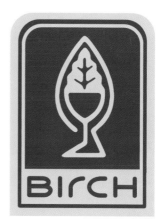

4.

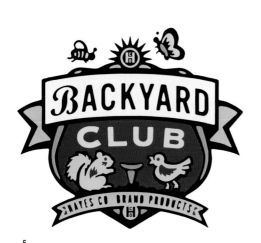

5.

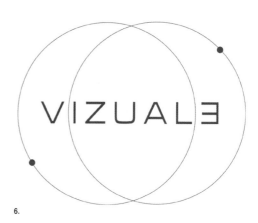

6.

7.

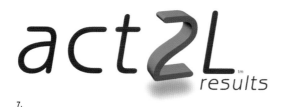

8.

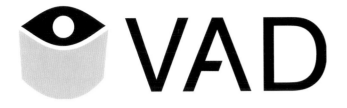 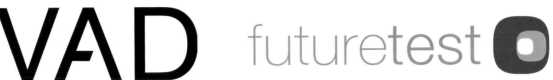

9.

futuretest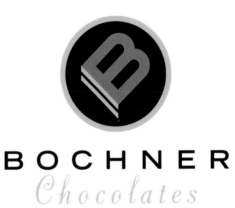

10.

COLLECTIVE CAPACITY™

11.

BOCHNER
Chocolates

12.

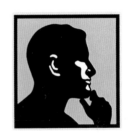

no boundaries™

13.

TALASKE
SOUND THINKING™

14.

PELICAN

15.

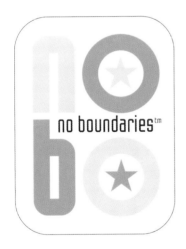

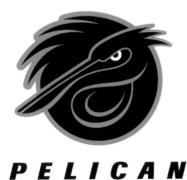

1 - 5
  Design Firm **Insight Design Communications**
6 - 8
  Design Firm **Keen Branding**
9 - 11
  Design Firm **Exit 33, Inc.**
12 - 15
  Design Firm **Mires>Design for Brands**

1.
  Client   *Cedar Creek*
  Designers   Tracy Holdeman,
              Lea Carmichael
2.
  Client   *Home National Bank*
  Designer   Tracy Holdeman
3.
  Client   *Land Escape*
  Designer   Tracy Holdeman
4.
  Client   *Birch*
  Designers   Tracy Holdeman,
              Lea Carmichael
5.
  Client   *The Hayes Co., Inc.*
  Designer   Tracy Holdeman
6.
  Client   *Vizuale*
  Designer   Mike Raveney

7.
  Client   *Act2L Results*
  Designer   Mike Raveney
8.
  Client   *Attus Technologies*
  Designer   Mike Raveney
9.
  Client   *McGraw Hill*
  Designer   Fodil Seddiki
10.
  Client   *Rob Reynolds & Vicki Woodward*
  Designer   Fodil Seddiki
11.
  Client   *Oliver Smith*
  Designer   Fodil Seddiki
12.
  Client   *Bochner Chocolates*
  Designers   José Serrano, Miguel Perez
13.
  Client   *Wal-Mart*
  Designers   Scott Mires, Miguel Perez
14.
  Client   *Talaske*
  Designers   Scott Mires and Neill,
              Leslie Quinn
15.
  Client   *Pelican Accessories*
  Designers   John Ball, Miguel Perez

PAUL
WU
+
ASSOCIATES
chartered accountants

604.734.7750

1.

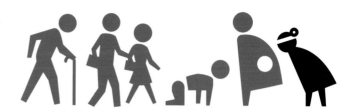

Dr. Winnie Su
FAMILY MEDICINE & OBSTETRICS

2.

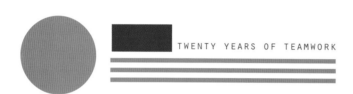

TWENTY YEARS OF TEAMWORK

3.

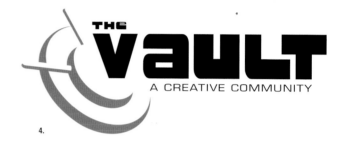

4.

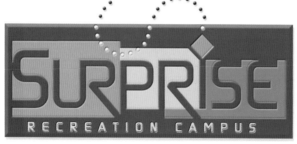

5.

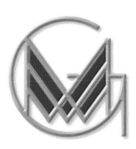

MOMENTUM GROUP

6.

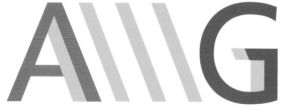

Associated Marketing Group

7.

1, 2
Design Firm **Nancy Wu Design**
3, 4
Design Firm **Iconix, Inc.**
5 - 7
Design Firm **Sullivan Marketing & Communications**

1.
Client   *Paul Wu & Associates Ltd.*
Designer   Nancy Wu
2.
Client   *Dr. Winnie Su, MD*
Designer   Nancy Wu
3.
Client   *GM/Toyota*
Designer   Paul Snyder
4.
Client   *Frenak Photo, Inc.*
Designer   Marina Savic
5.
Client   *City of Surprise AZ*
Designer   Jack Sullivan

6.
Client   *Momentum Group*
Designer   Jack Sullivan
7.
Client   *Associated Marketing Group*
Designer   Jack Sullivan
(opposite)
Client   *Fremont Bank*
Design Firm **Shawver Associates, Inc.**
Designer   Amy Krachenfels

FREMONT BANK

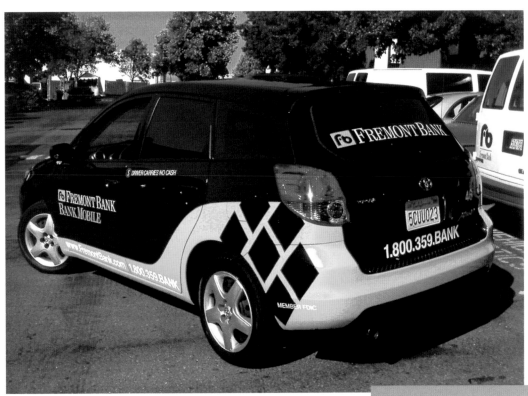

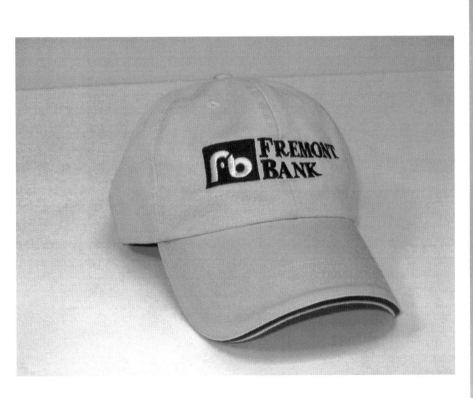

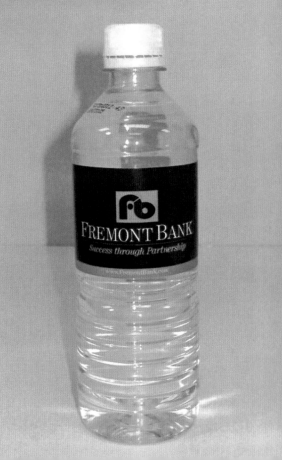

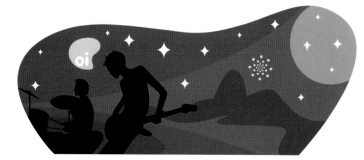

OI NOITES CARIOCAS

1.

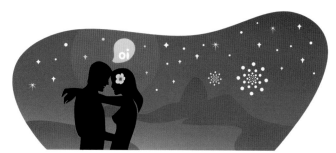

OI NOITES CARIOCAS

2.

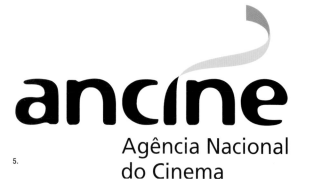

OI NOITES CARIOCAS

3.

OI NOITES CARIOCAS

4.

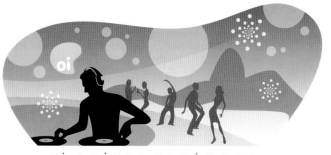

ancine

Agência Nacional
do Cinema

5.

VelaBrasil

6.

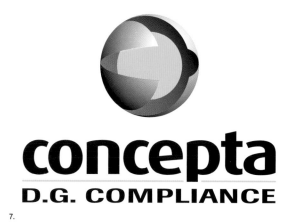

concepta
D.G. COMPLIANCE

7.

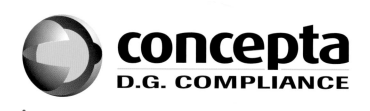

concepta
D.G. COMPLIANCE

8.

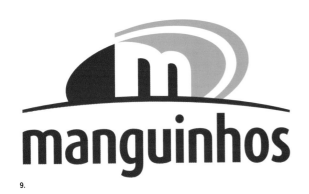

9.

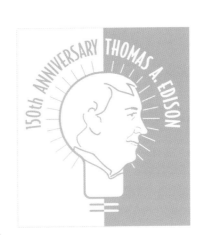

10.

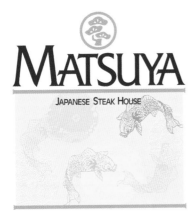

11.

12.

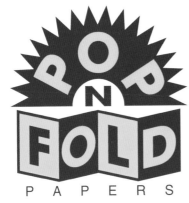

13.

STEPHEN LONGO 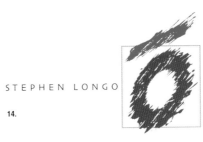 DESIGN ASSOCIATES

14.

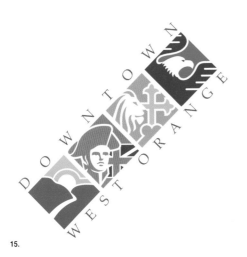

15.

1 - 5
  Design Firm **Pandora**
6 - 9
  Design Firm **Animus Design**
10 - 15
  Design Firm **Stephen Longo + Associates**

1 - 4.
  Client   *Oi Noites Cariocas*
  Designers   Silvia Grossmann,
              Lauro Machado

5.
  Client   *Ancine—National Cinema Agency*
  Designer   Silvia Grossmann

6.
  Client   *Vela Brasil*
  Designers   Marcus Fernandes,
              Rique Nitzche

7, 8.
  Client   *Concepta*
  Designers   Marcus Fernandes,
              Rique Nitzche

9.
  Client   *Manguinhos*
  Designers   Aldo Moura,
              Rique Nitzsche

10.
  Client   *U.S. Parks Service*
  Designer   Stephen Longo

11.
  Client   *Matsuya Restaurant*
  Designer   Stephen Longo

12.
  Client   *Nabisco*
  Designer   Stephen Longo

13.
  Client   *Pop N' Fold Papers*
  Designer   Stephen Longo

14.
  Client   *Stephen Longo*
              Design Associates
  Designer   Stephen Longo

15.
  Client   *Township of West Orange*
  Designer   Stephen Longo

165

1. MAKE 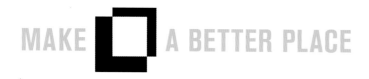 A BETTER PLACE

2.
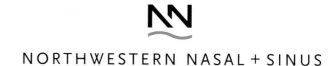
NORTHWESTERN NASAL + SINUS

3.
NSX **National Stock**^{SM} **Exchange**

4.
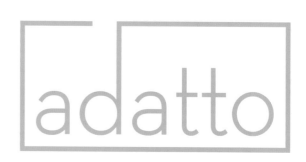
adatto

5.
fuse

6.
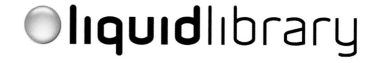
liquidlibrary

7.

HUBBARD STREET DANCE CHICAGO

1 - 7
Design Firm **Liska + Associates, Inc.**
1.
    Client   *Make A Better Place*
    Designer Fernando Munoz
2.
    Client   *Northwestern Nasal + Sinus*
    Designer Hans Krebs
3.
    Client   *National Stock Exchange*
    Designers Liska + Associates Staff
4.
    Client   *Adatto*
    Designer Jonathan Seeds
5.
    Client   *Fuse*
    Designer Brian Graziano

6.
    Client   *liquidlibrary*
    Designers Liska + Associates Staff
7.
    Client   *Hubbard Street Dance Chicago*
    Designer Steve Liska
(opposite)
    Client   St. John's University
    Design Firm **BrandLogic**
    Designers Wynn Medinger,
                Karen Lukas Hardy

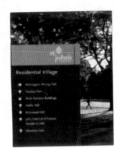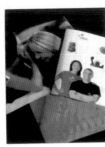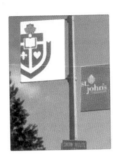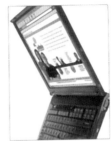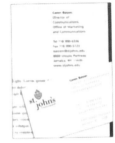

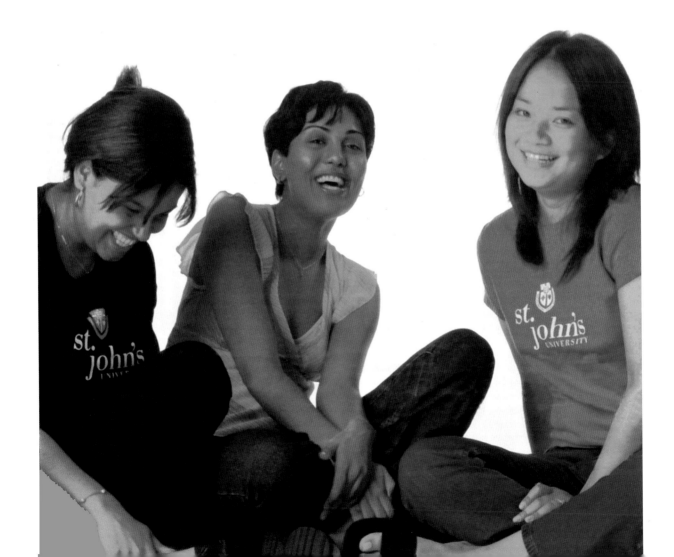

DOUBLEGREEN
L A N D S C A P E S

1.

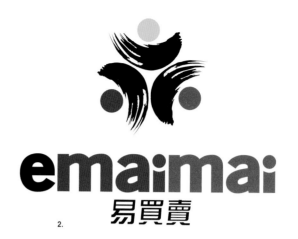

emaimai
易買賣

2.

AVENUE B
Consulting Inc.

3.

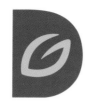

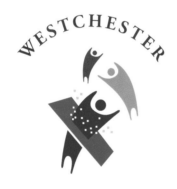

WESTCHESTER

NEIGHBORHOOD
SCHOOL

5.

GALLERY C

4.

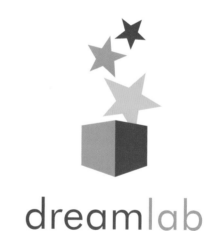

dreamlab

6.

[premis]
communications

7.

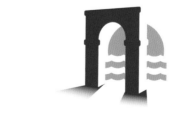

VISTAMAR
S C H O O L

8.

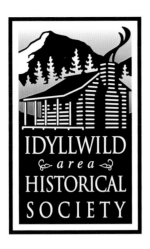

9.

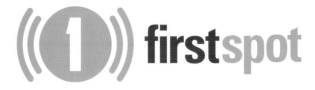

10.

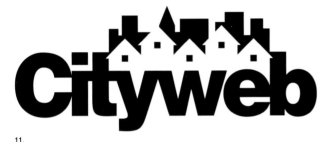

11.

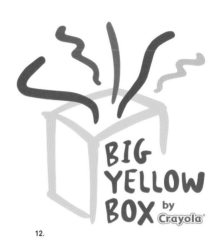

12.

Move Line

13.

LUXI

14.

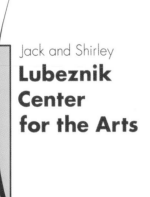

Jack and Shirley
**Lubeznik
Center
for the Arts**

15.

1 - 13
Design Firm **Evenson Design Group**
14, 15
Design Firm **Liska + Associates, Inc.**

1.
Client   *Doublegreen Landscapes*
Designer   Judy Lee

2.
Client   *Emaimai*
Designers   Judy Lee, Mark Sojka

3.
Client   *Avenue B Consulting Inc.*
Designer   Tricia Rauen

4.
Client   *Gallery C*
Designer   Mark Sojka

5.
Client   *Westchester Neighborhood School*
Designers   Ken Loh, Ondine Jarl

6.
Client   *Honda*
Designers   Mark Sojka, John Han

7.
Client   *Premis Communications*
Designer   Mark Sojka

8.
Client   *Vistamar School*
Designer   Mark Sojka

9.
Client   *Idyllwild Area Historical Society*
Designer   Mark Sojka

10.
Client   *FirstSpot*
Designer   Kera Scott

11.
Client   *Warner Bros. Online*
Designer   Mark Sojka

12.
Client   *Crayola*
Designers   Glen Sokamoto, Kera Scott

13.
Client   *Move Line*
Designer   Mark Sojka

14.
Client   *Luxi*
Designer   Jonathan Seeds

15.
Client   *Lubeznik Center for the Arts*
Designer   Laura Litman

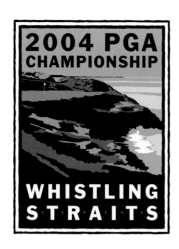

1.

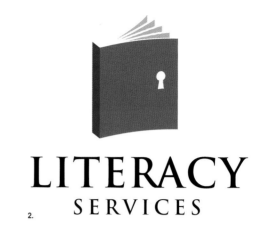

2.

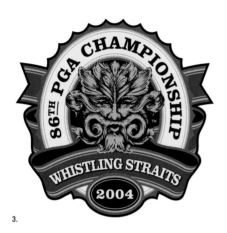

3.

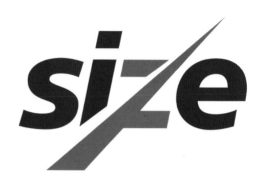

4.

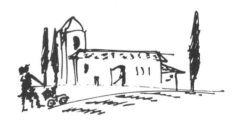

5.

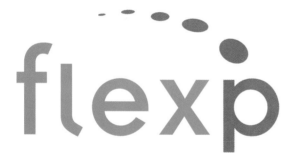

6.

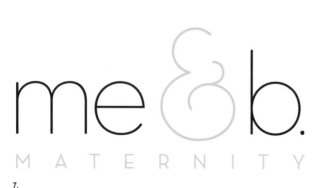

7.

1 - 3
Design Firm **McDill Design Milwaukee**
4 - 6
Design Firm **Look Design**
7
Design Firm **Liska + Associates, Inc.**
1.
Client   *Kohler Company*
Designer Joel Harmeling
2.
Client   *Literacy Services of Wisconsin*
Designer Brad Bedessem
3.
Client   *Kohler Company*
Designer Joel Harmeling
4.
Client   *Size Technologies*
Designers Look Design

5.
Client   *Flex P*
Designers Look Design
6.
Client   *Ciao Bambino!*
Designers Look Design
7.
Client   *me&b Maternity*
Designer Danielle Akstein
(opposite)
Client   Cubby's Coffee House
Design Firm **Evenson Design Group**
Designer John Krause

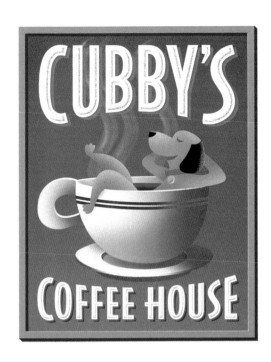

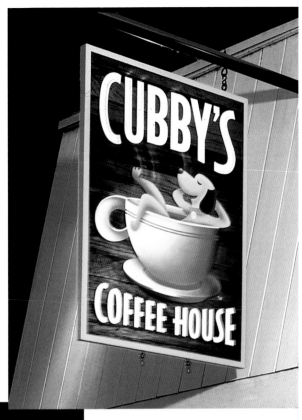

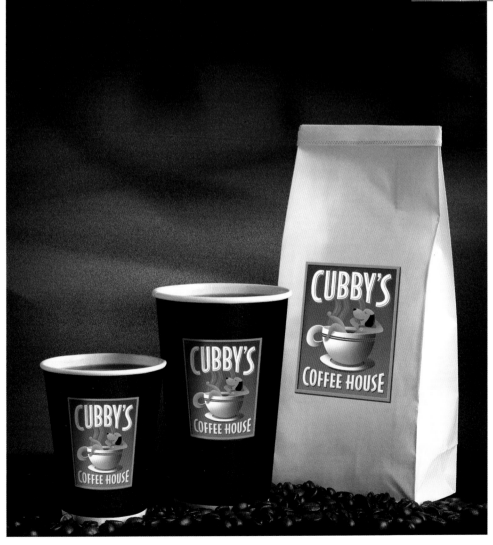

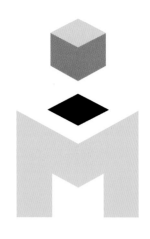

1.

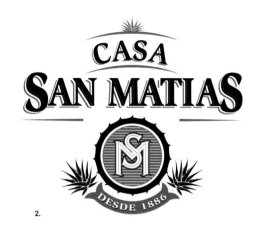

2.

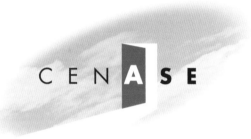

3.

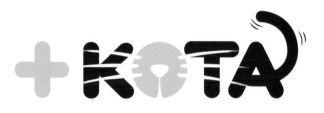

4.

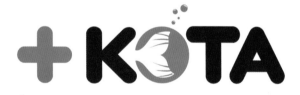

5.

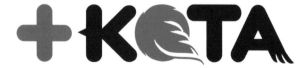

6.

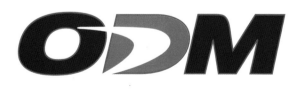

7.

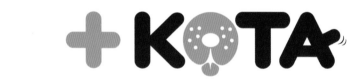

8.

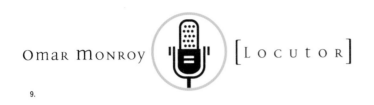

9.

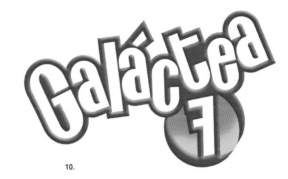

10.

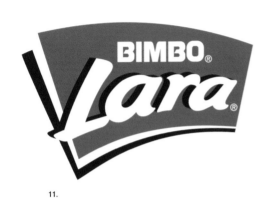

11.

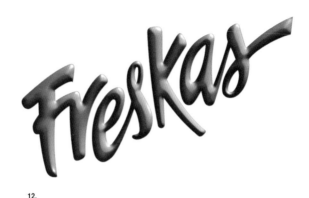

12.

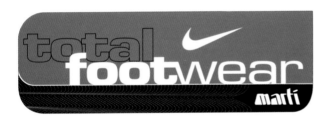

13.

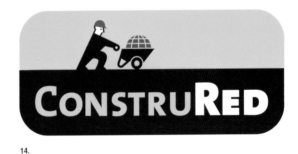

14.

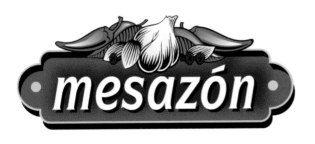

15.

1 - 15		
Design Firm	**TD2, S.C. Consultores en Identidad**	
1.		
Client	*A la Medida*	
Designers	Jose Luis Patiño, Rafael Treviño M.	
2.		
Client	*Casa San Matías (Tequila)*	
Designers	R. Rodrigo Córdova, Rafael Treviño M., Adalberto Arenas	
3.		
Client	*CENASA*	
Designer	Rafael Treviño M.	
4 - 7.		
Client	*+KOTA*	
Designers	Rafael Treviño, Erika Bravo	
8.		
Client	*ODM de México*	
Designer	Rafael Treviño M	

9.	
Client	*Omar Monroy*
Designer	Rafael Rodrigo Córdova
10.	
Client	*NESTLE Helados*
Designer	Rafael Rodrigo Córdova
11.	
Client	*BIMBO*
Designers	Rafael Treviño M., Rafael Rodrigo Córdova
12.	
Client	*Nestle Chocolates*
Designer	Rafael Treviño M.
13.	
Client	*Nike Mexico*
Designer	Rafael Treviño M.
14.	
Client	*Cementos Chihuahua*
Designer	Rafael Treviño
15.	
Client	*Mesazón*
Designers	José Luis Patiño, Rafael Treviño M.

1.

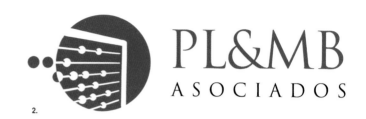

2.

PL&MB
ASOCIADOS

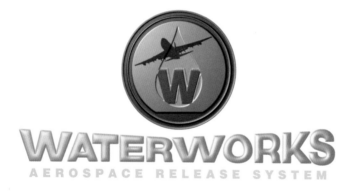

3.

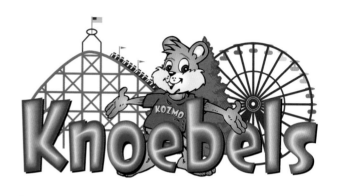

Knoebels

4.

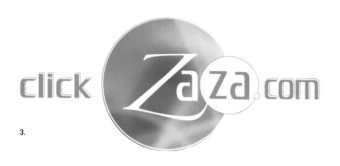

WATERWORKS
AEROSPACE RELEASE SYSTEM

5.

Rentalunits.com

6.

bestlodging.com

7.

1, 2
Design Firm **TD2, S.C. Consultores en Identidad**
3
Design Firm **T-1 Productions**
4, 5
Design Firm **PhaseOne Marketing & Design**
6, 7
Design Firm **Bondepus Graphic Design**

1.
Client   *Erika Rodríguez*
Designers   R. Rodrigo Córdova,
            Miguel Ríos
2.
Client   *Juana Pérez*
Designers   R. Rodrigo Córdova,
            Sergio Enriquez
3.
Client   *Click Zaza*
Designer   Parisa Chum

4.
Client   *Knoebels Amusement Park*
Designer   Michael Tobin
5.
Client   *Zyvax, Inc.*
Designer   Matthew Korbar
6.
Client   *Bestlodging.com*
Designer   Gary Epis, Geordie Lynch
7.
Client   *Bestlodging.com*
Designers   Gary Epis, Amy Bond
(opposite)
Client   Boomerang
Design Firm **Evenson Design Group**
Designer   Mark Sojka

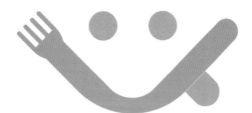

boomerang™

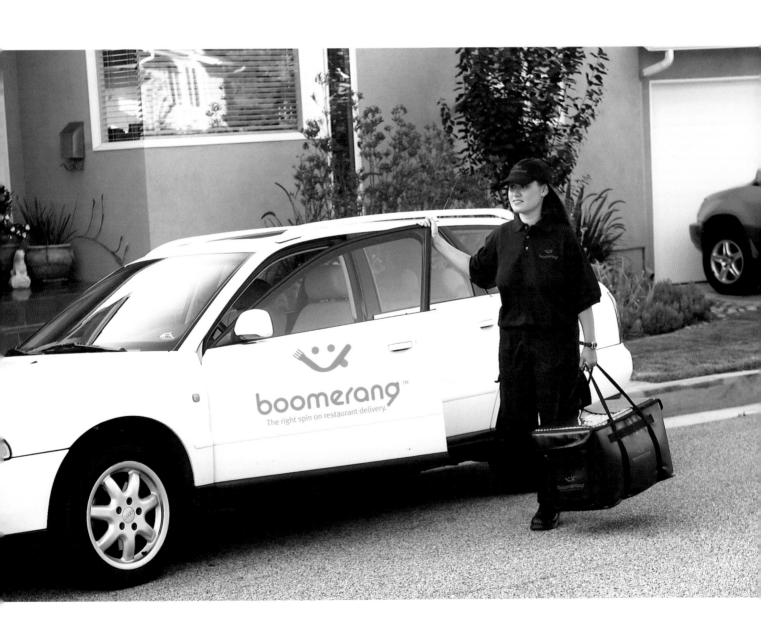

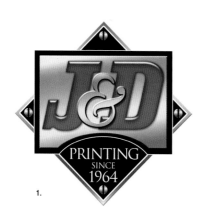

1.

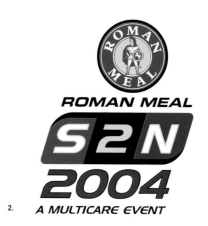

2.

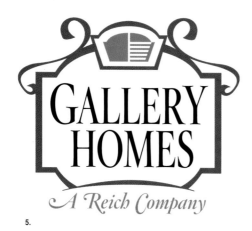

3.

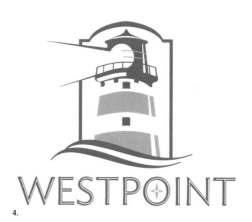

4.

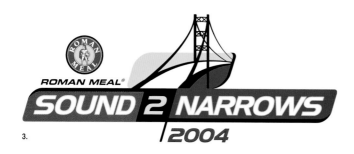

5.

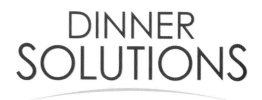

6.

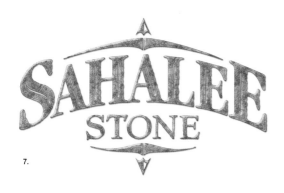

7.

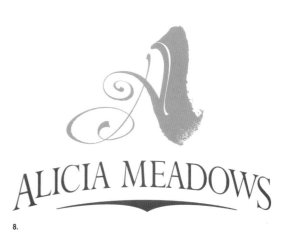

8.

ulmer | berne | llp
ATTORNEYS

9.

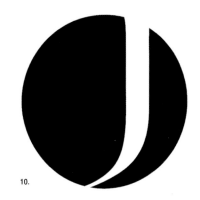

10.

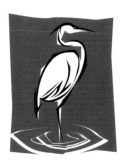

Nature Center
AT SHAKER LAKES

11.

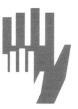

the althans foundation

12.

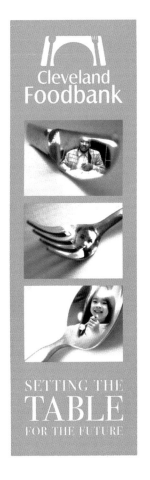

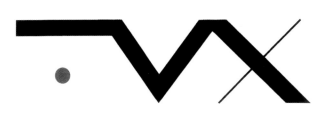

14.

1 - 8
Design Firm **Colin Magnuson Creative**
9 - 14
Design Firm **Epstein Design Partners, Inc.**

1.
Client   *J&D Printing Company*
Designer   Colin Magnuson

2, 3.
Client   *Multicare of Pierce County & Roman Meal*
Designer   Colin Magnuson

4.
Client   *Reich Construction*
Designer   Colin Magnuson

5.
Client   *Gallery Homes, A Reich Company*
Designer   Colin Magnuson

6.
Client   *Dinner Solutions*
Designer   Colin Magnuson

7.
Client   *WestBlock Systems*
Designer   Colin Magnuson

8.
Client   *Reich Construction*
Designer   Colin Magnuson

9.
Client   *Ulmer & Berne, LLP*
Designer   John Okal

10.
Client   *Josh Gottlieb Companies*
Designer   John Okal

11.
Client   *The Nature Center at Shaker Lakes*
Designer   Brian Jasinski

12.
Client   *Foundation Management Services, Inc.*
Designer   Brian Jasinski

13.
Client   *Cleveland Foodbank*
Designers   John Okal, Brian Jasinski

14.
Client   *The Value Exchange*
Designer   Brian Jasinski

13.

UVSolutions

1.

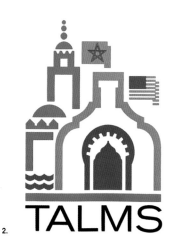

2.

BLUE RIDGE
POTTERS GUILD

3.

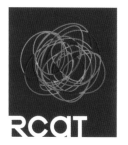

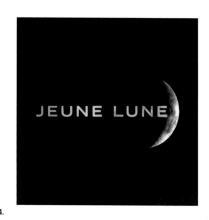

4.

3¹

Productions

5.

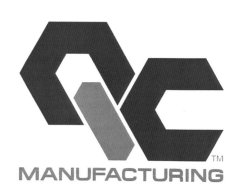

MANUFACTURING

6.

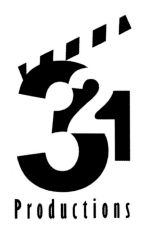

RCAT

REGIONAL
CONTRACT
ACADEMY
TRAINING

7.

1, 2
Design Firm **Frank D'Astolfo Design**
3
Design Firm **The Speidell Group**
4
Design Firm **Design Guys**
5
Design Firm **Purdue Student**
6
Design Firm **2g Marketing Communications, Inc.**
7
Design Firm **BBM & D**

1.
Client — UV Solutions Inc.
Designer — Frank D'Astolfo
2.
Client — Tangier American Legation Museum Society
Designer — Frank D'Astolfo

3.
Client — Blue Ridge Potters Guild
Designer — Rebekah E.W. Hoskins
4.
Client — Theatre de la Jeune Lune
Designers — Steven Sikora, Jay Theige
5.
Client — 3-2-1 Productions
Designer — Eric Beckner
6.
Client — Queen City Manufacturing
Designers — Ken Adams, Larry Livaudais
7.
Client — Regional Contract Academy Training
Designers — Ari Matson, Jon A. Leslie, Barbara Brown
(opposite)
Client — Rocamojo
Design Firm **Evenson Design Group**
Designer — Kera Scott

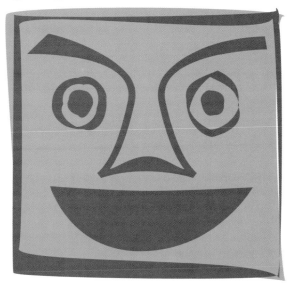

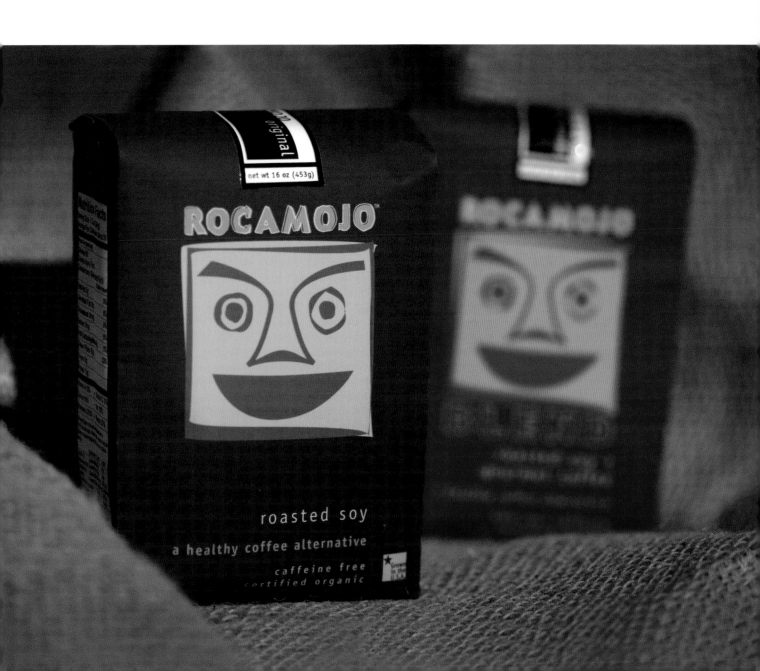

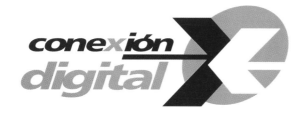

1.

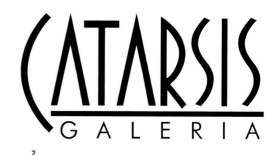

2.

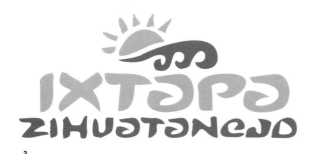

3.

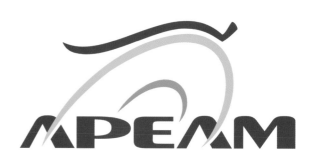

4.

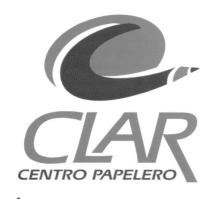

5.

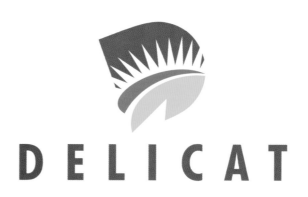

6.

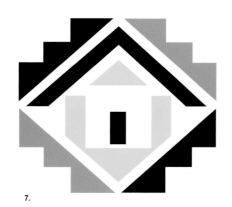

7.

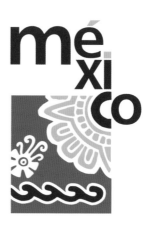

8.

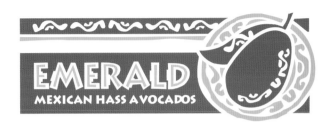

9.

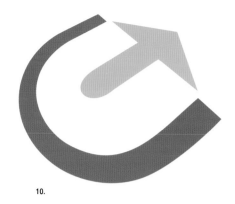

10.

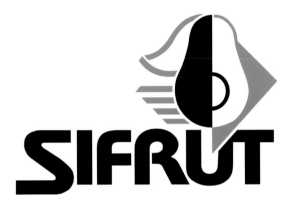

11.

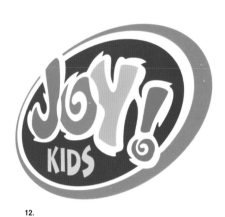

12.

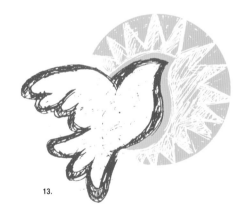

13.

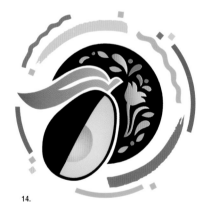

14.

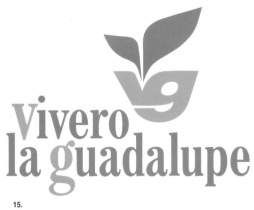

15.

1 - 15
Design Firm **Kenneth Diseño**

1.
Client   Cell Phone & Satellite TV Shop
Designer   Kenneth Treviño

2.
Client   Catarsis Art Gallery
Designers   Kenneth Treviño, Dolores Arroyo

3.
Client   Ixtapa Touristic Map
Designer   Kenneth Treviño

4.
Client   Assoc. of Avocado
Exporters Michoacan
Designer   Kenneth Treviño

5.
Client   Clar Paper Store
Designer   Kenneth Treviño

6.
Client   Delicat Fine Meats & Cheese
Designer   Kenneth Treviño

7.
Client   Hogar Y Ceramica
Designer   Kenneth Treviño

8.
Client   Playeras Michoacanas T Shirts
Designer   Kenneth Treviño

9.
Client   Amimex
Designer   Kenneth Treviño

10.
Client   City of Uruapan Chambers Assoc.
Designer   Kenneth Treviño

11.
Client   Sifrut Avocado Exporters
Designer   Kenneth Treviño

12.
Client   Joy Kids Fun Center
Designer   Kenneth Treviño

13.
Client   Hope For A Better
Future Conference
Designer   Kenneth Treviño

14.
Client   Uruapan City Fair
Designer   Kenneth Treviño

15.
Client   La Guadalupe Nursery
Designer   Kenneth Treviño

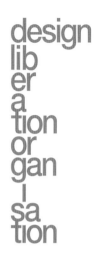

1.

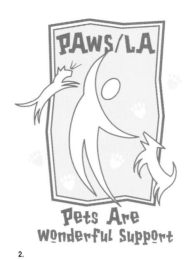

2.

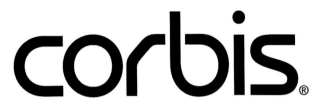

corbis®

3.

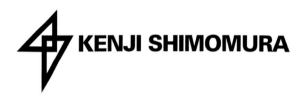

KENJI SHIMOMURA

4.

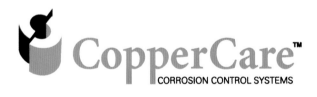

CopperCare™
CORROSION CONTROL SYSTEMS

5.

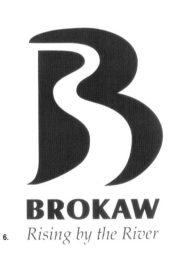

BROKAW
Rising by the River

6.

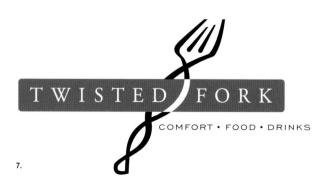

TWISTED FORK
COMFORT • FOOD • DRINKS

7.

1
Design Firm **Design Liberation Organisation**
2
Design Firm **Bradfield Design, Inc.**
3
Design Firm **Segura Inc.**
4
Design Firm **Kenji Shimomura**
5
Design Firm **DCG Solutions**
6
Design Firm **Foth & Van Dyke**
7
Design Firm **Becker Design**
1.
Client   *Design Liberation Organisation*
Designer   Greg Gutbezahl
2.
Client   *PAWS/LA*
Designer   Debra Bradfield

3.
Client   *Corbis*
Designer   TNOP
4.
Designer   Kenji Shimomura
5.
Client   *Copper Care, Inc.*
Designer   Marc E. Hedges
6.
Client   *Village of Brokaw*
Designer   Daniel Green
7.
Client   *Twisted Fork Restaurant*
Designer   Neil Becker
(opposite)
Client   Old Orchard Brande
Design Firm **The Bailey Group**
Designers   Steve Perry, Dave Fiedler

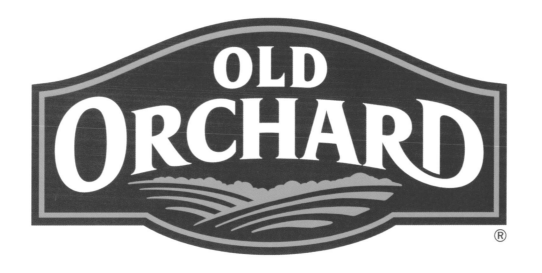

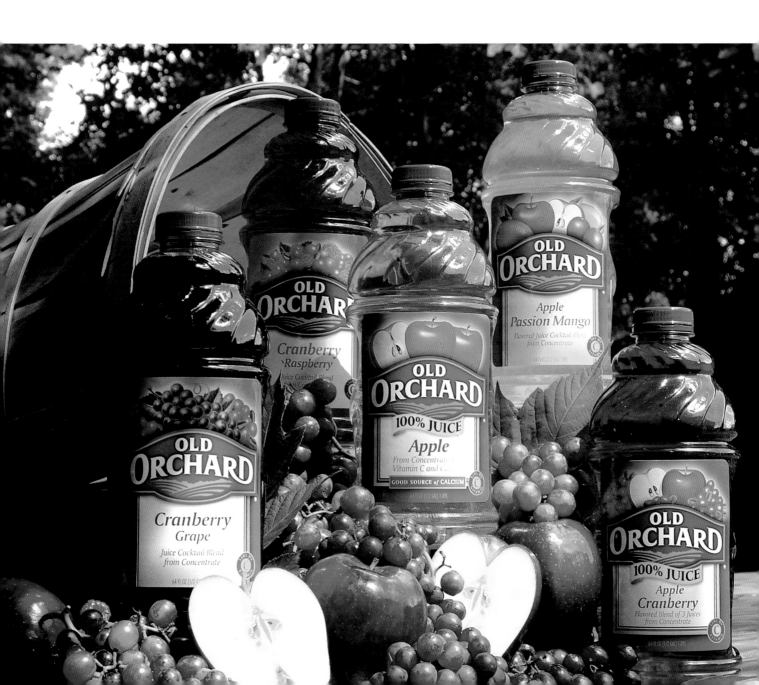

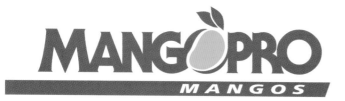

1.

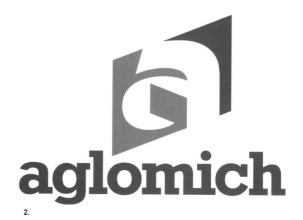

2.

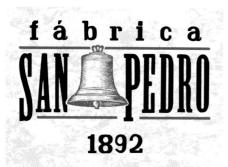

3.

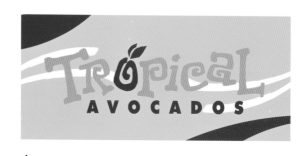

4.

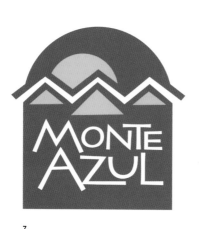

5.

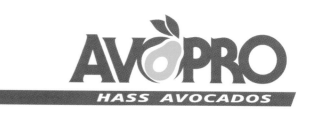

6.

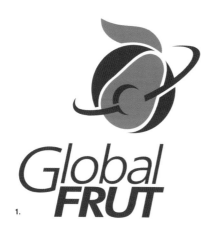

7.

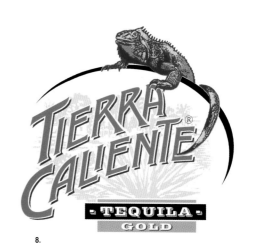

8.

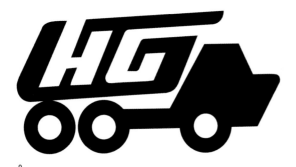

9.

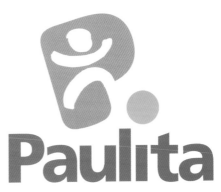

10.

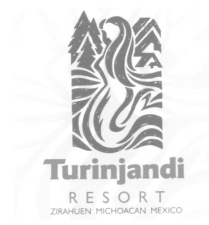

Turinjandi
R E S O R T
ZIRAHUEN MICHOACAN MEXICO

11.

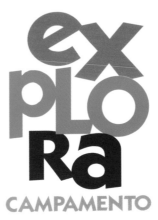

CAMPAMENTO

12.

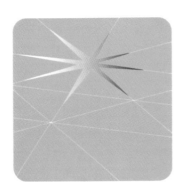

13.

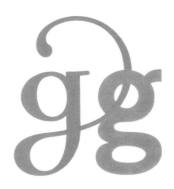

14.

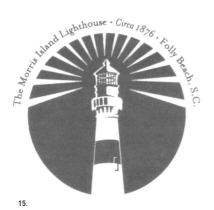

15.

1 - 12		
Design Firm	**Kenneth Diseño**	
13 - 15		
Design Firm	**Garfinkel Design**	
1.		
Client	*Global Frut Avocado Exporters*	
Designer	Kenneth Treviño	
2.		
Client	*Monroy Panel Factory*	
Designer	Kenneth Treviño	
3.		
Client	*San Pedro Old Textile Mill*	
Designer	Kenneth Treviño	
4.		
Client	*Fresh Directions International*	
Designer	Kenneth Treviño	
5, 6.		
Client	*Fresh Directions Mexicana*	
Designer	Kenneth Treviño	
7.		
Client	*Monte Azul Housing Development*	
Designer	Kenneth Treviño	

8.	
Client	*Industrial Mulsa Tequilas*
Designer	Kenneth Treviño
9.	
Client	*Hermanos Gudiño Transport*
Designer	Kenneth Treviño
10.	
Client	*Paulita Day Care Center*
Designer	Kenneth Treviño
11.	
Client	*Turinjandi Hotel-Resort*
Designer	Kenneth Treviño
12.	
Client	*Explora Summer Camp*
Designer	Kenneth Treviño
13.	
Client	*Advanced Wellness Technology*
Designer	Wendy Garfinkel-Gold
14.	
Client	*Garfinkel Design*
Designer	Wendy Garfinkel-Gold
15.	
Client	*Save the Light, Inc.*
Designer	Wendy Garfinkel-Gold

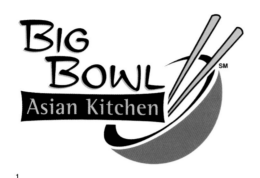

1.

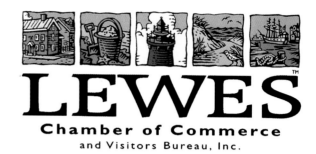

2.

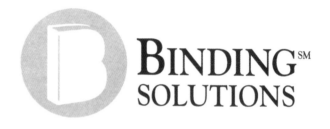

3.

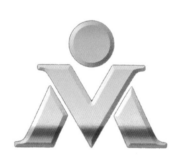

4.

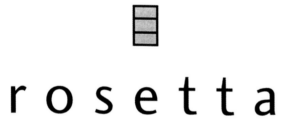

5.

6.

MARKETPLACE VISION

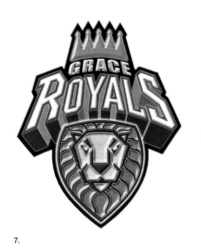

7.

1
Design Firm **Addison Whitney**
2
Design Firm **Dean Design/Marketing Group, Inc.**
3
Design Firm **Susan Meshberg Graphic Design**
4, 5
Design Firm **Stan Gellman Graphic Design Inc.**
6, 7
Design Firm **Dotzler Creative Arts**

1.
Client   *Brinker International*
Designers   Kimberlee Devis, Lisa Johnston, David Houk
2.
Client   *Lewes Chamber of Commerce*
Designer   Jeff Phillips
3.
Client   *Museum of the American Piano*
Designers   Susan Meshberg, Michele Kane

4.
Client   *Binding Solutions*
Designers   Teresa Thompson, Erin Goter
5.
Client   *Rosetta Financial Advisors*
Designers   David Kendall, Teresa Thompson
6.
Client   *Marketplace Vision*
Designers   Dotzler Creative Arts
7.
Client   *Grace University*
Designers   Dotzler Creative Arts
(opposite)
Client   Ameristar Casino
Design Firm **Visual Asylum**
Designer   Joel Sotelo

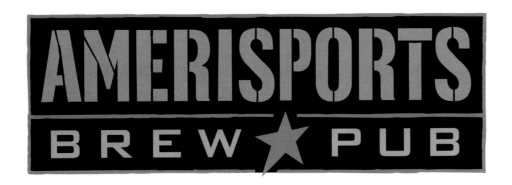

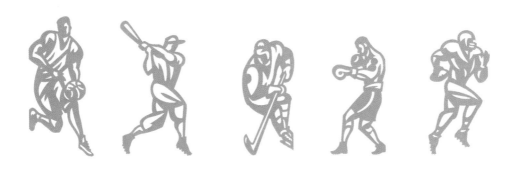

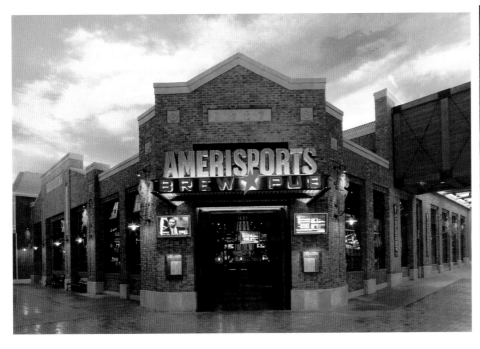

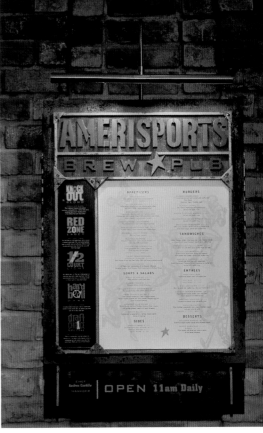

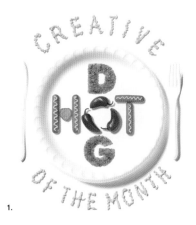

1.

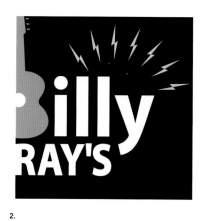

2.

3.

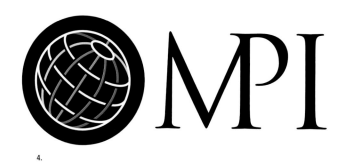

4.

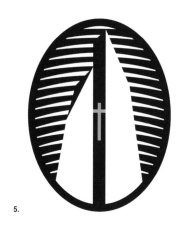

5.

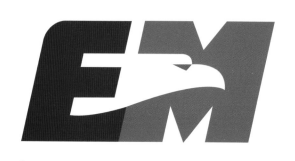

6.

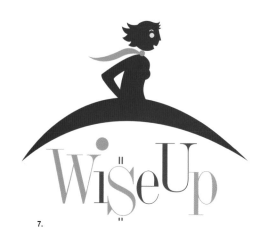

WiSeUp

7.

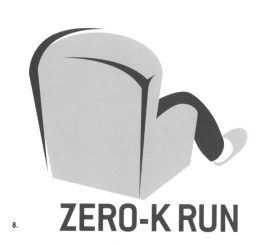

ZERO-K RUN

8.

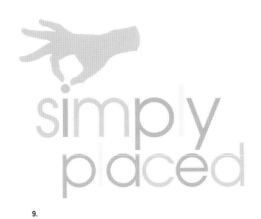

9.

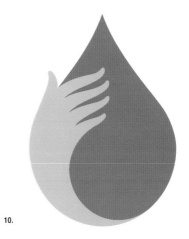

10.

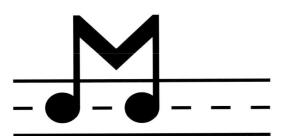

11.

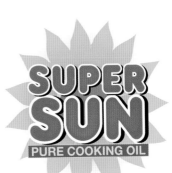

12.

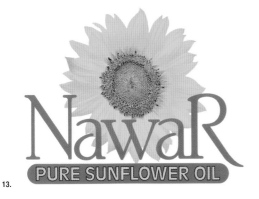

13.

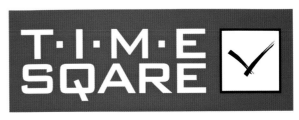

14.

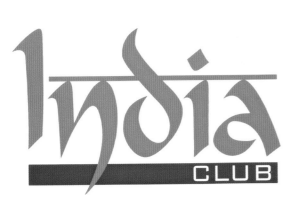

15.

1 - 11		
Design Firm	**Peterson & Company**	
12 - 15		
Design Firm	**Inca Tanvir Advertising LLC**	

1.
Client *Dallas Society of Visual Comm.*
Designer Scott Ray

2.
Client *Billy Ray*
Designer Scott Ray

3.
Client *Trophy Dental*
Designer Nhan Pham

4.
Client *MPI Meeting Prof. Int.*
Designer Nhan Pham

5.
Client *George Fox University*
Designer Bryan Peterson

6.
Client *Eagle Materials*
Designer Bryan Peterson

7.
Client *US Dept. of Labor,*
Womens Bureau
Designer Dorit Suffness

8.
Client *SMU Libraries*
Designer Miler Hung

9.
Client *Simply Placed*
Designer Miler Hung

10.
Client *Liquidity International*
Designer Nhan Pham

11.
Client *Jimmy LaFave,*
Music Road Records
Designer Scott Ray

12, 13.
Client *United Foods Company (psc)*
Designer Rajan Amrute

14.
Client *Arabian Trading Agency*
Designer Suresh Pawar

15.
Client *India Club, Dubai*
Designer Suresh Pawar

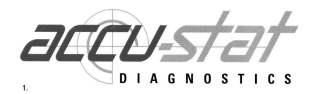

1.

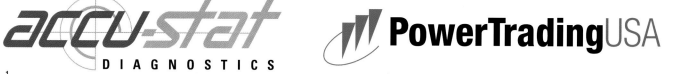

2.

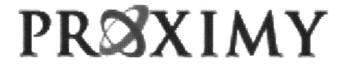

3.

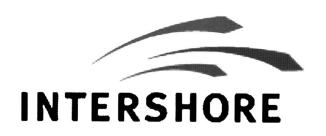

4.

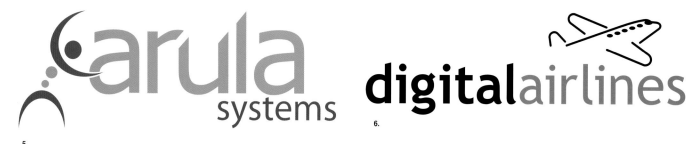

5.

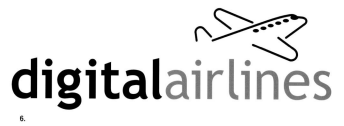

6.

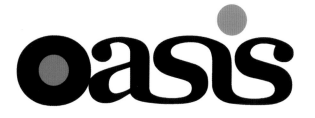

7.

1, 2
   Design Firm **Vince Rini Design**
3, 4
   Design Firm **Baker Brand Communications**
5, 6
   Design Firm **angryporcupine_design**
7
   Design Firm **Seran Design**
1.
   Client   *Accu-Stat Diagnostics*
   Designer   Vince Rini
2.
   Client   *Power Trading USA*
   Designer   Vince Rini
3.
   Client   *Proximy*
   Designer   Melissa Rosen
4.
   Client   *Intershore*
   Designer   Melissa Rosen

5.
   Client   *Arula Systems, Inc.*
   Designer   Cheryl Roder-Quill
6.
   Client   *Novell, Inc.*
   Designer   Cheryl Roder-Quill
7.
   Client   *Oasis Gallery*
   Designer   Sang Yoon
(opposite)
   Client   Pita Products
   Design Firm **Flowdesign, Inc.**
   Designer   Dan Matauch

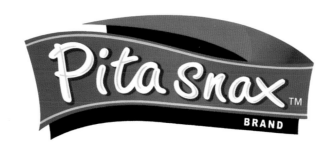

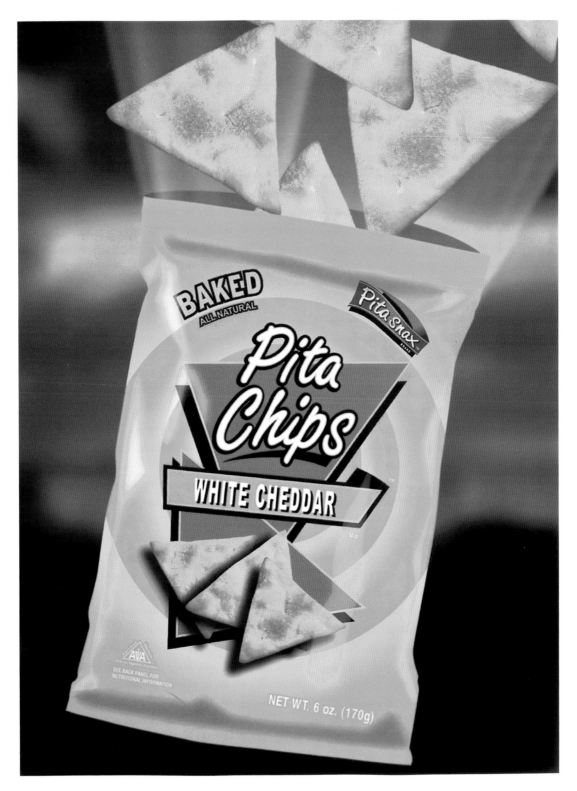

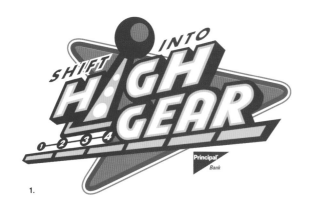

1.

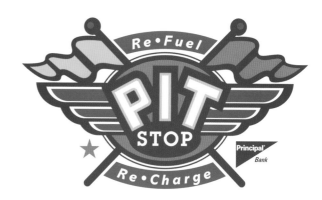

2.

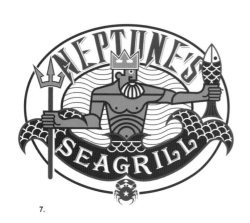

3.

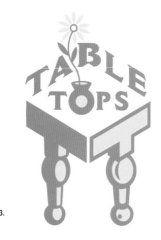

4.

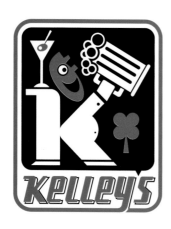

5.

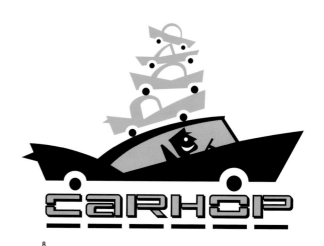

6.

7.

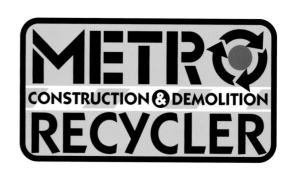

8.

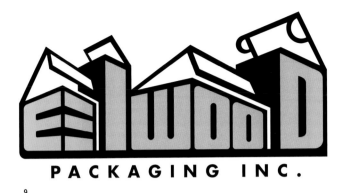

PACKAGING INC.

9.

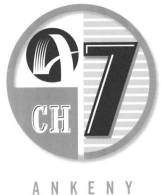

CH 7

A N K E N Y

10.

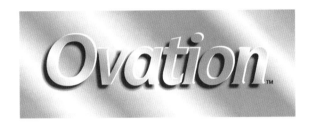

11.

LucencePhotographic

12.

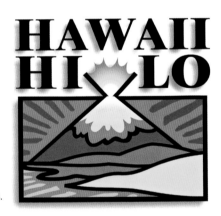

13.

Full House Gaming

14.

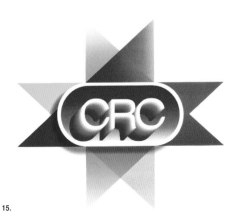

15.

1 - 10
Design Firm **Sayles Graphic Design, Inc.**
11 - 15
Design Firm **Lee Communciations, Inc.**
1, 2.
   Client   *Principal Bank*
   Designer John Sayles
3.
   Client   *Table Tops*
   Designer John Sayles
4.
   Client   *Kirke Financial Services*
   Designer John Sayles
5.
   Client   *Kelley's Pub and Grille*
   Designer John Sayles
6.
   Client   *Metro C&D Recycler*
   Designer John Sayles
7.
   Client   *Neptune's Seagrill*
   Designer John Sayles
8.
   Client   *Carhop*
   Designer John Sayles

9.
   Client   *Elwood Packaging*
   Designer John Sayles
10.
   Client   *City of Ankeny*
   Designer John Sayles
11.
   Client   *Essilor of America, Inc.*
   Designer Bob Lee
12.
   Client   *Lucence Photographic, Ltd.*
   Designer Bob Lee
13, 14.
   Client   *Full House Gaming, Inc.*
   Designer Bob Lee
15.
   Client   *Capitol Risk Concepts, Ltd.*
   Designer Bob Lee

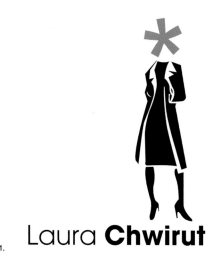

Laura **Chwirut**

1.

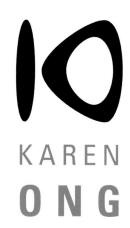

KAREN
ONG

2.

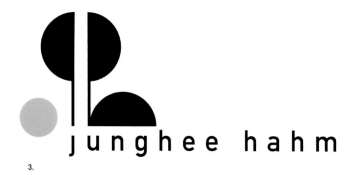

junghee hahm

3.

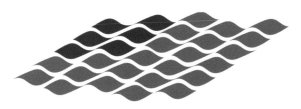

Boston ★ 2004
Nothing conventional about it.

4.

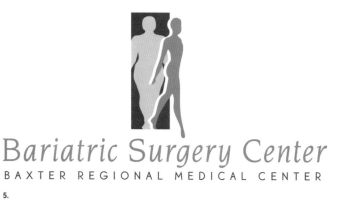

Bariatric Surgery Center
BAXTER REGIONAL MEDICAL CENTER

5.

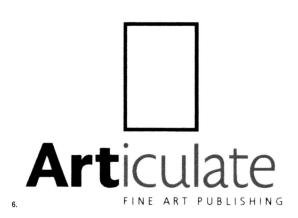

Articulate
FINE ART PUBLISHING

6.

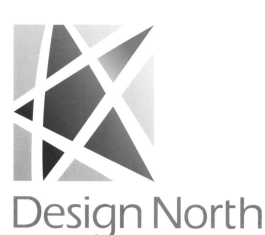

Design North

7.

1 Design Firm **Laura Chwirut**		**3.**	
		Client	*Junghee Hahm*
2 Design Firm **Karen Ong**		Designer	Junghee Hahm
		4.	
3 Design Firm **Junghee Hahm Design**		Client	*Democratic National Convention*
		Designer	Vic Ceroli, Sean Westgate
4 Design Firm **Hill Holliday**		**5.**	
		Client	*Bariatric Surgery Center*
5 Design Firm **Brooks-Jeffrey Marketing, Inc.**			*Baxter Regional Medical Center*
		Designers	Brooks-Jeffrey Marketing
6 Design Firm **Robert Meyers Design**			Creative Team
		6.	
7 Design Firm **Design North, Inc.**		Client	*Articulate*
1.		Designer	Robert Meyers
Client	*Laura Chwirut*	**7.**	
Designer	Laura Chwirut	Client	*Design North, Inc.*
2.		**(opposite)**	
Client	*Karen Ong*	Client	Xango
Designer	Karen Ong	Design Firm	**Flowdesign, Inc.**
		Designer	Dan Matauch

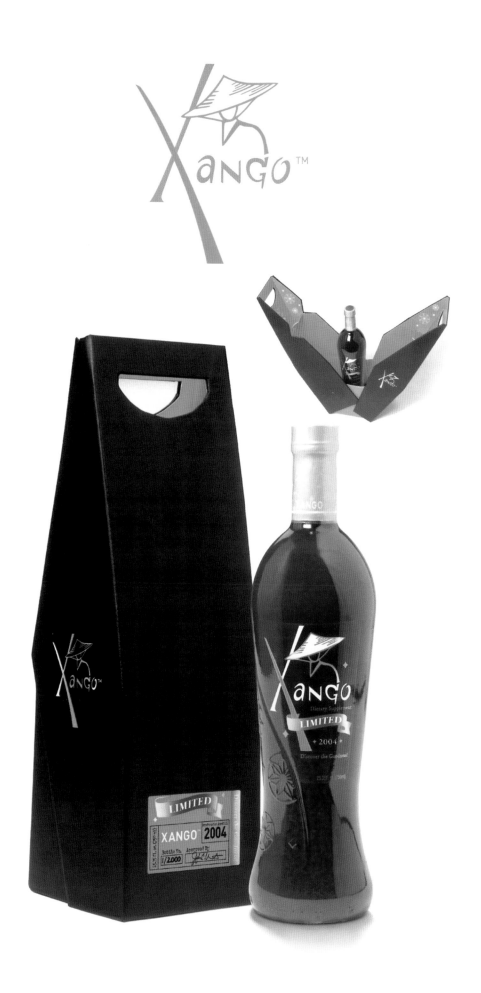

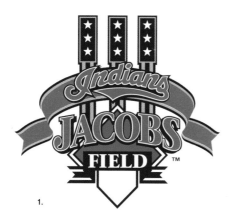

1.

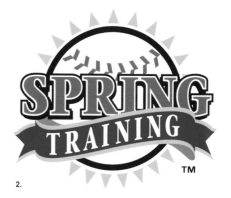

2.

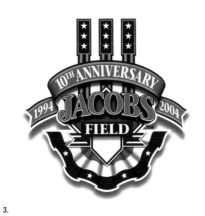

3.

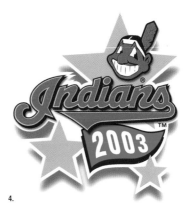

4.

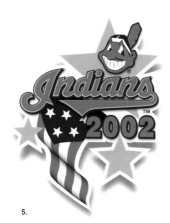

5.

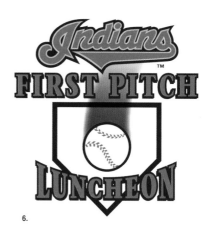

6.

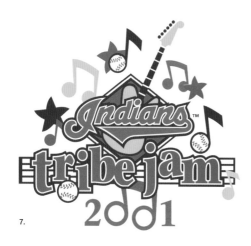

7.

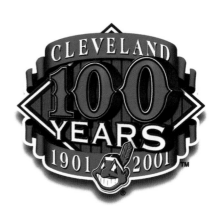

8.

196

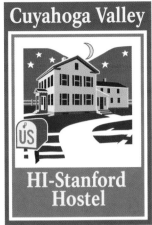

Cuyahoga Valley

HI-Stanford Hostel

9.

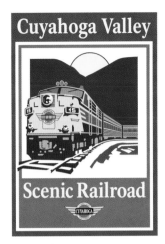

Cuyahoga Valley

Scenic Railroad

10.

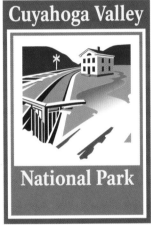

Cuyahoga Valley

National Park

11.

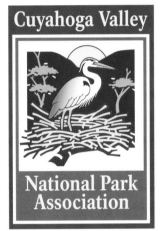

Cuyahoga Valley

National Park Association

12.

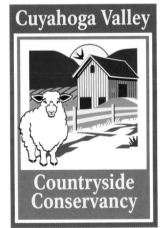

Cuyahoga Valley

Countryside Conservancy

13.

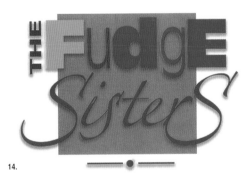

14.

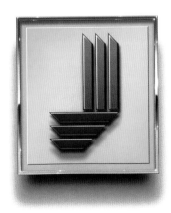

15.

1 - 15
Design Firm **Herip Design Associates, Inc.**
1 - 8.
Client   *Cleveland Indians*
Designers Walter M. Herip,
         John R. Menter
9 - 13.
Client   *Cuyhoga Valley National Park*
Designers Walter M. Herip,
         John R. Menter
14.
Client   *The Fudge Sisters*
Designer Walter M. Herip
15.
Client   *The Richard E. Jacobs Group, Inc.*
Designers Walter M. Herip,
         John R. Menter

1.

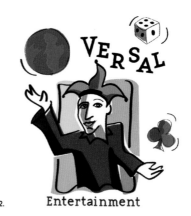

2.

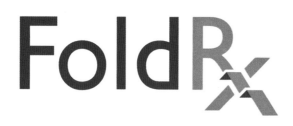

3.

4.

5.

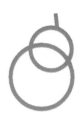

Pear Design

6.

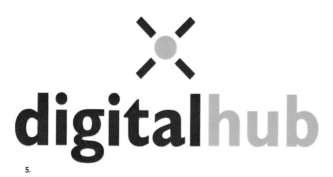

7.

1, 2
    Design Firm **Fassino/Design**
3, 4
    Design Firm **RS+K**
5, 6
    Design Firm **Pear Design**
7
    Design Firm **Walsh Design**

1.
    Client   *FoldRx*
    Designers   Chris Connors,
        Diane Fassino

2.
    Client   *Versal Entertainment*
    Designer   Angela Nannini

3.
    Client   *RS+K*
    Designer   Scot Kemp

4.
    Client   *Venture Investors*
    Designer   Kathleen Mitchell-Abendroth

5.
    Client   *Digitalhub*
    Designers   Linda Jackson,
        Norbert Marszalek

6.
    Client   *Pear Design*
    Designers   Linda Jackson,
        Norbert Marszalek

7.
    Client   *Rözana Cuizine*
    Designers   Miriam Lisco,
        Cathy Burnell

(opposite)
    Client   ISI International
    Design Firm **Walsh Design**
    Designers   Miriam Lisco,
        Andrew MacDonald

PACIFIC DRAGON

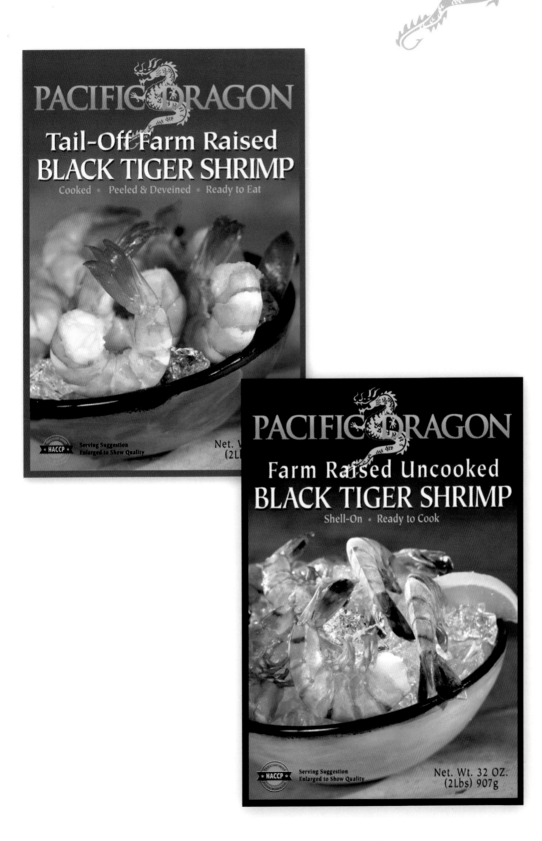

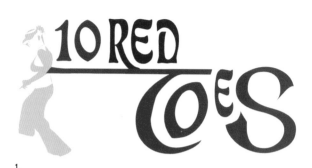

1.

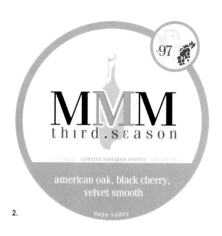

2.

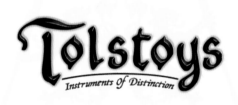

3.

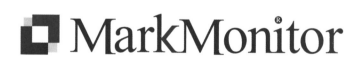

4.

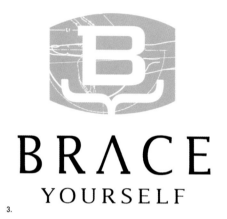

5.

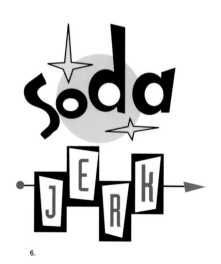

6.

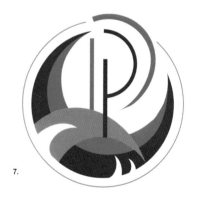

7.

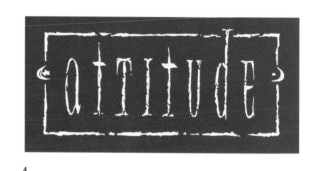

8.

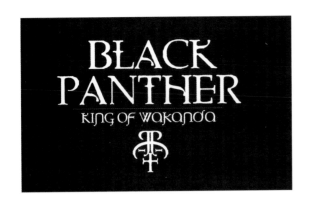

BLACK PANTHER
KING OF WAKANDA

9.

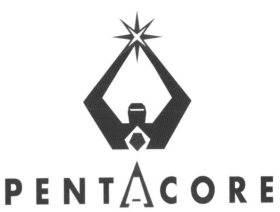

PENTACORE

10.

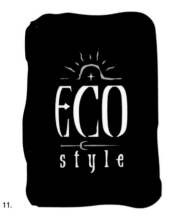

ECO style

11.

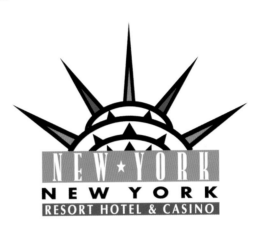

NEW YORK
NEW YORK
RESORT HOTEL & CASINO

12.

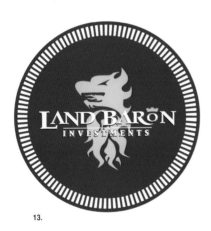

LAND BARON
INVESTMENTS

13.

LAND CAPITAL
FINANCIAL

14.

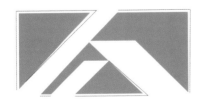

LUTTRELL
ASSOCIATES, INC.

15.

1 - 15
Design Firm **M3AD.com**

1.
Client   *Chronos 3*
Designers   Dan McElhattan III,
     Lauren M. Brown

2.
Client   *Chronos 3*
Designer   Dan McElhattan III

3.
Client   *Brace Yourself*
Designers   Dan McElhattan III,
     Raymond Perez

4.
Client   *Attitude Clothier*
Designer   Dan McElhattan III

5.
Client   *Navegante Group, Evolution*
Designers   Dan McElhattan III,
     Raymond Perez

6.
Client   *dm design lab*
Designer   Dan McElhattan III

7.
Client   *Paramount Professional Plaza*
Designer   Dan McElhattan III

8.
Client   *Elisa Cooper, Mark Monitor*
Designer   Dan McElhattan III

9.
Client   *M3 Advertising Design*
Designer   Dan McElhattan III

10.
Client   *Pentacore Engineering*
Designer   Dan McElhattan III

11.
Client   *Eco Style*
Designer   Dan McElhattan III

12.
Client   *Primm Investments*
Designer   Dan McElhattan III

13.
Client   *Land Baron Investments*
Designer   Dan McElhattan III

14.
Client   *Land Capital Financial*
Designer   Dan McElhattan III

15.
Client   *Luttrell Associates*
Designer   Dan McElhattan III

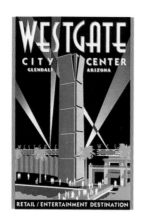

1.

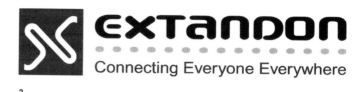

2.

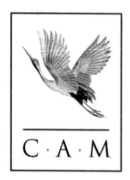

CRANE ASSET MANAGEMENT, LLC

3.

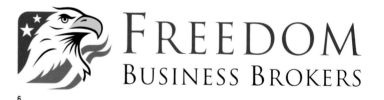

STUDIO G

4.

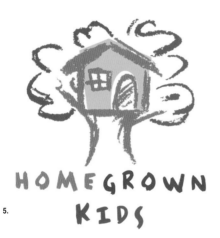

HOMEGROWN KIDS

5.

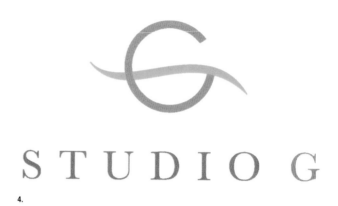

FREEDOM BUSINESS BROKERS

6.

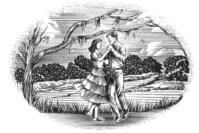

FLORIDA

FOLK FESTIVAL

7.

1		
Design Firm	**Development Design Group, Inc.**	
2		
Design Firm	**Crendo**	
3		
Design Firm	**Bloch + Coulter Design Group**	
4		
Design Firm	**Studio G**	
5, 6		
Design Firm	**Vince Rini Design**	
7		
Design Firm	**GOLD & Associates, Inc.**	

1.
Client — *The Ellman Companies*
Designer — Valerie Cataffa

2.
Client — *Extandon Inc.*
Designer — Tamra Heathershaw-Hart

3.
Client — *Crane Asset Management LLC*
Designer — Ellie Young Suh

4.
Client — *Studio G*
Designer — Gretchen Wills

5.
Client — *Homegrown Kids*
Designer — Vince Rini

6.
Client — *Freedom Business Brokers*
Designer — Vince Rini

7.
Client — *Florida Folk Festival*
Designers — Keith Gold, Peter Butcavage

(opposite)
Client — *Good Humor-Breyers*
Design Firm — **Smith Design**
Designer — Carol Konkowski

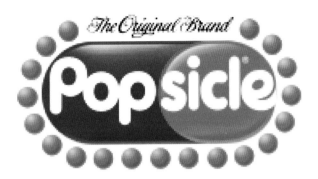

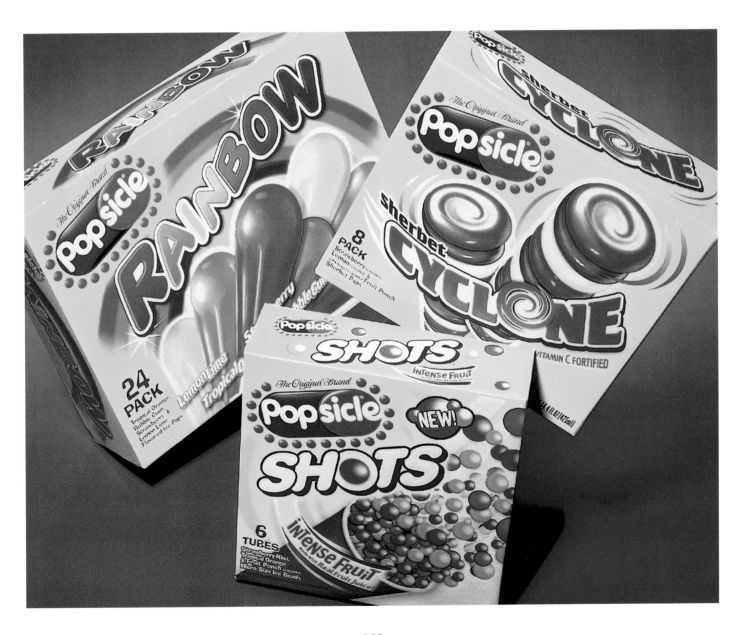

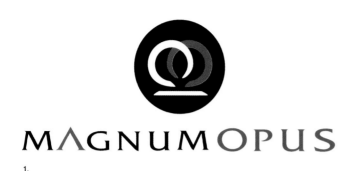

MAGNUMOPUS

1.

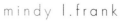

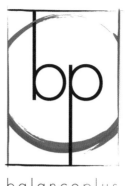

balanceplus

2.

BLEU
GOURMET

3.

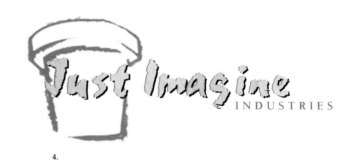

INDUSTRIES

4.

C H R O S N O S

5.

M3 ADVERTISING DESIGN

6.

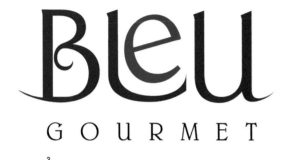

LIFE OR DEATH
LEADERSHIP

7.

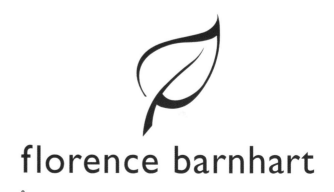

florence barnhart

8.

204

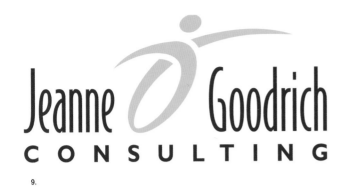

9.

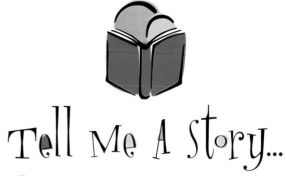

10.

VERB | creative

11.

BLACKST⬤NE

12.

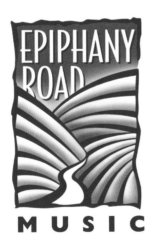

13.

PHOTON Light.COM

14.

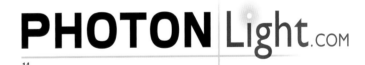

15.

1 - 6
Design Firm **M3AD.com**
7 - 15
Design Firm **Defteling Design**

1.
Client   MagnuMOpus
Designers   Dan McElhattan III,
             David Araujo

2.
Client   Balance Plus
Designer   Dan McElhattan III

3.
Client   Sonny Ahuja
Designers   Dan McElhattan ,
             David Araujo

4.
Client   Just Imagine Industries
Designer   Dan McElhattan III

5, 6.
Client   M3 Advertising Design
Designer   Dan McElhattan

7.
Client   Life or Death Leadership
Designer   Alex Wijnen

8.
Client   Florence Barnhart
Designer   Alex Wijnen

9.
Client   Jeanne Goodrich Consulting
Designer   Alex Wijnen

10.
Client   Tell Me A Story
Designer   Alex Wijnen

11.
Client   Verb Creative
Designer   Alex Wijnen

12.
Client   Blackstone, Inc.
Designer   Alex Wijnen

13.
Client   Epiphany Road Music
Designer   Alex Wijnen

14.
Client   Photon Light
Designer   Alex Wijnen

15.
Client   Paradise Media, Inc.
Designer   Alex Wijnen

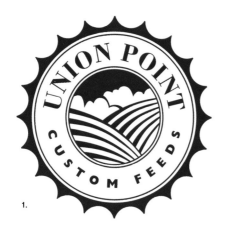

1.

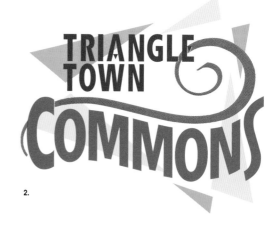

6.

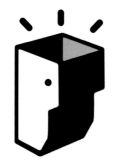

3.

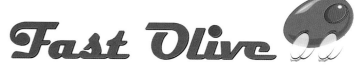

4.

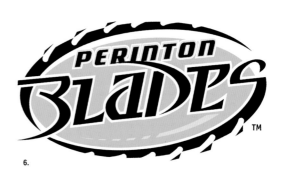

2.

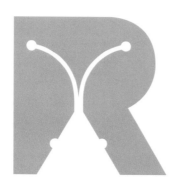

5.

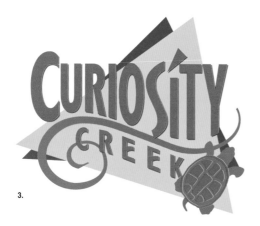

7.

1
Design Firm **Defteling Design**
2, 3
Design Firm **Herip Design Associates, Inc.**
4
Design Firm **GOLD & Associates, Inc.**
5, 6
Design Firm **Icon Graphics Inc.**
7
Design Firm **Lesniewicz Associates**

1.
Client   *Union Point Custom Feeds*
Designer   Alex Wijnen
2, 3.
Client   *The Richard E. Jacobs Group, Inc.*
Designers Walter M. Herip, John R. Menter
4.
Client   *Fast Olive*
Designer   Jan Hanak

5.
Client   *Cranial Capital, LLC*
Designers Icon Graphics Inc.
6.
Client   *Perinton Youth Hockey*
Designers Icon Graphics Inc.
7.
Client   *Roach Graphics*
Designer   Terry Lesniewicz
(opposite)
Client   *Food Collage, Inc.*
Design Firm **Flowdesign, Inc.**
Designer   Dan Matauch

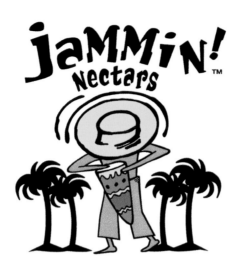

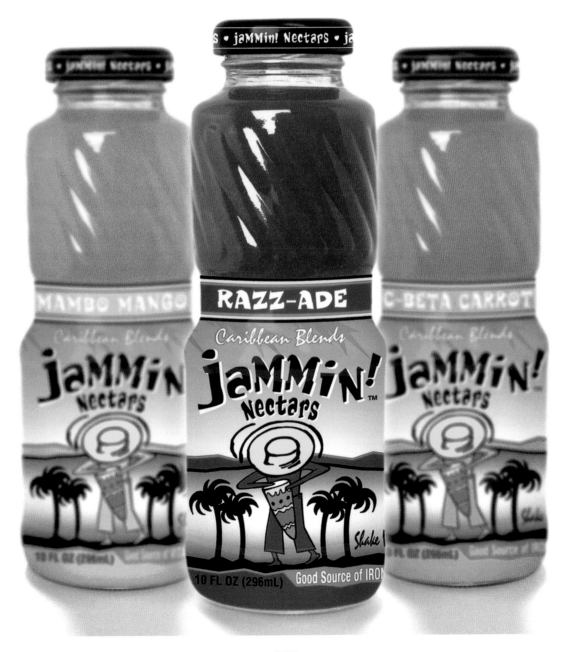

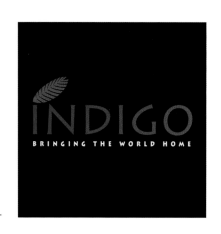

1.

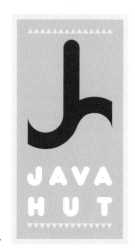

2.

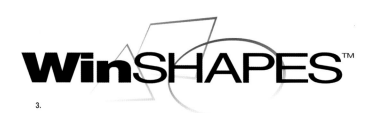

3.

4.

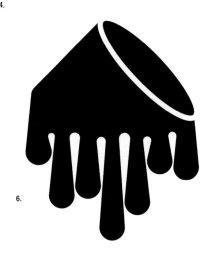

5.

6.

7.

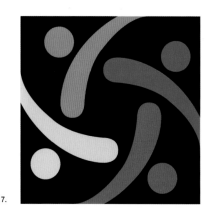

8.

stepxstep

208

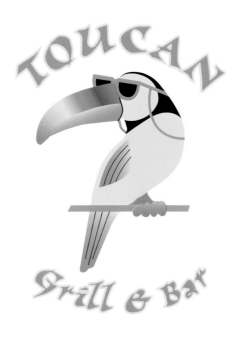

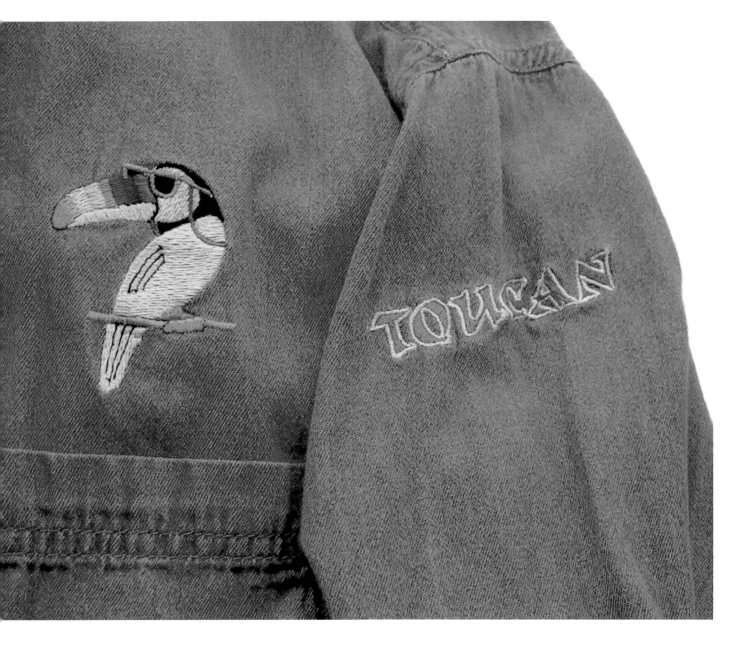

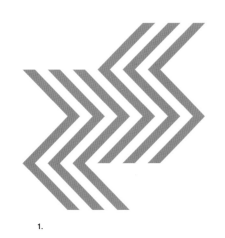

1.

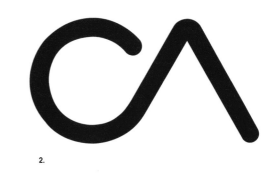

2.

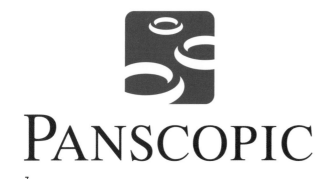

3.

front path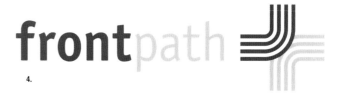

4.

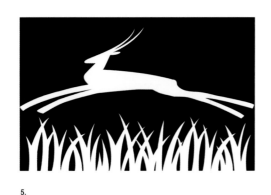

5.

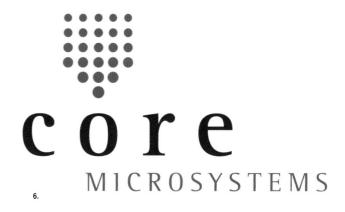

6.

PANSCOPIC

7.

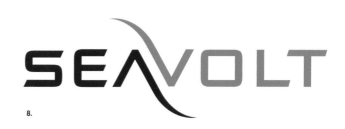

8.

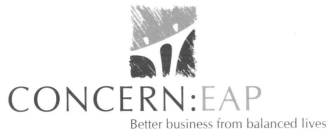

CONCERN:EAP

Better business from balanced lives

9.

efficēon ™

10.

Transmeta
C O R P O R A T I O N

11.

aftermedia ®

12.

BETA BREAKERS
SOFTWARE QUALITY ASSURANCE LABS

13.

SIX ◆ DEGREES

14.

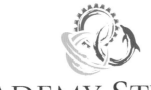

ACADEMY STUDIOS

15.

1 - 5
Design Firm **Lesniewicz Associates**
6 - 15
Design Firm **Plumbline Studios Inc.**
1.
Client   *Zyndorf/Serchuk*
Designer   Terry Lesniewicz
2.
Client   *Construction Architects*
Designer   Terry Lesniewicz
3.
Client   *Racing For Recovery*
Designer   Amy Lesniewicz
4.
Client   *FrontPath Health Coalition*
Designer   Jack Bollinger
5.
Client   *Owens Corning*
Designer   Jack Bollinger
6.
Client   *Core Microsystems*
Designer   Dom Moreci
7.
Client   *Panscopic*
Designer   Dom Moreci

8.
Client   *Sea Volt*
Designer   James Eli
9.
Client   *Concern:EAP*
Designer   Dom Moreci
10, 11.
Client   *Transmeta Corp*
Designers   James Eli, Dom Moreci
12.
Client   *AfterMedia*
Designer   Dom Moreci
13.
Client   *Beta Breakers*
Designer   Dom Moreci
14.
Client   *Six Degrees*
Designer   Ariel Villasol
15.
Client   *Academy Studios*
Designers   James Eli, Ariel Villasol,
          Dom Moreci, Mike Eli

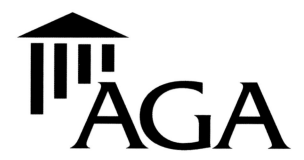

1.

GLOBAL IMPACT

2.

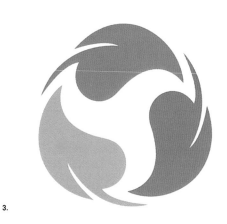

3.

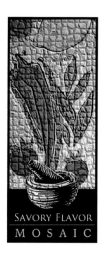

SAVORY FLAVOR
MOSAIC

4.

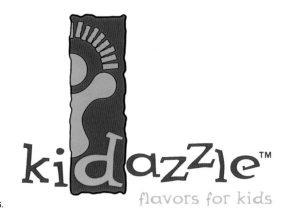

kidazzle™
flavors for kids

5.

MARIN
EDUCATION
FUND

Creating Educational Equity

6.

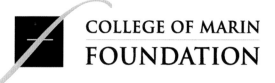

COLLEGE OF MARIN
FOUNDATION

7.

1 - 3
    Design Firm **TGD Communications**
4, 5
    Design Firm **AJF Marketing**
6, 7
    Design Firm **Ann Hill Communications**
1.
    Client   *Association of Government Accountants*
    Designer   Jennifer Cedoz
2.
    Client   *Global Impact*
    Designer   Gloria Vestal
3.
    Client   *Centennial Contractors Enterprises*
    Designer   Gloria Vestal

4.
    Client   *IFF-International Flavors & Fragrances*
    Designer   Justin Brindisi
5.
    Client   *IFF-International Flavors & Fragrances*
    Designer   Paul Borkowski
6.
    Client   *Marin Education Fund*
    Designer   Jack Zoog
7.
    Client   *College of Marin Foundation*
    Designer   Jack Zoog
(opposite)
    Client   *21st Century Spirits*
    Design Firm **Flowdesign, Inc.**
    Designer   Dan Matauch

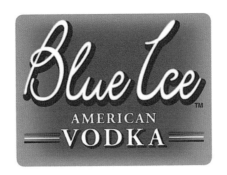

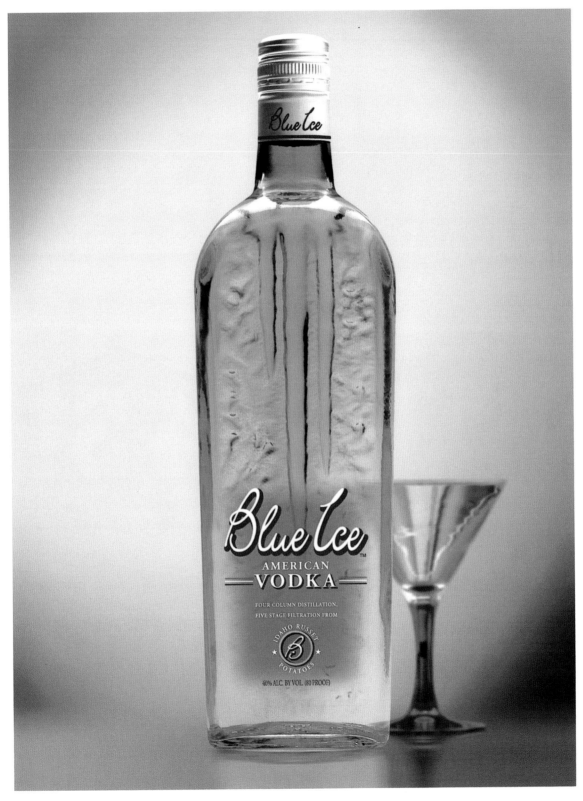

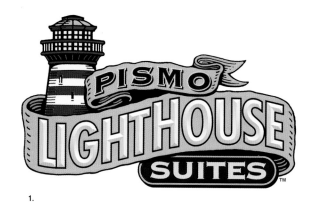

1.

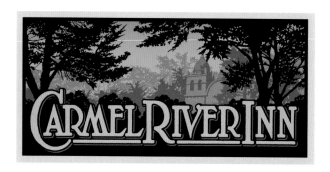

OceanParkHotels

2.

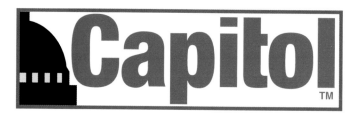

3.

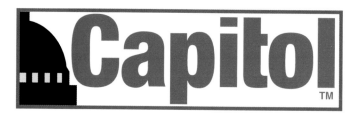

4.

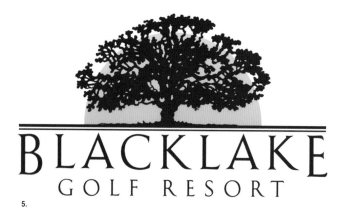

BLACKLAKE
GOLF RESORT

5.

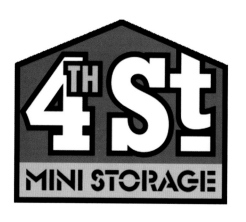

4TH St
MINI STORAGE

6.

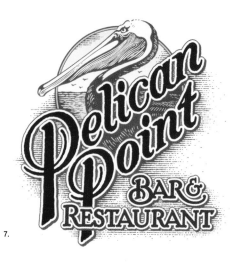

7.

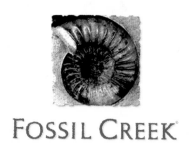

FOSSIL CREEK

8.

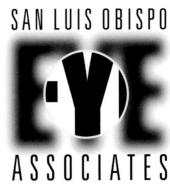

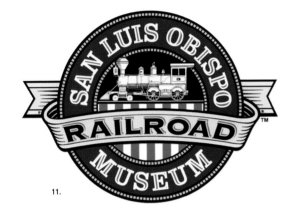

9.

10.

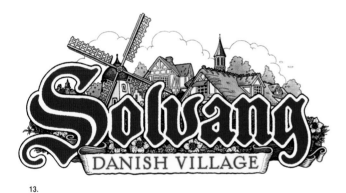

11.

12.

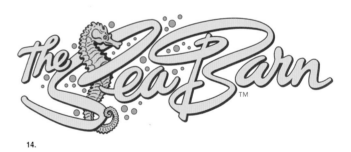

13.

14.

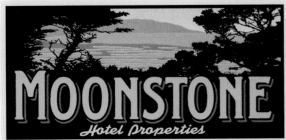

15.

1 - 15
Design Firm **Pierre Rademaker Design**

1.
Client   Martin Resorts
Designers   Debbie Shibata, Pierre Rademaker

2.
Client   Ocean Park Hotels
Designers   Anne Bussone, Pierre Rademaker

3.
Client   Moonstone Hotel Properties
Designers   Debbie Shibata, Pierre Rademaker

4.
Client   Capitol Outdoor
Designers   Anne Bussone, Pierre Rademaker

5.
Client   Infinite Horizon's
Designers   Debbie Shibata, Pierre Rademaker

6.
Client   Martin & Hobbs
Designers   Anne Bussone, Sierra Slade,
              Pierre Rademaker

7.
Client   Martin Resorts
Designers   Pierre Rademaker, Debbie Shibata

8.
Client   Fossil Creek Winery
Designers   Anne Bussone, Pierre Rademaker

9.
Client   Petite Soleil
Designers   Anne Bussone, Pierre Rademaker

10.
Client   San Luis Obispo Eye Associates
Designers   Kenny B. Swete, Dusty Davis,
              Pierre Rademaker

11.
Client   San Luis Railroad Museum
Designers   Elisa York, Anne Bussone,
              Pierre Rademaker

12.
Client   San Luis Obispo
Designer   Pierre Rademaker

13.
Client   Solvang
Designers   Pierre Rademaker, Debbie Shibata

14.
Client   The Sea Barn
Designers   Elisa York, Pierre Rademaker,
              Debbie Shibata

15.
Client   Moonstone Hotel Properties
Designers   Pierre Rademaker, Debbie Shibata

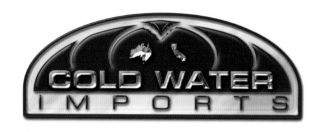

1.

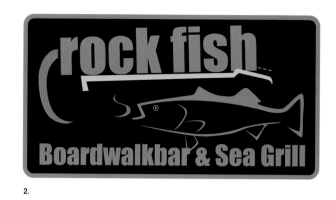

2.

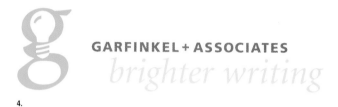

3.

GARFINKEL + ASSOCIATES
brighter writing

4.

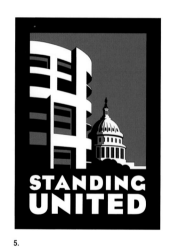

5.

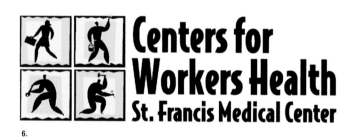

6.

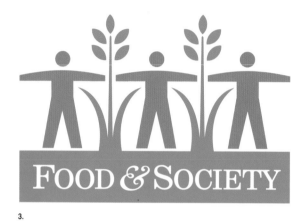

7.

1, 2
Design Firm **Medialias Creative**
3 - 5
Design Firm **Levine & Associates**
6, 7
Design Firm **Zoe Graphics**
1.
Client   *Cold Water Imports*
Designers   Gregg Holda,
       Shaun Menestrina
2.
Client   *Rockfish Boardwalk Bar & Sea Grill*
Designers   Gregg Holda,
       Shaun Menestrina
3.
Client   *Kellogg Foundation*
Designer   Lena Markley
4.
Client   *Garfinkel + Associates*
Designer   Jennie Jariel

5.
Client   *United Brotherhood of*
       Carpenters & Joiners of America
Designer   Steve Ofner
6.
Client   *St. Francis Medical Ctr.*
Designers   Kim Waters, Kathy Pagano
7.
Client   *Digital Brand Expressions*
Designers   Kim Waters, Kathy Pagano
(opposite)
Client   *American Beverage Marketers*
Design Firm **Flowdesign, Inc.**
Designer   Dan Matauch

218

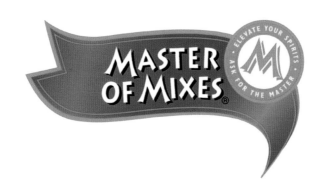

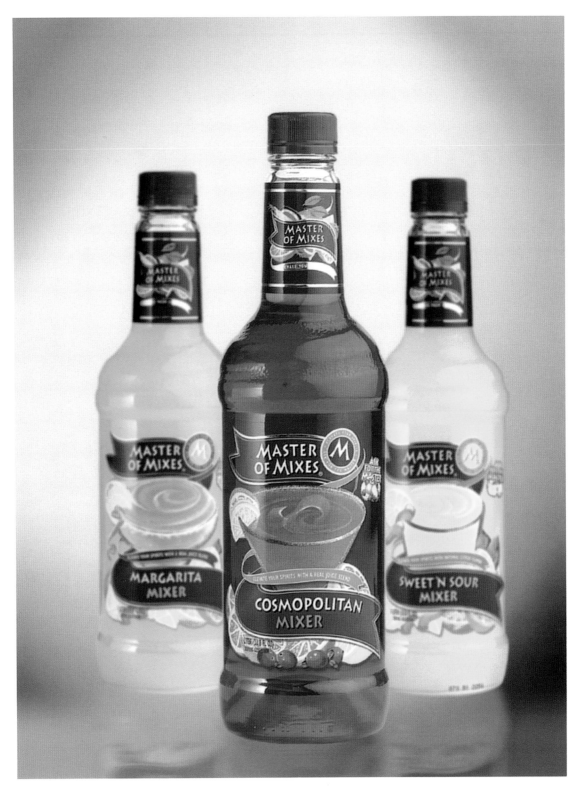

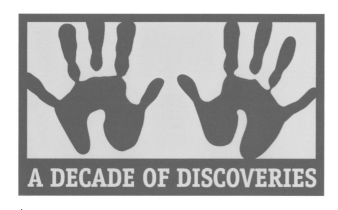

A DECADE OF DISCOVERIES

1.

eyePhysicians™

2.

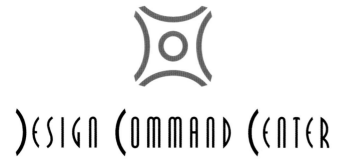

)esign (ommand (enter

3.

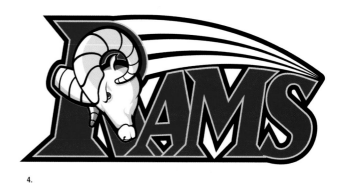

RAMS

4.

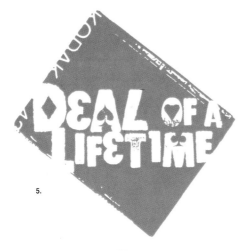

DEAL OF A LIFETIME

5.

ROCK the DOCK

6.

YO PHilly BLOCK PARTY

7.

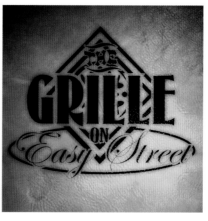

THE GRILLE ON Easy Street

8.

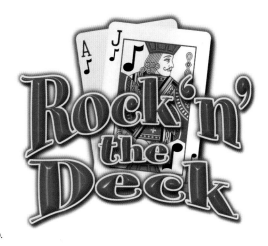

9.

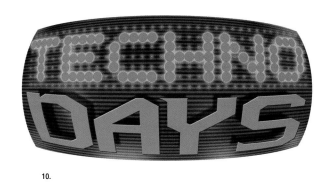

10.

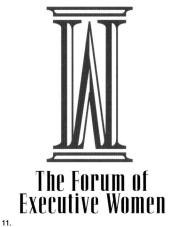

The Forum of Executive Women

11.

SKYLINE
TERRACE

12.

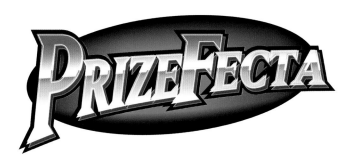

13.

WEsT EnD

CITY APARTMENTS

14.

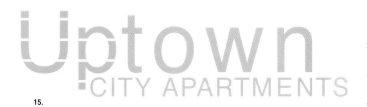

15.

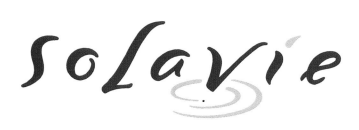

1.

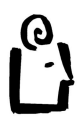

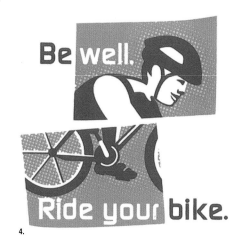
University
Book Store

2.

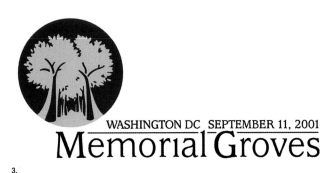

3.

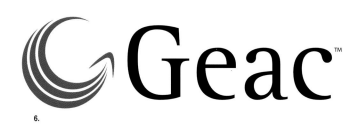

4.

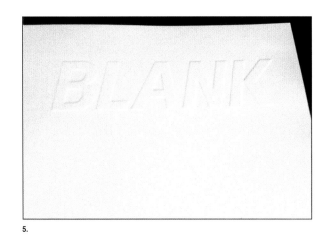

5.

Geac™

6.

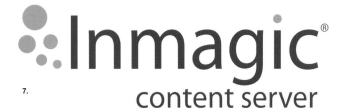

7.

1, 2
Design Firm **Hornall Anderson Design Works**
3 - 5
Design Firm **Blank Inc.**
6, 7
Design Firm **Hull Creative Group**

1.
Client   *Solavie*
Designers Jack Anderson, Kathy Saito,
           Gretchen Cook, Sonja Max,
           Henry Yiu, Alan Copeland
2.
Client   *University Book Store*
Designers John Hornall, Mary Hermes,
           Belinda Bowling, Holly Craven
3.
Client   *Greenspaces for DC*
Designers Danielle Willis, Robert Kent Wilson

4.
Client   *League of American Bicyclists*
Designers Robert Kent Wilson,
           Jay Kokernak,
           Christine Dzieciolowski
5.
Client   *Blank Inc.*
Designers Robert Kent Wilson,
           Christine Dzieciolowski
6.
Client   *Geac Corporation*
Designer Amy Braddock
7.
Client   *Inmagic Corporation*
Designer Carolyn Colonna
(opposite)
Client   *Oliver Winery*
Design Firm **Flowdesign, Inc.**
Designer Dan Matauch

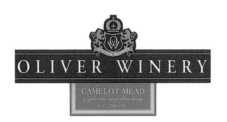

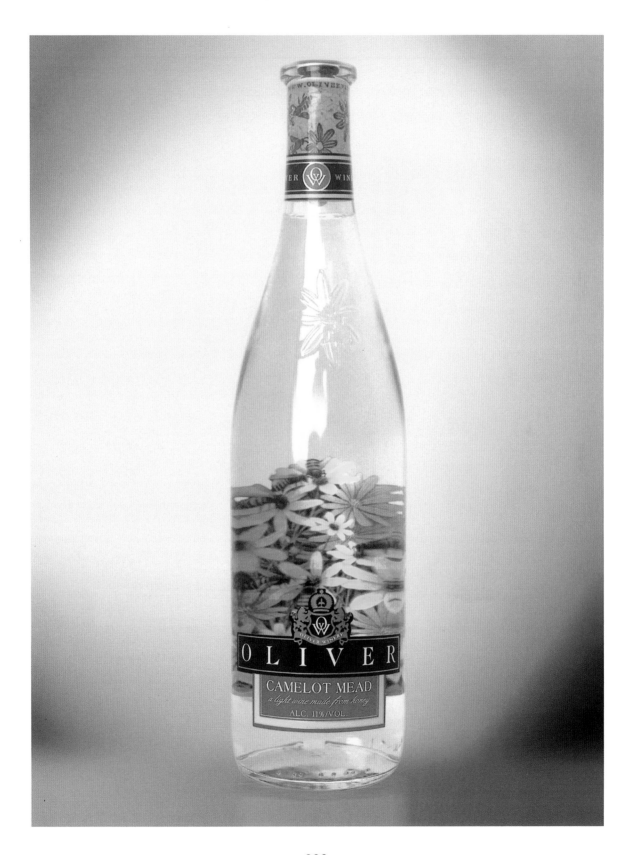

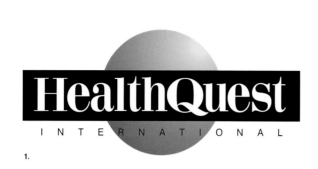

1.

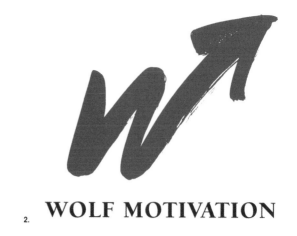

WOLF MOTIVATION

2.

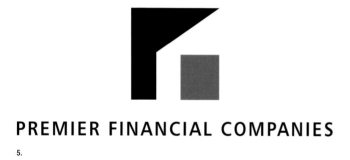

Chicago Avenue Evanston

3.

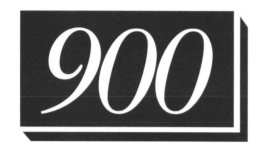

R O Y A L   O A K

4.

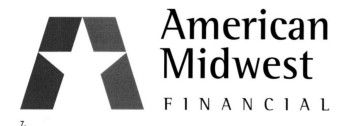

PREMIER FINANCIAL COMPANIES

5.

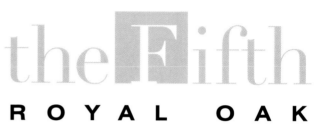

Center For
Financial
Innovation

6.

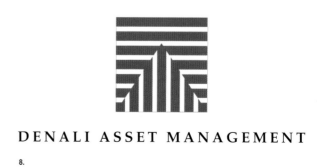

American
Midwest
F I N A N C I A L

7.

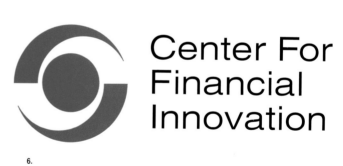

DENALI ASSET MANAGEMENT

8.

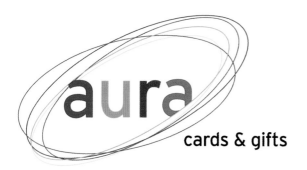

aura

cards & gifts

9.

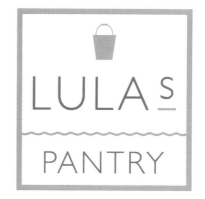

LULAS

PANTRY

10.

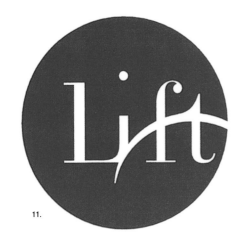

Lift

11.

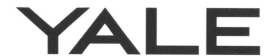

YALE

APPLIANCE + LIGHTING

12.

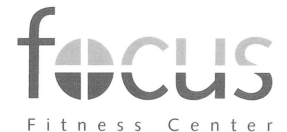

focus

Fitness Center

13.

SHADES

14.

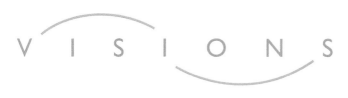

VISIONS

15.

1 - 8
Design Firm **Lienhart Design**
9 - 15
Design Firm **Kor Group**

1.
Client — *Healthquest International*
Designer — James Lienhart

2.
Client — *Wolf Motivation*
Designer — James Lienhart

3.
Client — *900 Chicago Avenue Evanston*
Designer — James Lienhart

4.
Client — *The Fifth Royal Oak*
Designer — James Lienhart

5.
Client — *Premier Financial Companies*
Designer — James Lienhart

6.
Client — *Center for Financial Innovation*
Designer — James Lienhart

7.
Client — *American Midwest Financial*
Designer — James Lienhart

8.
Client — *Denali Asset Management*
Designer — James Lienhart

9.
Client — *Aura Cards & Gifts*
Designers — Karen Dendy Smith, MB Jarosik, Jim Gibson

10.
Client — *Lula's Pantry*
Designers — Karen Dendy Smith, Jim Gibson, James Grady

11.
Client — *Lift*
Designers — Karen Dendy Smith, Kjerstin Westguard

12.
Client — *Yale Appliance & Lighting*
Designers — Karen Dendy Smith, Brian Azer

13 - 15.
Client — *Southbridge Hotel & Conference Center*
Designers — MB Jarosik, Sandra Meyer

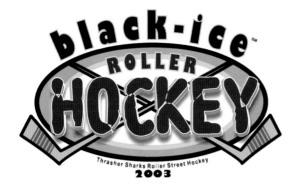

1.

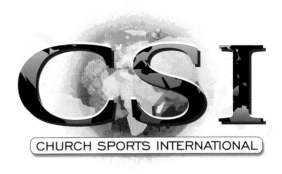

2.

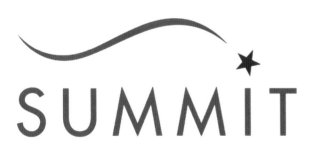

3.

4.

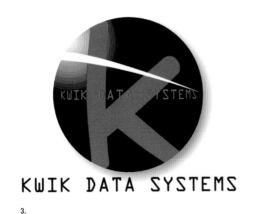

5.

AZIA
center
汇 亚 大 厦

6.

7.

1 - 3
Design Firm **imagineGrafx**
4 - 6
Design Firm **Calori & Vanden-Eynden**
7
Design Firm **FUSZION Collaborative**

1.
Client   *South Valley Christian Church*
Designer   Stephen Guy
2.
Client   *Church Sports Int'l*
Designer   Stephen Guy
3.
Client   *KWIK Data Systems*
Designer   Stephen Guy
4.
Client   *Greater Jamaica Development
            Corporation*
Designers   David Vanden-Eynden,
            Marisa Schulman

5.
Client   *City of Summit, NJ*
Designers   David Vanden-Eynden,
            Denise Funaro-Psoinos
6.
Client   *Shanghai Investment
            Real Estate Development*
Designers   David Vanden-Eynden,
            Chris Calori,
            Lindsay McCosh,
            Marisa Schulman
7.
Client   *uReach.com*
Designer   Steve Dreyer
(opposite)
Client   *Morinda, Inc.*
Design Firm **Flowdesign, Inc.**
Designer   Dan Matauch

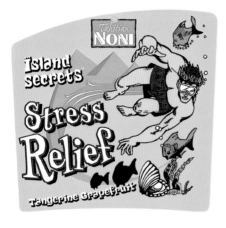

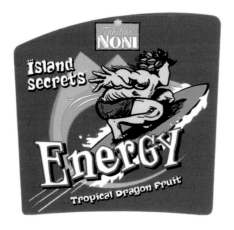

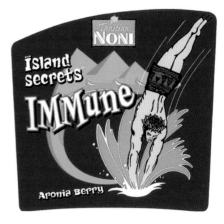

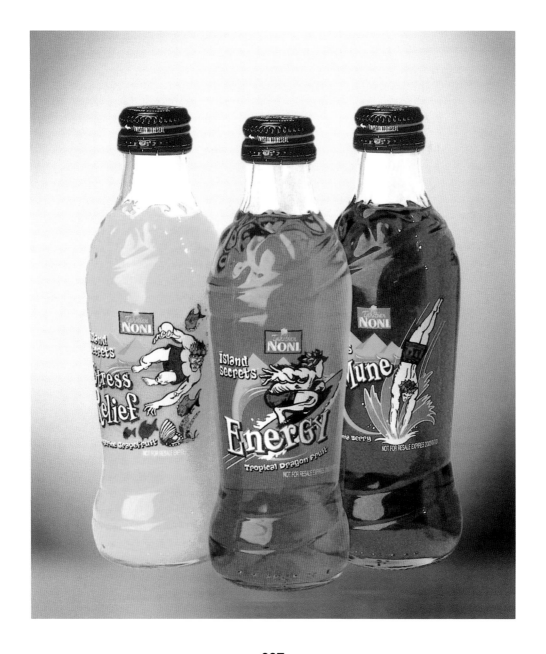

227

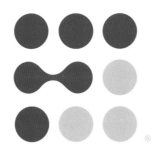

FUSZION | COLLABORATIVE

1.

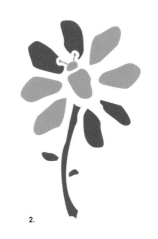

2.

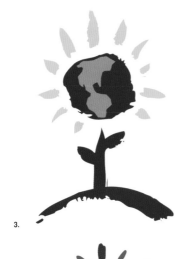

3.

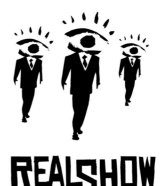

REALSHOW

4.

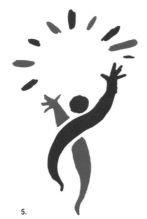

5.

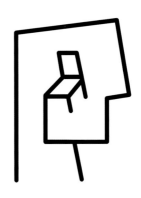

DECOTHERAPY

6.

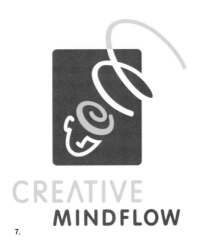

CREATIVE
MINDFLOW

7.

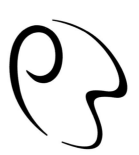

PALETTE

8.

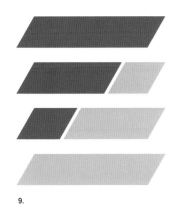

9.

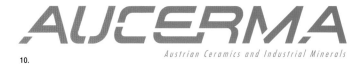

Austrian Ceramics and Industrial Minerals

10.

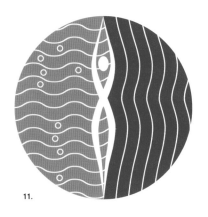

11.

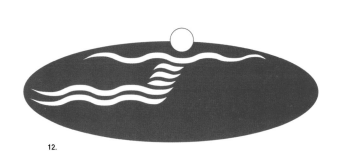

12.

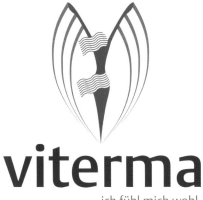

viterma
ich fühl mich wohl.

13.

ARCUTERM

14.

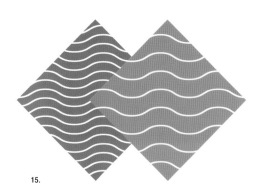

15.

1 - 8
Design Firm **FUSZION Collaborative**
9 - 15
Design Firm **motterdesign**

1.
Client   *FUSZION Collaborative*
Designers   Tony Fletcher, Rick Heffner

2.
Client   *Smith Fellows*
Designer   John Foster

3.
Client   *Community Anti-Drug Coalitions of America*
Designer   John Foster

4.
Client   *Art Director's Club of Metropolitan Washington*
Designer   John Foster

5.
Client   *Americans for the Arts*
Designer   John Foster

6.
Client   *Deco Therapy*
Designers   Steve Dreyer, Rick Heffner

7.
Client   *Creative Mindflow*
Designer   Christian Baldo

8.
Client   *Palette Restaurant*
Designers   Tony Fletcher, Rick Heffner

9.
Client   *Frewein & Farr*
Designer   Siegmund Motter

10.
Client   *Aucerma*
Designer   Siegmund Motter

11.
Client   *Unitec*
Designer   Siegmund Motter

12.
Client   *Ö-Bad**
Designer   Siegmund Motter

13.
Client   *Viterma*
Designer   Siegmund Motter

14.
Client   *Arcuterm*
Designer   Siegmund Motter

15.
Client   *Holzmüller*
Designer   Siegmund Motter

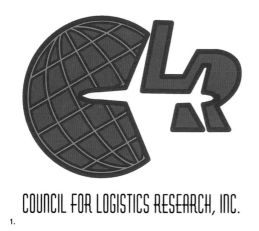

COUNCIL FOR LOGISTICS RESEARCH, INC.

1.

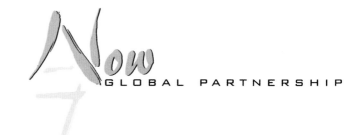

2.

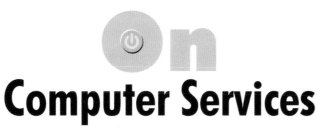

3.

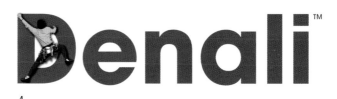

4.

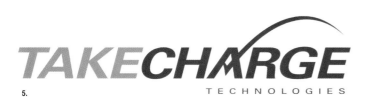

5.

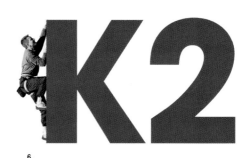

6.

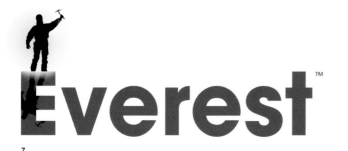

7.

1 - 3
Design Firm **MDVC Creative, Inc.**
4 - 7
Design Firm **Martin-Schaffer, Inc.**
1.
   Client   *Council for Logistics Research, Inc.*
2.
   Client   *Mitsui Bussan Logistics*
3.
   Client   *On Computer Services*
4.
   Client   *Grace Vydac*
   Designers Steve Cohn,
             Tina Martin

5.
   Client   *TakeCharge Technologies*
   Designers Kelly Mathieu,
             Tina Martin
6, 7.
   Client   *Grace Vydac*
   Designers Steve Cohn,
             Tina Martin
(opposite)
   Client   *Fuze Candy*
   Design Firm **Out Of The Box**
   Designer Rick Schneider

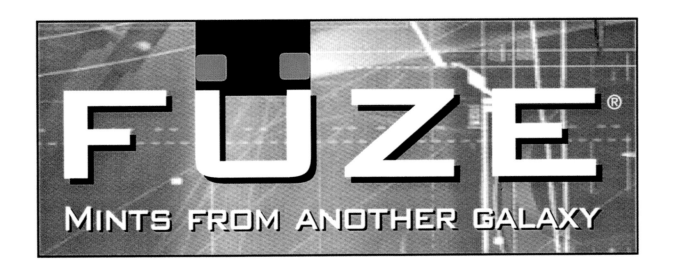

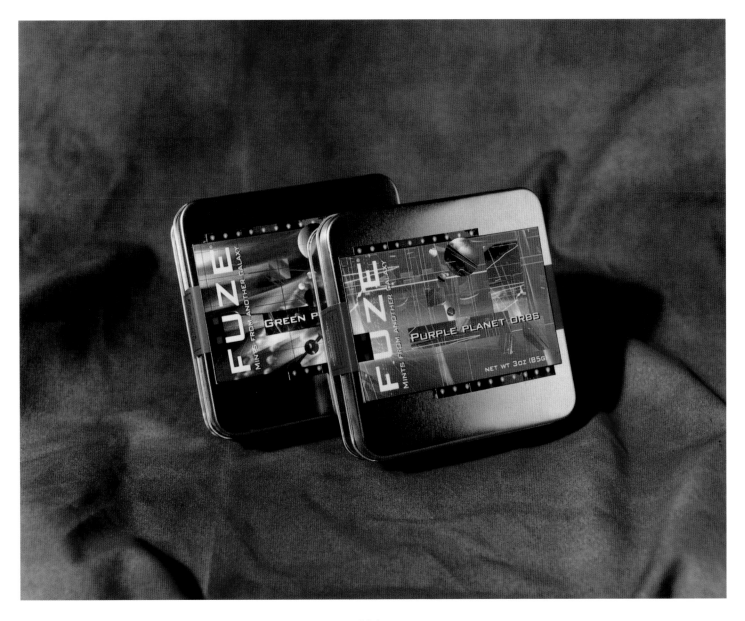

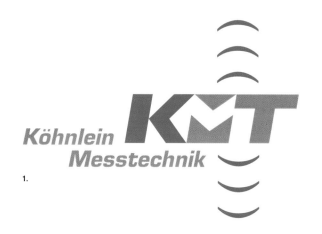

Köhnlein Messtechnik

1.

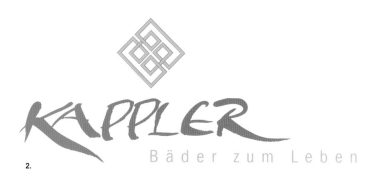

KAPPLER

Bäder zum Leben

2.

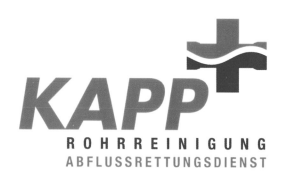

KAPP

ROHRREINIGUNG
ABFLUSSRETTUNGSDIENST

3.

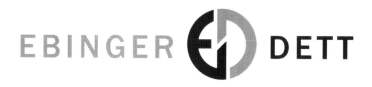

EBINGER DETT

4.

eigen **werk** !

5.

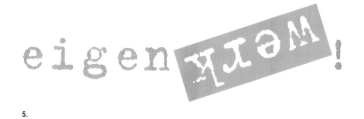

Ramah Wagner
business of health

6.

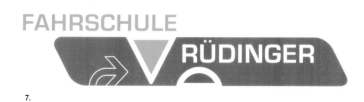

FAHRSCHULE RÜDINGER

7.

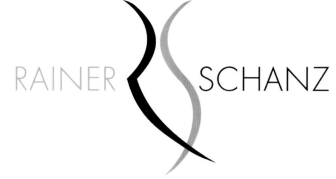

RAINER SCHANZ

8.

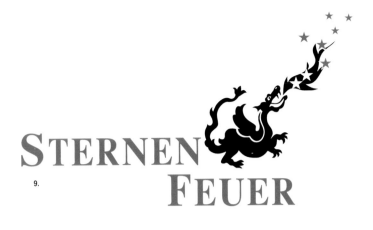

STERNEN
FEUER

9.

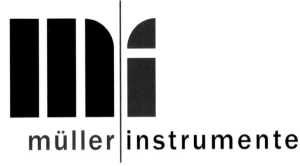

müller|instrumente

10.

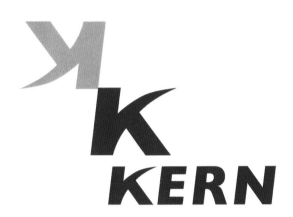

KERN

11.

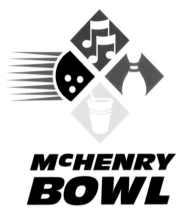

McHENRY
BOWL

12.

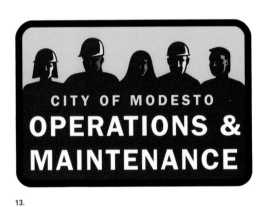

CITY OF MODESTO
OPERATIONS &
MAINTENANCE

13.

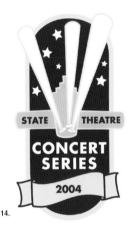

STATE THEATRE
CONCERT
SERIES
2004

14.

15.

1 - 11
Design Firm **revoLUZion**
Advertising and Design
12 - 15
Design Firm **Never Boring Design Associates**

1.
Client   *KMT Köhnlein Messtechnik*
Designer   Bernd Luz
2.
Client   *Kappler*
Designer   Bernd Luz
3.
Client   *Kapp*
Designer   Bernd Luz
4.
Client   *Ebinger Dett*
Designer   Bernd Luz
5.
Client   *Eigenwerk*
Designer   Bernd Luz
6.
Client   *Ramah Wagner*
Designer   Bernd Luz

7.
Client   *Fahrschule Rüdinger*
Designer   Bernd Luz
8.
Client   *Rainer Schanz*
Designer   Bernd Luz
9.
Client   *Verena Plein*
Designer   Bernd Luz
10.
Client   *Müller Instrumente*
Designer   Bernd Luz
11.
Client   *Kern Keto Design*
Designer   Bernd Luz
12.
Client   *McHenry Bowl*
Designer   Dyle Stoddard
13.
Client   *City of Modesto*
Designer   Dyle Stoddard
14.
Client   *State Theatre*
Designer   Dyle Stoddard
15.
Client   *Ooohlala*
Designer   Cheryl Cernigoj

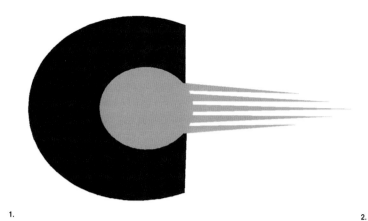

1.

MYC

2.

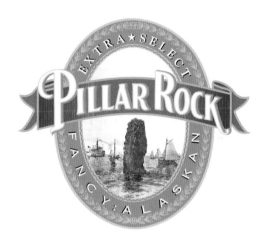

3.

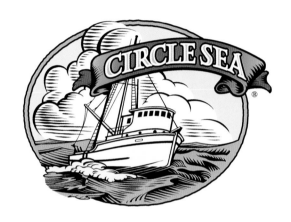

4.

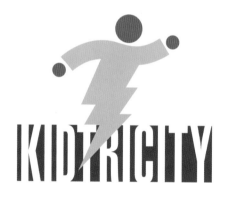

5.

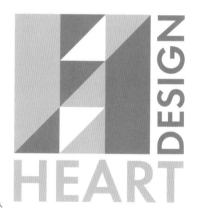

6.

www.rochesalon.com

7.

1, 2
Design Firm **Michael Lee Advertising & Design, Inc.**

3, 4
Design Firm **Mark Oliver, Inc.**

5, 6
Design Firm **Redpoint Design**

7
Design Firm **Lomangino Studio, Inc.**

1.
Client *Coastal Welding Supply*
Designers Michael Lee, Debby Stasinopoulou

2.
Client *Matagorda Yacht Club*
Designers Michael Lee, Debby Stasinopoulou

3.
Client *Ocean Beauty Seafoods*
Designers Mark Oliver, Harry Bates

4.
Client *Ocean Beauty Seafoods*
Designers Mark Oliver, Tom Hennessy

5.
Client *Kidtricity*
Designers Clark Most, Ty Smith

6.
Client *Heart Design*
Designer Clark Most

7.
Client *Roche Salon*
Designer Kristina Bonner

(opposite)
Client *Firenze Bread Co.*
Design Firm **Pandora**
Designer Silvia Grossman

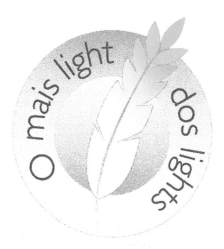

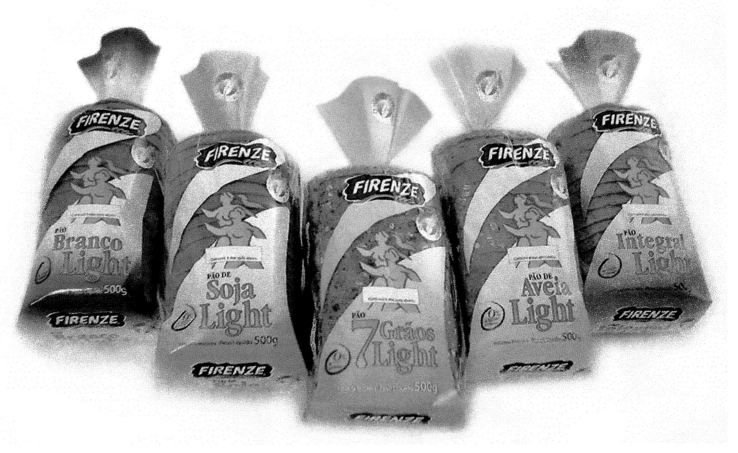

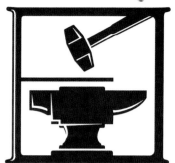

1.

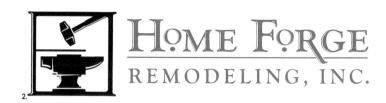

2.

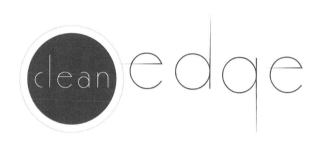

3.

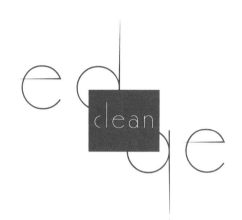

4.

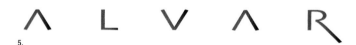

5.

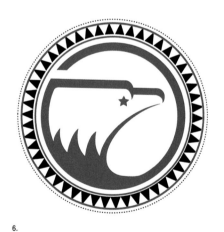

6.

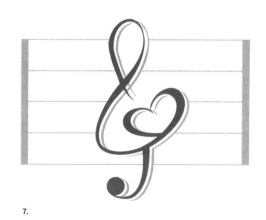

7.

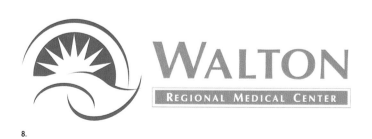

8.

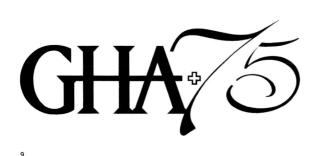

9.

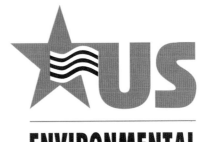

10.

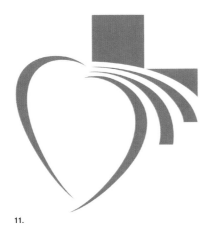

11.

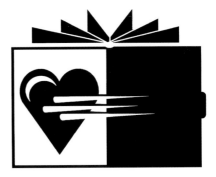

12.

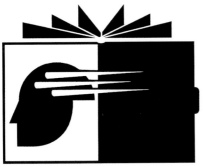

13.

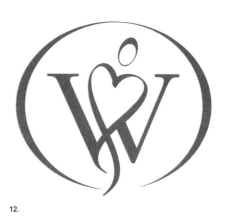

14.

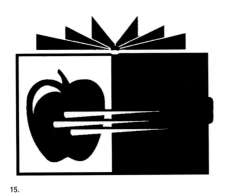

15.

1 - 15
Design Firm **WorldSTAR Design**
1, 2.
  Client   *Home Forge Remodeling, Inc.*
  Designer Greg Guhl
3, 4.
  Client   *Clean Edge*
           Domestic Services, Inc.
  Designer Greg Guhl
5.
  Client   *Decorative Expressions, Inc.*
  Designer Greg Guhl
6.
  Client   *Contingency*
           Management Group, LLC
  Designer Greg Guhl
7.
  Client   *American Heart Association*
  Designer Greg Guhl

8.
  Client   *Walton Regional*
           Medical Center
  Designer Greg Guhl
9.
  Client   *Georgia Hospital Association*
  Designer Greg Guhl
10.
  Client   *U.S. Environmental Services, Inc.*
  Designer Greg Guhl
11.
  Client   *The Specialty Hospital*
  Designer Greg Guhl
12.
  Client   *WellStar Health System*
  Designer Greg Guhl
13 - 15.
  Client   *Georgia Hospital Association*
  Designer Greg Guhl

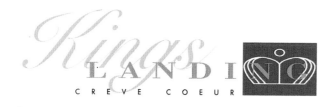

1.

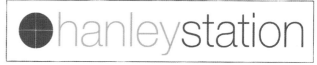

2.

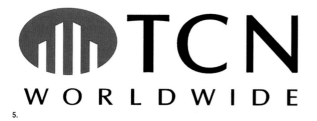

3.

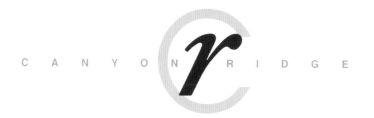

4.

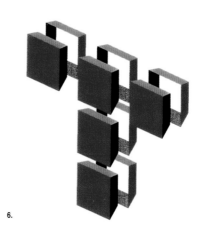

5.

6.

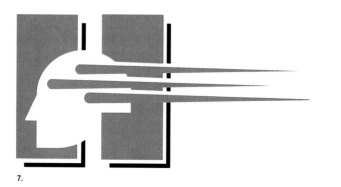

7.

1 - 3
Design Firm **Grizzell & Co.**
4 - 6
Design Firm **Lambert Design**
7
Design Firm **WorldSTAR Design**
1 - 3.
Client   *MLP*
Designer   John H. Grizzell
4.
Client   *Access HDTV*
Designer   Amy Sharp
5.
Client   *TCN Worldwide*
Designer   Christie Lambert

6.
Client   *TechLife Styles*
Designer   Christie Lambert
7.
Client   *Georgia Hospital Association*
Designer   Greg Guhl
(opposite)
Client   *Dr. Temt Laboratories*
                  (Cosmetics)
Design Firm **designbuero**
Designer   Thomas Stockhammer

go**4**elements

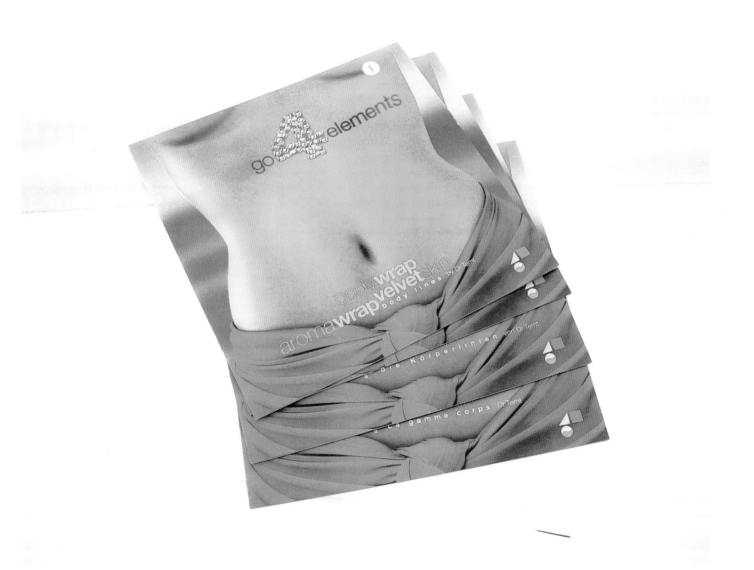

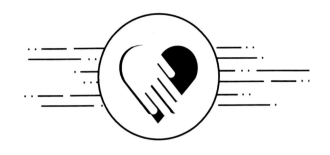

1.

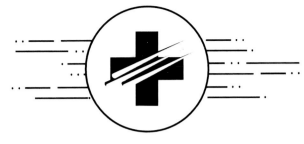

2.

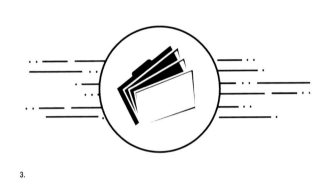

3.

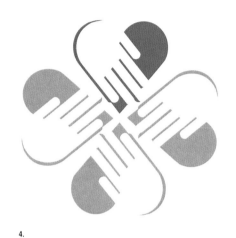

4.

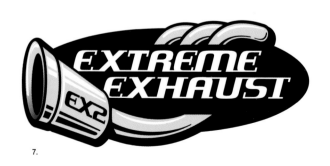

5.

6.

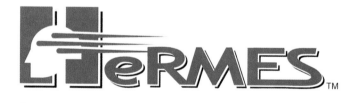

7.

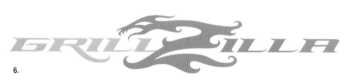

8.

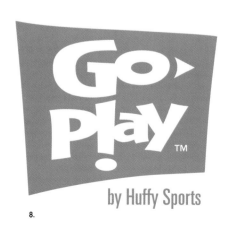

240

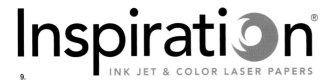

INK JET & COLOR LASER PAPERS

9.

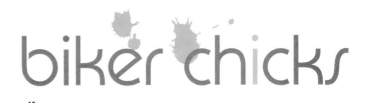

10.

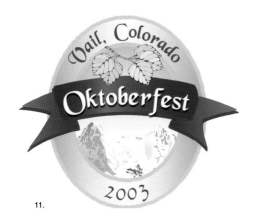

11.

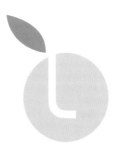

LemonAid Crutches

12.

 EAGLE HILL

13.

ΛCCESSCOMPLIANCE™

A CFM Partners Program

14.

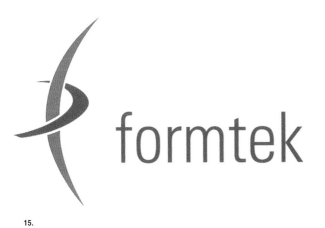

15.

1 - 5
Design Firm **WorldSTAR Design**
6 - 9
Design Firm **VMA, Inc.**
10 - 12
Design Firm **Studio One, Inc.**
13 - 15
Design Firm **Sightline Marketing**

1 - 5.
Client *Georgia Hospital Association*
Designer Greg Guhl
6.
Client *Char-Broil*
Designers Al Hidalgo, Joel Warneke
7.
Client *Huffy Bicycle Company*
Designer Greg Fehrenbach
8.
Client *Huffy Sports Company*
Designer Joel Warneke
9.
Client *Mead Westvaco Corporation*
Designers Rachel Botting, Kenneth Botts

10.
Client *Vail Biker Chicks*
Designer Margaret Cyphers
11.
Client *Vail Valley Chamber & Tourism Bureau*
Designer Margaret Cyphers
12.
Client *LemonAid Crutches*
Designer Margaret Cyphers
13.
Client *Eagle Hill Consulting*
Designers Clay Marshall, Lucinda Kennedy Ryan
14.
Client *CFM Partners*
Designers Robert McVearry, Lucinda Kennedy Ryan, Samantha Guerry
15.
Client *Formtek Inc.*
Designers Clay Marshall, Lucinda Kennedy Ryan, Samantha Guerry

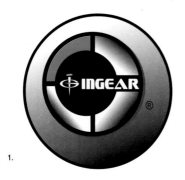

1.

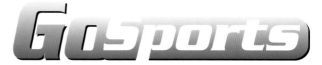

2.

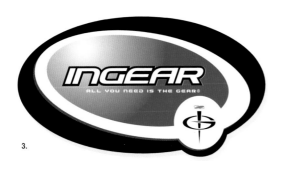

3.

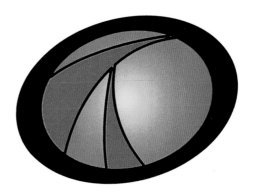

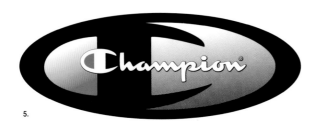

5.

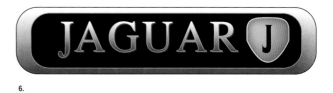

6.

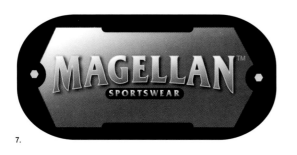

7.

1 - 7
Design Firm **InGEAR**
1.
   Client   *Meijer*
   Designer Matt Hassler
2.
   Client   *Target*
   Designer Matt Hassler
3.
   Client   *Kmart*
   Designer Matt Hassler
4.
   Client   *InGEAR Corporation*
   Designer Kurt Lichte

5, 6.
   Client   *JC Penney*
   Designer Matt Hassler
7.
   Client   *The Sports Authority*
   Designer Matt Hassler
(opposite)
   Client   *Sony Computer*
               Entertainment America
   Design Firm **CDI Studios**
   Designer Eddie Roberts

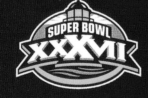
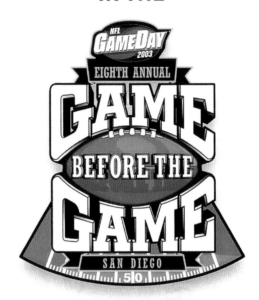
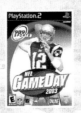

Emnak 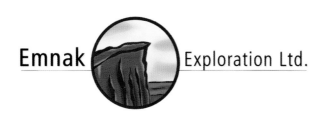 **Exploration Ltd.**

1.

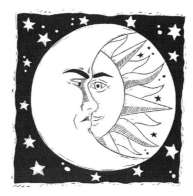

Creative Differences

2.

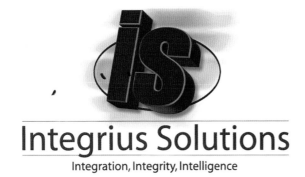

Integrius Solutions

Integration, Integrity, Intelligence

3.

E2E

Entrepreneur *to* Entrepreneur

4.

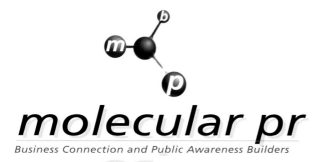

molecular pr

Business Connection and Public Awareness Builders

5.

Vision Exploration Inc.

6.

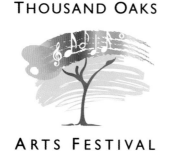

THOUSAND OAKS

ARTS FESTIVAL

7.

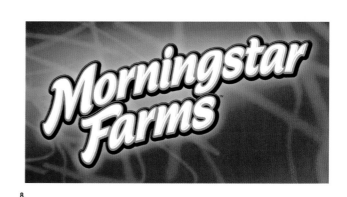

8.

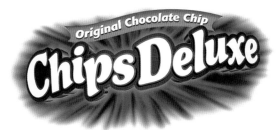

9.

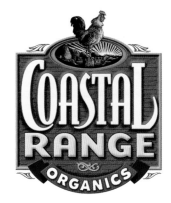

10.

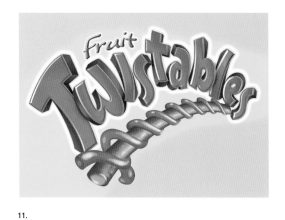

11.

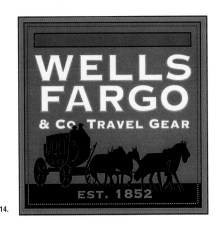

12.

THERMA
TECH

13.

WELLS
FARGO
& Co. TRAVEL GEAR

EST. 1852

14.

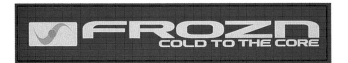

15.

1 - 6
Design Firm **Gabriella Sousa Designs**
7 - 12
Design Firm **DuPuis**
13 - 15
Design Firm **InGEAR**

1.
  Client   *Emnak Exploration Ltd.*
  Designer   Gabriella Sousa
2.
  Client   *Creative Differences*
  Designers   Gabriella Sousa, Anne Sinclair
3.
  Client   *Integrius Solutions*
4.
  Client   *The Enterprise Centre*
  Designer   Gabriella Sousa
5.
  Client   *Molecular pr*
  Designers   Gabriella Sousa, Laurie Campbell
6.
  Client   *Vision Exploration Inc.*
  Designer   Gabriella Sousa
7.
  Client   *Thousand Oaks Civic Arts Plaza*
  Designers   Bill Corridori, Al Nanakonpanom

8.
  Client   *Kelloggs Morningstar Farms*
  Designers   Steven DuPuis, Bill Pierce
9.
  Client   *Keebler*
  Designers   Steven DuPuis, Bill Pierce
10.
  Client   *Foster Farms*
  Designers   Steven DuPuis, John Silva
11.
  Client   *Kelloggs Fruit Twistables*
  Designers   Steven Dupuis,
               Al Nanakonpanom,
               John Silva, John Poll,
               Lindsay Evans
12.
  Client   *Kelloggs Pop Tarts*
  Designers   Steven DuPuis, Bill Pierce
               Damon Thompson
13.
  Client   *InGEAR*
  Designer   Jeremy Swanson
14, 15.
  Client   *Mass Merchants/Consumer*
  Designer   Derek Crenshaw

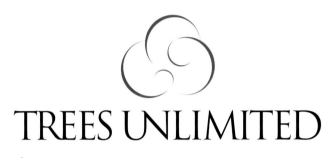

1.

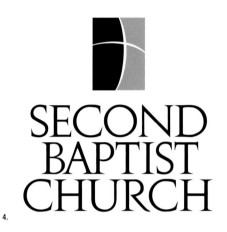

THE STORY OF GOD'S
PROMISE FOR ALL PEOPLE

2.

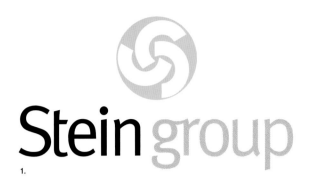

TREES UNLIMITED

3.

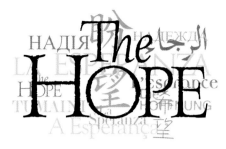

SECOND
BAPTIST
CHURCH

4.

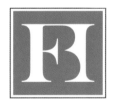

Integrated Electrical Services

5.

FISHER, BOYD, BROWN
BOUDREAUX & HUGUENARD LLP

6.   ATTORNEYS AT LAW

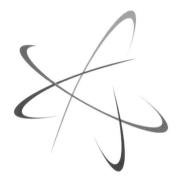

THE
TEXAN
TWO
STEP

7.

1 - 7
Design Firm **Loucks Designworks**
1.
   Client   *Stein Group*
   Designer   Jay Loucks
2.
   Client   *Mars Hill Productions*
   Designer   Jay Loucks
3.
   Client   *Trees Unlimited*
   Designer   Jay Loucks
4.
   Client   *Second Baptist Church*
   Designer   Jay Loucks

5.
   Client   *Integrated Electrical Services*
   Designer   Jay Loucks
6.
   Client   *Fisher Boyd*
   Designer   Jay Loucks
7.
   Client   *Ronald McDonald
               House of Houston*
   Designer   Jay Loucks
(opposite)
   Client   *Tumak's Bar & Grill*
   Design Firm **CDI Studios**
   Designer   Eddie Roberts

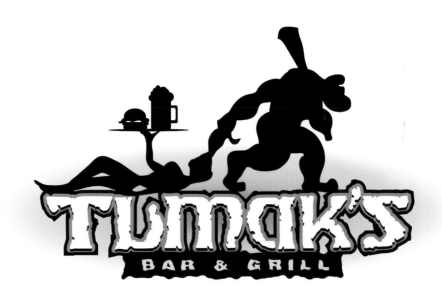

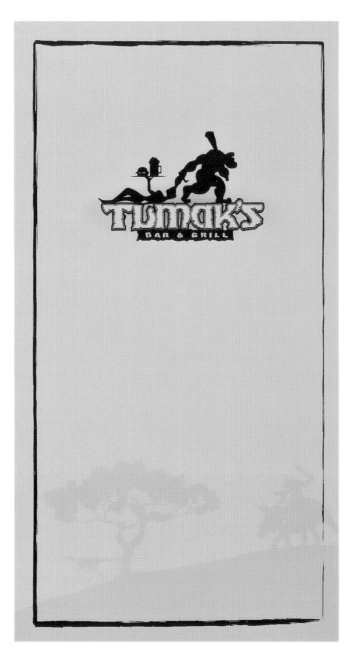

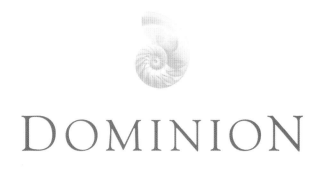

DOMINION

POST OAK

1.

firstbank

2.

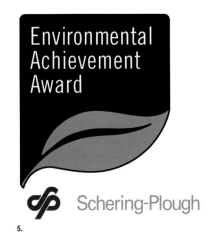

ISOLAGEN
The Science of   Living Cells

3.

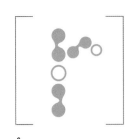

FifthWard
Pregnancy
HelpCenter

4.

Environmental
Achievement
Award

Schering-Plough

5.

rivet inc.

6.

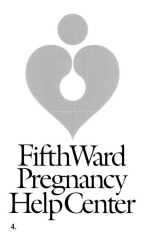

RED OAK
CONSULTING
A DIVISION OF MALCOLM PIRNIE

7.

FLM Graphics

8.

elucient

9.

dse | b®andesign

10.

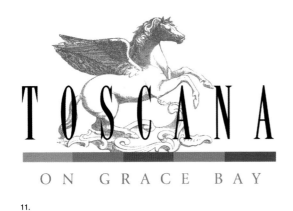

TOSCANA
ON GRACE BAY

11.

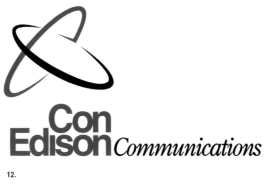

Con Edison *Communications*

12.

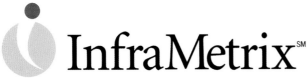

InfraMetrix℠
INFRASTRUCTURE DIAGNOSTIC SERVICES

13.

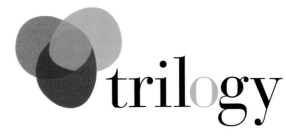

trilogy

14.

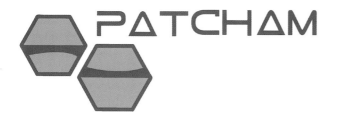

PATCHAM

15.

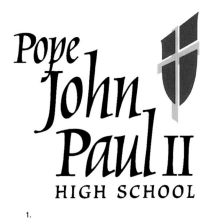

1.

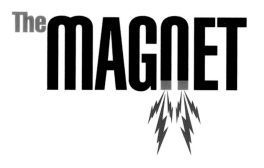

2.

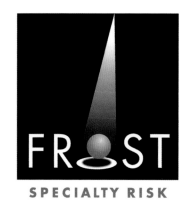

3.

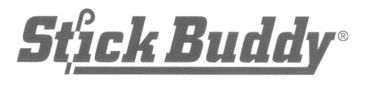

4.

THE DESIGN ACADEMY

5.

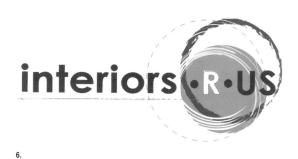

6.

D·TRAN

7.

1 - 4
   Design Firm **Ventress Design Group**
5 - 7
   Design Firm **T-1 Productions**
1.
   Client   *Pope John Paul II High School*
   Designer Tom Ventress
2.
   Client   *The Magnet Music Group*
   Designer Tom Ventress
3.
   Client   *Frost Specialty Risk*
   Designer Tom Ventress

4.
   Client   *T.A.C.K. Inc.*
   Designer Tom Ventress
5.
   Client   *The Design Academy*
   Designers Pallav Patel, Parisa Chum
6.
   Client   *Interiors R Us*
   Designers Parisa Chum, Pallav Patel
7.
   Client   *D-TRAN.com*
   Designer Pallav Patel
(opposite)
   Client   *Ambiance design group*
   Design Firm **CDI Studios**
   Designer Michelle Georgilas

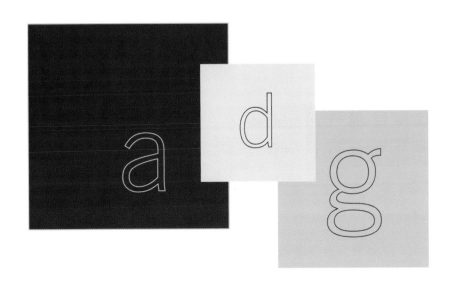

AMBIANCE design group*

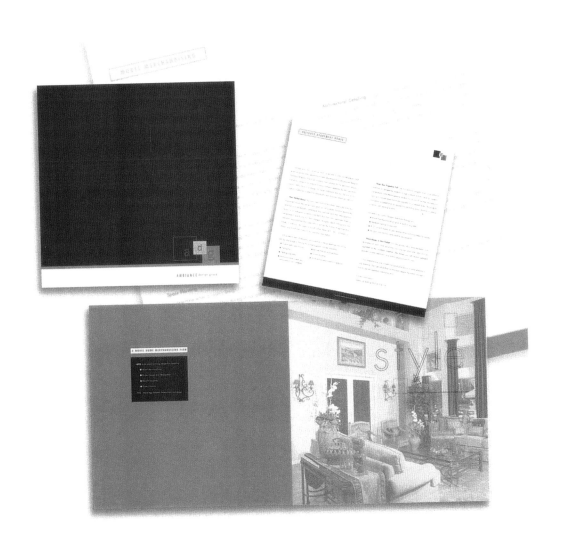

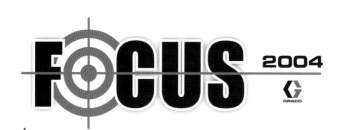

1.

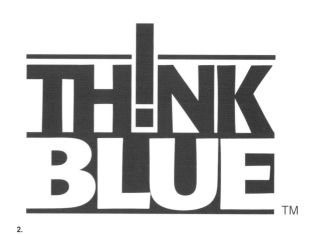

2.

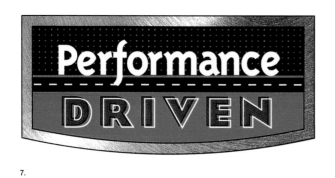

3.

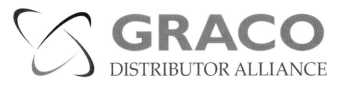

4.

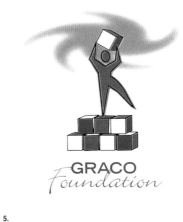

5.

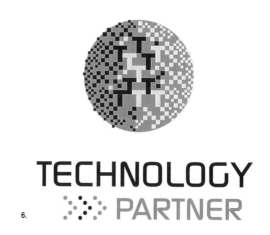

6.

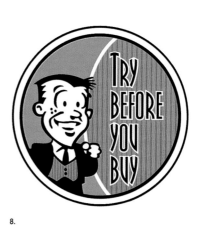

7.

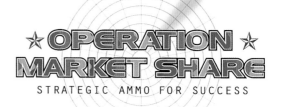

8.

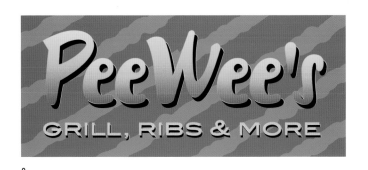

9.

Autoridad de Acueductos y Alcantarillados

10.

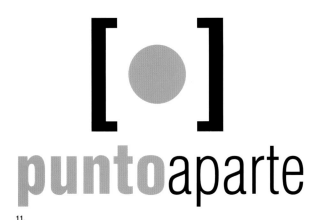

puntoaparte

11.

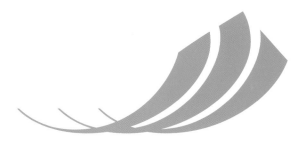

FUNDACIÓN COMUNITARIA
DE PUERTO RICO

12.

COOPERATIVA DE
SEGUROS MULTIPLES
DE PUERTO RICO

13.

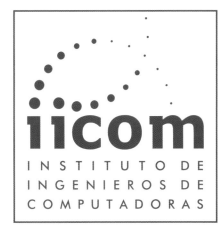

14.

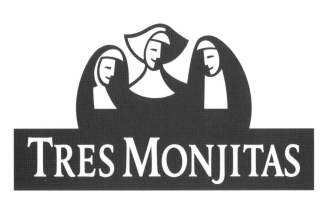

15.

1 - 8		
Design Firm	**Graco Inc.**	
9 - 15		
Design Firm	**ID Group**	
1.		
Client	*Contractor Division*	
Designer	Todd Safgren	
2.		
Client	*Contractor Division*	
Designer	David Orwoll	
3 - 7.		
Client	*Industrial Division*	
Designer	Gary Schmidt	
8.		
Client	*Corporate*	
Designer	Gary Schmidt	
9.		
Client	*PeeWee's Grill*	
Designers	Carolina Carezis, Abner Gutiertuez	

10.		
Client	*Autoridad de Acueductos y Alcantarillados*	
Designers	Jorge Colon, Abner Gutierrez	
11.		
Client	*Punto Aparte Publicidad*	
Designers	Sofiá Saenz, Abner Gutierrez	
12.		
Client	*Fundacion Comunitaria De PR*	
Designer	Mayra Maldonado	
13.		
Client	*Cooperativa Seguros Multiples PR*	
Designers	Mayra Maldonado, Abner Gutierrez	
14.		
Client	*Instituto Ingenieros De Computadoras*	
Designer	Mayra Maldonado	
15.		
Client	*Tres Monjitas Dairy*	
Designers	Abner Gutierrez, Mayra Maldonado	

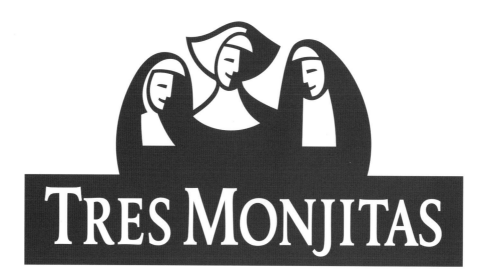

Design Firm **ID Group**
Client   *Tres Monjitas Dairy*
Designers Abner Gutierrez,
          Mayra Maldonado

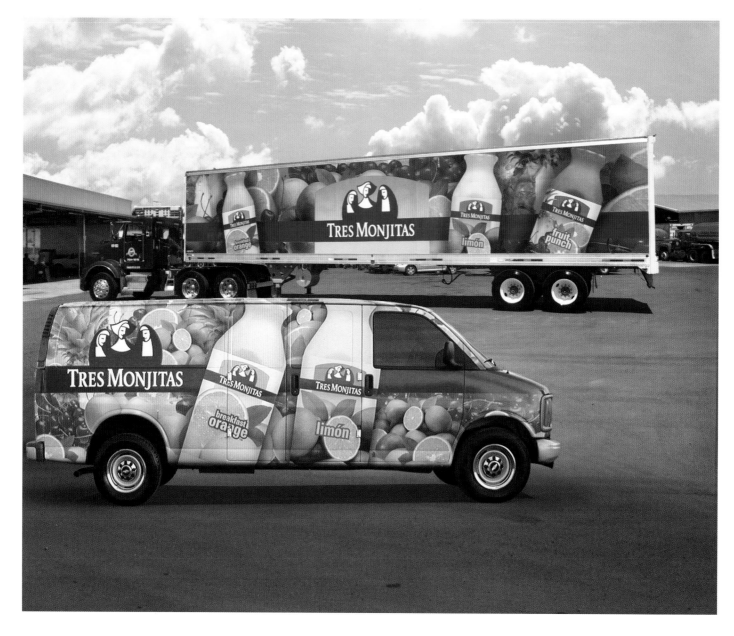

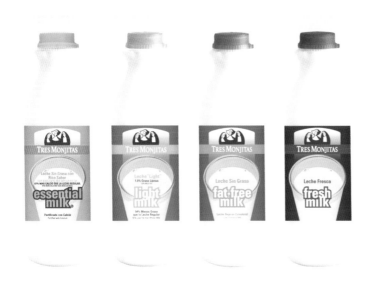

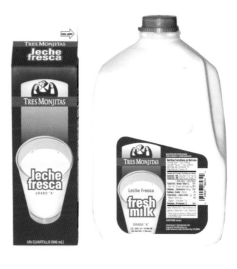

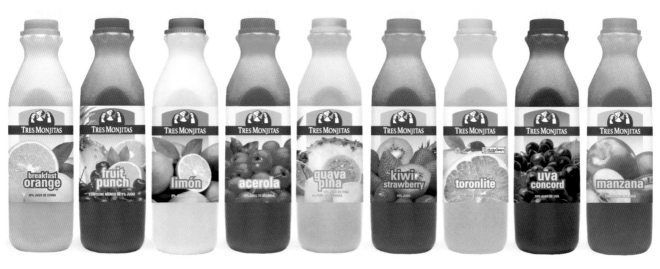

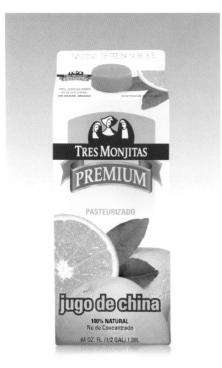

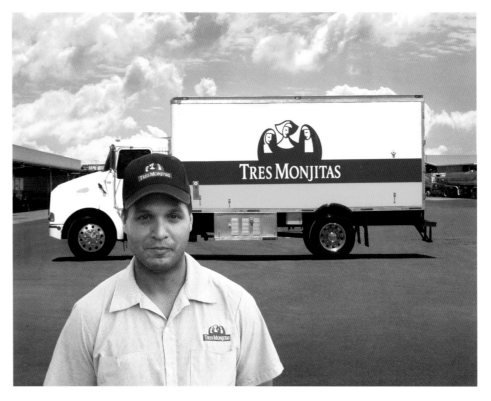

255

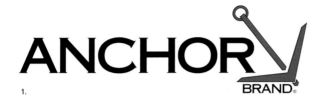

1.

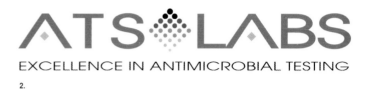

2.

EXCELLENCE IN ANTIMICROBIAL TESTING

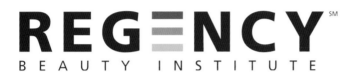

3.

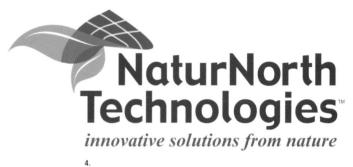

4.

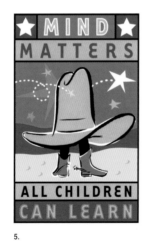

5.

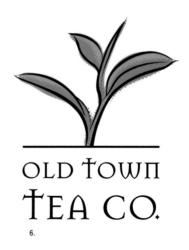

6.

7.

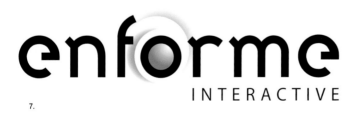

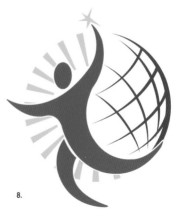

8.

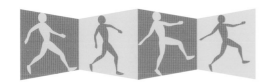

STRUT YOUR STUFF
Displays & Exhibits

9.

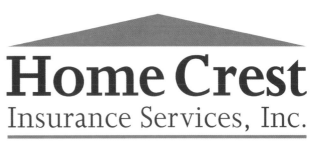

10.

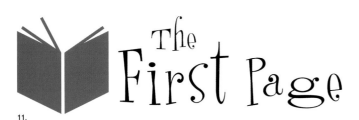

11.

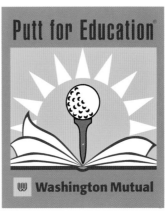

12.

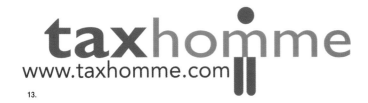

www.taxhomme.com

13.

medicalalumni association

14.

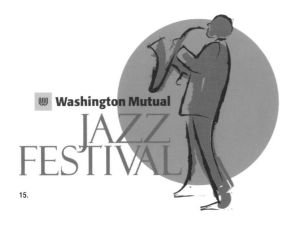

15.

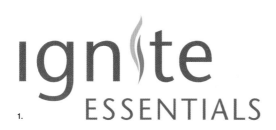

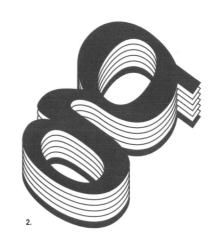

1.

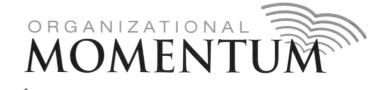

IT's different here.™

3.

STUTT KITCHENS & FINE CABINETRY

4.

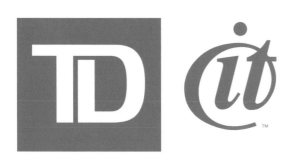

5.

ORGANIZATIONAL MOMENTUM

6.

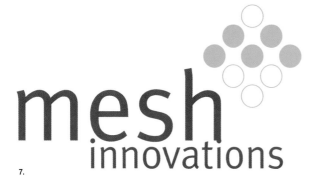

7.

1 - 7
Design Firm **Provoq Inc.**

1.
Client   *Ignite Essentials Leadership Development*
Designer   Jeffrey Chow

2.
Client   *The Gallanough Resource Centre*
Designer   Jeffrey Chow

3.
Client   *TD Bank Financial Group*
Designer   Jeffrey Chow

4.
Client   *Stutt Kitchens & Fine Cabinetry*
Designer   Jeffrey Chow

5.
Client   *University of Toronto Engineering Alumni Association*
Designer   Jeffrey Chow

6.
Client   *Organizational Momentum*
Designer   Jeffrey Chow

7.
Client   *Mesh Innovations Inc.*
Designer   Jeffrey Chow

(opposite)
Client   *Sony Computer Entertainment America*
Design Firm **CDI Studios**
Designer   Eddie Roberts

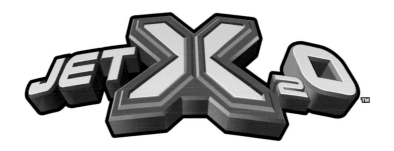

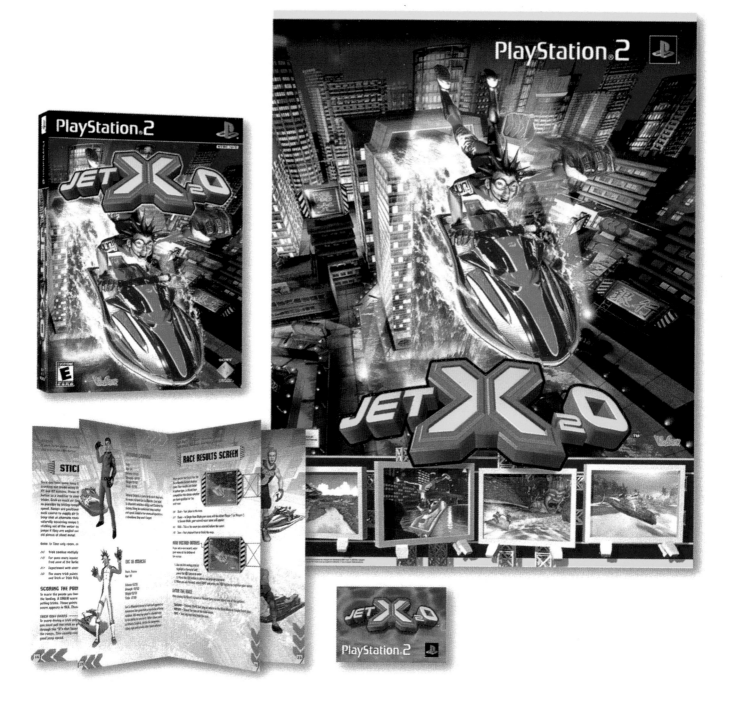

icon style guide

To maintain the CHOC brand image, any icon created and used to represent the hospital or its affiliates follows the same visual style as that established by the masterbrand signature, the mascot, and the affiliate icons. The examples below show various icons created for use in conjunction with newsletters and other collateral materials. Their shared characteristics include energetic, gestural pen strokes and simplified graphic treatments. Extend this same illustrative style when creating new iconic artwork.

CHOC Institute

CHOC Foundation
for Children

Kids Health: Calendar

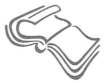

Literacy

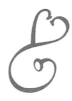

Physician Connection Logo

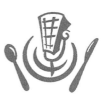

P.C: CME Lectures/Dinners

P.C: This & That

P.C: Case Study

P.C: Welcome

15

ICON USAGE

Our affiliates are fund-raising groups that support our organization and are an integral part of CHOC. Each has an icon that visually ties into the brand image. These icons are used to represent Guild activities that promote our hospital. It is important that these icons be used with as much respect and care as the CHOC Mascot. Like the mascot, these icons may be cropped and screened in their specified color, as long as they maintain their unique characteristics and recognizability. Be sure to leave a clear space of at least ½" around each icon when used as a logo. Each icon prints in one color, using the specified color, in black, or reversed to white.

Mad Hatter Guild
PMS 347

Small World Guild
PMS 660

Little Red Wagon Guild
PMS 200

Littlest Angel Guild
PMS 310

Lamp Lighter Guild
PMS 129

Jack & Jill Guild
PMS 660

Mother Goose Guild
PMS 200

11

Design Firm **Hornall Anderson Design Works**
Client *CHOC (Children's Hospital of Orange County)*
Designers Jack Anderson, Lisa Cerveny, Debra McCloskey, Steffanie Lorig, Jana Wilson Esser, Gretchen Cook, Jana Nishi, Darlin Gray

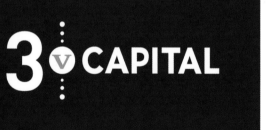

AIMCO

1.

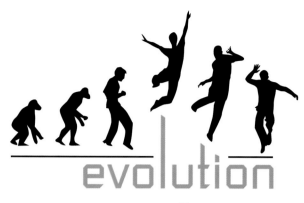

evolution
sports & music

2.

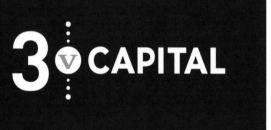

SoftPro
2004
USER GROUP
conference

3.

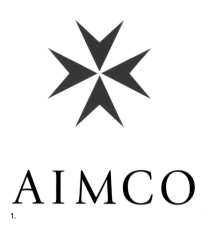

SoftPro
CORPORATION

2003
user group conference

4.

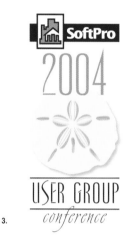

3 v CAPITAL

5.

M○NTAGGI○
european style for the american lifestyle

6.

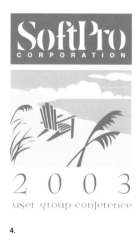

7.

1 - 4
Design Firm **CAI Communications**
5, 6
Design Firm **OrangeSeed Design**
7
Design Firm **Rickabaugh Graphics**
1.
Client   *Key Risk*
Designer Steve McCulloch
2.
Client   *Evolution Technologies*
Designer Beth Greene
3, 4.
Client   *SoftPro*
Designer Beth Greene

5.
Client   *3v Capital*
Designers Damien Wolf, Phil Hoch
6.
Client   *Montaggio*
Designers Damien Wolf, Phil Hoch
7.
Client   *Run for Christ*
Designer Eric Rickabaugh
(opposite)
Client   *AIGA Las Vegas*
Design Firm **CDI Studios**
Designers Michelle Georgilas,
          MacKenzie Walsh

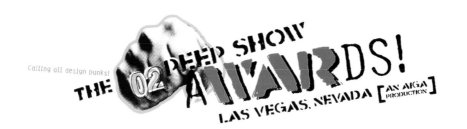

Calling all design punks!

THE 02 PEEP SHOW AWARDS!
LAS VEGAS, NEVADA [AN AIGA PRODUCTION]

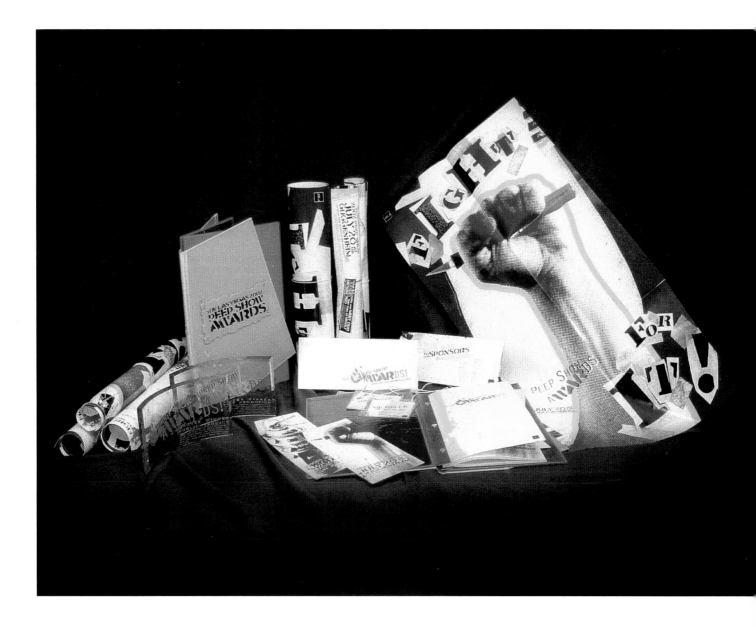

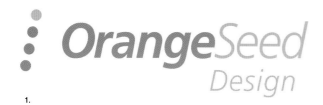

1.

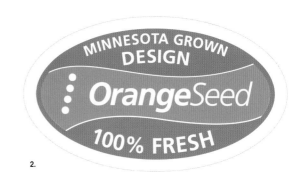

2.

EVERCIDE mc

3.

exponent ™

4.

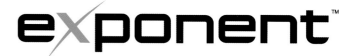

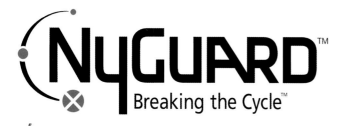

NyGUARD ™
Breaking the Cycle ™

5.

RIPTIDE ™

6.

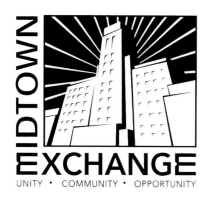

MIDTOWN EXCHANGE
UNITY • COMMUNITY • OPPORTUNITY

7.

LAKESHORE GRILL

8.

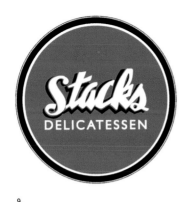

9.

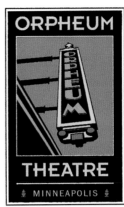

10.

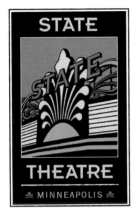

11.

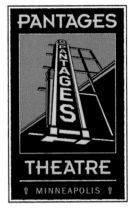

12.

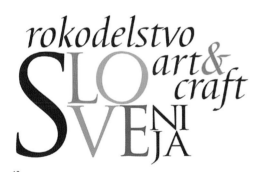

13.

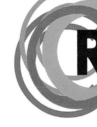

CENTER ROKODELSTVA LJUBLJANA

14.

15.

1 - 6
Design Firm **OrangeSeed Design**
7 - 12
Design Firm **Shea, Inc.**
13 - 15
Design Firm **KROG**

1, 2.
Client   *OrangeSeed Design*
Designer   Damien Wolf
3 - 6.
Client   *McLaughlin Gormley King Company*
Designers   Damien Wolf, Phil Hoch
7.
Client   *Ryan Companies*
Designer   Jason Wittwer
8.
Client   *Marshall Fields*
Designers   Michele Leitner, Mark Whitenack

9.
Client   *Stacks/American Retrospect Inc.*
Designer   Jason Wittwer
10 - 12.
Client   *Historic Theatre District*
Designers   James Rahn, Viera Hartmanova
13.
Client   *Obrtna zbornica Slovenije, Ljubljana*
Designer   Edi Berk
14.
Client   *Center rokodelstva Ljubljana*
Designer   Edi Berk
15.
Client   *Vodovod-Kanalizacija, Ljubljana*
Designer   Edi Berk

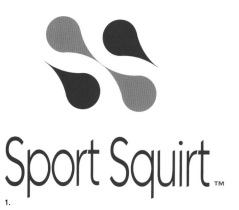

Sport Squirt™

1.

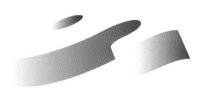

Flexo Impressions, Inc.

2.

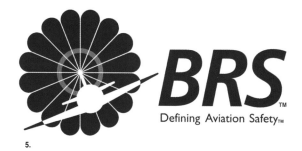

EQUITY BANK

3.

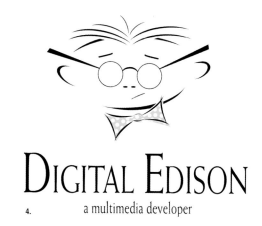

DIGITAL EDISON
a multimedia developer

4.

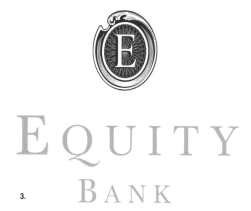

BRS
Defining Aviation Safety™

5.

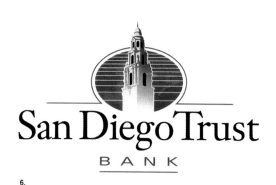

San Diego Trust
BANK

6.

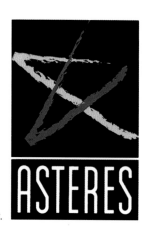

7.

1 - 5
Design Firm **Hendler-Johnston**
6, 7
Design Firm **Crouch and Naegeli/ Design Group West**
1.
　Client　*Sport Squirt*
　Designer　Chris Hendler
2.
　Client　*Flexo Impressions, Inc.*
　Designer　Chris Hendler
3.
　Client　*Equity Bank*
　Designer　Chris Hendler

4.
　Client　*Digital Edison*
　Designer　Chris Hendler
5.
　Client　*BRS*
　Designer　Chris Hendler
6.
　Client　*San Diego Trust Bank*
　Designer　Jim Naegeli
7.
　Client　*Asteres*
　Designer　Jim Naegeli
(opposite)
　Client　*Project Sunshine*
　Design Firm **CDI Studios**
　Designer　Michelle Georgilas

🔥 RED HOT $^{02°}$

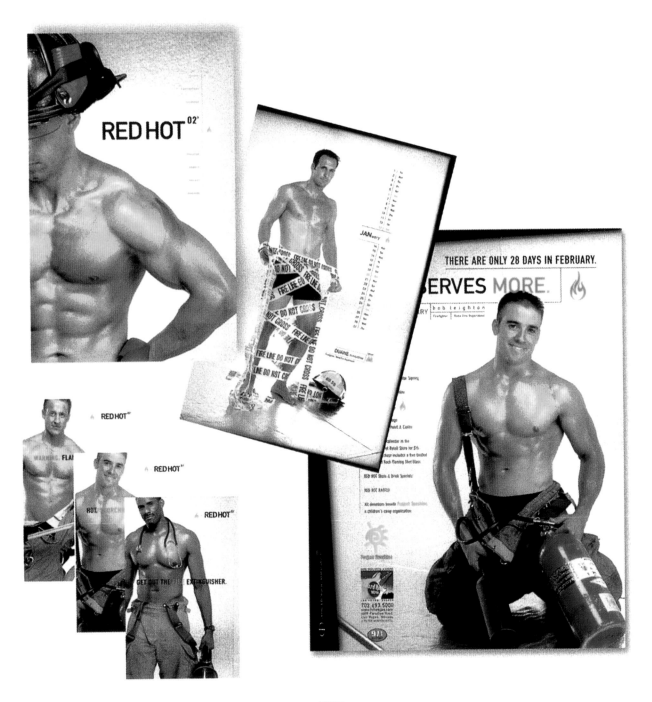

Gersh
Hospitality
Group

1.

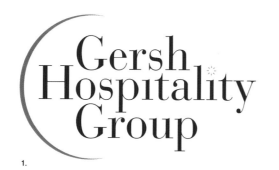

2.

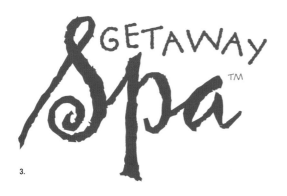

3.

水
WATER

4.

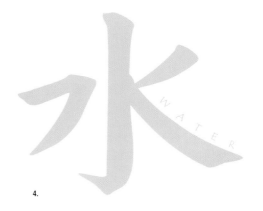
Willow Creek
WELLNESS

5.

advantix

6.

Venus™

7.

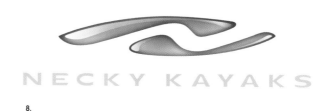
NECKY KAYAKS

8.

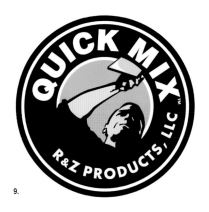

9.

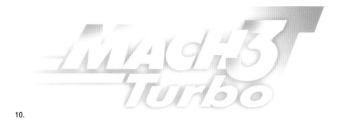

10.

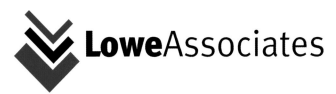

11.

 stress**design**

12.

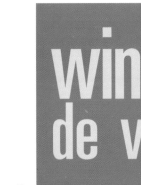

Unwin Development
Support for Public Broadcasting

13.

wines de vine

14.

 **nice.**

15.

1 - 5
  Design Firm **ANNADESIGN**
6 - 10
  Design Firm **Wallace Church, Inc.**
11 - 15
  Design Firm **stressdesign**

1.
  Client   *Gersh Hospitality Group*
  Designer Anna Christian
2 - 4.
  Client   *Creations by Alan Stuart*
  Designer Anna Christian
5.
  Client   *Willow Creek Wellness*
  Designer Anna Christian
6.
  Client   *Eastman Kodak Company*
  Designer Lawrence Haggerty
7.
  Client   *The Gillette Company*
  Designer Lawrence Haggerty

8.
  Client   *Ocean Kayak*
  Designer Lawrence Haggerty
9.
  Client   *R&Z Products*
  Designers Akira Yasuda
10.
  Client   *The Gillette Company*
  Designers Lawrence Haggerty,
               Jeremy Creighton
11.
  Client   *Lowe Associates*
  Designer Marc Stress
12.
  Client   *stressdesign*
  Designers Marc Stress, Kelly Lear
13.
  Client   *Unwin Development*
  Designers Marc Stress, Kelly Lear
14.
  Client   *Wines De Vine*
  Designer Marc Stress
15.
  Client   *Nice Productions*
  Designers Marc Stress, Marc Tucci

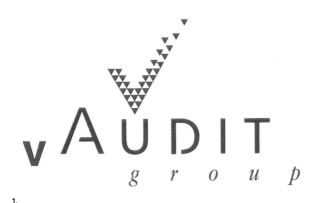

1.

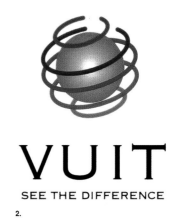

2.

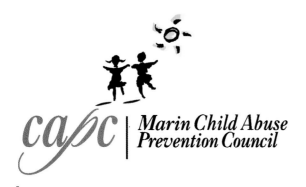

3.

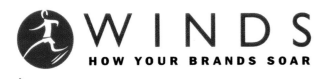

4.

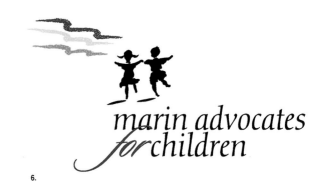

5.

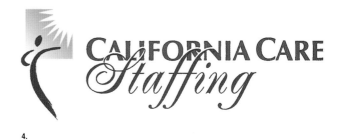

6.

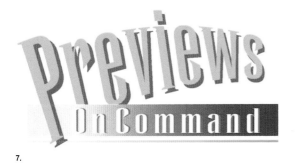

7.

1 - 3
Design Firm **Crouch and Naegeli/
Design Group West**
4 - 7
Design Firm **Dan Liew Design**
1.
   Client   *Vaudit*
   Designer *Jim Naegeli*
2.
   Client   *Vuit*
   Designer *Jim Naegeli*
3.
   Client   *Winds*
   Designers *Megan Boyer,
                  Jim Naegeli*
4.
   Client   *California Care Staffing*
   Designers *Dan Liew, Chris Ardito*

5.
   Client   *Marin Child Abuse
               Prevention Center*
   Designer *Dan Liew*
6.
   Client   *Marin Advocates for Children*
   Designer *Dan Liew*
7.
   Client   *OnCommand*
   Designers *Dan Liew, Phorest Bateson*
(opposite)
   Client   *Sony Computer
               Entertainment America*
   Design Firm **CDI Studios**
   Designer *Eddie Roberts*

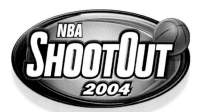

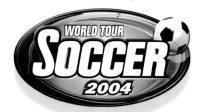

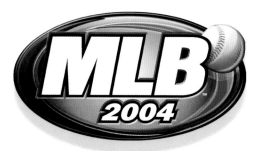

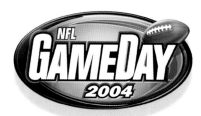

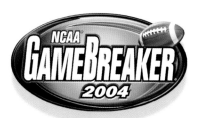

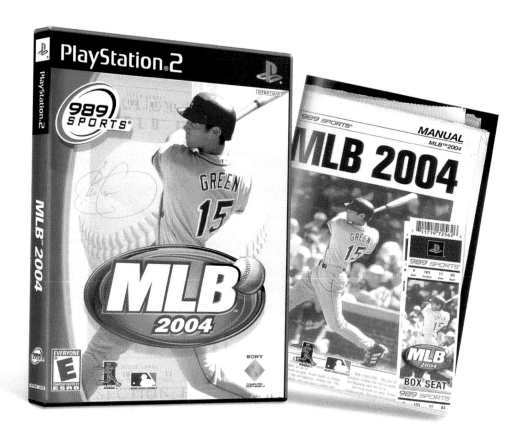

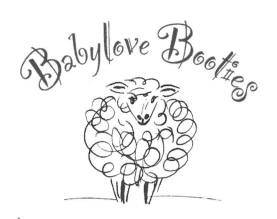

1.

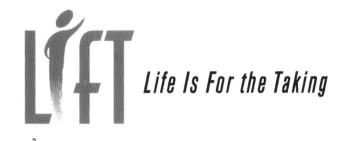

Life Is For the Taking

2.

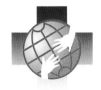

GLOBAL CARE STAFFING

3.

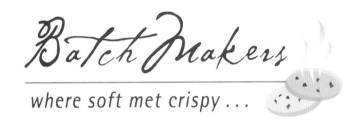

4.

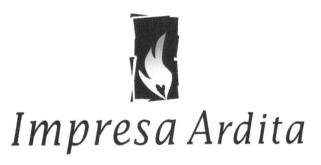

Impresa Ardita

5.

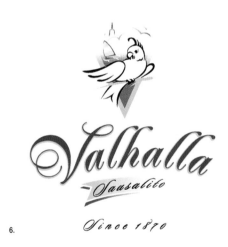

6.

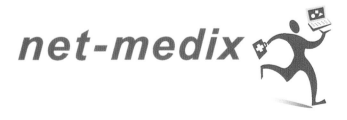

7.

8. SITESCAPES

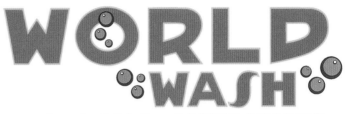

ibrain

9.

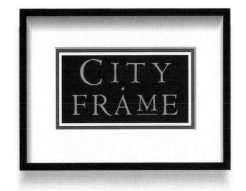

CITY FRAME

10.

zaphers

11.

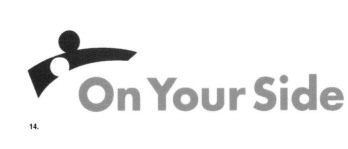

WORLD WASH

WASH & FOLD • ALTERATIONS

12.

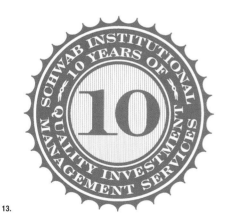

SCHWAB INSTITUTIONAL
10 YEARS OF
QUALITY INVESTMENTS
MANAGEMENT SERVICES
10

13.

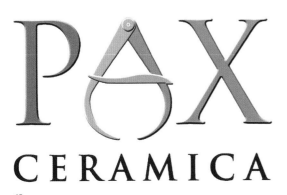

On Your Side

14.

PAX
CERAMICA

15.

1 - 8
Design Firm **Dan Liew Design**
9 - 15
Design Firm **Mitten Design**

1.
Client Margurite Holloway
Designer Dan Liew

2.
Client Lift
Designers Dan Liew, Chris Ardito

3.
Client Global Care Staffing
Designers Dan Liew, Chris Ardito

4.
Client BatchMakers
Designer Dan Liew

5.
Client Chris Ardito/Impresa Ardita
Designers Dan Liew, Chris Ardito

6.
Client Valhalla Restaurant
Designers Dan Liew, Linda Kelly,
Jet Lim

7.
Client Net Medix
Designers Dan Liew, Chris Ardito

8.
Client Sitescapes
Designers Dan Liew, Linda Kelly

9.
Client Ibrain, Inc.
Designer Marianne Mitten

10.
Client City Frame
Designer Marianne Mitten

11.
Client Hingston Consulting Group
Designers Marianne Mitten, Audrey Dufresne

12.
Client World Wash
Designers Marianne Mitten, Audrey Dufresne

13.
Client Schwab Institutional
Designer Marianne Mitten

14.
Client On Your Side
Designers Marianne Mitten, Baykal Askar

15.
Client Pax Ceramica
Designer Marianne Mitten

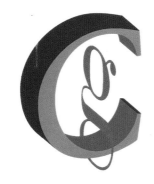

1. The Cata*lyst* Group, Inc.

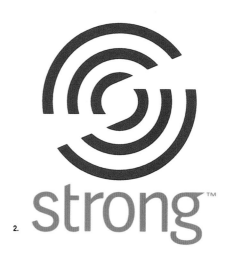

2. strong™

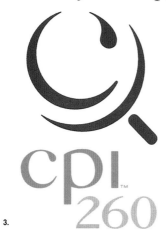

cpi™
260

3.

Circle
B A N K

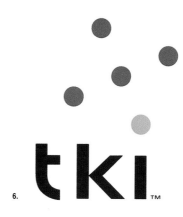

4.

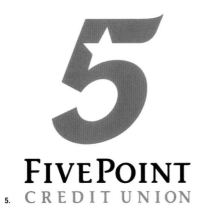

5 FIVE POINT
CREDIT UNION

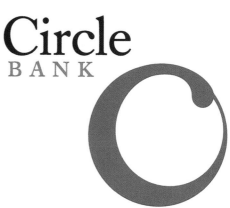

tki™

6.

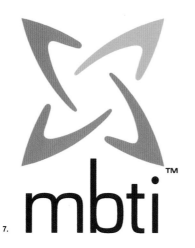

7. mbti™

1
  Design Firm **Mitten Design**
2 - 7
  Design Firm **Mortensen Design Inc.**
1.
  Client   *The Catalyst Group*
  Designer   Marianne Mitten
2, 3.
  Client   *CPP Inc.*
  Designers   Helena Seo,
              Gordon Mortensen
4.
  Client   *Circle Bank*
  Designers   Ann Jordan,
              Gordon Mortensen

5.
  Client   *FivePoint Credit Union*
  Designers   Helena Seo,
              Gordon Mortensen
6, 7.
  Client   *Cpp Inc.*
  Designers   Helena Seo,
              Gordon Mortensen
(opposite)
  Client   *Sony Computer
              Entertainment America*
  Design Firm **CDI Studios**
  Designers   Eddie Roberts,
              Casey Corcoran

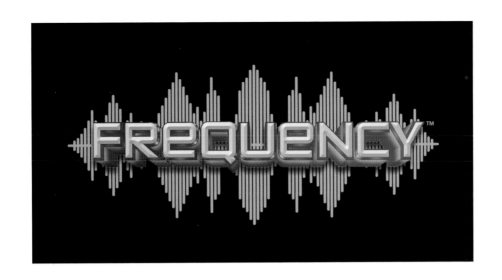

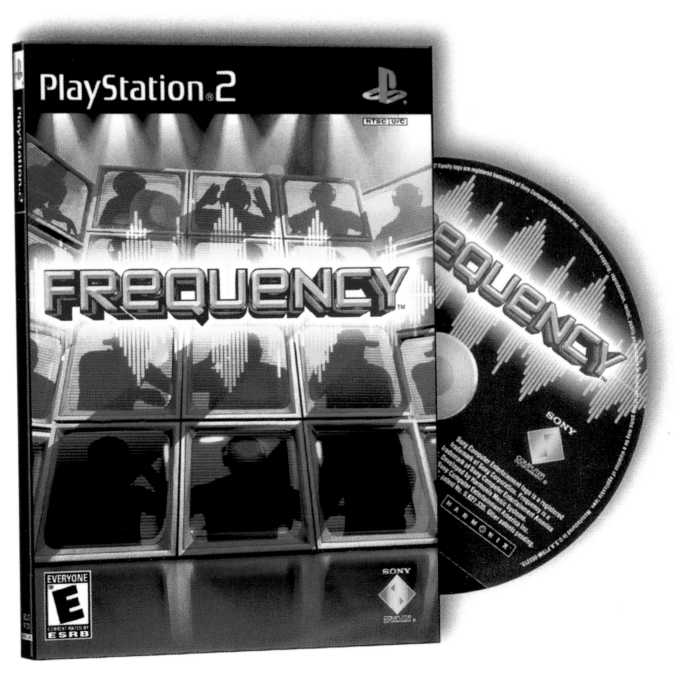

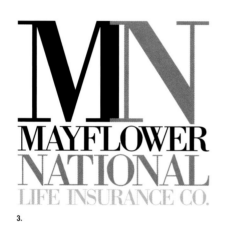

THE ROOSEVELT INVESTMENT GROUP

1.

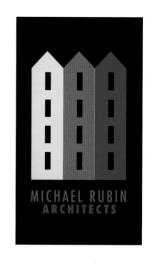

MICHAEL RUBIN
ARCHITECTS

2.

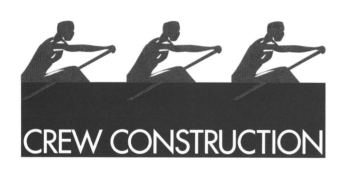

MN
MAYFLOWER
NATIONAL
LIFE INSURANCE CO.

3.

DIRTWORKS, PC

LANDSCAPE ARCHITECTURE

4.

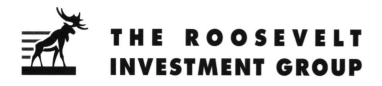

CREW CONSTRUCTION

5.

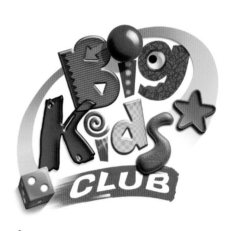

Big Kids Club

6.

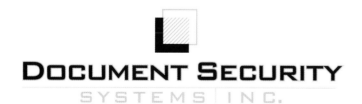

DOCUMENT SECURITY
SYSTEMS INC.

7.

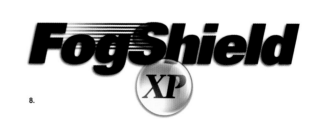

FogShield XP

8.

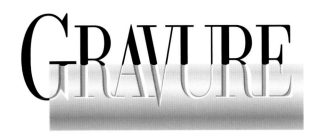

9.

HERON HILL

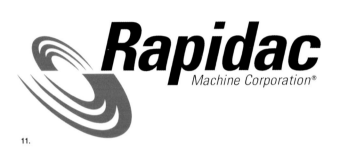

11.

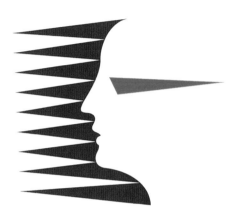

12.

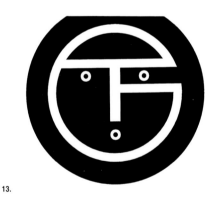

13.

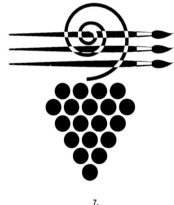

14.

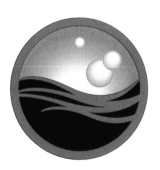

GLOBAL LIQUIDS TEAM

15.

1 - 5		**7.**	
Design Firm **Acme Communications, Inc.**		Client	*Document Security Systems Inc.*
6 - 11		Designers	William McElveney, Lisa Gates
Design Firm **McElveney & Palozzi**		**8.**	
Design Group Inc.		Client	*Bausch & Lomb*
12 - 15		Designer	Steve Palozzi
Design Firm **Tom Fowler, Inc.**		**9.**	
1.		Client	*Gravure Magazine*
Client	*The Roosevelt Investment Group*	Designers	William McElveney, Lisa Gates
Designers	Kiki Boucher, Jon Livingston	**10.**	
2.		Client	*Heron Hill Winery*
Client	*Michael Rubin Architects*	Designers	Steve Palozzi, William McElveney
Designer	Kiki Boucher	**11.**	
3.		Client	*Rapidac Machine Corporation*
Client	*Mayflower National*	Designers	Matt Nowicki, Lisa Gates
	Life Insurance Co.	**12.**	
Designers	Andrea Ross Boyle, Kiki Boucher	Client	*CPS Communications*
4.		Designer	Thomas G. Fowler
Client	*Dirtworks, PC*	**13.**	
Designers	Kiki Boucher, Jon Livingston	Client	*Inua Gallery*
5.		Designer	Thomas G. Fowler
Client	*Crew Construction Corp.*	**14.**	
Designer	Kiki Boucher	Client	*Table to Table*
6.		Designer	Thomas G. Fowler
Client	*McElveney & Palozzi*	**15.**	
	Design Group Inc.	Client	*Unilever HPC NA*
Designers	Gloria Kreitzberg, Steve Palozzi,	Designers	Mary Ellen Butkus,
	William McElveney		Jennifer Lipsett

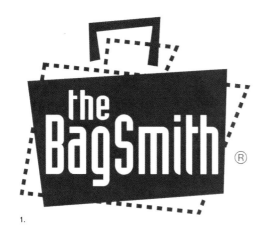

1.

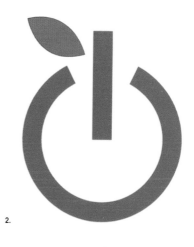

2.

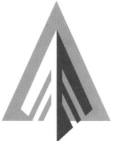

3.

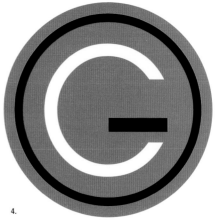

4.

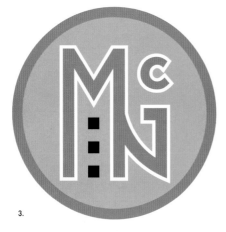

5.

Northamerican
Financial
Corporation

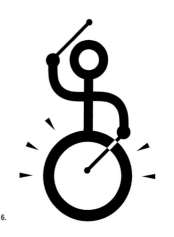

6.

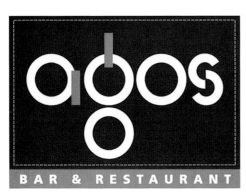

7.

1
   Design Firm **Karen Skunta & Company**
2
   Design Firm **Kellum McClain Inc.**
3 - 5
   Design Firm **McGaughy Design**
6, 7
   Design Firm **Tom Fowler, Inc.**
1.
   Client   *Smith International*
   Designers   Karen A. Skunta,
                Christopher Suster,
                Barbara Chin
2.
   Client   *Primedia*
   Designers   Beverly McClain,
                Ron Kellum

3.
   Client   *McGaughy Design*
   Designer   Malcolm McGaughy
4.
   Client   *Carole Goeas*
   Designer   Malcolm McGaughy
5.
   Client   *Northamerican Financial Corp*
   Designers   McGaughy Design
6.
   Client   *Gideon Cardozo
                Communications*
   Designer   Thomas G. Fowler
7.
   Client   *Agos Bar and Restaurant*
   Designer   Thomas G. Fowler
(opposite)
   Client   *Westwood Studios*
   Design Firm **CDI Studios**
   Designer   Victoria Hart

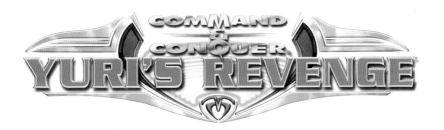

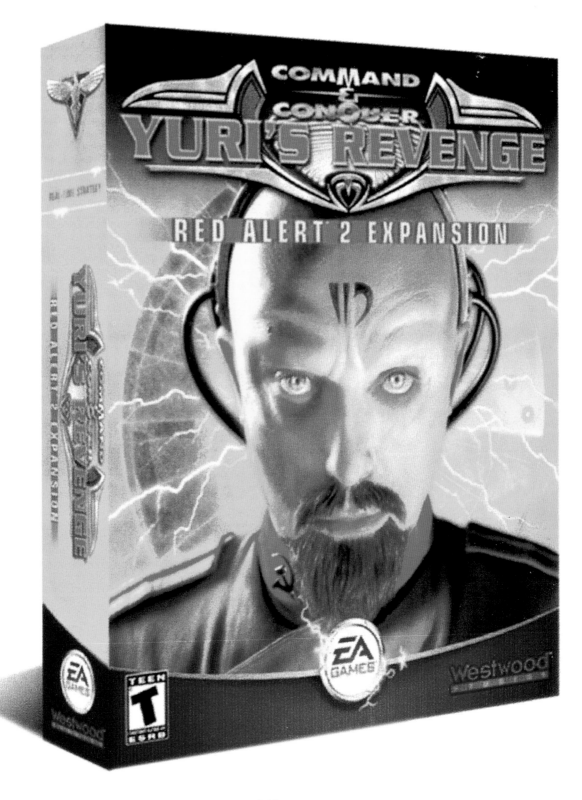

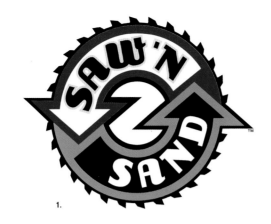

1.

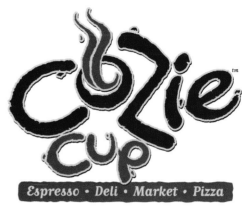

2.

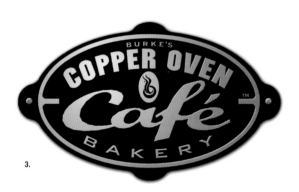

3.

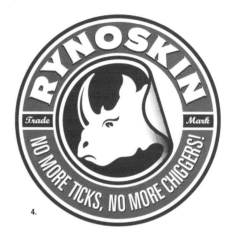

4.

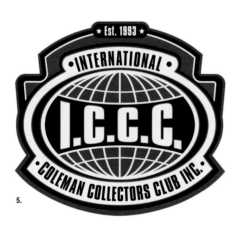

5.

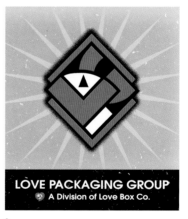

6.

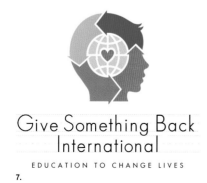

7.

RWI

G·R·O·U·P

8.

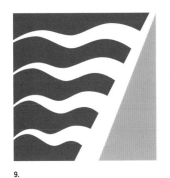 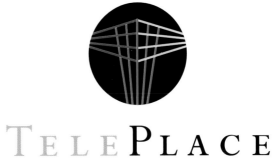

BAY AREA
AIRQUALITY
MANAGEMENT
DISTRICT

9.

TELEPLACE

10.

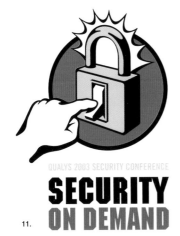

QUALYS 2003 SECURITY CONFERENCE

SECURITY
ON DEMAND

11.

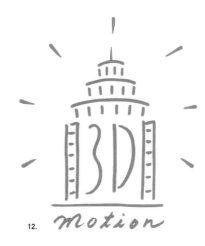

motion

12.

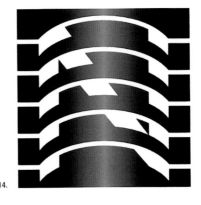

13.

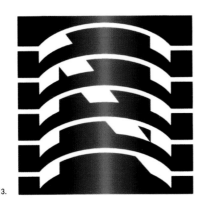

14.

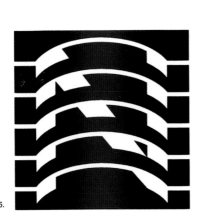

15.

1 - 6
Design Firm **LPG Design**
7 - 15
Design Firm **Gee + Chung Design**

1.
Client   *B-H Innovations*
Designer Dustin Commer
2, 3.
Client   *Burke Enterprise*
Designer Dustin Commer
4.
Client   *Har-son Inc.*
Designer Dustin Commer
5.
Client   *International Coleman
         Collectors Club Inc.*
Designer Dustin Commer
6.
Client   *Love Packaging Group*
Designer Rick Gimlin

7.
Client   *Give Something Back
         International Foundation*
Designer Earl Gee
8.
Client   *RWI Group, LLP*
Designer Earl Gee
9.
Client   *Bay Area Air Quality
         Management District*
Designer Earl Gee
10.
Client   *TelePlace*
Designer Earl Gee
11.
Client   *Qualys, Inc.*
Designer Earl Gee
12.
Client   *3-D Motion*
Designer Fani Chung
13 - 15.
Client   *Nanocosm Technologies, Inc.*
Designer Fani Chung

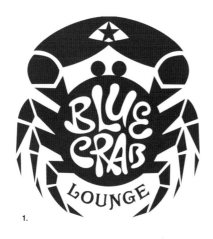

1.

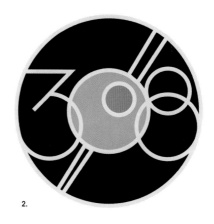

2.

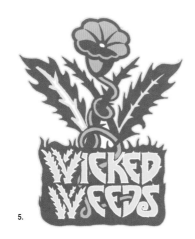

3.

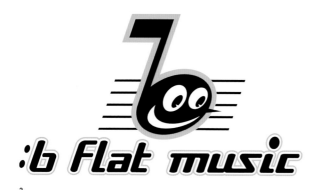

4.

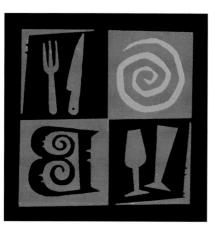

5.

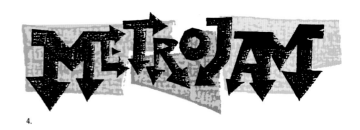

6.

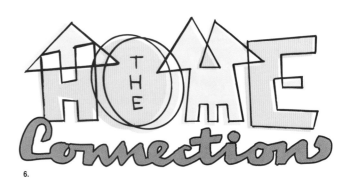

7.

1 - 7
Design Firm **Sayles Graphic Design, Inc.**

1.
Client   *Blue Crab Lounge*
Designer   John Sayles

2.
Client   *308 Martini Bar*
Designer   John Sayles

3.
Client   *B-Flat Music*
Designer   John Sayles

4.
Client   *MetroJam*
Designer   John Sayles

5.
Client   *Meredith Corporation*
Designer   John Sayles

6.
Client   *Home Connection*
Designer   John Sayles

7.
Client   *Backburner Grille and Cafe*
Designer   John Sayles
(opposite)
Client   *Westwood Studios*
Design Firm **CDI Studios**
Designer   Victoria Hart

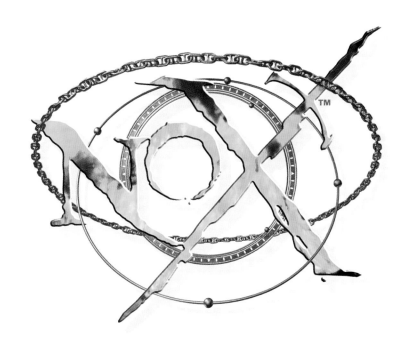

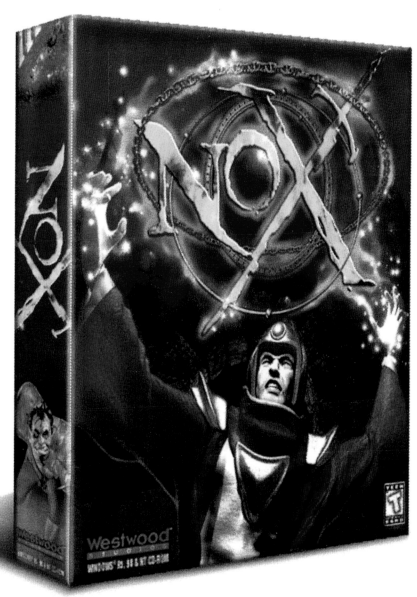

The corporate logo can be reversed out (appear all in white) of a virtually unlimited variety of bold and bright background colors. The key is to make sure there is adequate contrast between the logo and background. Background options range from our corporate colors (shown here) to Pantone cool and warm grays, four and darker, to any other color with appropriate contrast. Steer clear of pale, washed out, and neutral background colors.

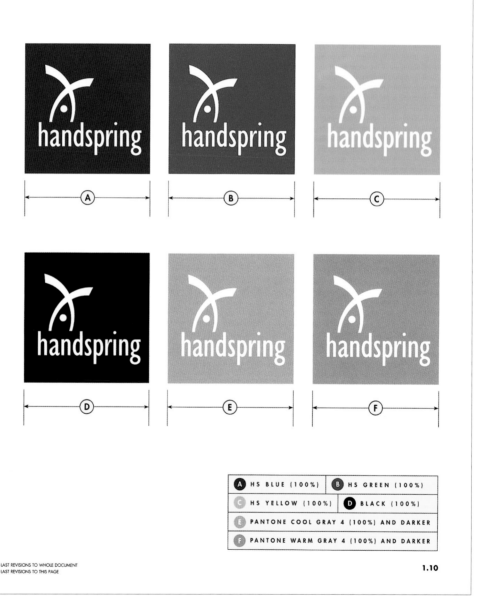

A HS BLUE (100%)	**B** HS GREEN (100%)	
C HS YELLOW (100%)	**D** BLACK (100%)	
E PANTONE COOL GRAY 4 (100%) AND DARKER		
F PANTONE WARM GRAY 4 (100%) AND DARKER		

7/99 DATE OF LAST REVISIONS TO WHOLE DOCUMENT
7/99 DATE OF LAST REVISIONS TO THIS PAGE

1.10

Design Firm **Mortensen Design**
Client *Handspring*
Designers Gorden Mortensen,
PJ Nidecker

A good background treatment can make the corporate symbol and/or signature pop off the page. After testing scores of options, we've determined the symbol is most compelling against a white background. If white isn't appropriate, Pantone's cool gray colors—one through eight—provide a complementary contrast without overshadowing the dynamics of the symbol. Use the following sample treatments to get a feel for effective background color usage.

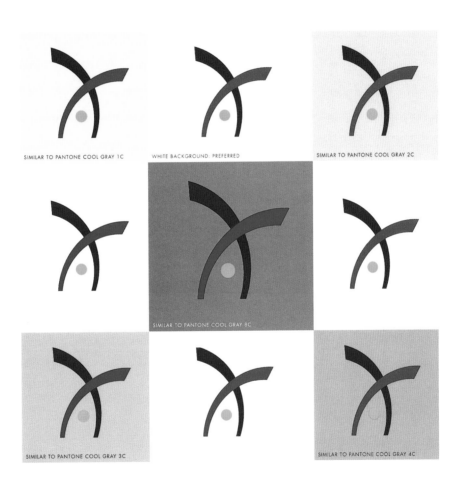

SIMILAR TO PANTONE COOL GRAY 1C

WHITE BACKGROUND: PREFERRED

SIMILAR TO PANTONE COOL GRAY 2C

SIMILAR TO PANTONE COOL GRAY 8C

SIMILAR TO PANTONE COOL GRAY 3C

SIMILAR TO PANTONE COOL GRAY 4C

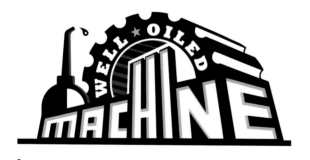

1.

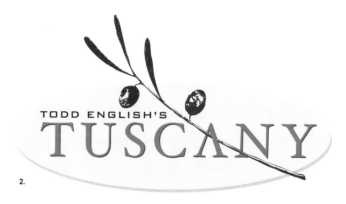

2.

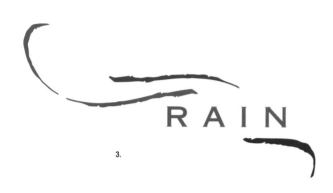

3.

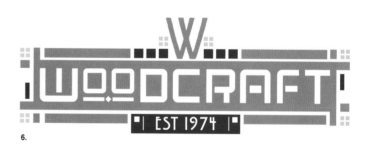

4.

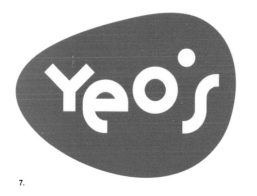

5.

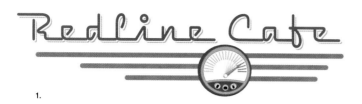

6.

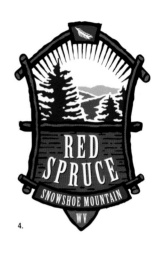

7.

1 - 4
Design Firm **Sonalysts, Inc.**
5, 6
Design Firm **Sayles Graphic Design, Inc.**
7
Design Firm **Ukulele Brand Consultants Pte Ltd**

1.
Client   *Southern Auto Auction*
Designers   Stephen Freitas, Rob King, Carol Hoyem, Rena DeBortoli

2.
Client   *Todd English's Tuscany*
Designers   Kathee Speranza-Ryan, Tracy Sainte Marie, John Visgilio

3.
Client   *Mohegan Sun*
Designers   Kathee Speranza-Ryan, Shannon Brenek, John Visgilio

4.
Client   *Intrawest*
Designers   Mike Skiles, Tracy Sainte Marie, John Visgilio

5.
Client   *Well-Oiled Machine*
Designer   John Sayles

6.
Client   *WoodCraft Architectural Millwork*
Designer   John Sayles

7.
Client   *Yeo Hiap Seng (Singapore) Pte Ltd*
Designers   Kim Chun-wei, Cheng Tze Tzuen

(opposite)
Client   *Herbal Philosophy Pte Ltd*
Design Firm **Ukulele Brand Consultants Pte Ltd**
Designers   Kim Chun-wei, Yvonne Lee

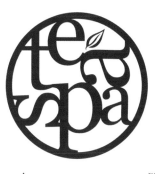

teaspa™

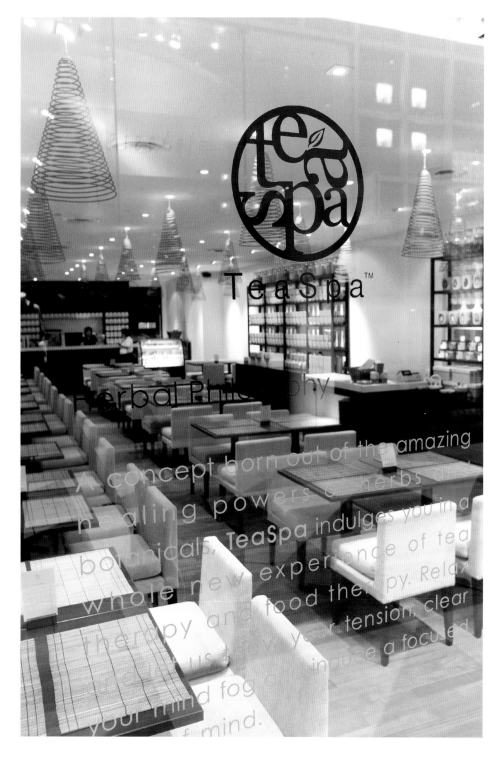

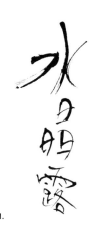

1.

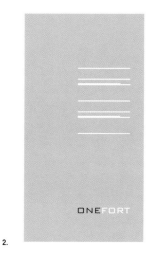

2.

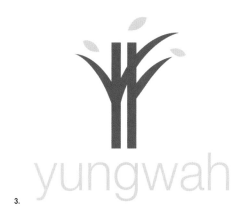

3.

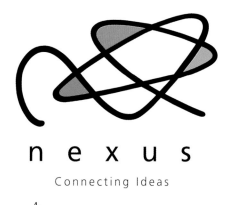

4.

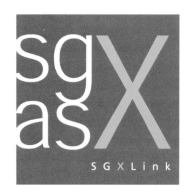

5.

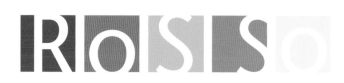

6.

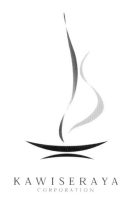

7.

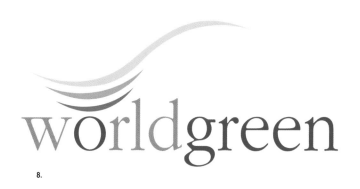

8.

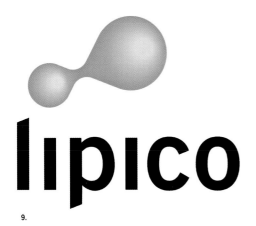

lipico

9.

10.

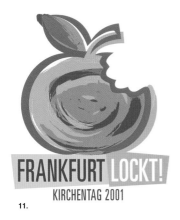

FRANKFURT LOCKT!
KIRCHENTAG 2001

11.

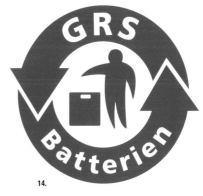

12.

 E R A C O N

13.

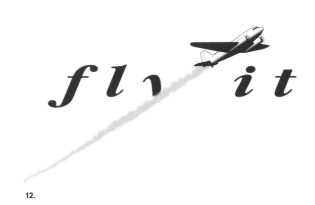

14.

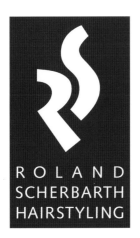

ROLAND
SCHERBARTH
HAIRSTYLING

15.

1 - 9
Design Firm **Ukulele Brand**
Consultants Pte Ltd
10 - 15
Design Firm **Aufgeweckte Werbung**
1.
Client   *Yeo Hiap Seng (Singapore) Pte Ltd*
Designers Kim Chun-wei, Stephanie Tan
2.
Client   *Chip Eng Seng Corporation Ltd*
Designers Kim Chun-wei, Cheng Tze Tzuen
3.
Client   *Yung Wah Industrial Co. (Pte) Ltd*
Designers Kim Chun-wei, Jessica Ang
4.
Client   *Ministry of Manpower*
Designers Kim Chun-wei, Jessica Ang
5.
Client   *Singapore Exchange*
Designers Kim Chun-wei, Yvonne Lee
6.
Client   *Office Libre Pte Ltd*
Designers Kim Chun-wei, Kok Yu Kim

7.
Client   *Kawiseraya Corporation*
Designers Kim Chun-wei, Daphne Chan
8.
Client   *Worldgreen Pte Ltd*
Designers Kim Chun-wei, Lynn Lim
9.
Client   *Lipico Technologies Pte Ltd*
Designers Kim Chun-wei, Cheng Tze Tzuen
10.
Client   *People-Connect*
Designer   Georg Hahn, Fout Simbolico
11.
Client   *Sound of Frankfurt*
Designer   Georg Hahn, Thomas Maritsdike
12.
Client   *fly-it*
Designers Georg Hahn, Sonja Bader
13.
Client   *Eracon*
Designer   Georg Hahn
14.
Client   *GRS*
Designer   Georg Hahn
15.
Client   *Roland Scherbarth*
Designer   Georg Hahn

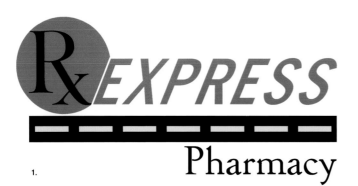

1.

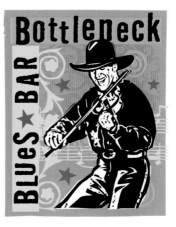

2. Ruffin' It

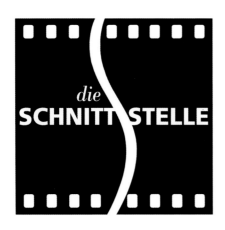

die
SCHNITT STELLE

3.

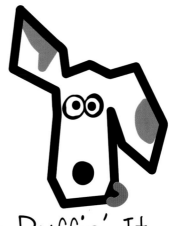

4.

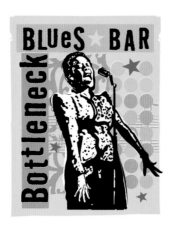

5.

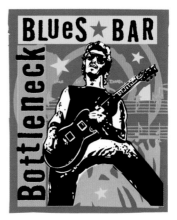

6.

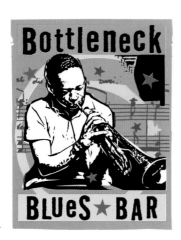

7.

1, 2
    Design Firm **Designs on You!**

3
    Design Firm **Aufgeweckte Werbung**

4 - 7
    Design Firm **Visual Asylum**

1.
    Client   *Rx Express*
    Designers Suzanna Stephens,
              Anthony B. Stephens

2.
    Client   *Ruffin' It*
    Designers Anthony B. Stephens,
              Suzanna Stephens

3.
    Client   *die Schnittstelle*
    Designer   George Hahn

4 - 7.
    Client   *Ameristar Casinos*
    Designer   Joel Sotelo
(opposite)
    Client   *O-Ton*
    Design Firm **Aufgeweckte Werbung**
    Designer   Georg Hahn

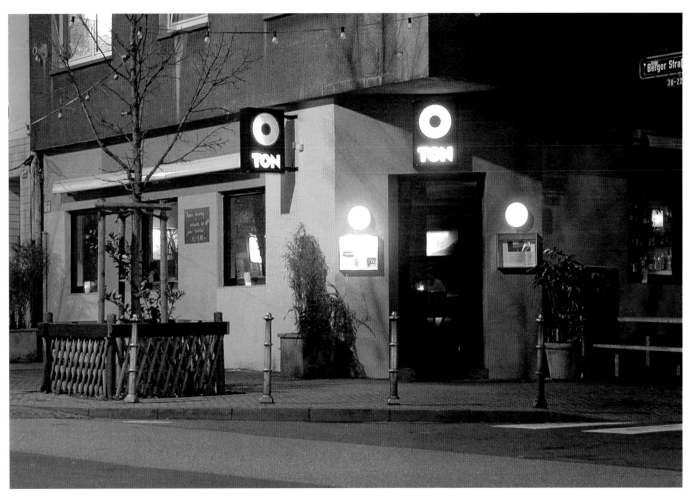

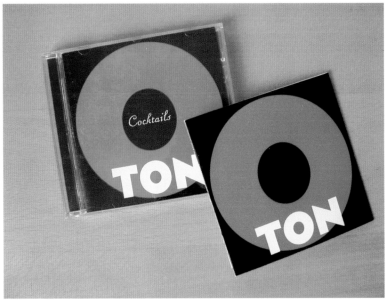

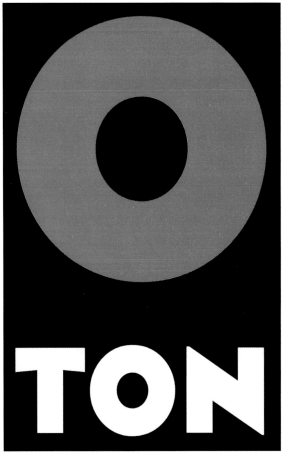

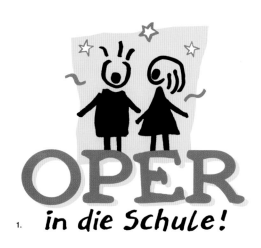

1. **OPER** *in die Schule!*

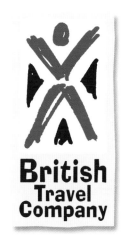

2. **British Travel Company**

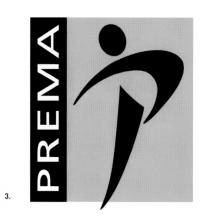

3. **PREMA**

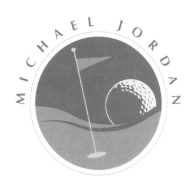

4. **LEFFINGWELLS**

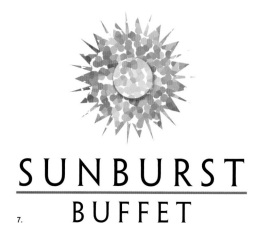

5. MICHAEL JORDAN
CELEBRITY
INVITATIONAL

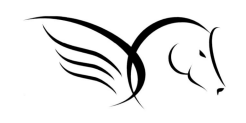

6. **PEGASUS**
RACE & SPORTS BOOK

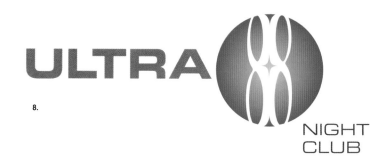

7. **SUNBURST** BUFFET

8. **ULTRA** NIGHT CLUB

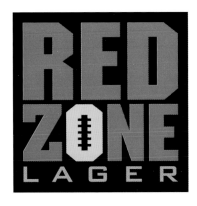

9.

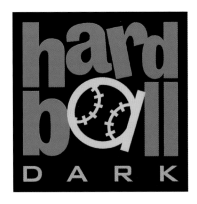

11.

13.

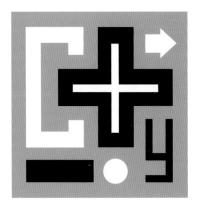

10.

12.

14.

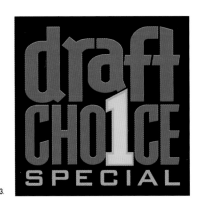

15.

1 - 3
Design Firm **Aufgeweckte Werbung**
4 - 8
Design Firm **Sonalysts, Inc.**
9 - 15
Design Firm **Visual Asylum**
1.
    Client   *Oper in die Schule*
    Designer   Georg Hahn
2.
    Client   *British Travel Company*
    Designer   Georg Hahn
3.
    Client   *Prema Show Productions Ltd.*
    Designer   Georg Hahn
4.
    Client   *Mohegun Sun*
    Designers   Kathee Speranza-Ryan,
                Carol Hoyem
5.
    Client   *Atlantis*
    Designer   Kathleen Damiata

6.
    Client   *Atlantis*
    Designers   Kathleen Damiata,
                Rena DeBortoli
7.
    Client   *Mohegan Sun*
    Designer   Rena DeBortoli
8.
    Client   *Patrick Lyon*
    Designer   Rena DeBortoli
9 - 13.
    Client   *Ameristar Casino*
    Designers   Visual Asylum
14.
    Client   *San Diego City College
                Graphic Design*
    Designer   Joel Sotelo
15.
    Client   *3 Squares "gourmet on the go"*
    Designer   Joel Sotelo

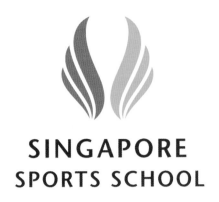

**SINGAPORE
SPORTS SCHOOL**

1.

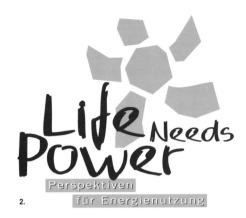

2.

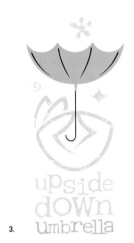

3.

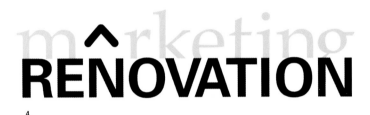

4.

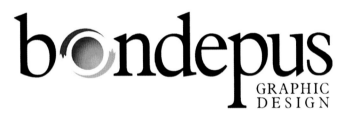

5.

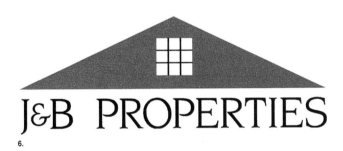

6.

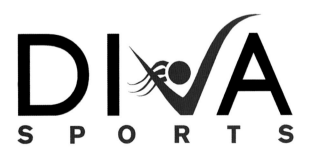

7.

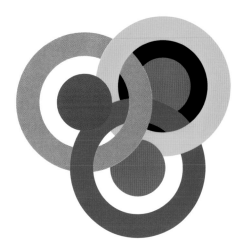

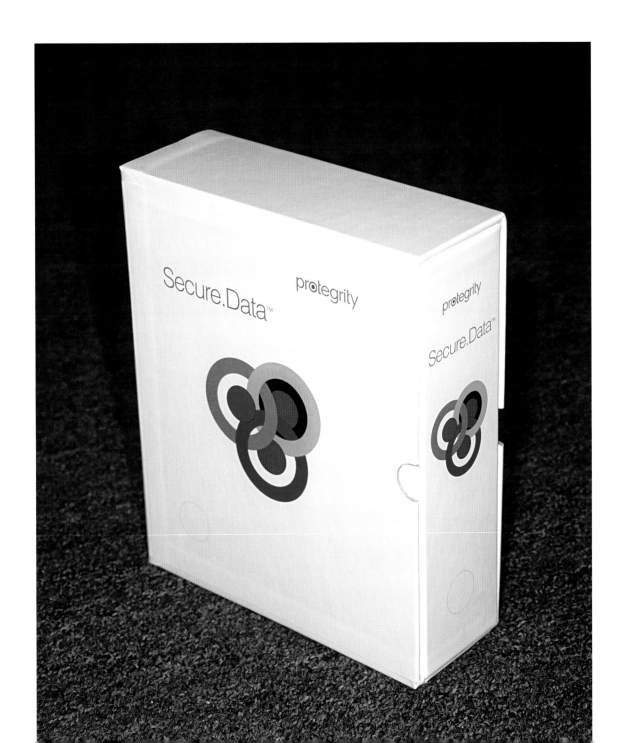

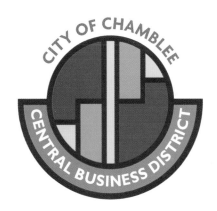
CITY OF CHAMBLEE
CENTRAL BUSINESS DISTRICT

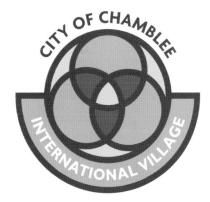
CITY OF CHAMBLEE
INTERNATIONAL VILLAGE

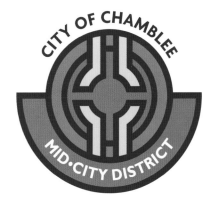
CITY OF CHAMBLEE
MID-CITY DISTRICT

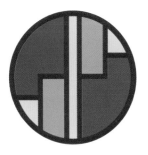

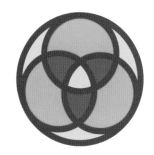

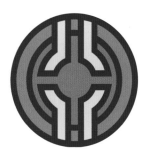

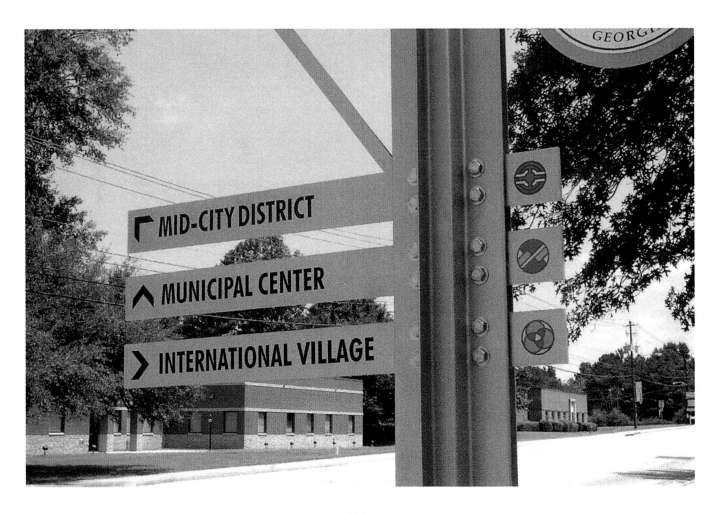

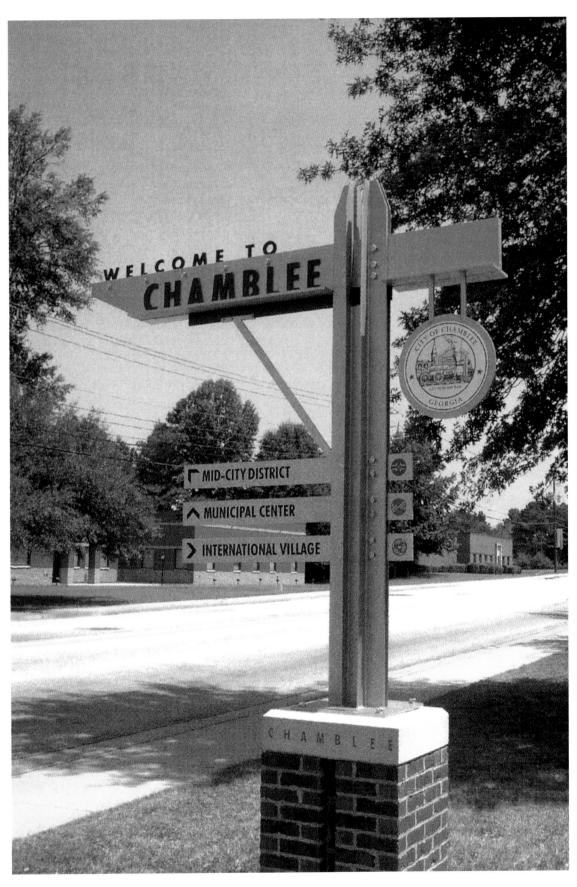

Design Firm **Sky Design**
Client   *City Of Chamblee, Ga.*
Designers   W. Todd Vaught,
            Carrie Brown

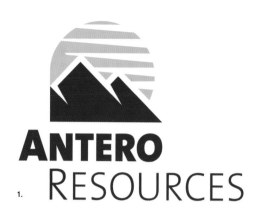

ANTERO RESOURCES

1.

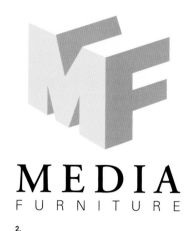

MEDIA FURNITURE

2.

ÂPEX DERMATOLOGY GROUP

3.

ExtendedPresence

Outsourced Sales Professionals

4.

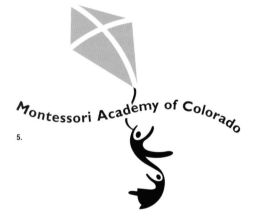

Montessori Academy of Colorado

5.

AMERICA AND THE WORLD

6.

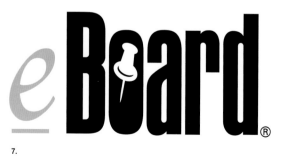

e**Board**®

7.

1 - 7
Design Firm **Convexus Consulting, Inc.**
1.
  Client   *Antero Resources*
  Designers   Karl Peters,
              David Warren
2.
  Client   *Media Furniture*
  Designer   Karl Peters
3.
  Client   *Apex Dermatology Group*
  Designers   Karl Peters,
              David Warren
4.
  Client   *Extended Presence*
  Designers   Karl Peters,
              David Warren
5.
  Client   *Montessori Academy of Colorado*
  Designers   Karl Peters,
              David Warren

6.
  Client   *America and the World*
  Designers   Karl Peters,
              David Warren
7.
  Client   *eBoard.com*
  Designer   Karl Peters
(opposite)
  Client   *Aga Khan Foundation USA*
  Design Firm **Poonja Design, Inc.**
  Designer   Suleman Poonja

298

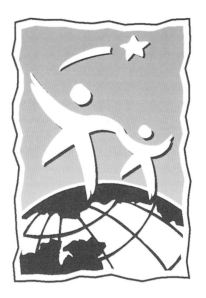

Partnership*Walk*

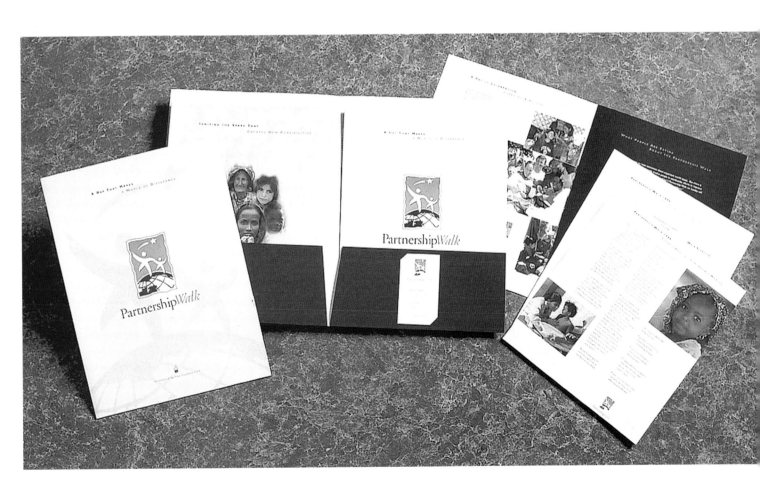

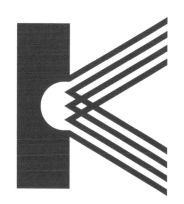 **Needed**Numbers

1.

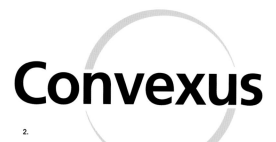 **Convexus**

2.

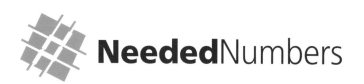

3.

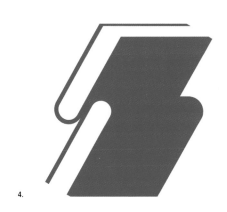

4.

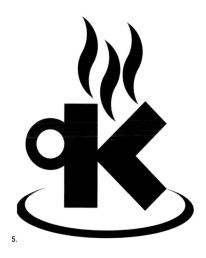

5.

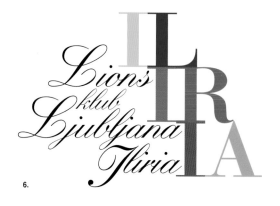 *Lions klub Ljubljana Iliria* ILIRIA

6.

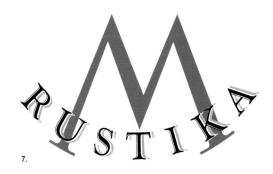 RUSTIKA

7.

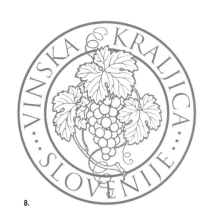 VINSKA & KRALJICA SLOVENIJE

8.

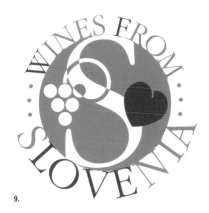

9.

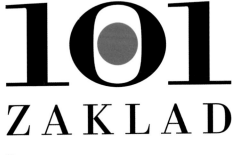

10.

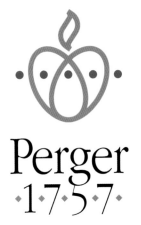

11.

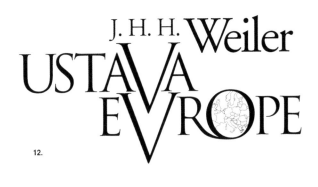

12.

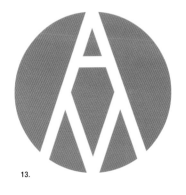

13.

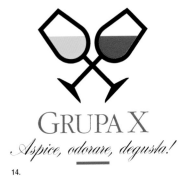

14.

LITTERA·SCRIPTA·MANET

15.

1, 2
Design Firm **Convexus Consulting, Inc.**
3 - 15
Design Firm **KROG**
1.
Client   *Optima Marketing*
Designer *Karl Peters*
2.
Client   *Convexus Consulting, Inc.*
Designers *Karl Peters, David Warren*
3, 4.
Client   *Presernova druzba, Ljubljana*
Designer *Edi Berk*
5.
Client   *Mladinska knjiga, Ljubljana*
Designer *Edi Berk*
6.
Client   *Lions klub Ljubljana Iliria*
Designer *Edi Berk*
7.
Client   *Janko in Zdena Mlakar, Ljubljana*
Designer *Edi Berk*
8.
Client   *Pomurski sejem, Gornja Radgona*
Designer *Edi Berk*

9.
Client   *Ministry of Agriculture of the*
          Republic of Slovenia, Ljubljana
Designer *Edi Berk*
10.
Client   *Kmecki glas, Ljubljana*
Designer *Edi Berk*
11.
Client   *Hrabroslav Perger, Slovenj Gradec*
Designer *Edi Berk*
12.
Client   *Pravna fakulteta, Ljubljana*
Designer *Edi Berk*
13.
Client   *Andrej Mlakar, Ljubljana*
Designer *Edi Berk*
14.
Client   *Grupa X, Ljubljana*
Designer *Edi Berk*
15.
Client   *Pravna fakulteta, Ljubljana*
Designer *Edi Berk*

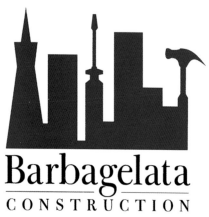

1.

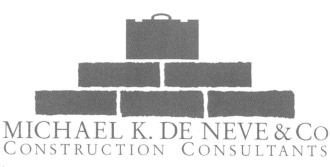

MICHAEL K. DE NEVE & Co
CONSTRUCTION CONSULTANTS

2.

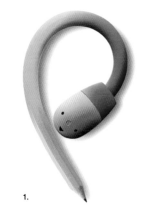

Barbagelata
CONSTRUCTION

3.

SKOV
CONSTRUCTION

4.

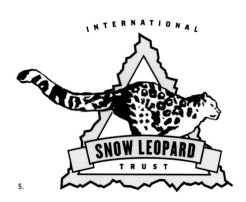

INTERNATIONAL

SNOW LEOPARD
TRUST

5.

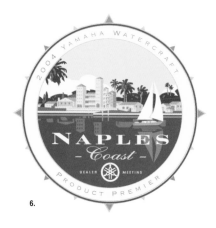

6.

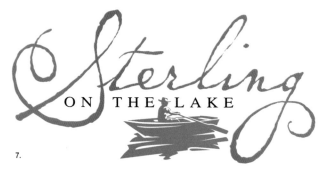

7.

1
　　Design Firm **KROG**
2 - 4
　　Design Firm **Bondepus Graphic Design**
5
　　Design Firm **Studio Rayolux**
6
　　Design Firm **Vitro Robertson**
7
　　Design Firm **Roni Hicks & Associates**
1.
　　Client　　　*Grafika Paradoks, Ljubljana*
　　Designer　　Edi Berk
2.
　　Client　　　*Michael K. De Neve & Co*
　　Designers　　Gary Epis, Amy Bond
3.
　　Client　　　*Barbagelata Construction*
　　Designers　　Gary Epis, Amy Bond

4.
　　Client　　　*SKOV Construction*
　　Designers　　Gary Epis, Amy Bond
5.
　　Client　　　*International Snow Leopard Trust*
　　Designer　　Thad Boss
6.
　　Client　　　*Yamaha Watercraft*
　　Designers　　Tracy Sabin, Mike Brower
7.
　　Client　　　*Sterling on the Lake*
　　Designers　　Tracy Sabin, Stephen Sharp
(opposite)
　　Client　　　*Innovative Foods Corp.*
　　Design Firm **LOGOSBRANDS**
　　Designers　　Denise Barac,
　　　　　　　　Franca Di Nardo

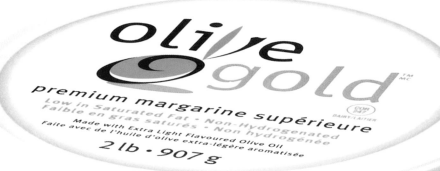

olive
gold ™ MC
premium margarine supérieure
Low in Saturated Fat · Non-Hydrogenated
Faible en gras saturés · Non hydrogénée
Made with Extra Light Flavoured Olive Oil
Faite avec de l'huile d'olive extra-légère aromatisée
2 lb · 907 g

olive
gold ™

premium margarine
Low in Saturated Fat
Non-Hydrogenated

INGREDIENTS: CANOLA OIL AND EXTRA LIGHT OLIVE OIL 69.5%, WATER 16%, MODIFIED PALM OIL 10.5%, SALT 1.8%, WHEY POWDER 1.4%, VEGETABLE MONO AND DIGLYCERIDES 0.4%, SOY LECITHIN 0.2%, POTASSIUM SORBATE 0.1%, ARTIFICIAL FLAVOUR, ALPHA TOCOPHEROL, VITAMIN A PALMITATE, VITAMIN D3, BETA CAROTENE, CITRIC ACID. KEEP REFRIGERATED. GOOD FOR COOKING AND BAKING. ONE ASPECT OF A HEALTHY DIET IS TO HAVE NOT MORE THAN 10% OF ENERGY FROM SATURATED FAT.

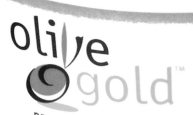

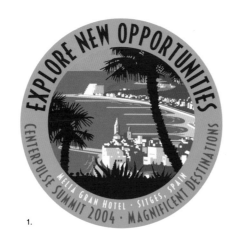

1.

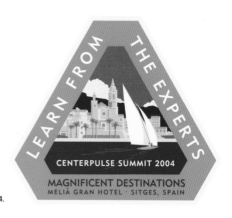

2.

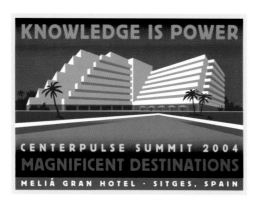

3.

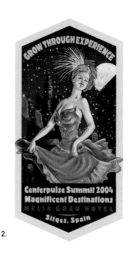

4.

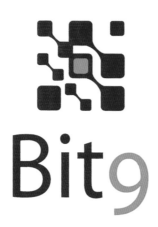

5.

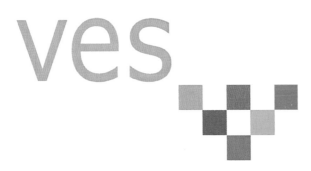

6.

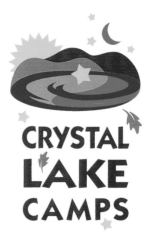

7.

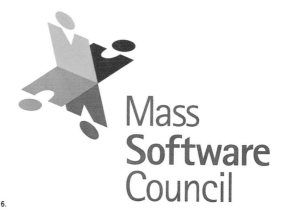

8.

304

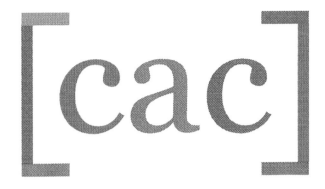

PeerBridge

9.

[cac]

10.

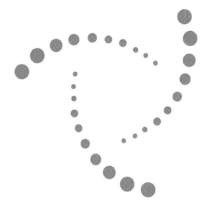

New Center
for ARTS *and* CULTURE

11.

12.

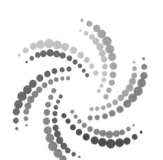

Taralon

13.

Clifton Heights

LA COSTA OAKS

14.

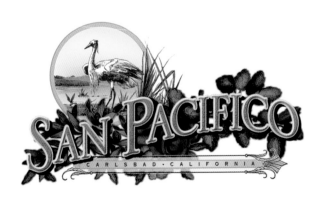

15.

1 - 4
  Design Firm **Parker/White**
5 - 12
  Design Firm **Gill Fishman Associates**
13, 14
  Design Firm **Roni Hicks & Associates**
15
  Design Firm **Sabingrafik, Inc.**
1 - 4.
  Client   *Centerpulse*
  Designers   Tracy Sabin, Dylan Jones
5.
  Client   *Harvard VES*
  Designer   Alicia Ozyjowski
6.
  Client   *Mass Software Council*
  Designers   Alicia Ozyjowski,
              Michael Persons
7.
  Client   *Bit9 Inc.*
  Designer   Alicia Ozyjowski

8.
  Client   *Crystal Lake Camps*
  Designer   Michael Persons
9.
  Client   *Peerbridge Group*
  Designer   Michael Persons
10.
  Client   *Brown University*
  Designer   Gill Fishman
11.
  Client   *New Jewish Center for Arts*
  Designer   Alicia Ozyjowski
12.
  Client   *Trine Pharmaceuticals*
13.
  Client   *Taralon*
  Designers   Tracy Sabin, Stephen Sharp
14.
  Client   *Clifton Heights*
  Designers   Tracy Sabin, Stephen Sharp
15.
  Client   *San Pacifico*
  Designer   Tracy Sabin

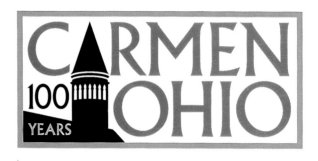

1.

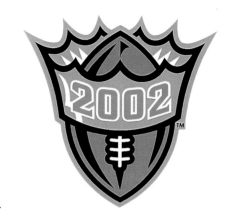

2.

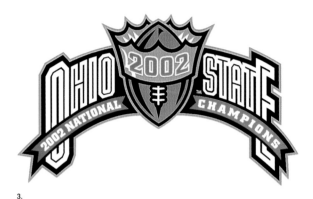

3.

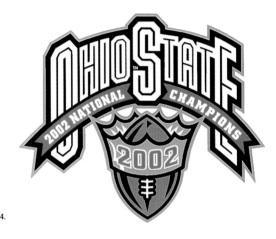

4.

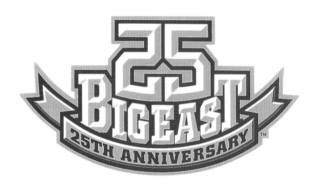

5.

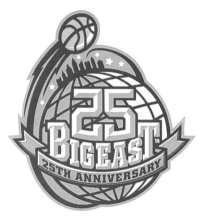

6.

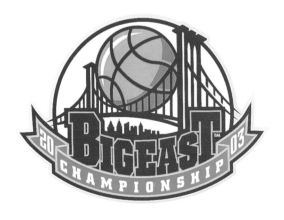

7.

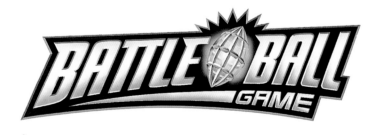

8.

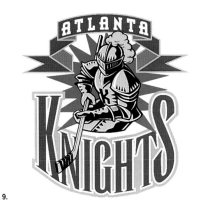

9.

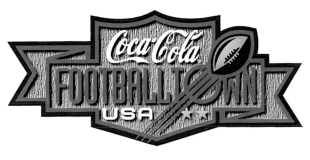

10.

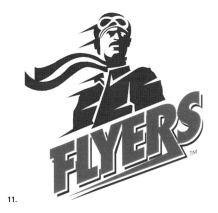

11.

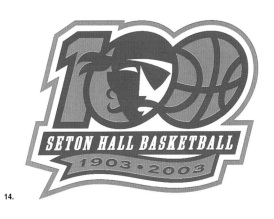

12.

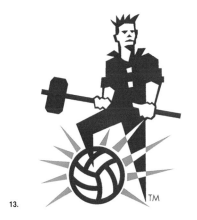

13.

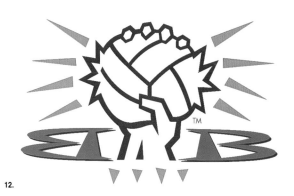

14.

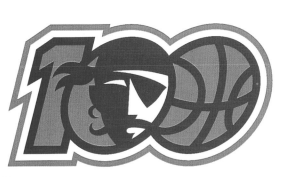

15.

1 - 15
Design Firm **Rickabaugh Graphics**
1 - 4.
Client   *The Ohio State University*
Designers   Eric Rickabaugh, Dave Cap
5 - 7.
Client   *The Big East Conference*
Designers   Eric Rickabaugh, Rob Carolla
8.
Client   *Hasbro, Inc.*
Designers   Bill Concannon, Dave Cap
9.
Client   *Atlanta Knights*
Designers   Eric Rickabaugh, Mike Linley

10.
Client   *Coca-Cola/Momentum*
Designers   Nathan Forness, Eric Rickabaugh
11.
Client   *University of Dayton*
Designer   Eric Rickabaugh
12, 13.
Client   *The Ball Busters*
Designer   Eric Rickabaugh
14, 15.
Client   *Seton Hall University*
Designers   Eric Rickabaugh, Dave Cap

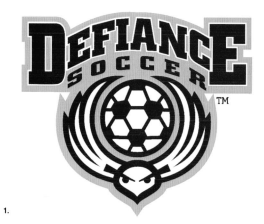

1.

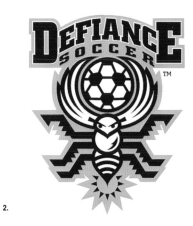

4.

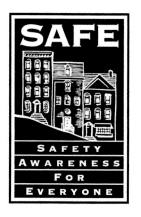

3.

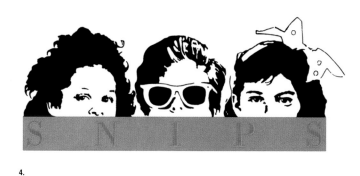

6.

5.

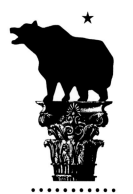

Northern California Investments

7.

1 - 3
Design Firm **Rickabaugh Graphics**
4 - 7
Design Firm **Steven Lee Design**
1 - 3.
   Client   *Defiance College*
   Designer   Eric Rickabaugh
4.
   Client   *SNIPS*
   Designer   Steven Lee
5.
   Client   *Safety Awareness for Everyone*
   Designer   Steven Lee
6.
   Client   *Prime Pacific Global
               Management Corporation*
   Designer   Steven Lee

7.
   Client   *Northern California Investments*
   Designer   Steven Lee
(opposite)
   Client   *Saint John's Health Center*
   Design Firm **Poonja Design, Inc.**
   Designer   Suleman Poonja

JIMMY STEWART

RELAY MARATHON

2001

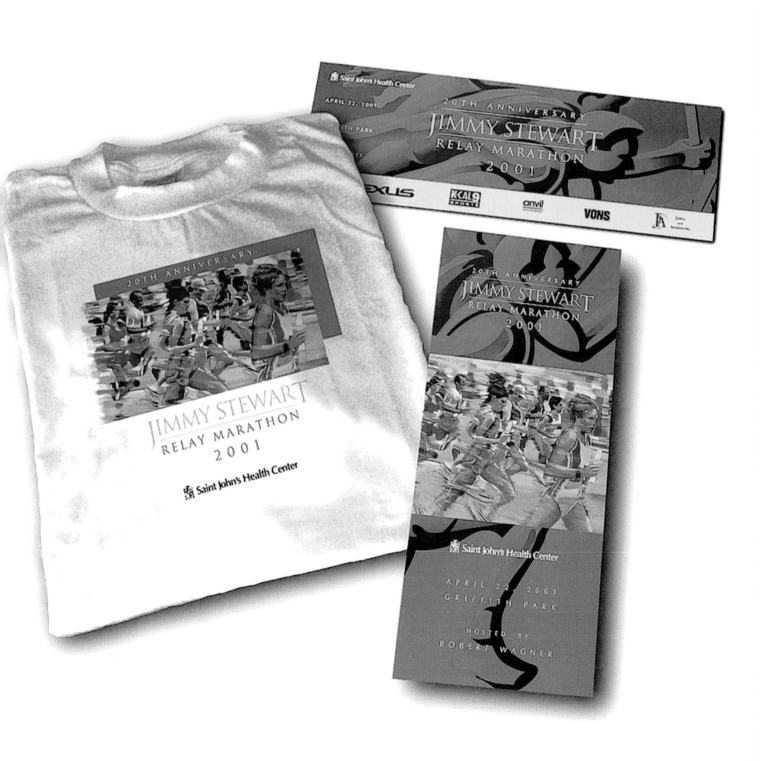

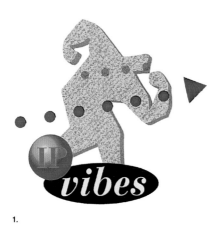

1.

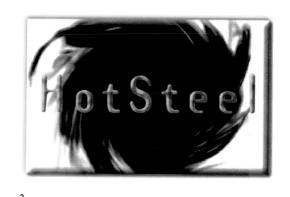

2.

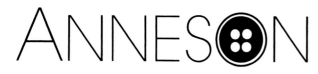

3.

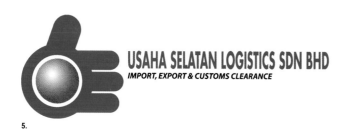

4.

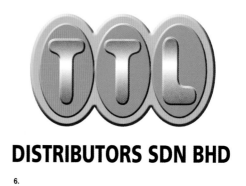

5.

DISTRIBUTORS SDN BHD

6.

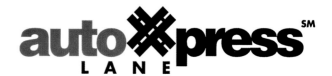

7.

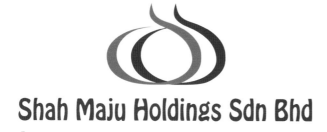

8.

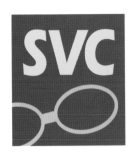

STANDARD VISION CARE SDN BHD

9.

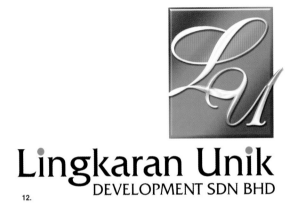

TCL PLASTIC INDUSTRIES SDN. BHD.

10.

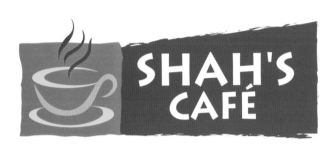

SHAH'S CAFÉ

11.

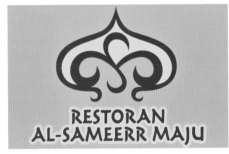

Lingkaran Unik
DEVELOPMENT SDN BHD

12.

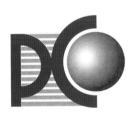
PLANO-COMP

13.

RESTORAN AL-SAMEERR MAJU

14.

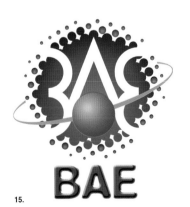
BAE

15.

1 - 4				8.		
Design Firm **Steven Lee Design**					Client	Stargate Resources
5 - 15					Designer	Allen Tan
Design Firm **FGA**				9.		
1.					Client	Standard Vision Care Sdn Bhd
	Client	IPvibes			Designers	FGA Creative Team
	Designer	Steven Lee		10.		
2.					Client	TCL Plastic Industries Sdn Bhd
	Client	HotSteel			Designers	FGA Creative Team
	Designer	Steven Lee		11.		
3.					Client	Shah Maju Holdings Sdn Bhd
	Client	Anneson			Designers	FGA Creative Team
	Designer	Steven Lee		12.		
4.					Client	Lingkaran Unik Development Sdn Bhd
	Client	autoXpress Lane			Designer	Allen Tan
	Designer	Steven Lee		13.		
5.					Client	Plano-Comp Sdn Bhd
	Client	Usaha Selatan Logistics Sdn Bhd			Designer	Allen Tan
	Designers	FGA Creative Team		14.		
6.					Client	Restoran Al-Sameerr Maju
	Client	TTL Distributors Sdn Bhd			Designers	FGA Creative Team
	Designers	FGA Creative Team		15.		
7.					Client	BAE International Inc. Sdn Bhd
	Client	Shah Maju Holdings Sdn Bhd			Designers	FGA Creative Team
	Designers	FGA Creative Team				

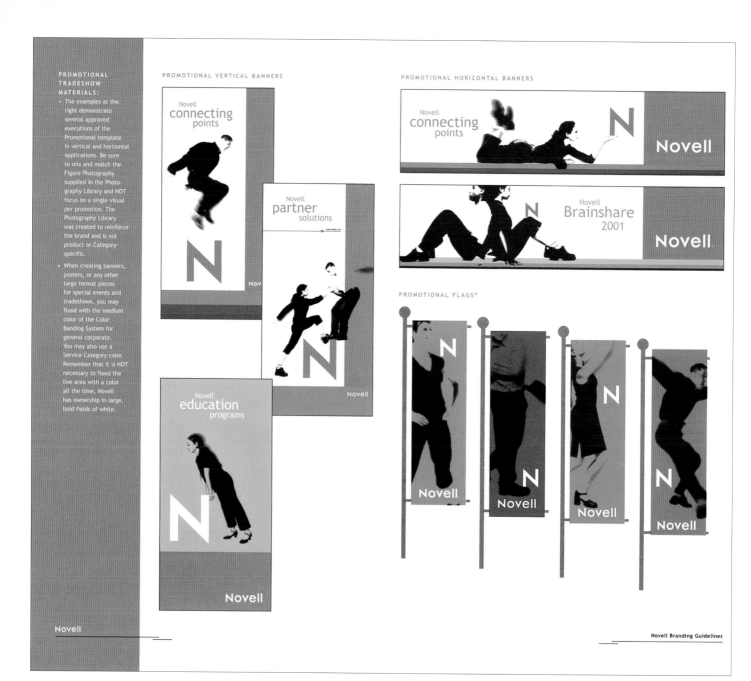

PROMOTIONAL TRADESHOW MATERIALS:

- The examples at the right demonstrate several approved executions of the Promotional template in vertical and horizontal applications. Be sure to mix and match the Figure Photography supplied in the Photography Library and NOT focus on a single visual per promotion. The Photography Library was created to reinforce the brand and is not product or Category-specific.

- When creating banners, posters, or any other large format pieces for special events and tradeshows, you may flood with the medium color of the Color Banding System for general corporate. You may also use a Service Category color. Remember that it is NOT necessary to flood the live area with a color all the time, Novell has ownership in large, bold fields of white.

PROMOTIONAL VERTICAL BANNERS

Novell
connecting
points

Novell
partner
solutions

Novell
education
programs

Novell

PROMOTIONAL HORIZONTAL BANNERS

Novell
connecting
points

N
Novell

Novell
Brainshare
2001

N
Novell

PROMOTIONAL FLAGS*

Novell

Novell

Novell

Novell

Novell

Novell Branding Guidelines

Design Firm **Hornall Anderson Design Works, Inc.**
Client *Novell, Inc.*
Designers Larry Anderson, Jack Anderson, James Tee, Holly Craven,
Michael Brugman, Kaye Farmer, Taro Suzuki, Jay Hilburn,
Belinda Bowling

MERCHANDISE:

- Using a sparse look to build brand equity is a mandate from Novell Corporate Marketing.
- All Corporate Merchandise should include the Novell Logo, preferably in Novell Red.
- All Corporate T-shirts should ONLY have the Novell Logo on the front of the shirt. Any deviation from this must be approved by Novell Corporate Marketing.
- The N Graphic and Figure Photography should appear on the back of the T-shirt. (You can use any of the images included on the CD.)
- Corporate Hats should have the N Graphic on the front and the Novell Logo on the back. The Logo appears in Novell Red on a white or light colored hat or white on a red hat.

T-SHIRT

MOUSEPAD

BUTTON

HAT

NAMETAG

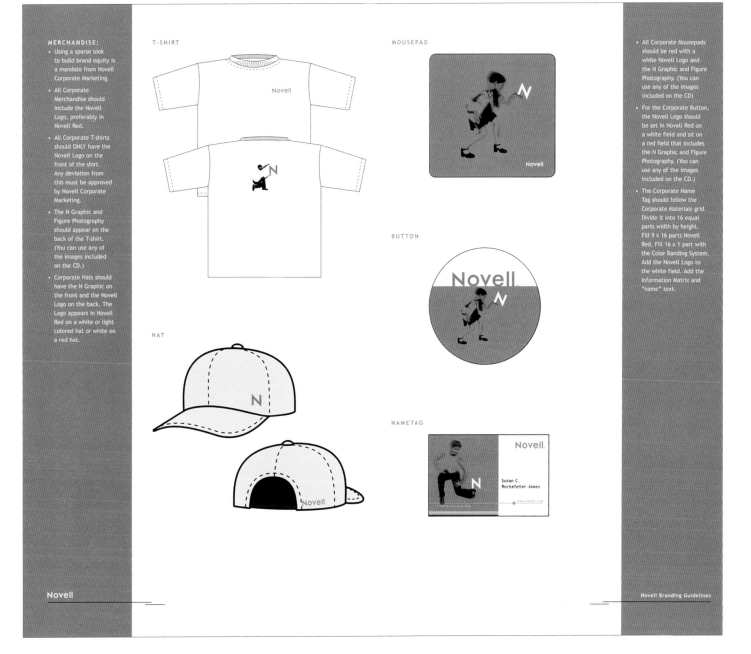

- All Corporate Mousepads should be red with a white Novell Logo and the N Graphic and Figure Photography. (You can use any of the images included on the CD)
- For the Corporate Button, the Novell Logo should be set in Novell Red on a white field and sit on a red field that includes the N Graphic and Figure Photography. (You can use any of the images included on the CD.)
- The Corporate Name Tag should follow the Corporate Materials grid. Divide it into 16 equal parts width by height. Fill 9 x 16 parts Novell Red. Fill 16 x 1 part with the Color Banding System. Add the Novell Logo to the white field. Add the Information Matrix and "name" text.

- The N Graphic and Figure Photography is a combination of the Novell Logo "N" with Photography.

- The N Graphic and Figure Photography always appear in conjunction with the Novell Logo.

- There is an established relationship between the N Graphic and the Figure Photography. DO NOT modify the established spatial relationship.

- These images were created to be used generously. No one image represents a specific Service Category or product. Use all images within the library, and mix and match as much as possible.

- The N Graphic and Figure Photography shown in its entirety is referred to as a Stand-alone Graphic.

- Stand-alone Graphics are used on all Corporate materials.

- A Supergraphic is an enlarged, close crop of the Figure Photography. The N Graphic may be removed from its locked position and placed in general proximity of the figure.

- Supergraphics are used for Promotional materials only.

Novell

 Novell Logo

 N Graphic

Figure Photography

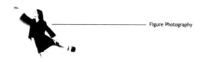 N Graphic

Stand-alone Graphic

Figure Photography

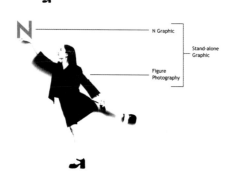

STAND-ALONE GRAPHIC   SUPERGRAPHIC

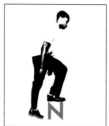   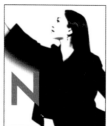

ON WHITE BACKGROUND   ON NOVELL RED

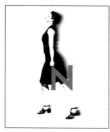   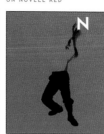

ON LIGHT BACKGROUND   ON DARK COLORS

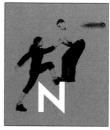   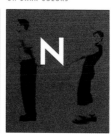

ONE COLOR ("N" IS 30%
SCREEN OF BLACK)   ON COLOR BANDING SYSTEM

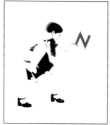   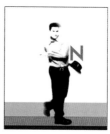

- The Figure Photography always appears as black on a white background OR black on one of the Novell Colors.

- The N Graphic is always Novell Red on a white background OR white on a colored background.

- If only one color is available, the N graphic prints 30% screen of black on a white background. DO NOT place the Figure Photography on a black background.

- For Promotional materials, the Figure Photography can overlap the Color Banding System.

- The images were created to be used as they are. Do NOT manipulate or distort the images found in the Figure Photography Library.

- Figure Photography is always used in conjunction with the N Graphic— never without.

NOTE: The complete directory of the Figure Photography can be found in the Reference section of these Guidelines. Figure Photography images are provided on the Branding Guidelines CDs as 1) high resolution Photoshop tiff files, 2) Illustrator eps files with the N Graphic and 3) as a combined lock-up saved as a 4-color process tiff file. A "How To" Photoshop file has been included to help guide in adding back-ground colors to the Figure Photography.

PRODUCT BOX

UPGRADE BOX

CD LABELS

Product CD   Beta CD   Evaluation CD

CD ENVELOPES

DOCUMENTATION

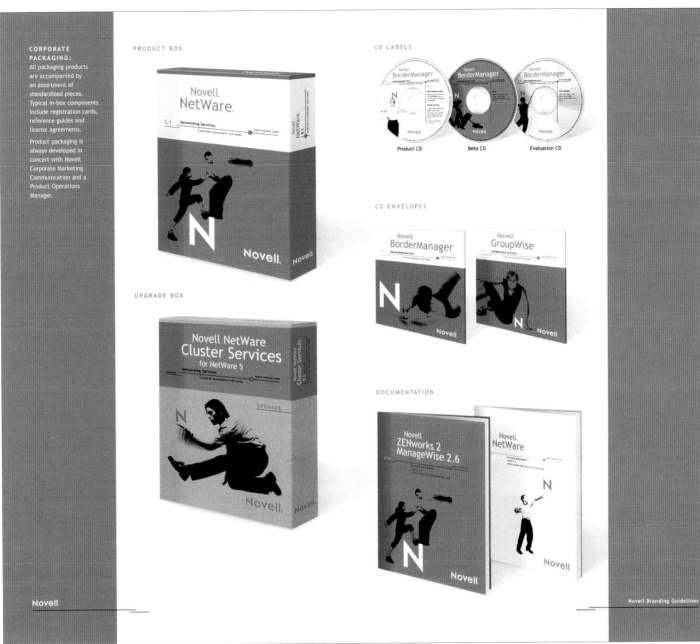

(continued)
Design Firm **Hornall Anderson Design Works**
Client   *Novell, Inc.*

315

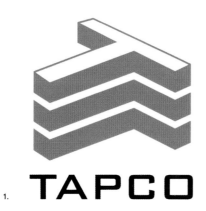

1. TAPCO

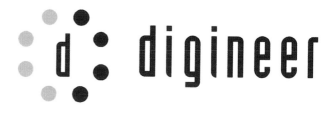

2.

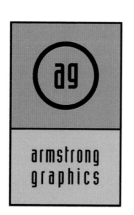

stirsby
-EST. '01-

3.

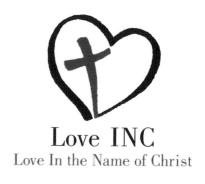

Love INC
Love In the Name of Christ

4.

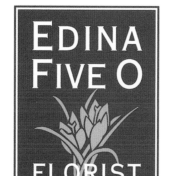

EDINA FIVE O FLORIST

5.

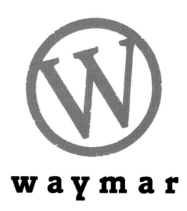

waymar

6.

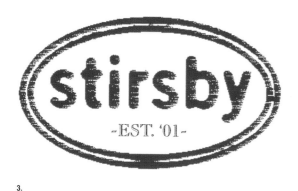

ag
armstrong graphics

7.

1 - 7
Design Firm **Armstrong Graphics**
1.
 Client *Tapco*
 Designer R. Bruce Armstrong
2.
 Client *Digineer*
 Designer R. Bruce Armstrong
3.
 Client *John Danicic*
 Designer R. Bruce Armstrong
4.
 Client *Love Inc.*
 Designer R. Bruce Armstrong
5.
 Client *Edina Five-O Florist*
 Designer R. Bruce Armstrong

6.
 Client *Waymar Restaurant Furniture*
 Designer R. Bruce Armstrong
7.
 Client *Armstrong Graphics*
 Designer R. Bruce Armstrong
(opposite)
 Client *Malaysian Institute of Baking*
 Design Firm **FGA**
 Designers FGA Creative Team

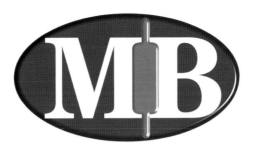

MALAYSIAN INSTITUTE OF BAKING

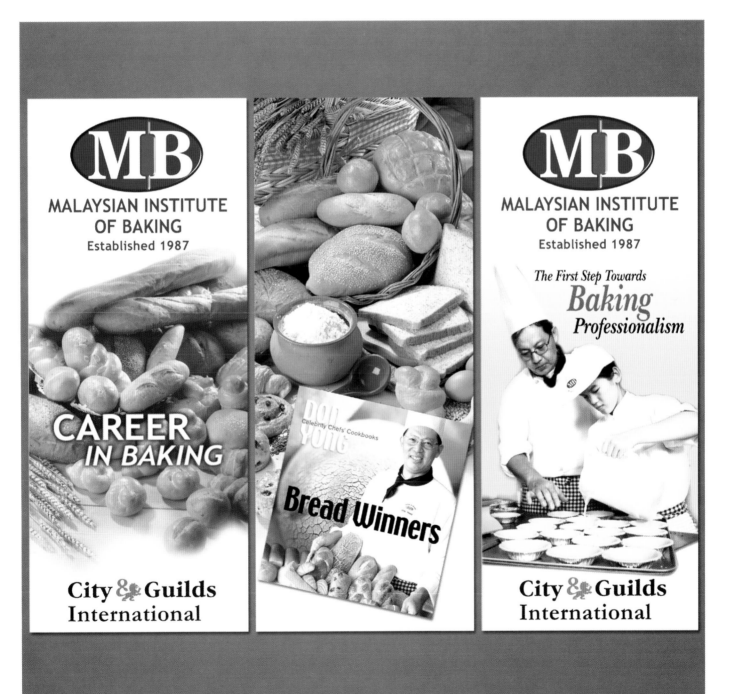

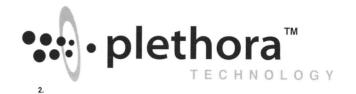

1.

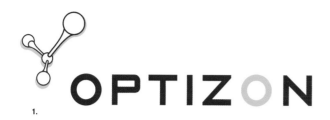

2.

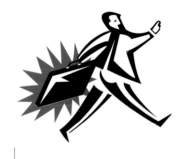

3.

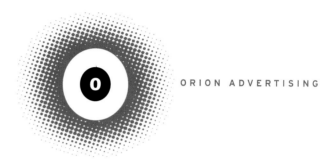

4.

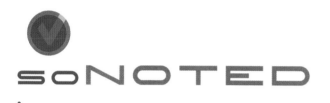

re | salzman designs

5.

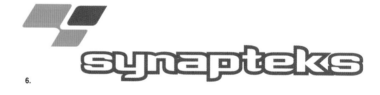

6.

TJW VENTURES

7.

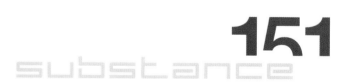

8.

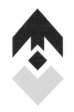

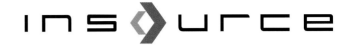

10.

APEX

9.

 MiND INVENTIONS

11.

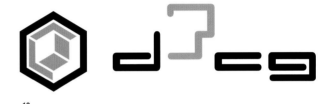

12.

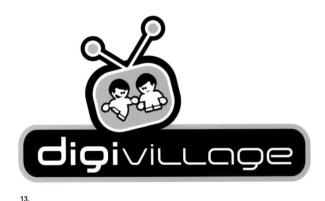

alphainsight

14.

13.

LITECAST

15.

1 - 15
Design Firm **substance 151**

1.
Client — Optizon
Designers — Ida Cheinman, Rick Salzman

2.
Client — Plethora Technology
Designers — Ida Cheinman, Rick Salzman

3.
Client — soNoted
Designers — Ida Cheinman, Rick Salzman

4.
Client — Orion Advertising
Designers — Ida Cheinman, Rick Salzman

5.
Client — re:salzman designs
Designers — Ida Cheinman, Rick Salzman

6.
Client — synapteks
Designers — Ida Cheinman, Rick Salzman

7.
Client — TJW Ventures
Designers — Ida Cheinman, Rick Salzman

8.
Client — substance 151
Designers — Ida Cheinman, Rick Salzman

9.
Client — Apex SEO
Designers — Ida Cheinman, Rick Salzman

10.
Client — inSource
Designers — Ida Cheinman, Rick Salzman

11.
Client — Mind Inventions
Designers — Ida Cheinman, Rick Salzman

12.
Client — d3cg
Designers — Ida Cheinman, Rick Salzman

13.
Client — digivillage
Designers — Ida Cheinman, Rick Salzman

14.
Client — AlphaInsight Corporation
Designers — Ida Cheinman, Rick Salzman

15.
Client — Litecast
Designers — Ida Cheinman, Rick Salzman

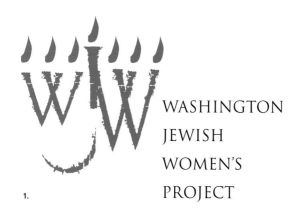

WASHINGTON
JEWISH
WOMEN'S
PROJECT

1.

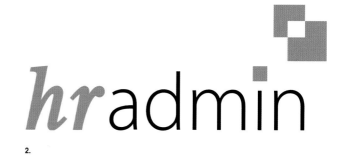

2.

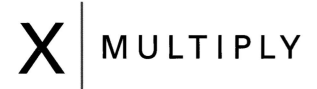

3.

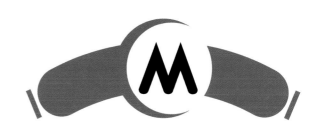

4.

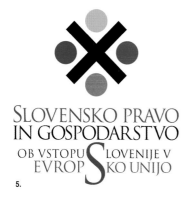

SLOVENSKO PRAVO
IN GOSPODARSTVO
OB VSTOPU SLOVENIJE V
EVROPSKO UNIJO

5.

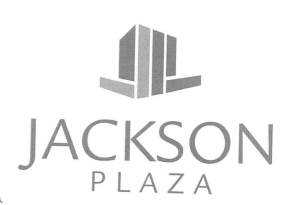

6.

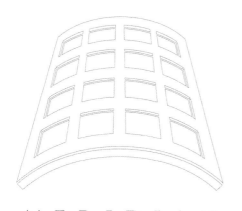

7. MERIDIAN

1, 2
Design Firm **substance 151**
3
Design Firm **Armstrong Graphics**
4, 5
Design Firm **KROG, Ljubljana**
6, 7
Design Firm **Sky Design**
1.
Client   *Washington Jewish
              Women's Project*
Designers   Ida Cheinman, Rick Salzman
2.
Client   *hrAdmin*
Designers   Ida Cheinman, Rick Salzman
3.
Client   *Multiply Communications*
Designer   R. Bruce Armstrong

4.
Client   *Mesarstvo Mlinaric, Lesce*
Designer   Edi Berk
5.
Client   *Pravna fakulteta. Ljubljana*
Designer   Edi Berk
6.
Client   *Gateway Management*
Designers   Celie Goforth, Carrie Brown
7.
Client   *Holder Properties*
Designers   W. Todd Wright, Carrie Brown,
              Matt Worsham
(opposite)
Client   *Maju Avenue*
Design Firm   **FGA**
Designers   FGA Creative Team

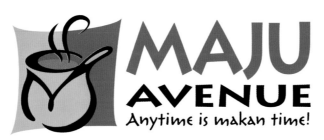

MAJU
AVENUE
Anytime is makan time!

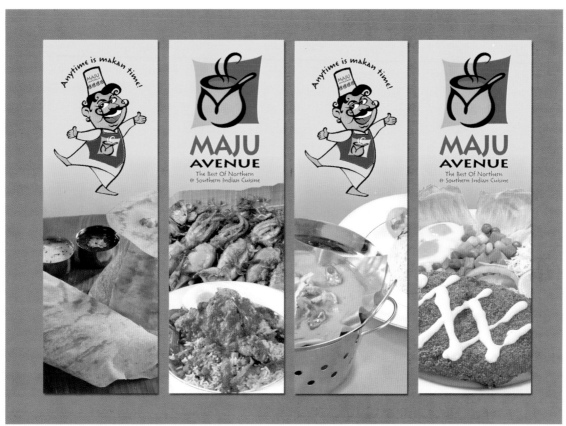

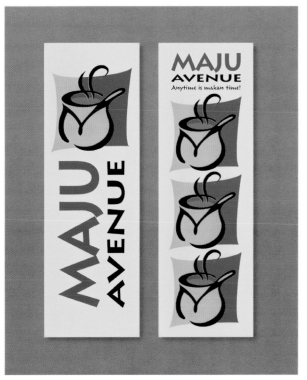

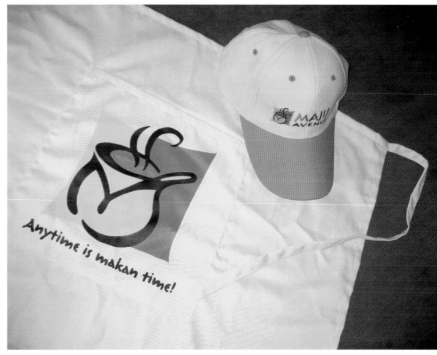

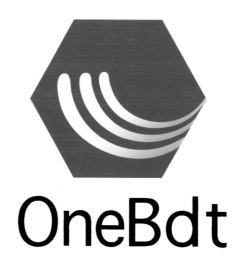

OneBdt

Design Firm **Longwater & Co., Inc.**
Client   *One Bolt, Inc.*
Designers   Kathryn Strozier,
            Elaine Longwater,
            Anastasia Kontos

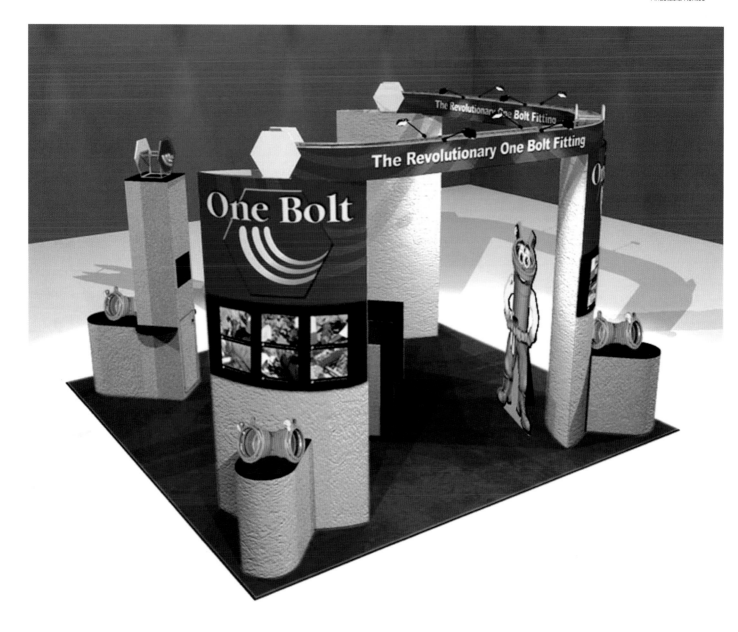

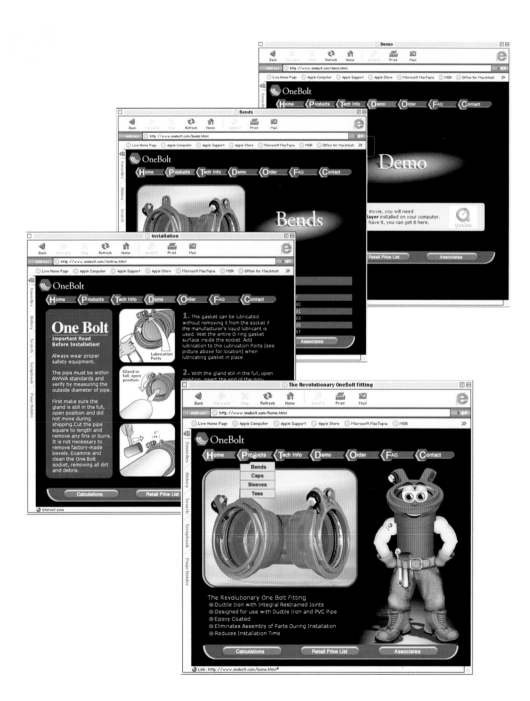

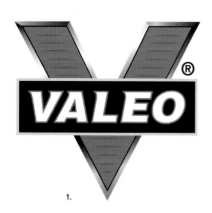

1.

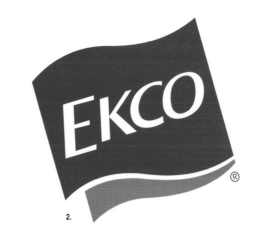

2.

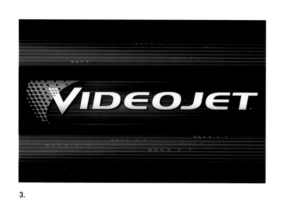

3.

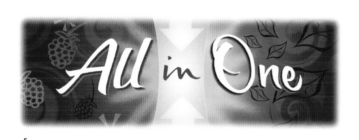

4.

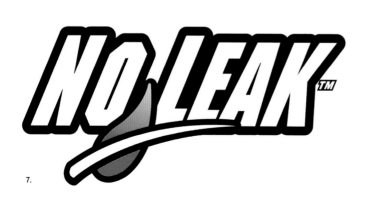

5.

burnes group

6.

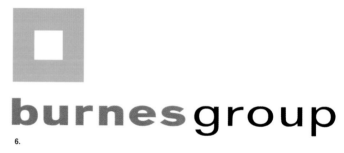

7.

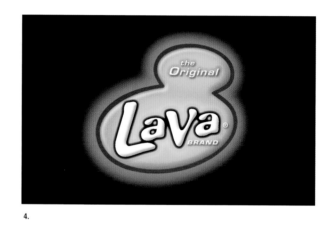

8.

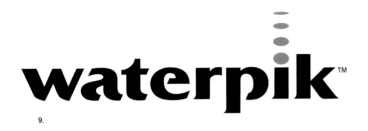

waterpik™

9.

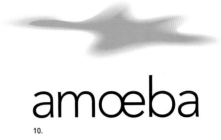

amœba

10.

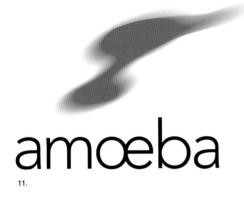

amœba

11.

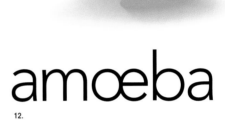

amœba

12.

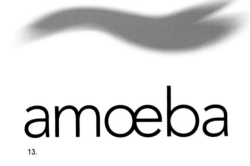

amœba

13.

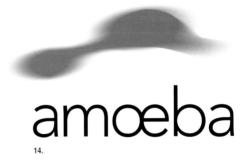

amœba

14.

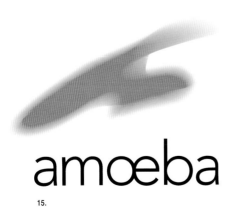

amœba

15.

1 - 9
Design Firm **Source/Inc.**
10 - 15
Design Firm **Bright Strategic Design**

1.
Client   *Valeo, Inc.*
Designers Susan Hartline, Sarrah Trembley,
          Bernie Dolph, Mike Nicholson

2.
Client   *World Kitchen Inc.*
Designers Sabrina Chan, Adrienne Nole,
          Mike Nicholson

3.
Client   *Videojet Technologies*
Designers Scott Burns, Mike Nicholson

4.
Client   *Haggerty Enterprises*
Designers Sabrina Chan, Adrienne Nole,
          Mike Nicholson

5.
Client   *Chatlem, Inc.*
Designers Mike Nicholson, Bernie Dolph

6.
Client   *The Burnes Group*
Designers Adrienne Nole, Mike Nicholson

7.
Client   *Gold Eagle Co.*
Designers Scott Burns, Mike Nicholson

8.
Client   *Kraft Foods Inc.*
Designers Scott Burns, Adam Ferguson,
          Mike Nicholson, Michael Bast

9.
Client   *Waterpik Technologies*
Designers Sabrina Chan, Adrienne Nole,
          Mike Nicholson

10 - 15.
Client   *Amoeba*
Designers Keith Bright, Glenn Sakamoto

325

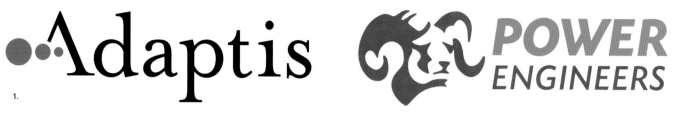

1.

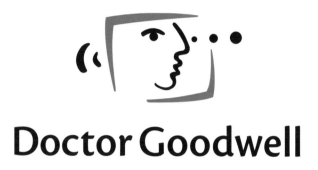

2.

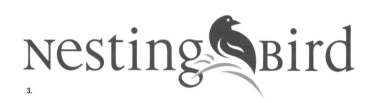

3.

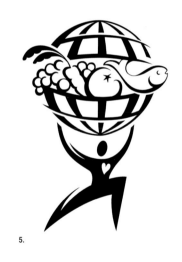

Doctor Goodwell

4.

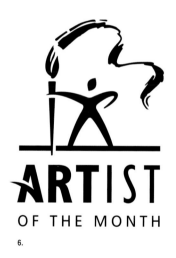

ARTIST
OF THE MONTH

5.

6.

Captaris

7.

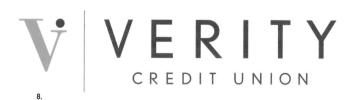

8.

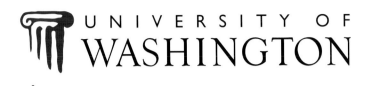

UNIVERSITY OF
WASHINGTON

9.

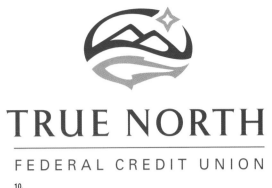

TRUE NORTH
FEDERAL CREDIT UNION

10.

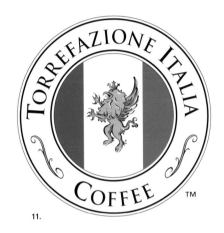

11.

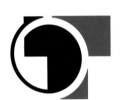

TĒLA

12.

SOUND HEART

13.

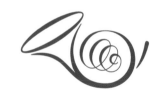

SUN VALLEY SUMMER
Symphony

14.

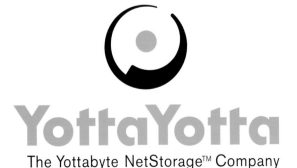

YottaYotta
The Yottabyte NetStorage™ Company

15.

1 - 15
Design Firm **Phinney/Bischoff Design House**

1.
Client   *Adaptis*
Designer   Brian Buckner

2.
Client   *Power Engineers, Inc.*
Designer   Cody Rasmussen

3.
Client   *Nesting Bird*
Designer   Dean Hart

4.
Client   *Doctor Goodwell*
Designers   Dean Hart, Lorie Ransom

5.
Client   *Children's Hospital Seattle*
Designer   Cody Rasmussen

6.
Client   *Children's Hospital Seattle*
Designer   Lorie Ransom

7.
Client   *Captaris*
Designer   Dean Hart

8.
Client   *Verity Credit Union*
Designer   Cody Rasmussen

9.
Client   *University of Washington*
Designer   Lorie Ransom

10.
Client   *True North Federal Credit Union*
Designer   Lorie Ransom

11.
Client   *Torrefazione Italia*
Designers   Dean Hart, Brian Buckner

12.
Client   *Tela*
Designer   Lorie Ransom

13.
Client   *Sound Heart*
Designer   Dean Hart

14.
Client   *Sun Valley Summer Symphony*
Designer   Dean Hart

15.
Client   *Yotta Yotta*
Designer   Cody Rasmussen

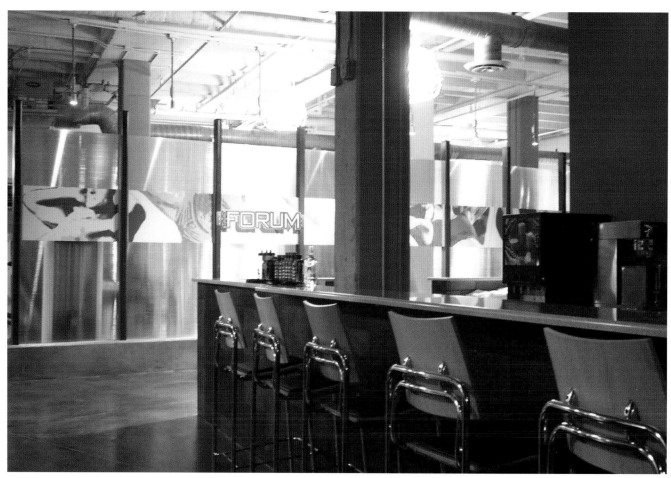

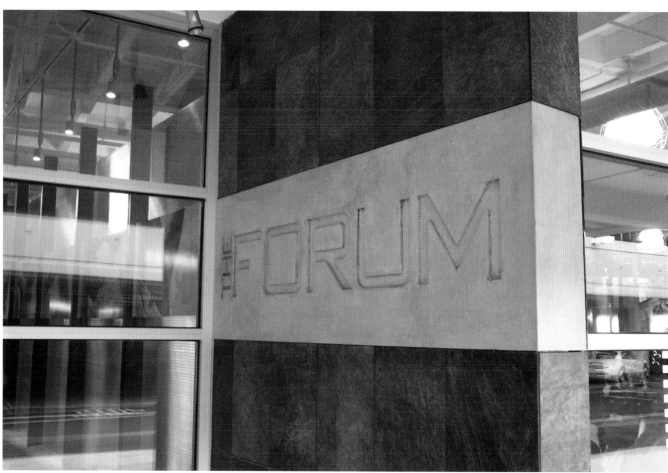

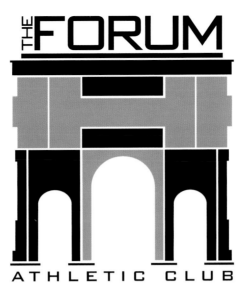

THE FORUM
ATHLETIC CLUB

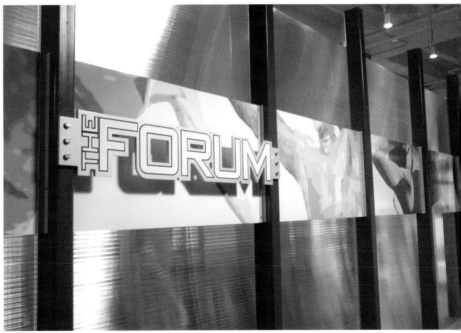

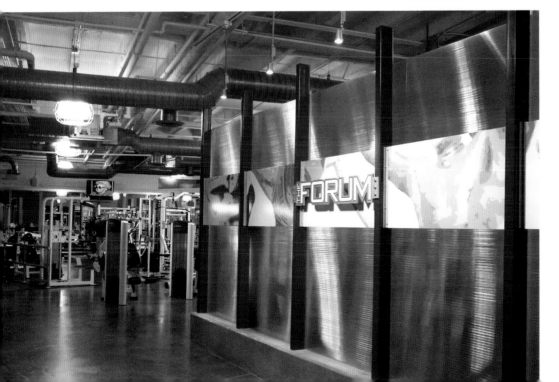

Design Firm **Sky Design**
Client *The Forum*
Designers W. Todd Vaught,
Celie Goforth

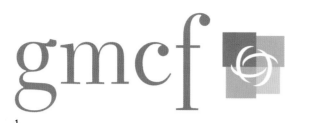

1.

MEADOWS, ICHTER & BOWERS
ATTORNEYS AT LAW

2.

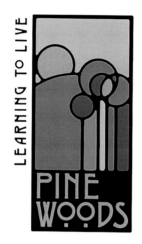

LEARNING TO LIVE

PINE WOODS

3.

HALO

4.

greenHOUSE

5.

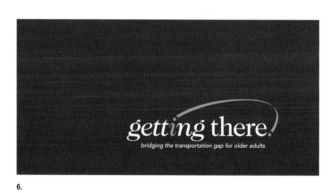

getting there.
bridging the transportation gap for older adults

6.

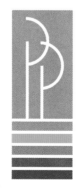

PENTERRA PLAZA

7.

1 - 4
Design Firm **Sky Design**
5 - 7
Design Firm **Noble Erickson Inc.**
1.
　　Client　　　*Georgia Medical Care Foundation*
　　Designers　Celie Goforth, W. Todd Vaught,
　　　　　　　Carrie Brown
2.
　　Client　　　*Meadows, Ichter & Bowers*
　　Designers　W. Todd Vaught, Matt Worsham
3.
　　Client　　　*Pinewoods*
　　Designers　W. Todd Vaught,
　　　　　　　Carrie Brown
4.
　　Client　　　*Halo*
　　Designers　W. Todd Vaught,
　　　　　　　Thom Williams

5.
　　Client　　　*Zeppelin Development*
　　Designer　　Jackie Noble
6.
　　Client　　　*The Rose Foundation*
　　Designer　　Robin Ridley
7.
　　Client　　　*Simpson Housing*
　　Designers　Steven Erickson, Jackie Noble,
　　　　　　　Robin Ridley
(opposite)
　　Client　　　*DataPeer, Inc.*
　　Design Firm **Design Source East**
　　Designer　　Mark Lo Bello

330

power²sync

Powered by DataPeer, Inc.

power²share

Powered by DataPeer, Inc.

power²search

Powered by DataPeer, Inc.

power²network

Powered by DataPeer, Inc.

power²store

Powered by DataPeer, Inc.

power²host

Powered by DataPeer, Inc.

power²protect

Powered by DataPeer, Inc.

power²govern

Powered by DataPeer, Inc.

power²educate

Powered by DataPeer, Inc.

power²profit

Powered by DataPeer, Inc.

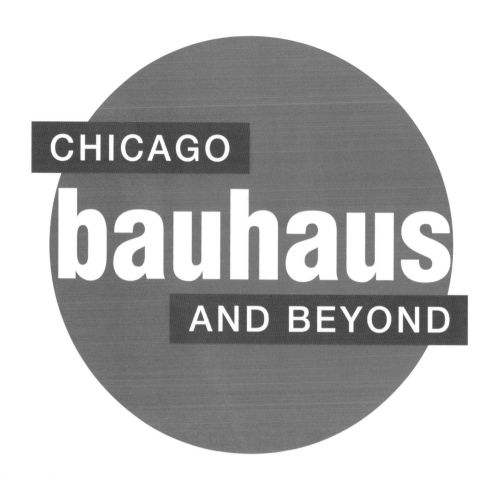

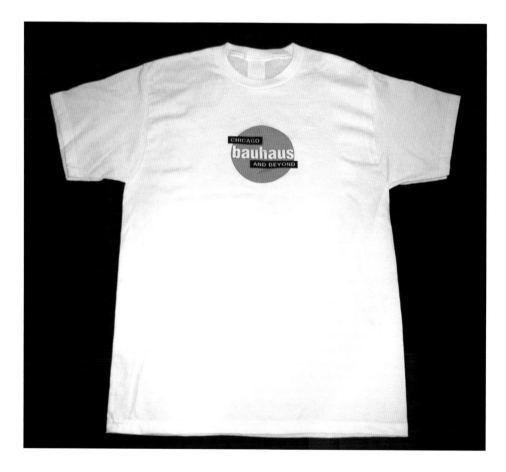

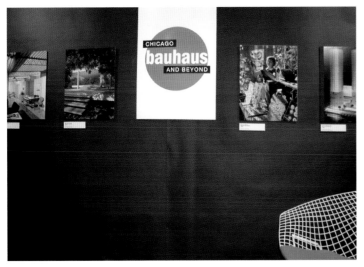

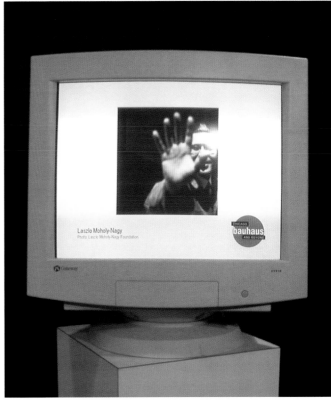

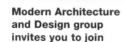

Modern Architecture and Design group invites you to join

Why we're here — why you should join

A diverse group of architects, designers, collectors, dealers, curators and enthusiasts have organized in response to a need for a forum in which to gather information...
creative 20...
migration...
continued...
its influenc...

Chicago B...
events rela...
graphic de...
and desig...

Modernism...
will play a...

Founding m...
writer and d...
known colle...
in libraries, t...
clients, and...
past. The G...
but not to th...

A non-profit organization celebrating and promoting awareness of 20th Century modern architecture and design. For detailed information check out our web site:

www.chicagobauhausbeyond.org
or call: 312.371.0986

Join Cl

Modern Architecture and Design group invites you to join

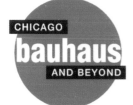

A non-profit organization celebrating and promoting awareness of 20th Century modern architecture and design. For detailed information check out our web site:

www.chicagobauhausbeyond.org
or call: 312.371.0986

Events and Future Plans

Our next event: Sunday, April 18, 2004 / 1-3 pm
will be a guided tour of the Bauhaus Apprenticeship Institute 1757 North Kimball Avenue, Chicago, Illinois. The BAI is a non-profit organization dedicated to rigorous, practical and professional education in American art and craft furniture.
"Show and Tell" — For those who wish to participate, bring one of your favorite small Modernist objects: pottery, glass, sculpture, photos, graphics, jewelry, artwork or whatever excites you. Share your stories about these pieces.
This event is **free** for members and a $5.00 donation for guests. Please RSVP to Joe Kunkel by email: joe@jetsetmodern.com or call Joan Gand: 847.445.6008

Chicago Bauhaus and Beyond invites you to join us for tours, seminars, lectures and special events exploring the rich architectural and design heritage of Chicago and the people who helped create it. Modernism is alive and active in the area and creating a new legacy in which we will play a part.

Join the exciting new modernism design group in Chicago

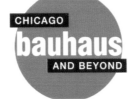

Design Firm **Allen Porter Design**
Client   *Chicago Bauhaus and Beyond*
Designer   Allen Porter

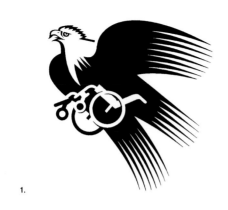

1.

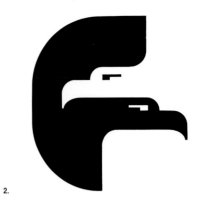

2.

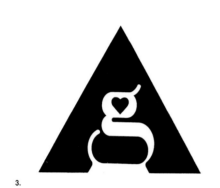

3.

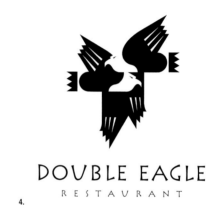

DOUBLE EAGLE
R E S T A U R A N T

4.

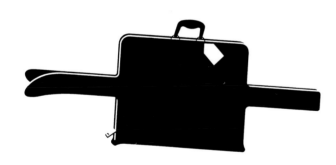

5.

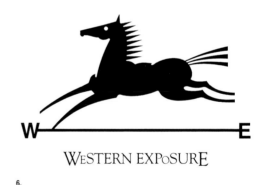

W━━━━━━━━━━E

WESTERN EXPOSURE

6.

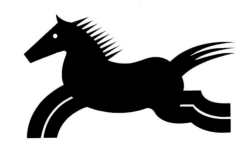

Polo Ridge
F A R M S

7.

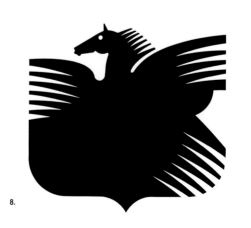

8.

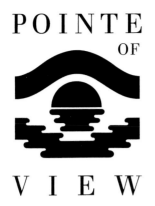

P O I N T E
OF
V I E W

9.

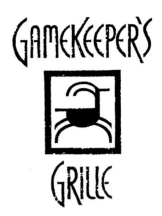

GAMEKEEPER'S

GRILLE

10.

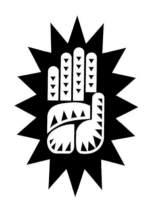

11.

12.

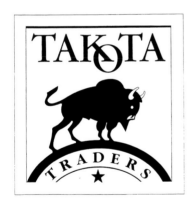

TAKOTA
TRADERS
★

13.

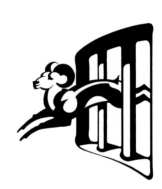

14. **ROCKY MOUNTAIN BAIL BONDS**

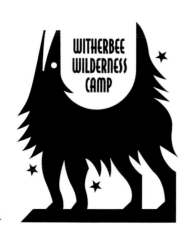

WITHERBEE
WILDERNESS
CAMP

15.

1 - 15
Design Firm **The Weller Institute**
for the Cure of Design, Inc.

1.
Client   *Park City Handicapped*
Sports Association
Designer   Don Weller

2.
Client   *Double Eagle Lodge at Deer Valley*
Designer   Don Weller

3.
Client   *Alpha Graphix*
Designer   Don Weller

4.
Client   *Double Eagle Restaurant*
Designer   Don Weller

5.
Client   *The Design Conference That Just*
Happens To Be In Park City
Designer   Don Weller

6.
Client   *Western Exposure*
Designer   Don Weller

7.
Client   *Polo Ridge Farms*
Designer   Don Weller

8.
Client   *The Weller Institute*
Designer   Don Weller

9.
Client   *Pointe of View*
Designer   Don Weller

10.
Client   *Gamekeeper's Grille Restaurant*
Designer   Don Weller

11.
Client   *Todd Ware Massage*
Designer   Don Weller

12.
Client   *Plyfibres, Inc.*
Designer   Don Weller

13.
Client   *Takota Traders*
Designer   Don Weller

14.
Client   *Rocky Mountain Bail Bonds*
Designer   Don Weller

15.
Client   *Witherbee Wilderness Camp*
Designer   Don Weller

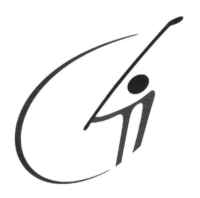

MatchRite™
Paint Matching Systems

1.

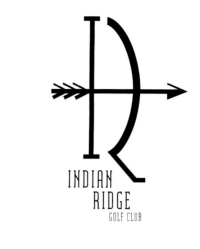

INDIAN
RIDGE
GOLF CLUB

2.

Partner

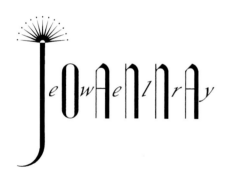

3.

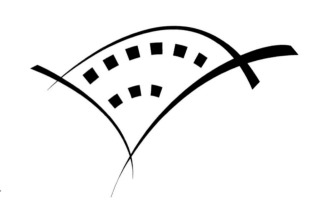

4.

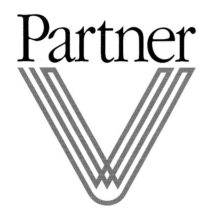

JeOwAenlrAy

5.

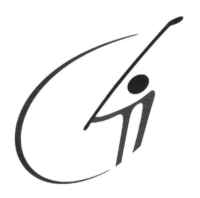

6.

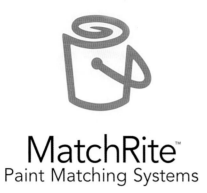

7.

1
Design Firm **Square One Design**
2
Design Firm **Peg Faimon Design**
3
Design Firm **KROG**
4
Design Firm **Robert Morris College Institute
of Art and Design**
5
Design Firm **Cube Advertising & Design**
6, 7
Design Firm **William Ho Design Associates
Ltd.**

1.
Client — *X-Rite*
Designers — Yolanda Gonzaez,
Lin Ver Meulen

2.
Client — *Indian Ridge Golf Club*
Designer — Peg Faimon

3.
Client — *Slovenska Knjiga, Ljubljana*
Designer — Edi Berk

4.
Client — *The Asian American Institute*
Designer — Andrea Polli

5.
Client — *Joanna Jewelry, Inc.*
Designer — David Chiow

6.
Client — *Alfred Dunhill*
Designer — William C.K. Ho

7.
Client — *Shun Feng Golf Club*
Designer — William C.K. Ho
(opposite)
Client — *Johnny Rockets*
Design Firm **Northten, Inc.**
Designers — Sandi Ciz,
Kevin Favell

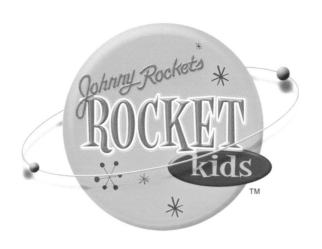

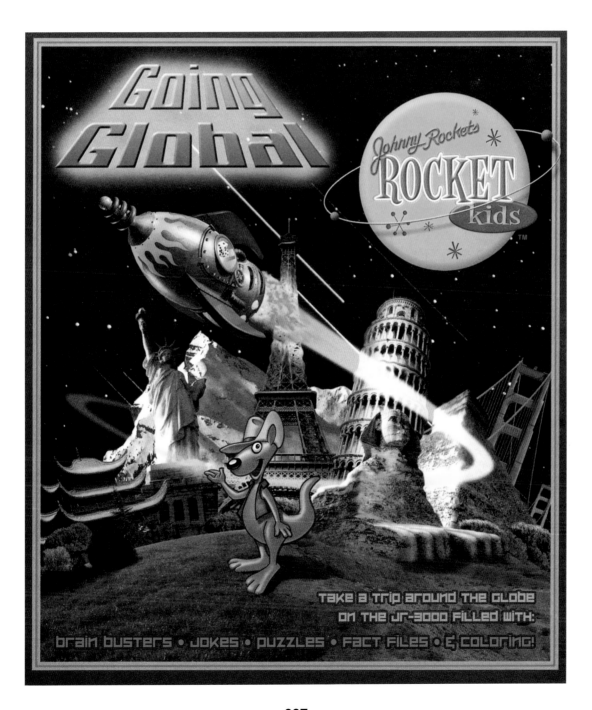

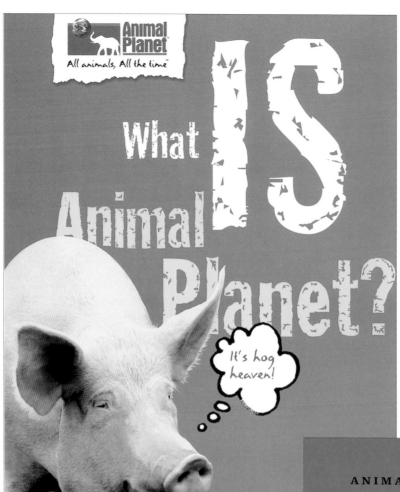

Client   *Animal Planet*
Design Firm **Animal Planet**

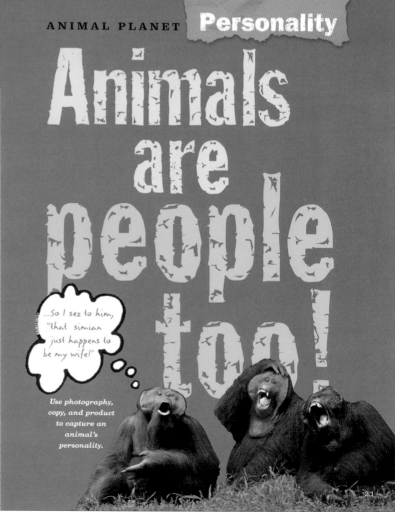

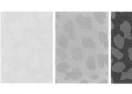**Patterns**

The most striking

artistic patterns

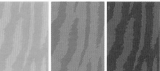

DALMATIAN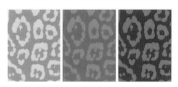

TIGER

CHEETAH

GIRAFFE

Silhouetting

Do it right—or there will be consequences. Trust me!

To focus attention on the animal rather than its habitat, remove the backgrounds from photographs whenever practical.

Use sharp, crisp photographs that silhouette cleanly.

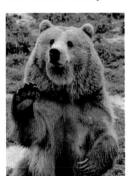

Before:
The background distracts from the star of the show.

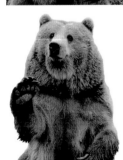

After:
By removing the background, attention is focused on the animal.

IMAGE DON'TS

Don't use complicated images. They should be well defined and easy to silhouette. If you must include a background, keep it simple.

Don't use images that look posed or premeditated. Animal Planet images should be full of character and expression.

Don't use images of expressionless animals. It's difficult, for example, to get a good sense of the personality of a shark.

Don't use aggressive or ferocious images.

3.5

Mix and match colors and patterns to produce interesting combinations beyond what is found in nature. Be sure to use stylized colors to avoid anything looking like actual fur.

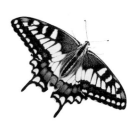

are inspired by animals

  BIRD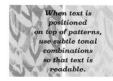

When text is positioned on top of patterns, use subtle tonal combinations so that text is readable.

  COW

  REPTILE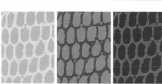

  ZEBRA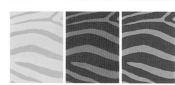

3.9

(continued)
Client *Animal Planet*
Design Firm **Animal Planet**

ANIMAL PLANET Animusings™

Thought balloons containing Animusings™ should be drawn to resemble soft, puffy clouds with a trail of three bubbles, descending in size, leading to the animal.

And remember, these are thought balloons...animals don't speak.

The use of these thought balloons helps humans to better understand OUR way of thinking.

ANIMUSINGS™

Samples of Animusings artwork can be downloaded from the Virtual Library.

3.11

(opposite)
Client *TrueFACES*
Design Firm **TrueFACES Creation**
Designer Allen Tan

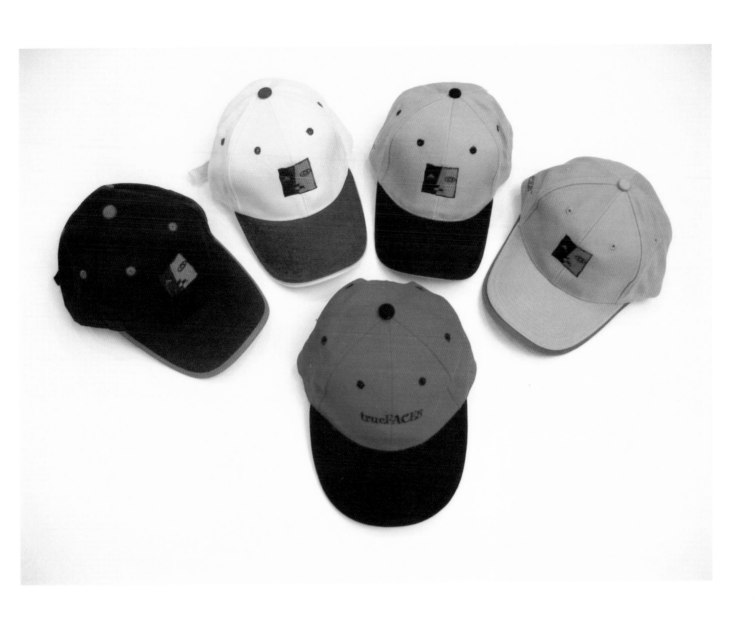

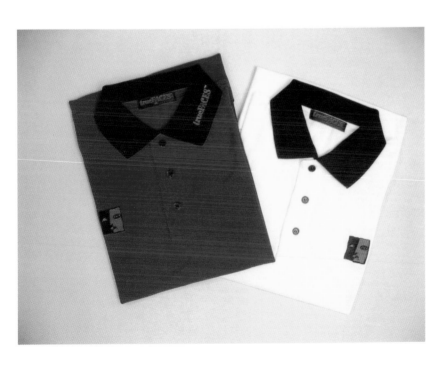

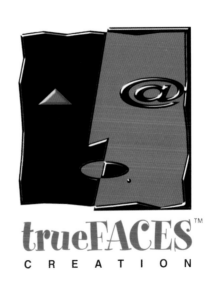

trueFACES™
CREATION

1.

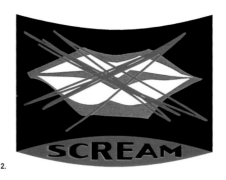

2.

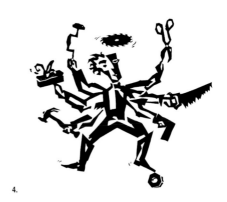

3.

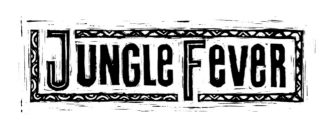

4.

5.

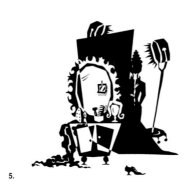

6.

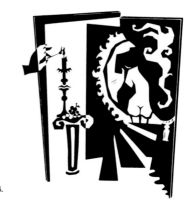

7.

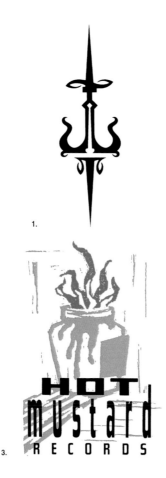

8.

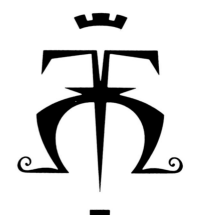

9.

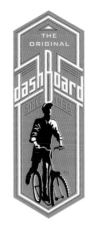

10.

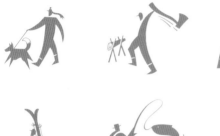

11.

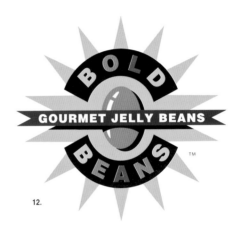

12.

A M E R I C A N

MUSEUM OF QUILTS

& T E X T I L E S

13.

GRILL

14.

Media-
Network

15.

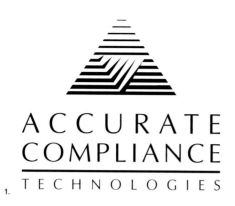

1.

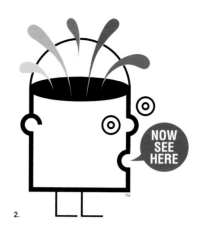

2.

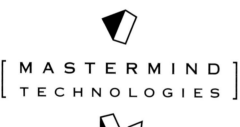

3.

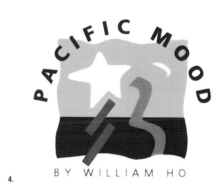

4.

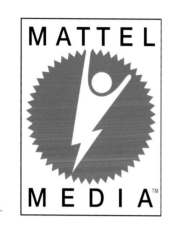

5.

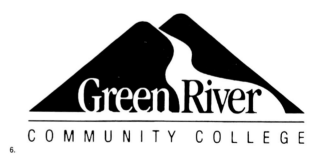

6.

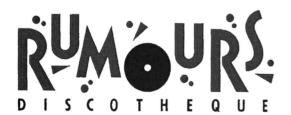

7.

1
Design Firm **GOLD & Associates**
2
Design Firm **Fairly Painless Advertising**
3
Design Firm **B.D. Fox & Friends, Advertising**
4
Design Firm **William Ho Design
Associates Ltd.**
5
Design Firm **Lomangino Studio Inc.**
6, 7
Design Firm **Hansen Design Company**

1.
Client   *Accurate Compliance Technologies*
Designer   Keith Gold

2.
Client   *Miller SQA*
Designers   Steve Frykholm,
              Brian Hauch

3.
Client   *Mattel*
Designer   Garrett Burke

4.
Client   *Pacific Mood*
Designer   William C.K. Ho

5.
Client   *Mastermind Technologies*
Designer   Arthur Hsu

6.
Client   *Green River
              Community College*
Designers   Pat Hansen, Jesse Doquilo

7.
Client   *Rumours Discotheque*
Designers   Pat Hansen, Sheila Schimpf
(opposite)
Client   *jstar Brands*
Design Firm **Cahan & Associates**
Designers   Michael Braley, Bill Cahan,
              Todd Simmons

344

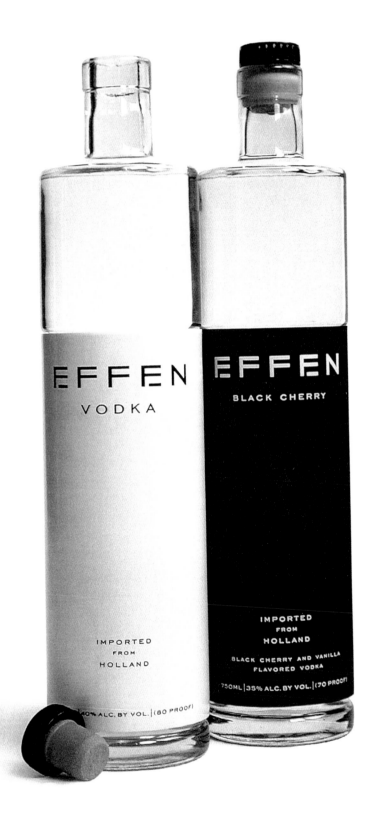

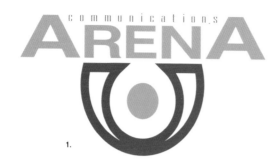

1.

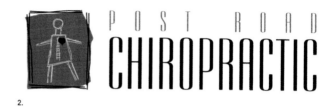

2.

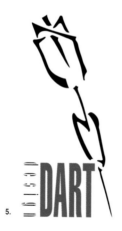

3.

4.

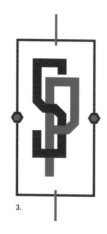

5.

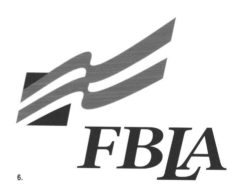

6.

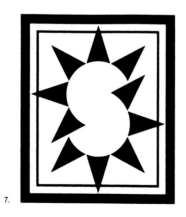

7.

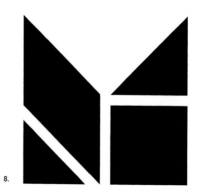

8.

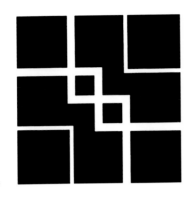

9.

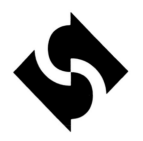

STRATEGIC CONCEPTS
INCORPORATED

10.

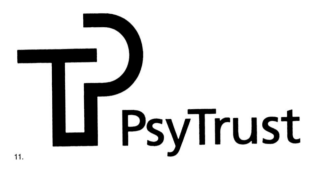PsyTrust

11.

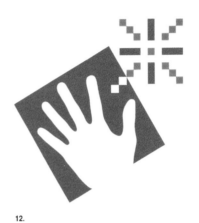

12.

I R S
SERVICE TEAM

13.

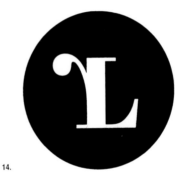

14.

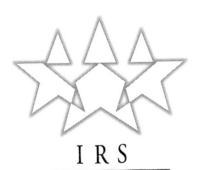

15.

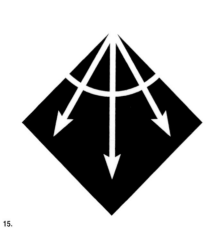

1 - 3, 5
Design Firm **Dart Design**
4
Design Firm **Kendrew Group**
6 - 15
Design Firm **Fuller Designs, Inc.**

1.
Client   *Arena Communications*
Designer   David Anderson

2.
Client   *Post Road Chiropractic*
Designer   David Anderson

3.
Client   *Success Printing*
Designer   David Anderson

4.
Client   *HBO*
Designer   David Anderson-Dart Design

5.
Client   *Dart Design*
Designer   David Anderson

6.
Client   *Future Business Leaders of America*
Designer   Doug Fuller

7.
Client   *Sharp Building Corp.*
Designer   Doug Fuller

8.
Client   *McDonald Management Solutions*
Designer   Doug Fuller

9.
Client   *Integrated Healthcare*
            Arlington Hospital
Designer   Doug Fuller

10.
Client   *Strategic Concepts, Inc.*
Designer   Doug Fuller

11.
Client   *PsyTrust, LLC*
Designer   Doug Fuller

12.
Client   *Florida Entech Corporation*
Designer   Doug Fuller

13.
Client   *Price Waterhouse*
Designer   Doug Fuller

14.
Client   *Regis Lefebure Photography*
Designers   Doug Fuller, Aaron Taylor

15.
Client   *Active Adventures*
Designer   Doug Fuller

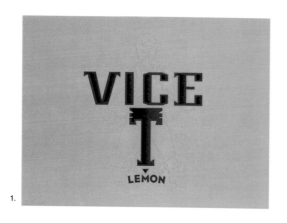

1.

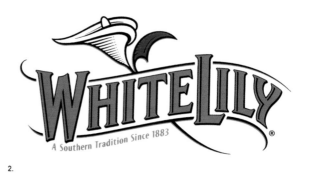

2.

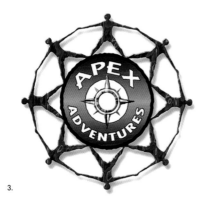

3.

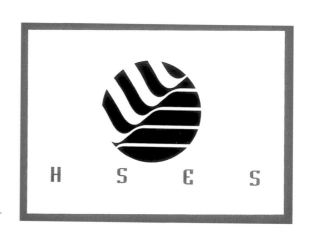
MUSIC & VIDEO

4.

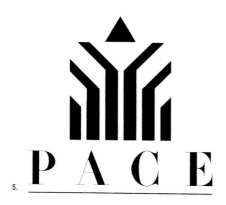
P A C E

5.

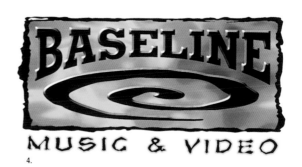
H   S   E   S

6.

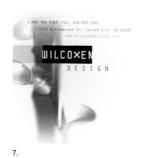

7.

1, 2
Design Firm **Pedersen Gesk**
3, 4
Design Firm **Jefrey Gunion**
Illustration & Design
5, 6
Design Firm **Grizzell & Co.**
7
Design Firm **IE Design + Communications**
1.
Client   *Lincoln Brewing*
Designers Rony Zibara, Roger Remaley
2.
Client   *White Lily*
Designers Rony Zibara, Andrea Williams
3.
Client   *APEX Adventures*
Designer   Jefrey Gunion

4.
Client   *Baseline Music & Video*
Designer   Jefrey Gunion
5.
Client   *Richfield Properties Inc.*
Designer   John H. Grizzell
6.
Client   *HSES*
Designer   John H. Grizzell
7.
Client   *Wilcoxen Design*
Designers Marcie Carson, Cya Nelson
(opposite)
Client   *Golden Triangle Association*
Design Firm **Noble Erickson Inc.**
Designers Jackie Noble,
            Lisa Scheideler

GTΔ

GOLDEN TRIANGLE

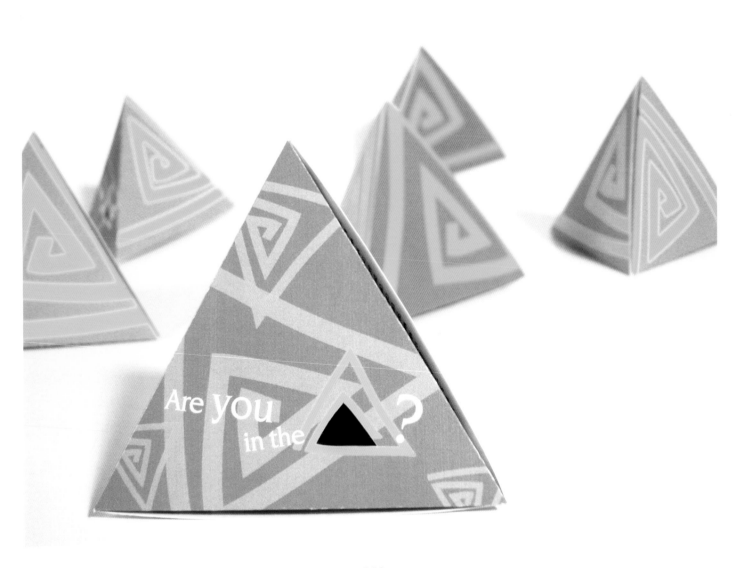

Are **you** in the ◢ ?

HEY ARNOLD! LOGO

Show Logos

Standard Full Color Logo

black
C= 40 M= 40
Y= 40 K= 100

PMS 122c
C= 0 M= 15
Y= 100 K= 0

Black & White Logo

black
C= 40 M= 40
Y= 40 K= 100

white

Full Color Logo on Dark Background

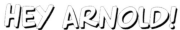

PMS 1795c
C= 10 M= 90
Y=100 K= 0

PMS 122c
C= 0 M= 15
Y= 100 K= 0

Full Color Packaging Logo with Nickelodeon Logo

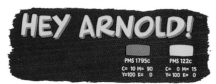

PMS 021c

black
C= 40 M= 40
Y= 40 K= 100

PMS 122c
C= 0 M= 15
Y= 100 K= 0

©

Design Firm **Nickelodeon**
Client *Nickelodeon*

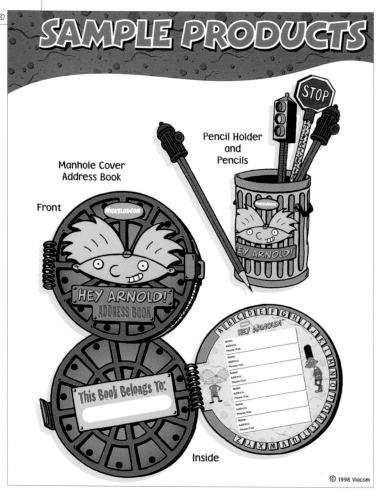

Manhole Cover
Address Book

Front

Pencil Holder
and
Pencils

This Book Belongs To:

Inside

© 1998 Viacom

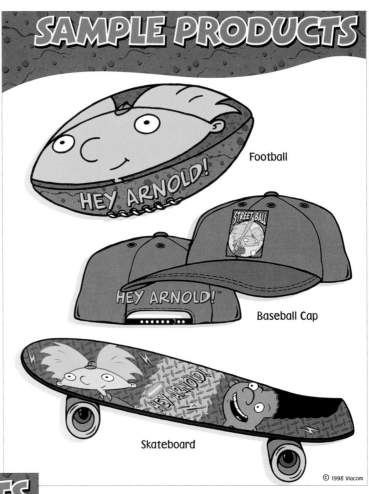

Football

Baseball Cap

Skateboard

© 1998 Viacom

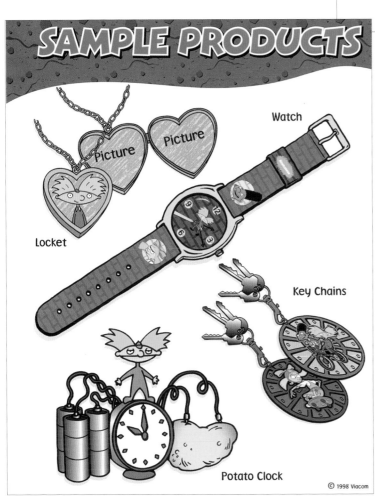

Watch

Picture Picture

Locket

Key Chains

Potato Clock

© 1998 Viacom

351

(continued)
Design Firm **Nickelodeon**
Client *Nickelodeon*

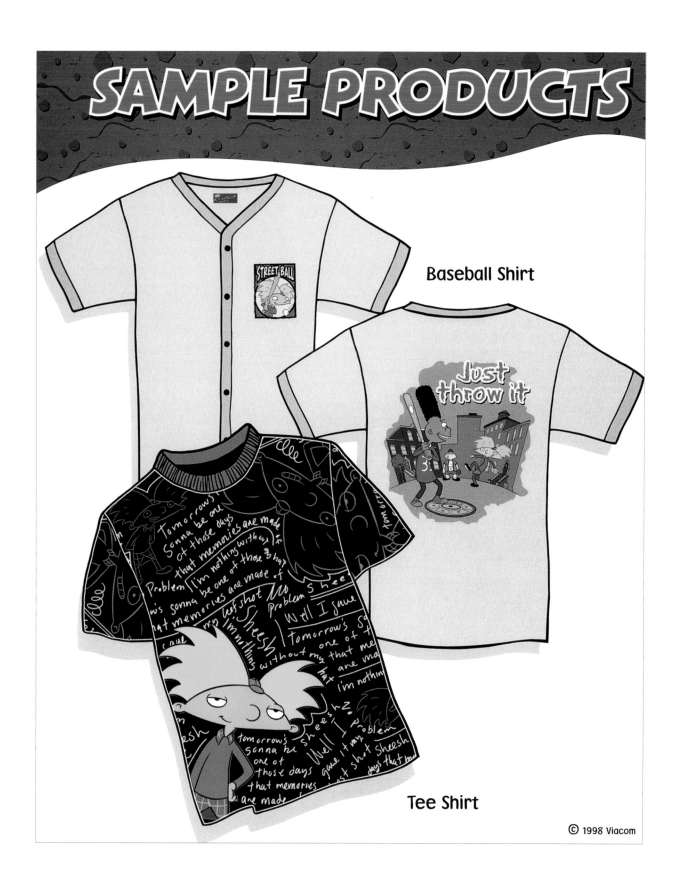

Baseball Shirt

Tee Shirt

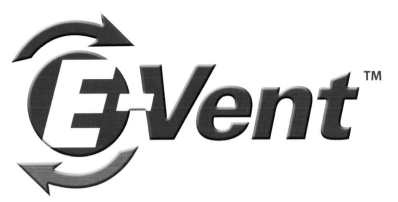

Design Firm **FGA**
Client   *Ecotint (M) Sdn Bhd*
Designers   FGA Creative Team

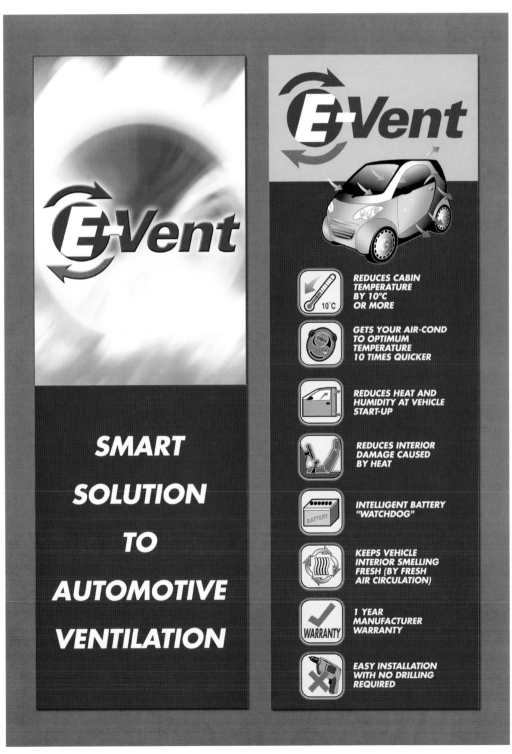

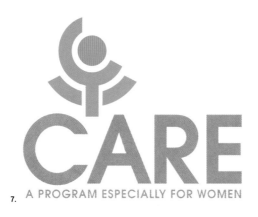

1.

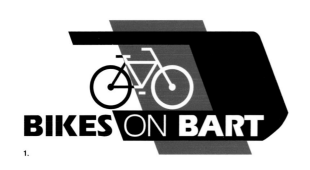

Creative Finds For Creative Minds
University Art

2.

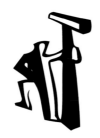

DecisionMaker®

3.

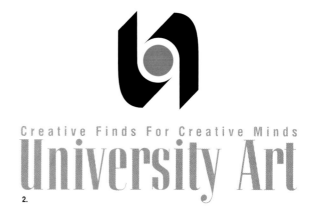

4.

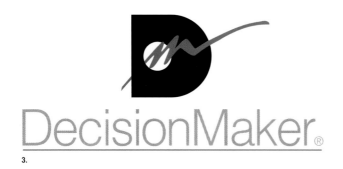

THORENFELDT CONSTRUCTION, INC.

5.

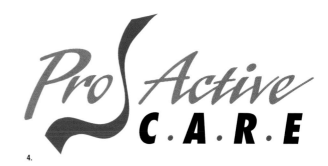

OUTSOURCE, INC.
Fulfillment and Distribution Services

6.

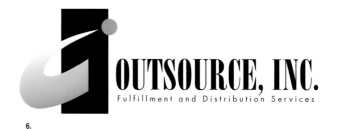

CARE
A PROGRAM ESPECIALLY FOR WOMEN

7.

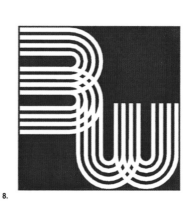

8.

354

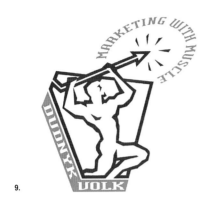

9.

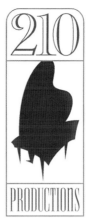

10.

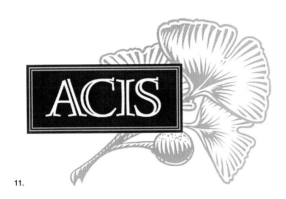

11.

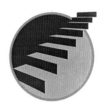

PENNSYLVANIA
EARLY STAGE PARTNERS

12.

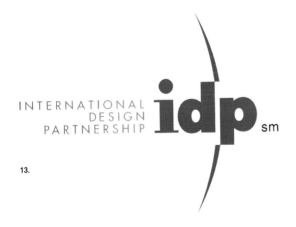

13.

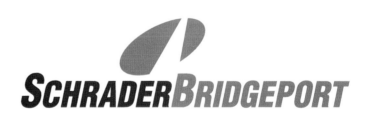

14.

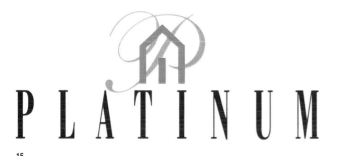

15.

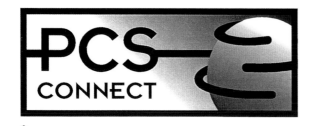

1.

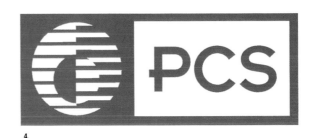

2.

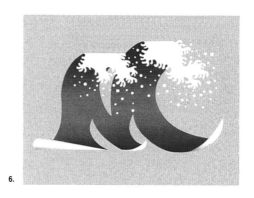

3.

4.

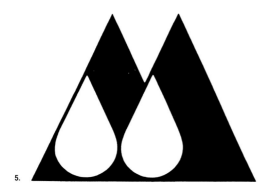

5.

6.

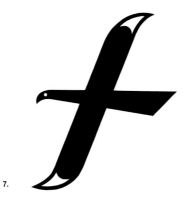

7.

1, 2
Design Firm **Rousso+Associates, Inc.**
3, 4
Design Firm **Torrisi Design Associates, Inc.**
5 - 7
Design Firm **Minoru Morita Graphic Design**
1.
   Client   *The Melamine Corporation*
   Designer   Steven B. Rousso
2.
   Client   *Taylor Mathis*
   Designer   Steven B. Rousso
3.
   Client   *PCS Connect*
4.
   Client   *Primary Consulting Services*

5.
   Client   *Design M*
   Designer   Minoru Morita
6.
   Client   *M Studio*
   Designer   Minoru Morita
7.
   Client   *Forgerty Family*
   Designer   Minoru Morita
(opposite)
   Client   *Retina Consultants of*
              Southwest Florida
   Design Firm **Cave**
   Designers   David Edmundson,
                Matt Cave

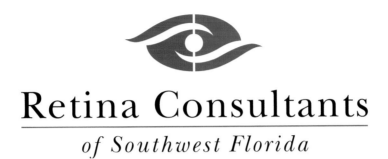

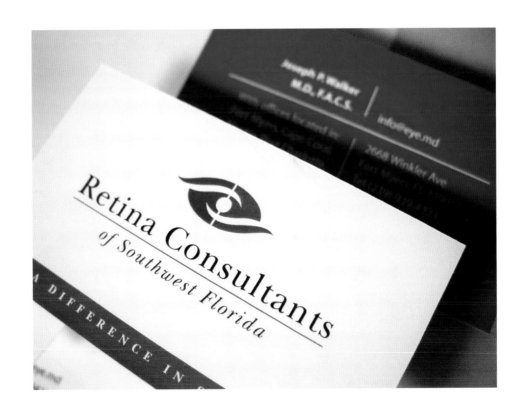

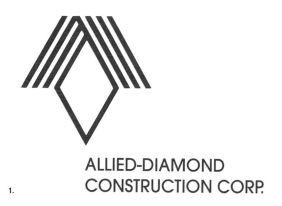

ALLIED-DIAMOND
CONSTRUCTION CORP.

1.

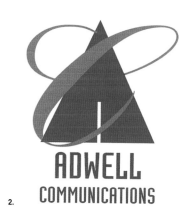

ADWELL
COMMUNICATIONS

2.

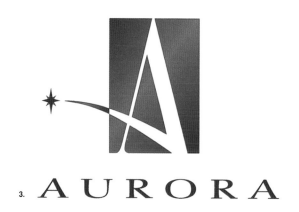

AURORA

3.

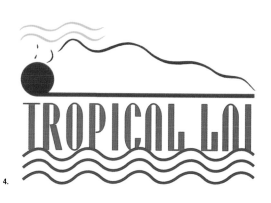

TROPICAL LAI

4.

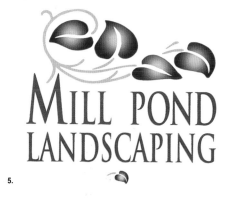

MILL POND
LANDSCAPING

5.

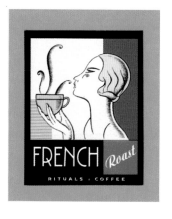

FRENCH Roast
RITUALS · COFFEE

6.

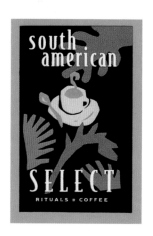

south american

SELECT
RITUALS · COFFEE

7.

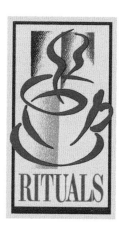

RITUALS

8.

HARBOR

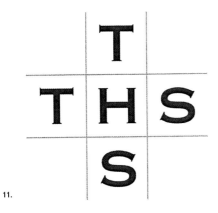

BANKS

9.

10. 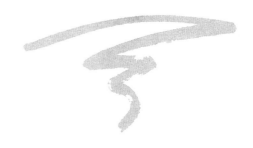 **Tecton**Architects | pc

11.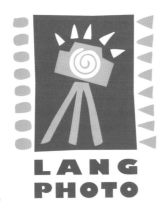
T
T H S
S

12.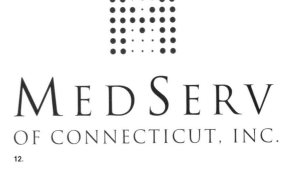
MEDSERV
OF CONNECTICUT, INC.

13.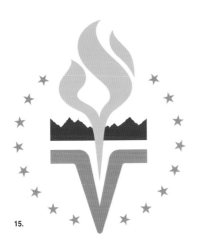
LANG
PHOTO

14.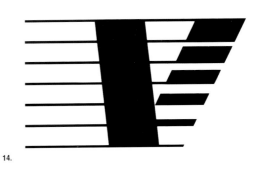

15.

1 - 5
Design Firm **Guarino Graphics, Ltd.**
6 - 9
Design Firm **Callahan and Company**
10 - 13
Design Firm **Ritz Henton Design Group**
14, 15
Design Firm **Robert W. Taylor Design, Inc.**
1.
 Client   *Allied Diamond Construction*
 Designer Jan Guarino
2.
 Client   *Adwell Communications*
 Designer Jan Guarino
3.
 Client   *Aurora Productions*
 Designer Jan Guarino
4.
 Client   *The Three Musketeers*
 Designer Jan Guarino

5.
 Client   *Mill Pond Landscaping*
 Designer Jan Guarino
6, 7.
 Client   *Rituals Coffee*
 Designers Paula Sloane, Jonathan Carlson
8, 9.
 Client   *JP Foodservice*
 Designer Paula Sloane
10.
 Client   *Tecton Architects, P.C.*
11.
 Client   *Total Healthcare Solutions, Inc.*
12.
 Client   *MedServ of Connecticut, Inc.*
13.
 Client   *Lang Photography*
14.
 Client   *Valleylab, Inc.*
 Designer Robert W. Taylor
15.
 Client   *Colorado Sports Hall of Fame*
 Designers Robert W. Taylor,
       Gwyn VanderVorste

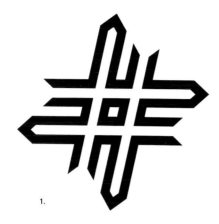

1.

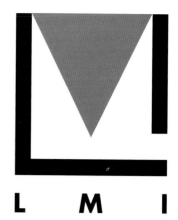

2. **L M I**

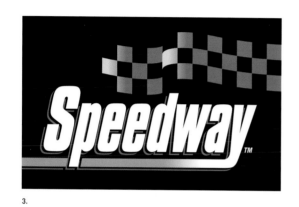

3.

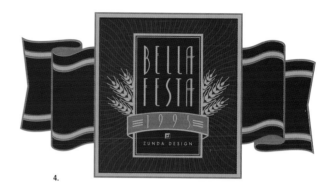

4.

SINGAPORE
INNOVATES

5.

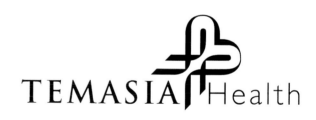

TEMASIA Health

6.

7.

1
Design Firm **Robert W. Taylor Design, Inc.**
2 - 4
Design Firm **Zunda Design Group**
5 - 7
Design Firm **Design Objectives Pte Ltd**

1.
Client   *Center for International
        Trade Development*
Designer Robert W. Taylor

2.
Client   *Liebhardt Mills, Inc.*
Designer Charles Zunda

3.
Client   *USA Detergents*
Designer Todd Nickel

4.
Client   *Zunda Design Group*
Designers Todd Nickel, Charles Zunda

5.
Client   *Singapore Economic
        Development Board*
Designer Ronnie S C Tan

6.
Client   *Temasia Health Pte Ltd*
Designer Ronnie S C Tan

7.
Client   *Lee Hwa Jewellery Pte Ltd*
Designer Ronnie S C Tan

(opposite)
Client   *Southern Specialties*
Design Firm **Cave**
Designers David Edmundson,
          Matt Cave

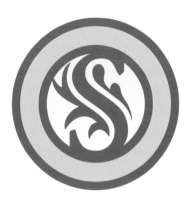

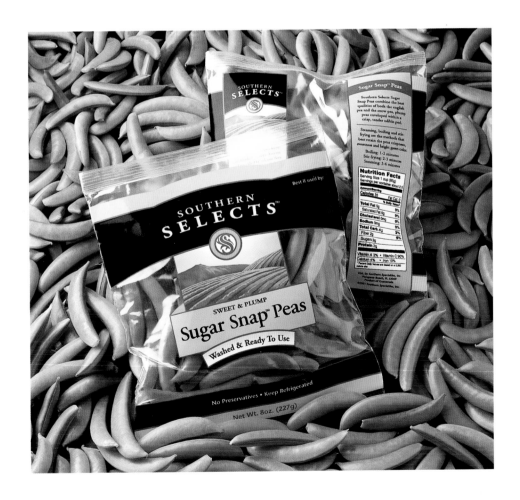

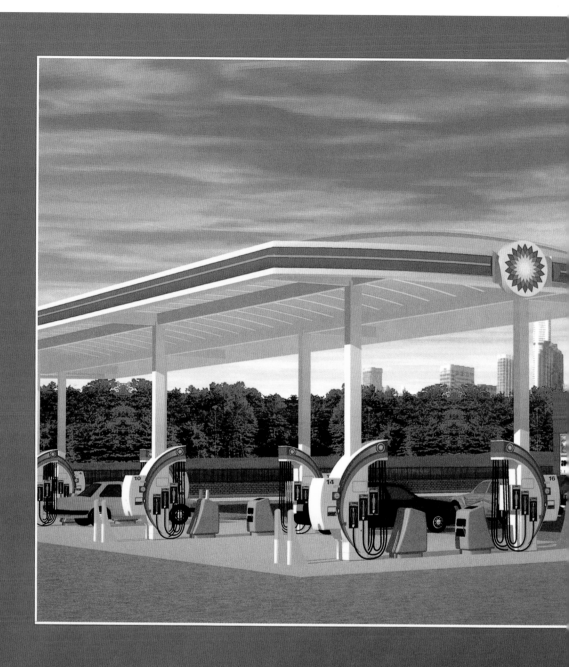

our new look

Our new identity stands for the essence of our company – it is a graphic representation of our core values. In a sense, our identity is a promise to customers, investors, competitors and the rest of our worldwide audience. It pledges that we will strive to act and communicate in an energetic, forthright and forward-thinking way in everything we do. As we show this new face to the world, we send a clear message: BP is leading the changes taking place in our industry. Our striking new look reflects the bold steps we're taking in every area, from technology to exploration to environmental protection. And this is just the beginning.

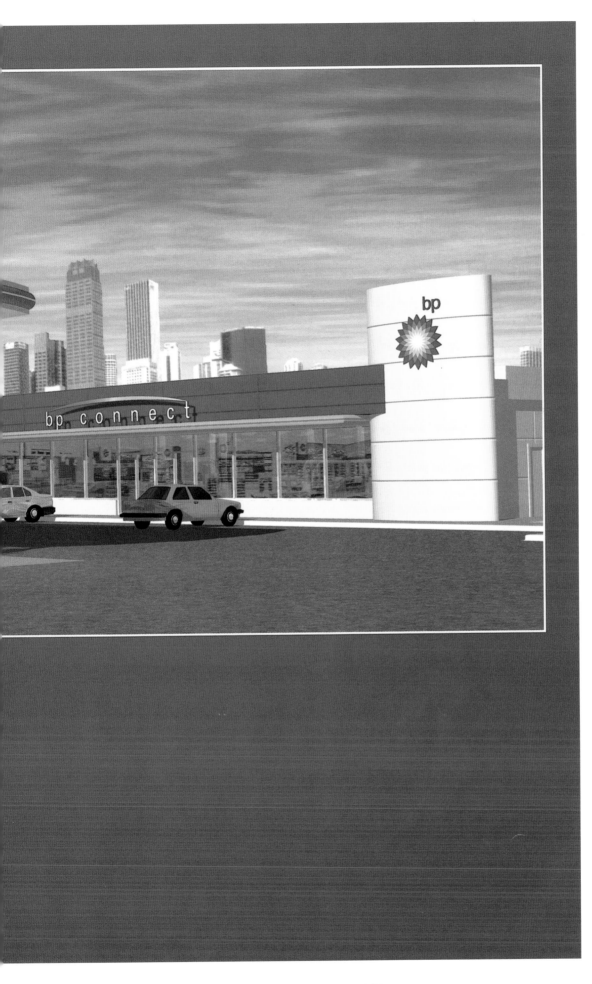

Design Firm **Landor Associates**
Client   *BP Amoco*
Designers Margaret Youngblood,
          Nancy Hoefig,
          Courtney Reeser,
          Peter Harleman,
          David Zapata,
          Brad Scott,
          Cynthia Murnane,
          Todd True,
          Frank Mueller,
          Michele Berry,
          Cameron Imani,
          Ivan Thelin,
          Ladd Woodland,
          Maria Wenzel,
          Jane Bailey,
          Susan Manning,
          Wendy Gold,
          Greg Barnell,
          Stephen Lapaz,
          Bryan Vincent,
          Russell DeHaven

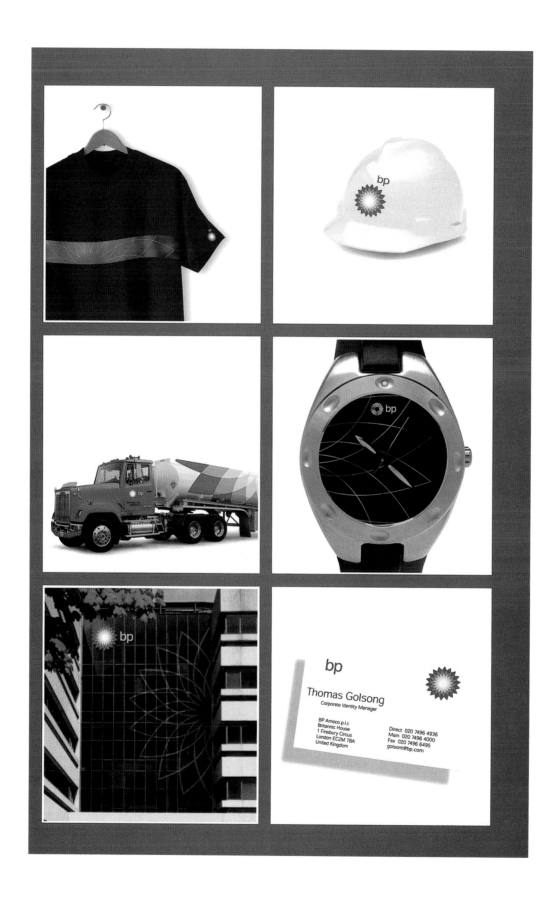

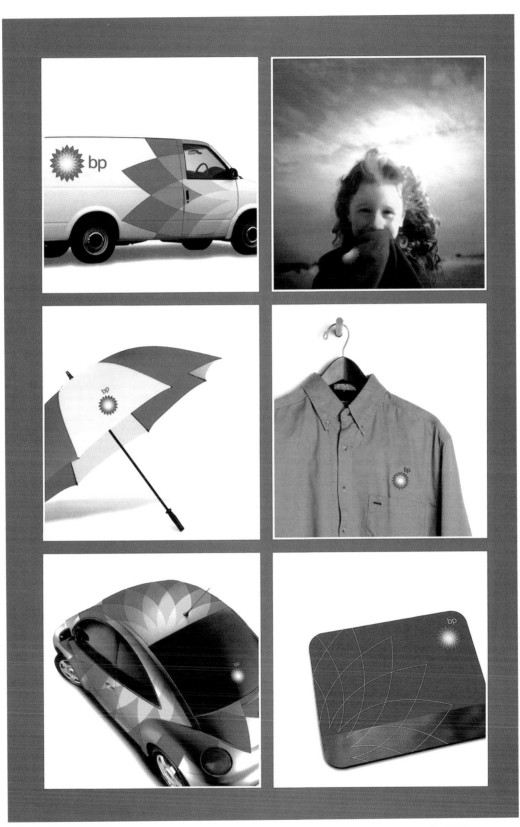

(continued)
Design Firm **Landor Associates**
Client   *BP Amoco*

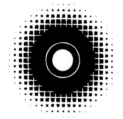

1.

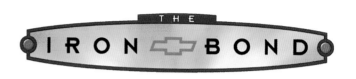

2.

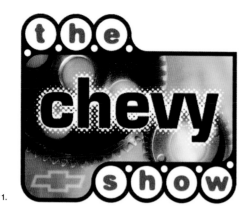

3.

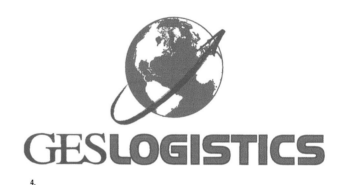

4.

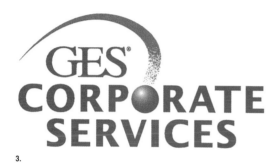

5.

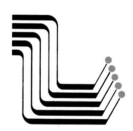

6. LITESOM CORPORATION

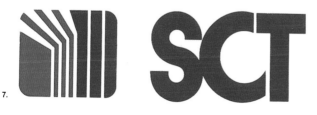

7.

1 - 5
Design Firm **Tieken Design**
& Creative Services
6, 7
Design Firm **The Corporate Identity People**
1.
Client   *Graham Associated Advertising*
Designers   Fred E. Tieken,
      Rik Boberg
2.
Client   *Graham Associated Advertising*
Designers   Fred E. Tieken,
      Sarah Spencer
3.
Client   *GES Exposition Services*
Designers   Fred E. Tieken
4.
Client   *GES Exposition Services*
Designers   Fred E. Tieken,
      Sarah Spencer
5.
Client   *PhotosOnCD*
Designers   Fred E. Tieken

6.
Client   *Litesom Corporation*
Designer   Joseph Finisdore
7.
Client   *SCT-Systems*
      & Computer Technology
Designer   Joseph Finisdore
(opposite)
Client   *Palermo's*
Design Firm **Design North, Inc.**

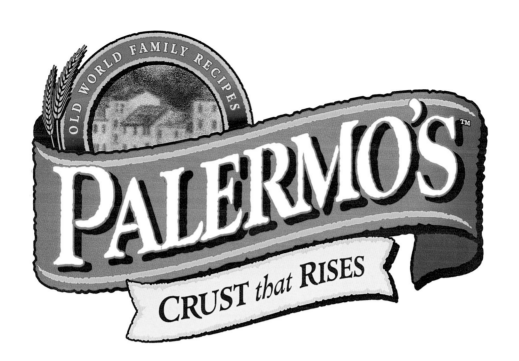

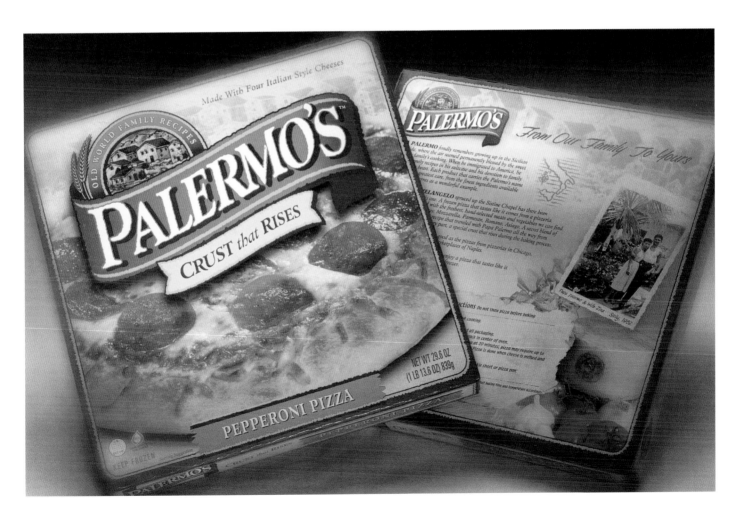

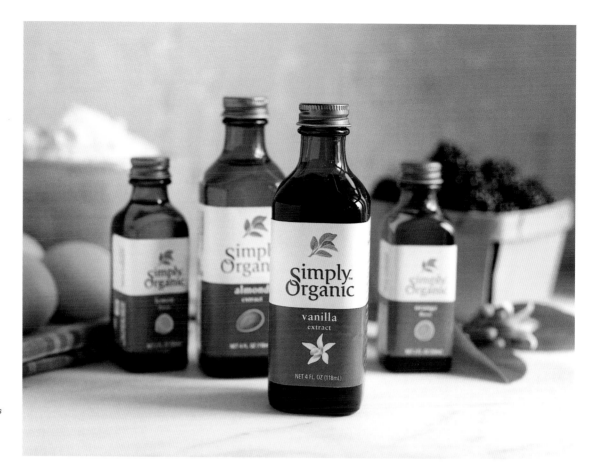

Design Firm **Be Design**
Client   *Frontier Natural Products*
Designers   Eric Read,
            Suzanne Hadden,
            Monica Vallejos,
            Will Burke

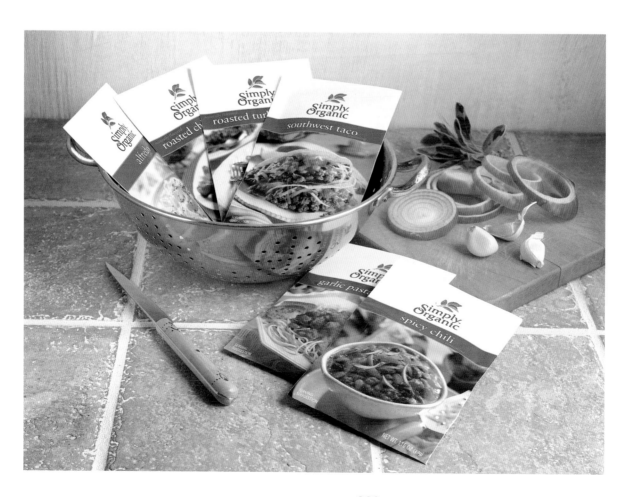

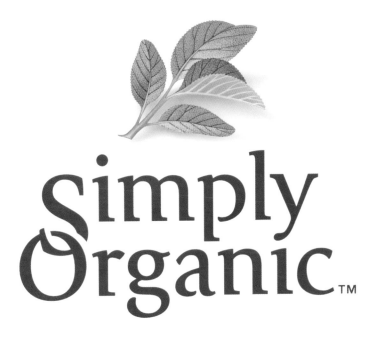

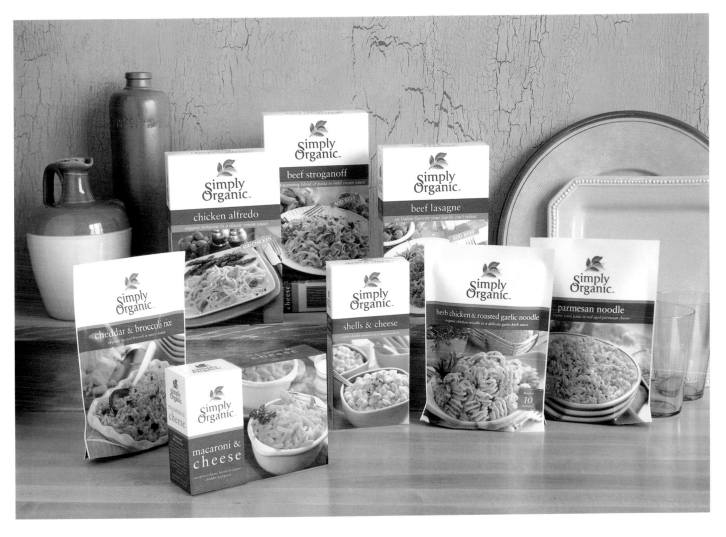

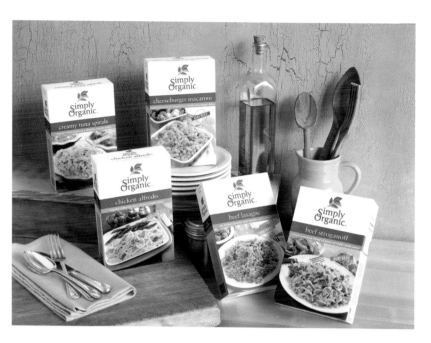

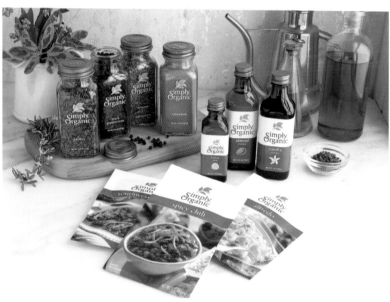

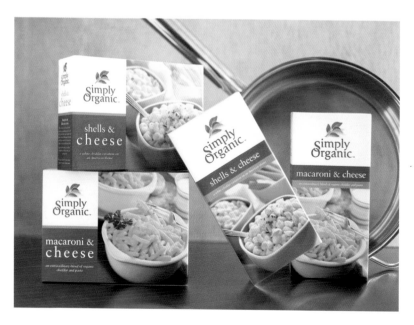

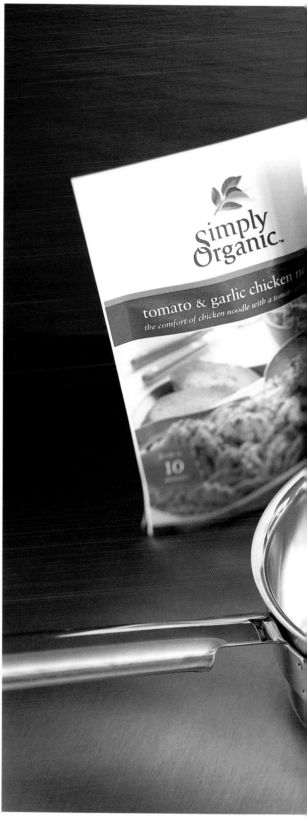

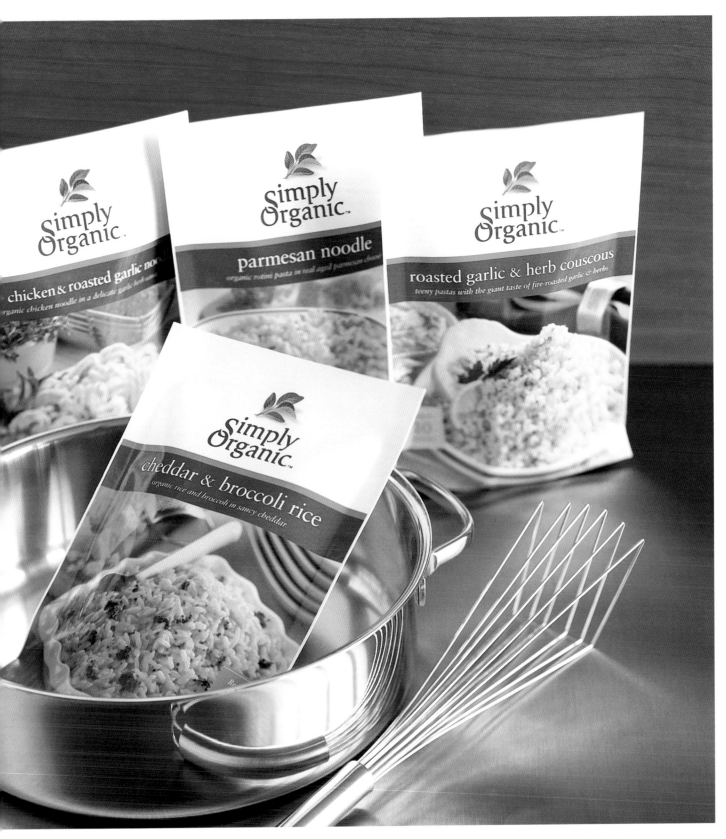

(continued)
Design Firm **Be Design**
Client *Frontier Natural Products*

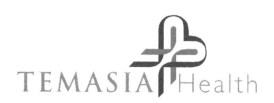

1.

YANGTZE COUNCIL

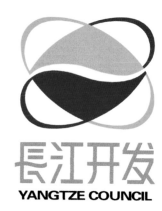

2.

4.

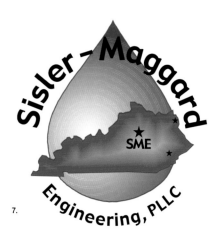

3.

CALIFORNIA

STAR OAK

PRIVATE RESERVE

alcohol 12.5% by volume

2001 CABERNET SAUVIGNON

5.

 SuzyPress agency

6.

Sisler-Maggard

SME

Engineering, PLLC

7.

1
    Design Firm **Design Objectives Pte Ltd**
2 - 4
    Design Firm **Kinggraphic**
5
    Design Firm **Will Winston Design**
6
    Design Firm **Mikael T. Zielinski**
7
    Design Firm **Designs On You!**

1.
Client   *Temasia Health Pte Ltd*
Designer   Ronnie S.C, Tan

2.
Client   *Shanghai-Hong Kong Council for the Promotion & Development of Yangtze*
Designer   Hon Bing-wah

3.
Client   *Sino Group*
Designer   Hon Bing-wah

4.
Client   *Far East Organization*
Designer   Hon Bing-wah

5.
Client   *Prince Michel/Kroger*
Designer   Will Casserly

6.
Client   *SuzyPress Agency*
Designer   Mikael T. Zielinski

7.
Client   *Sisler-Maggard Engineering, PLLC*
Designers   Suzanna Stephens, Anthony B. Stephens

(opposite)
Client   *Pekoe Siphouse*
Design Firm **Be Design**
Designers   Monica Schlaug, Will Burke

pekoe

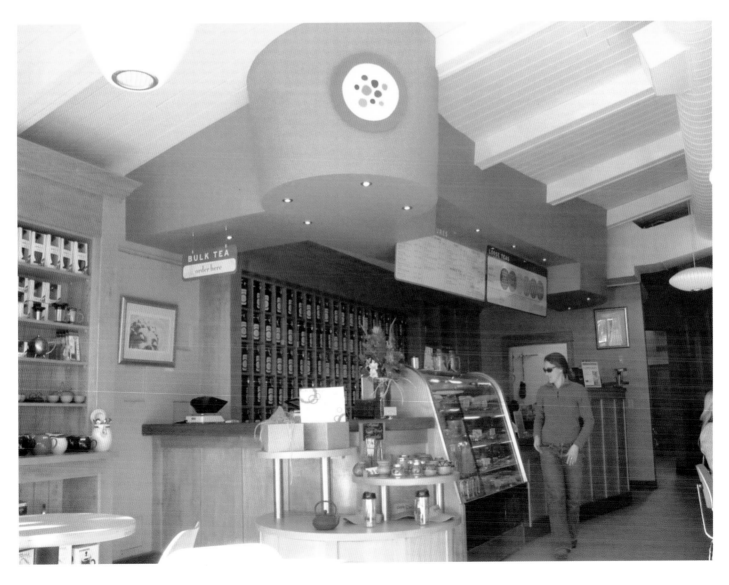

Design Firm **FutureBrand**
Client *UPS*
Designers Claude Salzberger,
Sven Seger,
Diego Kolsky,
Michael Thibodeau,
Alan Campbell,
Marco Acevedo,
Michael Matthews,
Marie Schabenbeck,
Mike Sheehan,
Phil Rojas,
Tom Li

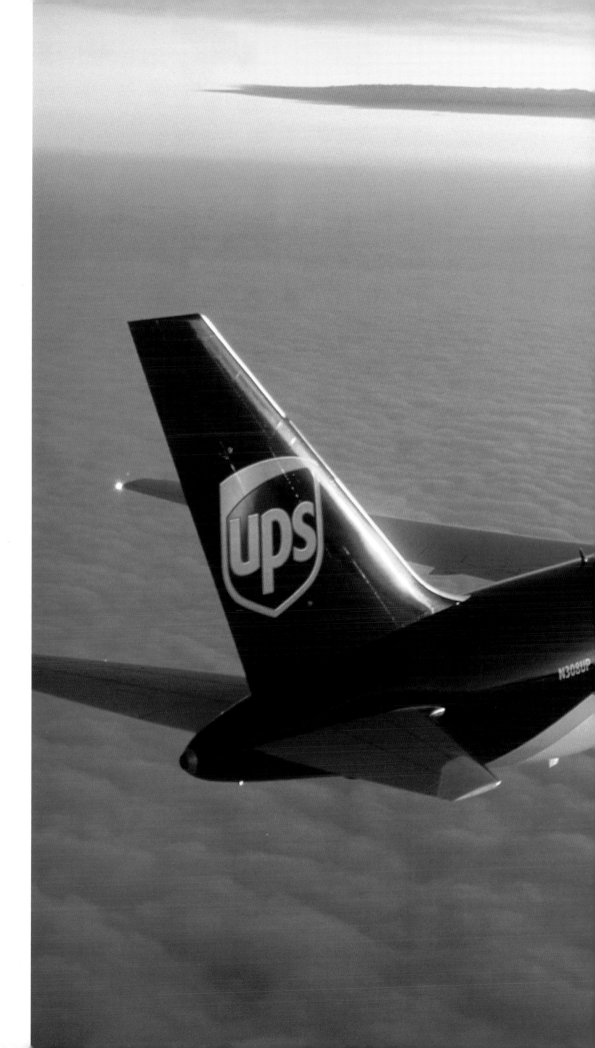

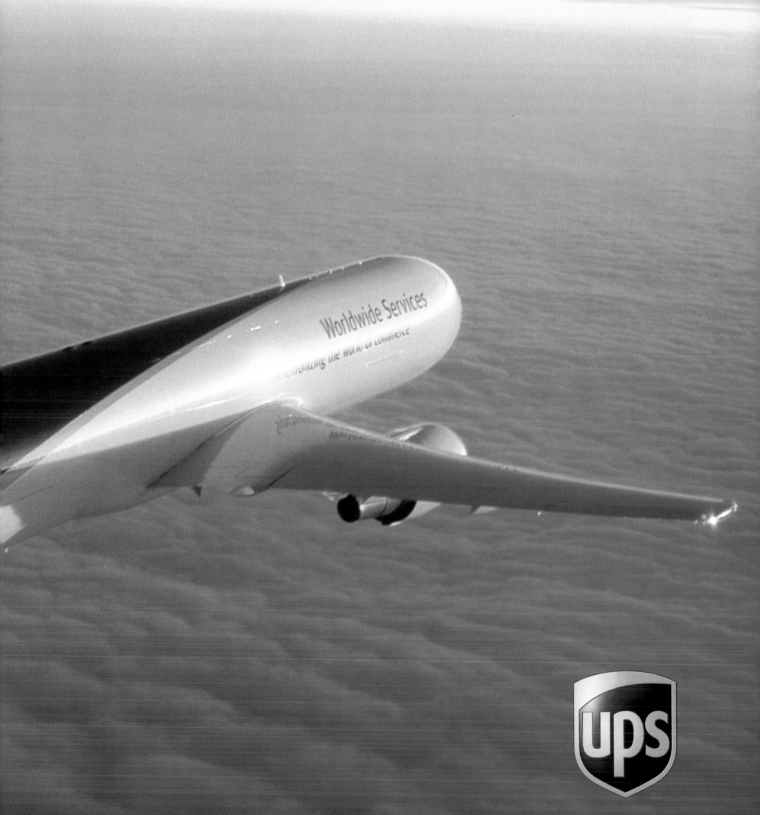

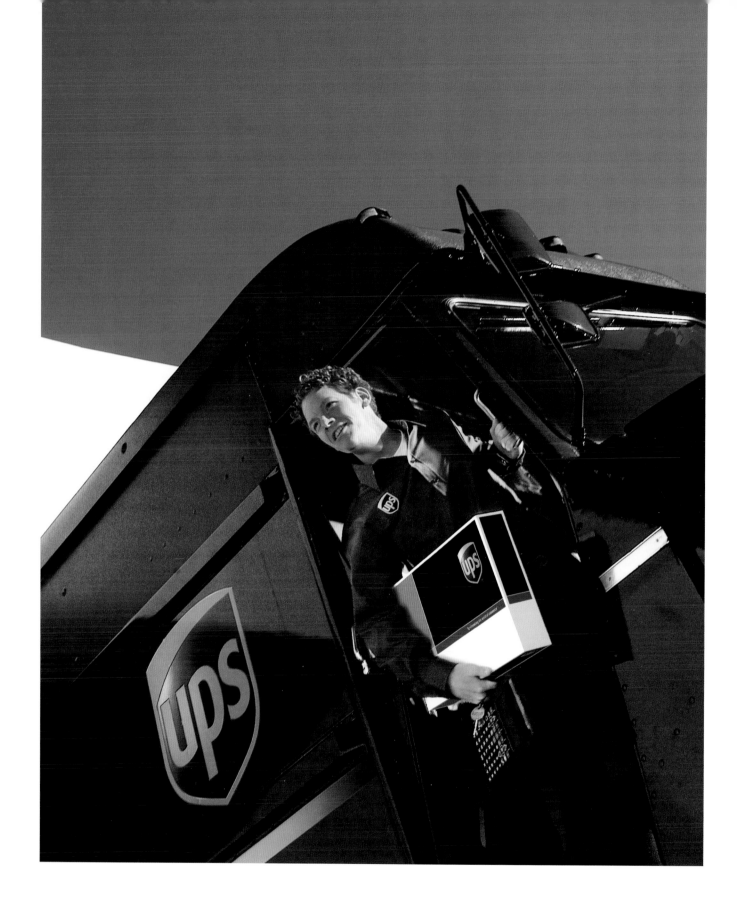

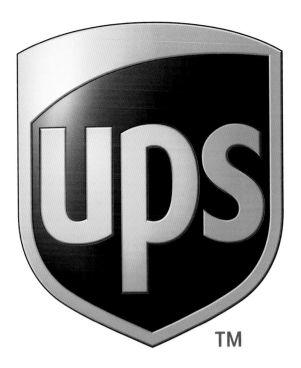

TM

(continued)
Design Firm **FutureBrand**
Client *UPS*

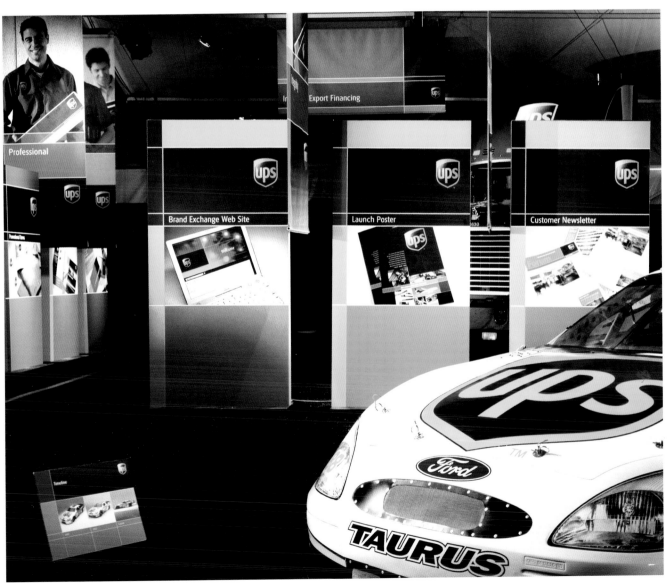

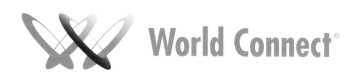

1.

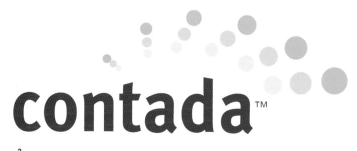

2.

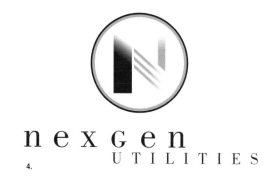

3.

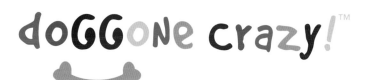

4.

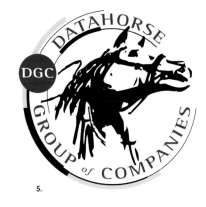

5.

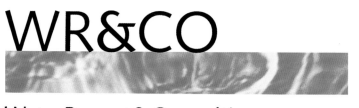

6.

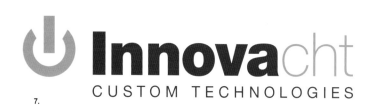

7.

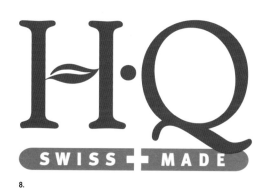

8.

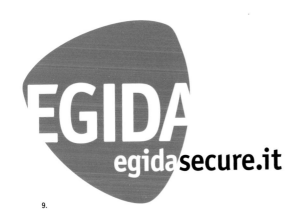

9.

CAMERA DI COMMERCIO
INDUSTRIA ARTIGIANATO AGRICOLTURA
DI VICENZA

10.

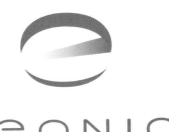

eyeonics™
evolving vision

11.

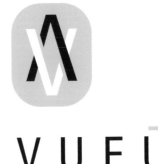

ADVUEŪ
YOUR WORLD, YOUR VIEW

12.

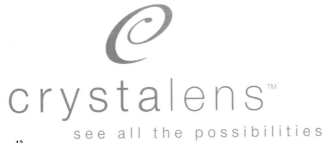

crystalens™
see all the possibilities

13.

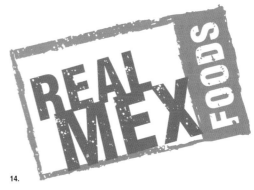

14.

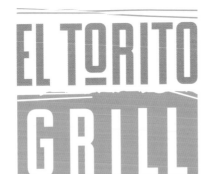

15.

1 - 5		
Design Firm	**Provoq Inc.**	
6 - 10		
Design Firm	**Tangram Strategic Design**	
11 - 15		
Design Firm	**Perceive**	
1.		
Client	*World Connect Inc.*	
Designer	Jeffrey Chow	
2.		
Client	*World Connect Inc.*	
Designer	Jeffrey Chow	
3.		
Client	*Doggone Crazy*	
Designer	Jeffrey Chow	
4.		
Client	*Nexgen Utilities*	
Designer	Jeffrey Chow	
5.		
Client	*Datahorse Group of Companies*	
Designer	Jeffrey Chow	
6.		
Client	*WaterReport & Consulting*	
Designers	Enrico Sempi, Andrea Sempi	
7.		
Client	*Innova*	
Designers	Enrico Sempi, Andrea Sempi	

8.		
Client	*Paglieri Sell System*	
Designers	Enrico Sempi, Antonella Trevisan	
9.		
Client	*Telecom & Capital Express*	
Designers	Enrico Sempi, Gianluca Barbero	
10.		
Client	*Camera di Commercio I.A.A. di Vicenza*	
Designers	Enrico Sempi, Antonella Trevisan, Guido Rosa	
11.		
Client	*Eyeonics*	
Designer	Ann Marie Siciliano	
12.		
Client	*Advueu*	
Designer	Jason Simon	
13.		
Client	*Crystalens*	
Designer	Christine McClain	
14.		
Client	*Real Mex Foods*	
Designer	Christine McClain	
15.		
Client	*El Torito*	
Designer	Ann Marie Siciliano	

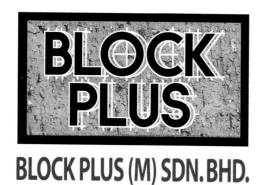

BLOCK PLUS (M) SDN. BHD.

1.

iju|inštitutzajavnoupravo

2.

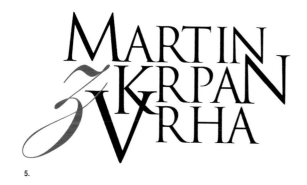

3.

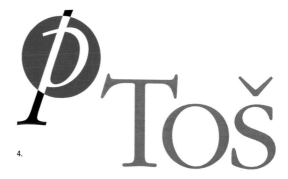

4.

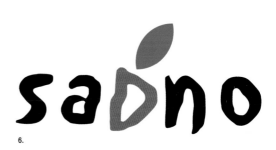

6.

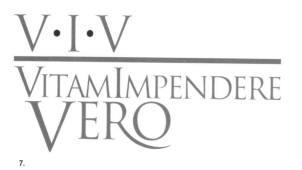

5.

V · I · V

VitamImpendere
VERO

7.

1
Design Firm **FIXGO ADVERTISING**
        (M) SDN BHD
2 - 7
Design Firm **KROG**
1.
  Client   *Block Plus (M) Sdn Bhd*
  Designers *FGA Creative Team*
2.
  Client   *Institut za javno upravo, Ljubljana*
  Designer   *Edi Berk*
3.
  Client   *Institut za primerjalno*
            pravo, Ljubljana
  Designer   *Edi Berk*
4.
  Client   *Peter Tos, Ljubljana*
  Designer   *Edi Berk*

5.
  Client   *Presernova druzba, Ljubljana*
  Designer   *Edi Berk*
6.
  Client   *Zlati gric, Slovenske Konjice*
  Designer   *Edi Berk*
7.
  Client   *Pravna fakulteta, Ljubljana*
  Designer   *Edi Berk*
(opposite)
  Client   *A&P Canada*
  Design Firm **LogosBrands**
  Designers *Gabriella Sousa,*
            Sunny Chan

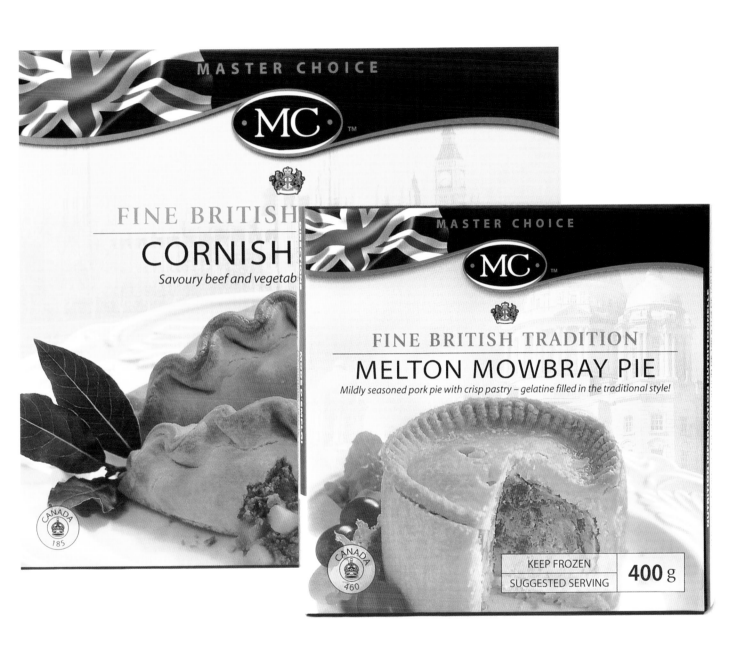

MASTER CHOICE

MC ™

FINE BRITISH

CORNISH

Savoury beef and vegetab

CANADA 185

MASTER CHOICE

MC ™

FINE BRITISH TRADITION

MELTON MOWBRAY PIE

Mildly seasoned pork pie with crisp pastry – gelatine filled in the traditional style!

CANADA 460

| KEEP FROZEN | 400 g |
| SUGGESTED SERVING | |

OHANA FARM

1.

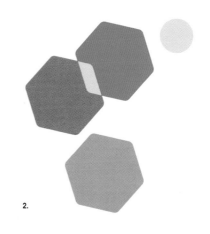

2.

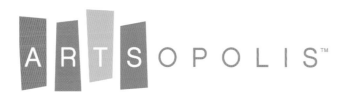

3.

James
Phillip
Wright Architects

4.

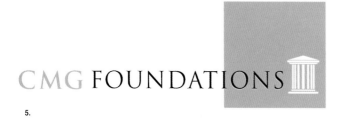

5.

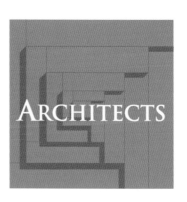

6.

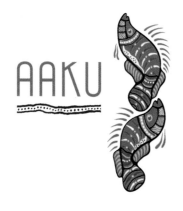

7.

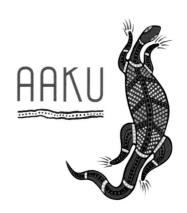

8.

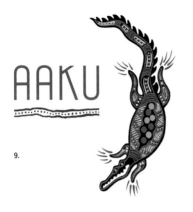

9.

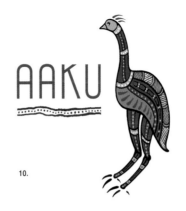

10.

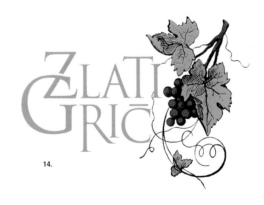

11.

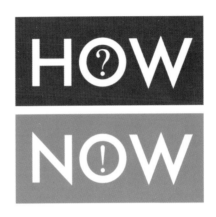

12.

S K Y L A R
+
H A L E Y

13.

ZLATI
GRIC

14.

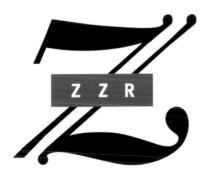

ZZR

15.

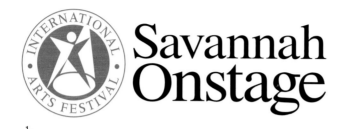

1.

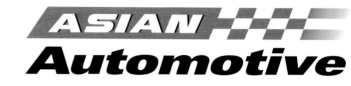

2.

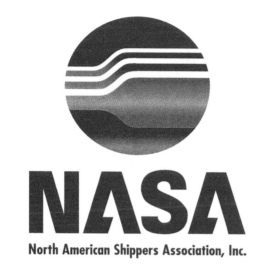

North American Shippers Association, Inc.

3.

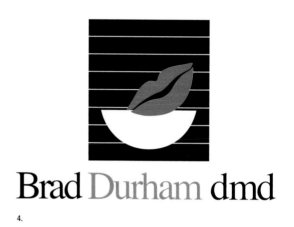

Brad Durham dmd

4.

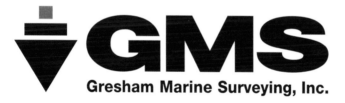

Gresham Marine Surveying, Inc.

5.

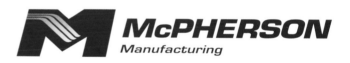

McPHERSON Manufacturing

6.

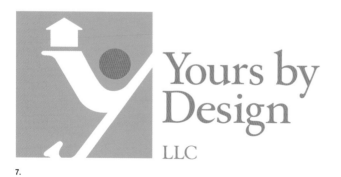

7.

1 - 7
Design Firm **Longwater & Co., Inc.**

1.
Client — *Savannah Onstage*
Designers — Kathryn Strozier,
Elaine Longwater,
Anastasia Kontos

2.
Client — *Asian Automotive*
Designers — Kathryn Strozier,
Elaine Longwater,
Anastasia Kontos

3.
Client — *North American
Shippers Association*
Designers — Kathryn Strozier,
Elaine Longwater,
Anastasia Kontos

4.
Client — *Brad Durham, DMD*
Designers — Kathryn Strozier,
Elaine Longwater,
Anastasia Kontos

5.
Client — *Gresham Marine
Surveying, Inc.*
Designers — Kathryn Strozier,
Elaine Longwater,
Anastasia Kontos

6.
Client — *McPherson Manufacturing*
Designers — Kathryn Strozier,
Elaine Longwater,
Anastasia Kontos

7.
Client — *Yours By Design, LLC*
Designers — Kathryn Strozier,
Elaine Longwater,
Anastasia Kontos

(opposite)
Client — *Ruffin' It Pet Supplies*
Design Firm **Designs On You!**
Designers — Anthony B. Stephens,
Suzanna Stephens,

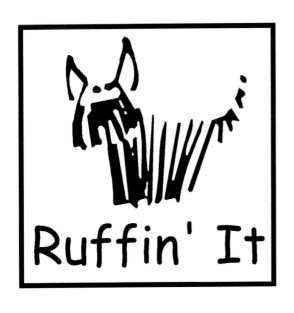

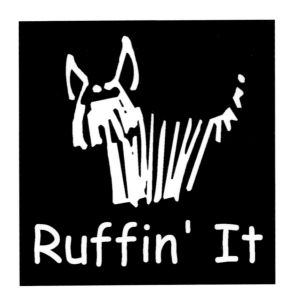

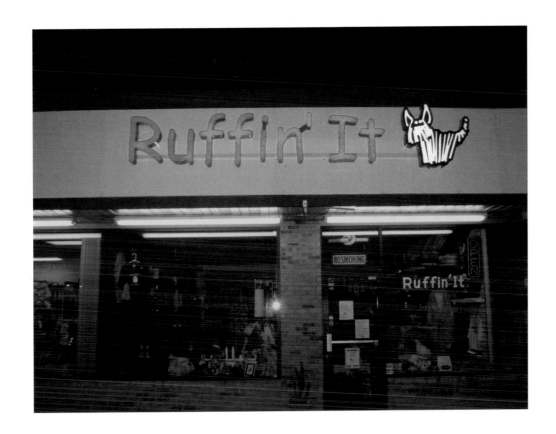

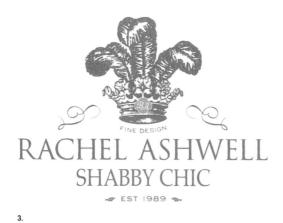

1.

CODE**C**ORRECT

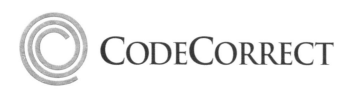

Stone Barns Center
for Food & Agriculture

2.

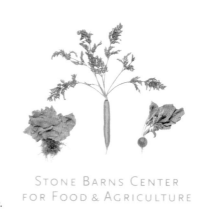

RACHEL ASHWELL
SHABBY CHIC
EST 1989

3.

COLOR PRESERVE™

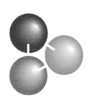

4.

5.

SENSA

6.

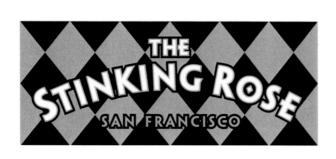

7.

8.

386

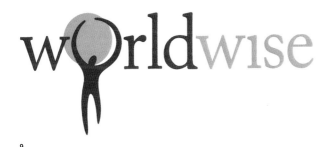

9.

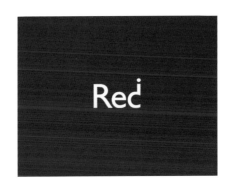

10.

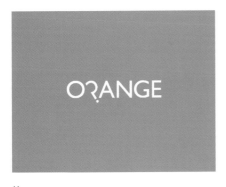

11.

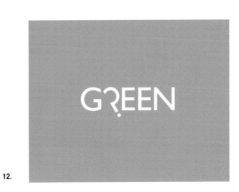

12.

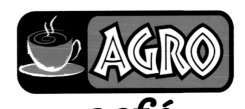

13.

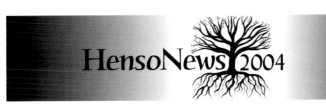

15.

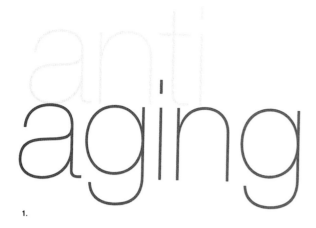

1.

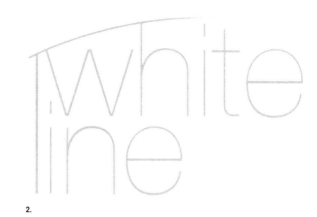

2.

LBI Unfallforschung

3.

viewpointsystem

4.

RESOLUTION
L I N E

5.

vogel&NOLL
verlag

6.

Brüd3r

7.

1 - 7
Design Firm **designbuero**
1, 2.
Client   *Dr. Temt Laboratories*
Designer   Thomas Stockhammer
3.
Client   *LBI Unfallforschung*
Designer   Thomas Stockhammer
4.
Client   *view point system*
Designer   Thomas Stockhammer
5.
Client   *Dr. Temt Laboratories*
Designer   Thomas Stockhammer
6, 7.
Client   *DOR Film*
Designer   Thomas Stockhammer

(opposite)
Client   *Cedar Bluff Middle School*
             Talented and Gifted Group
Design Firm **Designs On You!**
Designers Suzanna Stephens,
              Anthony B. Stephens

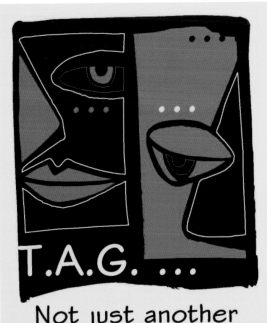

Not just another
pretty face!

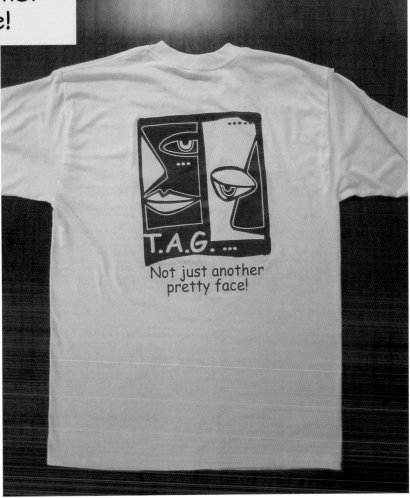

**Verizon:
Start-Up Standards**

Verizon Logo Key Applications

▶ Detailed specifications for specific key applications of the logo are being developed and are available through the Corporate Identity Manager.

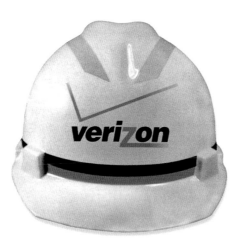

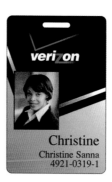

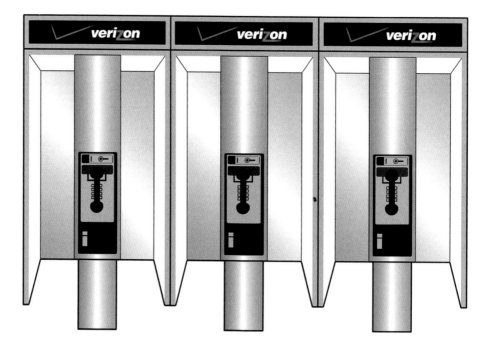

V.3.0 (06/23/00)

► Detailed specifications for fleet graphics are being developed and are available through the Corporate Identity Manager.

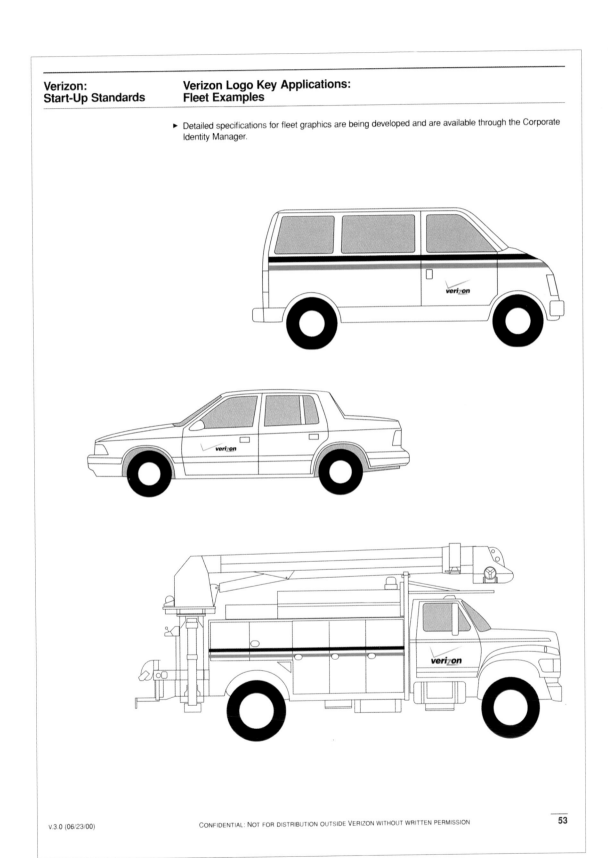

391

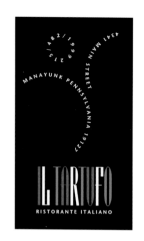

1.

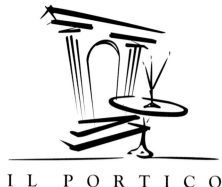

IL PORTICO

2. RISTORANTE ITALIANO

3.

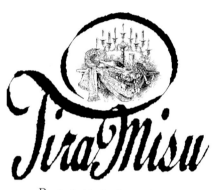

4.

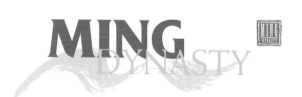

5.

6.

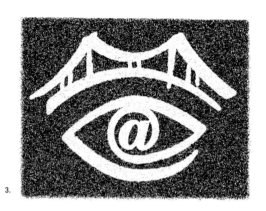

7.

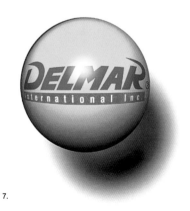

1 - 4
Design Firm **Zygo Communications**
5 - 7
Design Firm **66 communication inc.**
1.
   Client   *IL Tartufo*
   Designer Scott Laserow
2.
   Client   *IL Portico*
   Designer Scott Laserow
3.
   Client   *MindBridge*
   Designer Scott Laserow
4.
   Client   *TiraMisu*
   Designer Scott Laserow
5.
   Client   *Infinity Industries Inc.*
   Designer Chin C. Yang

6.
   Client   *Deco Enterprise Co., Ltd.*
   Designer Chin C. Yang
7.
   Client   *Delmar International Inc.*
   Designer Chin C. Yang
(opposite)
   Client   *CompanyB, Inc.*
   Design Firm **Finished Art, Inc.**
   Designers Donna Johnston, Kannex Fung,
               Barbara Dorn, Luis Fernandez,
               Li-Kim Goh, Mary Jane Hasek,
               Cory Langner, Ake Nimsuwan,
               Larry Peebles, Anne Vongnimitra

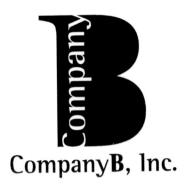

CompanyB, Inc.

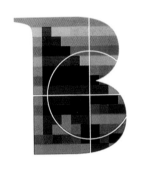

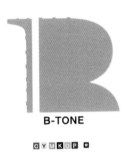

B-TONE

C Y M K O P ▪

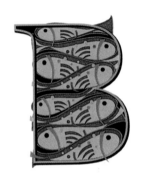

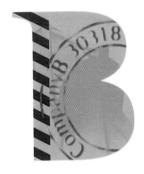

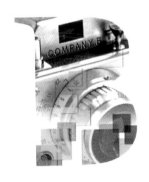

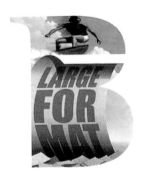

LARGE FOR MAT

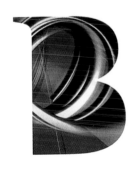

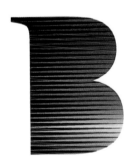

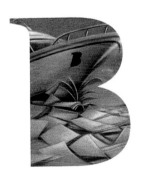

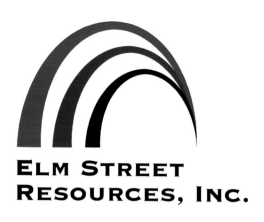

ELM STREET RESOURCES, INC.

1.

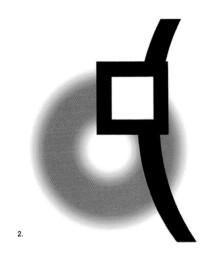

2.

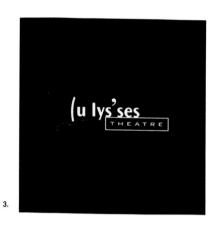

5.

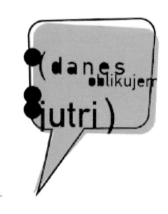

6.

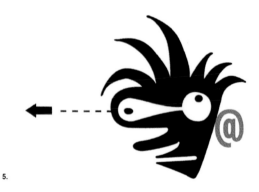

3.

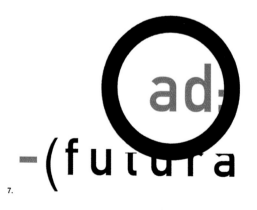

4.

7.

1
Design Firm **Designs On You!**
2 - 7
Design Firm **Design Center**
5 - 7
Design Firm **Design Objectives Pte Ltd**
1.
Client   *Chapman Printing* and *Elm Street Resources*
Designers   Anthony B. Stephens, Suzanna Stephens
2.
Client   *Design Center*
Designer   Eduard Cehovin
3.
Client   *Ulysses Theatre*
Designer   Eduard Cehovin

4.
Client   *Ministry for Ecology*
Designer   Eduard Cehovin
5.
Client   *Yo.Stream.Net*
Designer   Eduard Cehovin
6.
Client   *FYM Cosmetics*
Designer   Eduard Cehovin
7.
Client   *Ad Futura Foundation*
Designer   Eduard Cehovin
(opposite)
Client   *Birds Eye Foods*
Design Firm **Design North, Inc.**

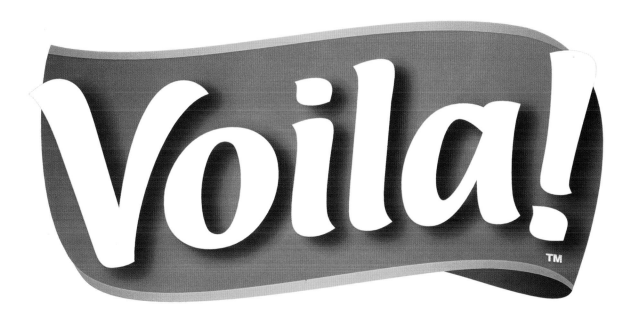

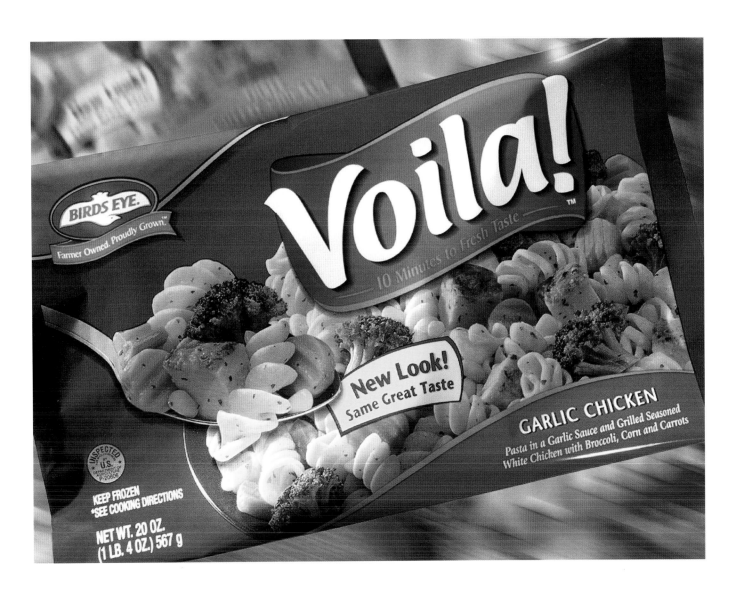

Index

400